ESTIANS

THE

D1539936

OSTROGOTHS

M

DACIA

Black Sea

THRACE

PONTUS

MACEDONIA

CAPPADOCIA

ASIA

SYRIA

e a

CYRENAICA

EGYPT

A Survey of the New Testament

Temple Area, Jerusalem

A SURVEY OF THE
NEW TESTAMENT

Robert H. Gundry

ZONDERVAN PUBLISHING HOUSE
GRAND RAPIDS, MICHIGAN

A Survey of the New Testament

© 1970 by Zondervan Publishing House
Grand Rapids, Michigan

Library of Congress Catalog Card Number: 78-106442

First printing   1970
Second printing 1971
Third printing   1972
Fourth printing 1973

Printed in the United States of America

Contents

PART ONE

THE BACKDROP:
POLITICAL, CULTURAL AND
RELIGIOUS ANTECEDENTS

PART TWO

THE CRUCIAL EVENT:
JESUS' CAREER

PART THREE

THE TRIUMPHANT AFTERMATH:
FROM JERUSALEM TO ROME

PART FOUR

THE EXPLANATION AND IMPLICATIONS
EPISTLES AND APOCALYPSE

Illustrations,
Maps,
and Charts

ILLUSTRATIONS

JACKET AND TITLE PHOTOS:
MARTIN H. HEICKSEN
LEVANT PHOTO SERVICE

MAPS

CHARTS

Preface

A survey textbook of the New Testament should bring together the most salient items from New Testament background, technical introduction, and commentary. Nearly all surveys of the New Testament suffer, however, from a deficiency of comments on the Biblical text. As a result, study of the survey textbook often nudges out reading of the primary and most important source — the New Testament itself. This is a serious omission, especially since many beginning students have never read the New Testament systematically or thoroughly.

In this survey the attempt has been to prompt the student into the Biblical text by carrying on a continual dialogue with it in the form of comments and references to the pertinent scriptural sections for reading. In this way, by tracing the flow of thought from section to section, the student is able to gain a sense of logical progression. Also, by this means it has been possible to move at least some of the background material concerning intertestamental history, Judaism, and other matters, which seem tortuous to many students, from the first part of the book to later sections for direct elucidation of the Biblical text. This is a superior method since it reduces the discouragingly long introduction to the typical college course in New Testament survey, better enables the student to see the relevance of background material for interpreting the text, and, above all, keeps the textbook from supplanting the New Testament.

To be sure, the procedure forces treatment of intertestamental and Roman history to be brief. But that is just as well for the beginning student, for at least we do not obscure the big picture by dwelling on the unessential details of Hasmonean family squabbles, political intrigues within the Herodian household, and similar incidental matters.

After the necessary introductory material, the gospels are treated both separately and harmonistically to enjoy the advantages of both approaches. In spite of the fact that they were not the first books of the New Testament to be written, the gospels come under consideration first because their subject matter provides the basis for all that follows. To avoid discontinuity, the study of Acts proceeds without interruption. The epistles of Paul, Hebrews, the general epistles, and Revelation follow in roughly chronological order (so far as that is determinable) with indications of their relationship to events in Acts. Throughout, comments on the Biblical text (in addition to introductory discussions) do not merely summarize or rehearse what is self-evident, but concentrate on what is not readily apparent to the uninitiated reader.

Leading questions introduce chapters and sections as a teaching device to invite expectancy, induce right questioning of the material by the student, and launch his thinking into the proper channels. Section headings and marginal headings for paragraphs and groups of related paragraphs keep the student oriented. Summary outlines systematize the foregoing material. Questions for further discussion assist not only review of the material, but also utilization of it and application to the contemporary scene. Suggestions for further investigation (collateral reading) include commentaries and other standard works, ancient primary sources, topical works, and related literature.

The theological and critical perspective of this textbook is evangelical and orthodox. In a survey, considerations of space and the purpose of the book rule out full substantiation of presuppositions and methodology as well as complete consideration of opposing views. Nevertheless, frequent note is taken of other positions; and unorthodox literature, so indicated, sometimes appears among the suggestions for collateral reading. Instructors will be able to guide their students further in evaluation of these supplementary sources.

Biblical quotations come from the Revised Standard Version and the New American Standard Bible: New Testament. However, the King James Version inevitably influences some of the theological terminology.

Grateful acknowledgment is made to The Lockman Foundation for permission to quote from The New American Standard Bible — New Testament, to the Division of Christian Education of the National Council of the Churches of Christ in the U.S.A. for permission to quote from the Revised Standard Version of the Bible, and to the publishers Charles Scribner's Sons and Harper & Row for permission to quote from works duly noted in the following pages.

My thanks go to Professors F. F. Bruce, Clark Pinnock, and Marchant King, who read the manuscript in whole or in part, kindly offering suggestions for improvement, and to Mrs. Christine Goudy and Miss Jill Dayton, who helped to upgrade the

English style. Remaining deficiencies are solely the author's responsibility. Finally, my students at Westmont College deserve credit for the inspiration they have given for the accumu-
lation and writing of this material.

ROBERT H. GUNDRY
Santa Barbara, California

INTRODUCTION

Approaching
the New Testament

The New Testament forms Part Two of the Bible. An an-
thology of twenty-seven books of varying lengths, it has only
one-third the bulk of Part One, the Old Testament.[1] But that is
understandable, for the Old Testament covers thousands of years
of history, the New Testament less than one century. The frac-
tion of the first century A.D. covered by the New Testament was
the crucial era during which, according to Christian belief,
Messianic prophecy began to be fulfilled, the divine plan for
human salvation was accomplished through the incarnate Son of
God, Jesus Christ, and the new people of God, the church,
was formed — all on the basis of the new covenant, under which
God offers to forgive the sin of those who believe in Jesus Christ
by the virtue of His vicarious death.

"New Testament," in fact, means "New Covenant," in contrast
to the old covenant (under which God forgave sins in virtue of
animal sacrifices only by provisional anticipation of the truly
adequate sacrifice of Christ). The term "testament" conveys the
idea of a last will and testament which goes into effect only
upon the death of the testator. So also the new covenant went
into effect with the death of Jesus (see Hebrews 9:15-17).

Written in Greek from about A.D. 45-95, the books of the New
Testament are traditionally ascribed to the apostles Peter, John,
Matthew, and Paul and to the other early Christian authors
John Mark, Luke, James, and Jude. In our Bibles the New Testament books do not occur in the chronological order of their
writing. For example, Paul's early epistles were the first to
have been written (with the possible exception of James), rather

---

[1]Old Testament and New Testament are Christian, not Jewish, designations, since the Jews accept only the Old Testament as scripture.

than the gospels. Even in the grouping of Paul's epistles the order is not chronological, for Galatians (or 1 Thessalonians) was written well before Romans, which stands first because it is the longest of the Pauline epistles; and among the gospels Mark, not Matthew, appears to have been written first.

The order of books, then, is logical and solely a matter of Christian tradition. The gospels appear at the beginning because they describe the crucial events of Jesus' career. Among them, Matthew appropriately comes first because of its length and close relationship to the immediately preceding Old Testament. (Matthew frequently cites the Old Testament and begins with a genealogy which reaches back into the Old Testament.) Then comes the triumphant aftermath of Jesus' life and ministry in the Acts of the Apostles, a stirring account of the successful upsurge and outreach of the Church in Palestine and throughout Syria, Asia Minor, Macedonia, Greece, and as far as Rome in Italy. (In actual writing, Acts was second in the two-volume work, Luke-Acts.) So much for the historical books of the New Testament.

The epistles and finally the Apocalypse (or Revelation) explain the theological significance of the redemptive history and draw ethical implications. Among the epistles, Paul's stand first — and within that grouping the order is primarily one of decreasing length, with the major exception of the Pastorals (1 and 2 Timothy, and Titus), which precede Philemon, the shortest surviving letter of Paul. The longest of the non-Pauline epistles, Hebrews (author unknown), is next, then the Catholic, or General, Epistles by James, Peter, Jude, and John. Finally, the book which looks forward to the future return of Christ, the Revelation, draws the New Testament to a fitting climax.

But why study such ancient documents as the New Testament contains? The historical reason is that in the New Testament we find the explanation for the phenomenon of Christianity. The cultural reason is that the influence of the New Testament has permeated Western civilization to the extent that one cannot be well-educated without a knowledge of what the New Testament contains. The theological reason is that the New Testament is the divinely inspired account of Jesus' redemptive mission into the world, and the standard of belief and practice for the Church. The devotional reason is that the Holy Spirit uses the New Testament to bring people into living and growing personal relationship with God through His son Jesus Christ. All reasons enough!

PART I

The Backdrop:
Political, Cultural, and
Religious Antecedents

ALEXANDER THE GREAT, *a brilliant soldier and conqueror, was also a mystic. He gave the world a new conception of unity for mankind.*

THE GREEK OF THE SEPTUAGINT *in a manuscript page of Isaiah. A by-product of hellenism, the translation of the Old Testament Scriptures into Greek started during the third century* B.C.

CHAPTER 1

Intertestamental and New Testament Political History

Leading questions:

What happened in the Middle East from the end of the Old Testament period through the intertestamental and New Testament periods?

How did the Jews fare?

What cultural developments took place?

What factions among the Jews did the political pressures, cultural changes, and religious questions produce?

Who were the leaders in these developments, and what did they contribute to the sweep of history?

THE GRECIAN PERIOD

Old Testament history closed with the Assyrian captivity of the northern kingdom of Israel, the subsequent Babylonian captivity of the southern kingdom of Judah, and the return to Palestine of some of the exiles under Persian rule in the sixth and fifth centuries B.C. The four centuries between the end of Old Testament history and the beginning of New Testament history comprise the intertestamental period (sometimes called "the four hundred silent years" because of the gap in the Biblical record and the silencing of the prophetic voice). During this hiatus Alexander the Great became master of the ancient Middle East by inflicting successive defeats upon the Persians at the battles of Granicus (334 B.C.), Issus (333 B.C.), and Arbela (331 B.C.).

Alexander The Great

The Greek culture, called *Hellenism*, had been spreading for some time through Greek trade and colonization, but Alexander's conquests provided far greater impetus than before. The Greek language became the *lingua franca*, or common trade and diplomatic language. By New Testament times Greek was the

Hellenization

3

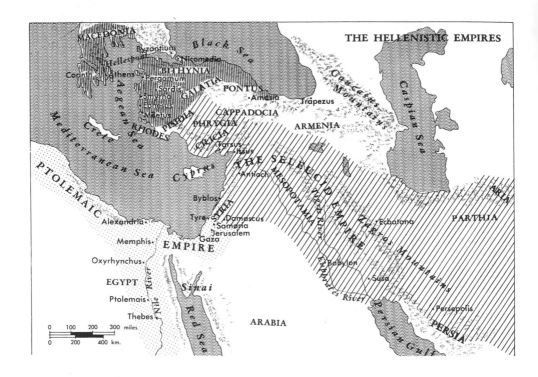

HELLENISTIC EMPIRES *after the career of Alexander the Great, continued for three hundred years to New Testament times.*

street language even in Rome, where the indigenous proletariat spoke Latin, but the great mass of slaves and freedmen spoke Greek. Alexander founded seventy cities, modeling them after the Greek style. He and his soldiers married Oriental women. Thus the Grecian and Oriental cultures mixed.

Upon the death of Alexander at the age of thirty-three (323 B.C.) his leading generals divided the empire into four parts, two of which are important for New Testament historical background, the Ptolemaic and the Seleucid. The Ptolemaic Empire centered in Egypt, having Alexandria as its capital. The succession of rulers over that empire were called the *Ptolemies.* Cleopatra, who died in 30 B.C., was the last of the Ptolemaic dynasty. The Seleucid Empire centered in Syria, having Antioch as its capital. A number of its rulers were named *Seleucus,* several others *Antiochus.* When Pompey made Syria a Roman province in 64 B.C., the Seleucid Empire came to an end.

The
Ptolemies

Sandwiched between Egypt and Syria, Palestine became a victim of rivalry between the Ptolemies and the Seleucids. At first the Ptolemies dominated Palestine for 122 years (320-198 B.C.). The Jews generally fared well during this period. According to early tradition, under Ptolemy Philadelphus (285-246 B.C.) seventy-two Jewish scholars began to translate the Hebrew

4

Old Testament into a Greek version called the Septuagint.
Translation of the Pentateuch came first, remaining sections of
the Old Testament later. The work was done in Egypt, apparently for Jews who understood Greek better than Hebrew, and
contrary to tradition, probably by Egyptian rather than Palestinian Jews. The Roman numeral LXX (seventy being the
nearest round number to seventy-two) is the common symbol
for this version of the Old Testament.

Seleucid attempts to gain Palestine, both by invasion and by
marriage alliance, failed, until Antiochus III defeated Egypt in
198 B.C. Among the Jews two factions developed, "the house of
Onias" (pro-Egyptian) and "the house of Tobias" (pro-Syrian).
The Syrian king Antiochus IV or Epiphanes (175-163 B.C.) replaced the Jewish high priest Onias III with Onias' brother Jason,

ANTIOCHUS IV (EPIPHANES)
*is portrayed on this coin
as himself (left) and as the
god Zeus (right), a de-
liberate attempt to iden-
tify the cult of the king
with the cult of Zeus.*

a Hellenizer, who planned to make Jerusalem into a Greek city.
A gymnasium with an adjoining race track was built. There
Jewish lads exercised nude in Greek fashion, to the outrage of
pious Jews. The track races opened with invocations to pagan
deities, and even the Jewish priests attended such events. Hellenization also included attendance at Greek theaters, adoption
of Greek dress, surgery to remove the marks of circumcision,
and exchange of Hebrew for Greek names. Jews who opposed
the paganization of their culture were called *Hasidim* or *Hasi-
deans*, "pious people," roughly equivalent to *Puritans*.

Before launching an invasion of Egypt, Antiochus Epiphanes
replaced his own appointee in the high priesthood, Jason, with
Menelaus, another Hellenizing Jew, who had offered Antiochus
higher tribute. Menelaus may not have even belonged to a
priestly family. Pious Jews naturally resented the selling of the
sacred office of high priest to the highest bidder.

In spite of initial successes, Antiochus' attempt to annex
Egypt failed. Ambitious Rome did not want the Seleucid Empire to increase in strength. Outside Alexandria, therefore, a   5

THE VILLAGE OF MODEIN *is visible in the distance. It was the home of the Maccabees and the place where the Jewish war of independence began.*

Roman envoy drew a circle on the ground around Antiochus and demanded that before he step out of the circle he promise to leave Egypt with his troops. Having learned to respect Roman power when he was a hostage for twelve years in Rome earlier, Antiochus acquiesced.

INTER-
TESTAMENTAL
AND
NEW TESTAMENT
POLITICAL
HISTORY

Persecution
by Antiochus
Epiphanes

Meanwhile, rumor reached the displaced high priest Jason that Antiochus had been killed in Egypt. Immediately returning to Jerusalem from his refuge in Transjordan, Jason seized control of the city from Menelaus. The embittered Antiochus, stung by his psychological defeat at the hands of the Romans, interpreted Jason's action as a revolt and sent his soldiers to punish the rebels and to reimpose Menelaus as high priest. In so doing, they ransacked the Temple and slaughtered many Jerusalemites. Antiochus himself returned to Syria. Two years later (168 B.C.) he sent his general Apollonius with an army of twenty-two thousand to collect tribute, outlaw Judaism, and enforce heathenism as a means of consolidating his empire and replenishing his treasury. The soldiers plundered Jerusalem, tore down its houses and walls, and burned the city. Jewish men were killed, women and children enslaved. It became a capital offense to circumcise, observe the Sabbath, celebrate Jewish festivals, or possess copies of the Old Testament. Many Old Testament scrolls were destroyed. Pagan sacrifices became compulsory, as did processional marching in honor of Dionysus (or Bacchus), the Greek god of wine. An altar to Zeus, and perhaps also his statue, was erected in the Temple. Animals abominable according to the Mosaic law were sacrificed on the altar, and "sacred" prostitution was practiced in the Temple precincts.

THE MACCABEAN PERIOD

Jewish resistance came quickly. In the village of Modein (or Modin) a royal agent of Antiochus urged an elderly priest named

JOPPA, *on the Palestinian coast, was one of the Greek city-states attacked by the Hasmoneans. Along with other cities Joppa was de-hellenized and integrated into the Jewish community.*

Mattathias to set an example for the villagers by offering a heathen sacrifice. Mattathias refused. When another Jew stepped forward to comply, Mattathias killed him, killed the royal agent, demolished the altar, and fled to the mountains with his five sons and other sympathizers. Thus the Maccabean Revolt began in 167 B.C. under the leadership of Mattathias' family, called the *Hasmoneans*, from Hasmon, great grandfather of Mattathias, or the *Maccabees*, from the nickname "Maccabeus" ("the Hammer") given to Judas, one of Mattathias' sons.

Judas Maccabeus led highly successful guerilla warfare, until the Jews were able to defeat the Syrians in pitched battle. The

THE HASMONEAN KINGDOM *gained its widest expansion under the reign of Alexander Jannaeus.*

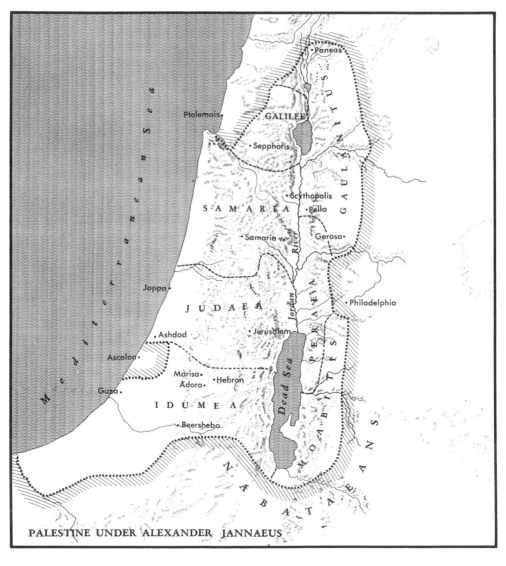

PALESTINE UNDER ALEXANDER JANNAEUS

INTER-
TESTAMENTAL
AND
NEW TESTAMENT
POLITICAL
HISTORY

BATH RUINS *of a Maccabean castle. Although the Hasmoneans attacked Greek cities, they adopted the court style of hellenistic kings.*

Maccabean Revolt, however, was also a civil war between pro-Hellenistic and anti-Hellenistic Jews. The struggle continued even after the death of Antiochus Epiphanes (163 B.C.). Ultimately the Maccabees regained religious freedom, rededicated the Temple, conquered Palestine, and expelled the Syrian troops from their citadel in Jerusalem.

After Judas Maccabeus was killed in battle (160 B.C.), his brothers Jonathan and then Simon succeeded him in leadership. By playing claimants to the Seleucid throne against one another, they were able to gain concessions for the Jews. Jonathan began to rebuild the damaged walls and buildings of Jerusalem. He also assumed the high priestly office. Simon gained recognition of Judean independence from Demetrius II, a contestant for the Seleucid crown, and renewed a treaty with Rome originally made under Judas. Proclaimed as "the great high priest and commander and leader of the Jews," Simon officially united in himself religious, military, and political headship over the Jewish state.

The subsequent history of the Hasmonean dynasty (142-37 B.C.) is a tale of internal strife caused by ambition for power. The political aims and intrigues of the Hasmoneans alienated many of the religiously minded Hasidim, who developed into the

Maccabean Independence

9

Pharisees and the Essenes, such as those who produced the Dead Sea Scrolls from Qumran.[1] The aristocratic and politically minded supporters of the Hasmonean priesthood became the Sadducees. Finally, the Roman general Pompey subjugated Palestine (63 B.C.), so that during the New Testament period Roman power dominated Palestine.

THE ROMAN PERIOD

Roman
Expansion

The eighth century B.C. saw the founding of Rome, and the fifth century B.C. the organization of a republican form of government there. Two centuries of war with the North African rival city of Carthage ended in victory for Rome (146 B.C.). Conquests in the eastern end of the Mediterranean Basin by Pompey and in Gaul by Julius Caesar extended Roman domination. After Julius Caesar's assassination, Octavian, later known as Augustus, defeated the forces of Antony and Cleopatra in naval battle off the coast of Actium, Greece, in 31 B.C. and became emperor. Thus Rome passed from a period of expansion to a period of peace, known as the *Pax Romana*. The province of Judea broke the peace by major revolts which the Romans crushed in A.D. 70 and 135. However, the prevailing unity and political stability of the civilized world under Rome facilitated the spread of Christianity upon its emergence.

Roman
Administration

Augustus set up a provincial system of government designed to keep proconsuls from administering foreign territories for their own aggrandizement. There were two kinds of provinces, sena-

[1]See pages 48-51.

THE ROMAN EMPIRE

TERRITORY IN 44 B.C.
ACQUIRED — 44 B.C. - 14 A.D.
ACQUIRED — 14 A.D. - 117 A.D.
TERRITORY HELD TEMPORARILY

torial and imperial. Proconsuls, appointed by the Roman senate over senatorial provinces usually for terms of only one year, were answerable to the senate. Alongside the proconsuls were procurators, appointed by the emperor usually over financial matters. Propraetors governed the imperial provinces. Appointed by the emperor, propraetors were answerable to him, and exercised their civil and military authority by means of standing armies.

INTER-
TESTAMENTAL
AND
NEW TESTAMENT
POLITICAL
HISTORY

The following Roman emperors, with the dates of their emperorships, touch the New Testament story:

Augustus (27 B.C.-A.D. 14), under whom the birth of Jesus, the census connected with His birth, and the beginning of the emperor cult occurred;

Tiberius (A.D. 14-37), under whom Jesus publicly ministered and died;

Caligula (A.D. 37-41), who demanded worship of himself, ordered his statue placed in the Temple at Jerusalem, but died before the order was carried out;

Claudius (A.D. 41-54), who expelled Jewish residents from Rome, among them Aquila and Priscilla (Acts 18:2), for civil disturbance;

Nero (A.D. 54-68), who persecuted Christians, probably only in the environs of Rome, and under whom Peter and Paul were martyred;

Vespasian (A.D. 69-79), who as a general began to crush a Jewish revolt, became emperor, and left completion of the task to his son Titus, the climax coming with the destruction of Jerusalem and the Temple in A.D. 70;

Domitian (A.D. 81-96), whose persecution of the church probably provided the background for the writing of the Apocalypse (Revelation) as encouragement to oppressed Christians.

The Romans allowed native vassal rulers in Palestine. One was Herod the Great, who ruled the country under the Romans from 37 to 4 B.C. His father Antipater, having risen to power and favor with the Romans, had launched him into a military and political career. The Roman senate approved the kingship of Herod, but he had to gain control of Palestine by force of arms. Of Idumean (Edomite) ancestry, he was therefore resented by the Jews. Herod was scheming, jealous, and cruel; he killed two of his own wives and at least three of his own sons. It was he who had the infants in Bethlehem slaughtered according to Matthew's nativity account. Augustus once said that it was better to be Herod's pig than his son (a word-play, since the Greek words for pig and son sound very much alike). But Herod

AUGUSTUS CAESAR, *a systematic and efficient ruler, initiated an era of peace and stability.*

NERO *was the Roman emperor when Paul was imprisoned in Rome. Probably both Peter and Paul were martyred under his reign.*

was also an efficient ruler and a clever politician, who managed to survive the struggles for power in the higher echelons of Roman government. For example, he switched allegiance from Mark Antony and Cleopatra to Augustus and successfully convinced Augustus of his sincerity. Secret police, curfew, and high taxes, but also free grain during famine and free clothing in other calamities characterized the administration of Herod. Among many building projects, his greatest contribution to the Jews was the beautification of the Temple in Jerusalem. This was not an expression of his sharing the Jewish faith (he did not), but an attempt to conciliate his subjects. The Temple, decorated with white marble, gold, and jewels, became proverbial for its splendor: "Whoever has not seen the Temple of Herod has seen nothing beautiful." Herod the Great died of intestinal cancer and dropsy in 4 B.C. He had commanded a number of leading Jews to be slaughtered when he died so that although there would be no mourning *over* his death, at least there would be mourning *at* his death. The order died with him.

Lacking their father's ability and ambition, the sons of Herod ruled separate parts of Palestine. Archelaus became ethnarch of Judea, Samaria, and Idumea; Herod Philip tetrarch of Iturea, Trachonitis, Gaulanitis, Auranitis, and Batanea; and Herod An-

CAESAREA, *now seafront ruins, was constructed by Herod the Great. The city became the Roman center of administration in Palestine.*

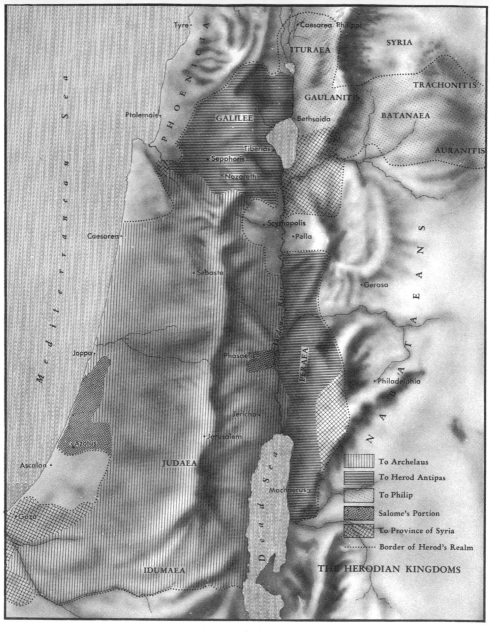

THE HOUSE OF HEROD. *After* A.D. *6 the territory formerly alloted to Archelaus was governed by successive Roman procurators.*

tipas tetrarch of Galilee and Perea.[2] John the Baptist rebuked Antipas for divorcing his wife to marry Herodias, the wife of his half brother. When Herodias induced her dancing daughter to demand the head of John the Baptist, Antipas yielded to the grisly request (Mark 6:17-29; Matthew 14:3-12). Jesus called Herod Antipas "that fox" (Luke 13:32) and later stood trial be-

14   [2]See map on this page.

fore him (Luke 23:7-12). Herod Agrippa I, grandson of Herod the Great, executed James the Apostle and son of Zebedee and imprisoned Peter (Acts 12). Herod Agrippa II, great grandson of Herod the Great, heard Paul's self-defense (Acts 25, 26).

INTER-
TESTAMENTAL
AND
NEW TESTAMENT
POLITICAL
HISTORY

The misrule of Archelaus in Judea, Samaria, and Idumea led to his removal from office and banishment by Augustus in A.D. 6. This same misrule had caused Joseph, Mary, and Jesus upon their return from Egypt to settle in Nazareth of Galilee instead of Bethlehem in Judea (Matthew 2:21-23). After Archelaus' removal, except for brief periods Roman governors ruled the territory. One of the governors, Pontius Pilate, was Jesus' judge. The governors Felix and Festus heard Paul's case (Acts 23-26). And Florus' raiding the Temple treasury ignited the Jewish revolt of A.D. 66-73. It must be remembered, however, that in spite of the Herods and the Roman governors, the Jewish priesthood and the Sanhedrin (a kind of Jewish Supreme Court) largely controlled local matters affecting daily life.

Temple worship with its sacrificial system ceased with the destruction of Jerusalem in A.D. 70. As a substitutionary measure Jewish rabbis established a school in the Mediterranean coastal town of Jamnia for more intensive study of the Torah, the Old Testament law. The unsettled situation in Palestine continued until Emperor Hadrian erected a temple to the Roman god Jupiter where the Jewish Temple had stood, and prohibited the rite of circumcision. The Jews revolted again, this time under the leadership of Bar Cochba,[3] hailed by many of them as the Messiah (A.D. 132). The Romans crushed the uprising in A.D. 135, rebuilt Jerusalem as a Roman city, and banned Jews from entering the city. Thus the Jewish state ceased to exist until its revival in 1948.

FROM THE BAR-COCHBA REBELLION *this wood bowl of olive stones and a child's shoe were among other items found in hide-out caves of the Judean wilderness.*

---

[3]The second part of Bar Cochba's name is subject to a variety of English spellings, the most common of which, besides Cochba, is Kokhba.

CENTURY	DOMINANT POWER	IMPORTANT EVENTS
B.C. 8th (700s)	Assyria	Captivity of the northern kingdom of Israel with the destruction of the capital city of Samaria in 722 B.C.
7th (600s)		
6th (500s)	Babylonia	Captivity of the southern kingdom of Judah with destruction of Jerusalem in 586 B.C.
	Persia	Return of some Jews to Palestine to rebuild their nation, Temple, and Jerusalem, beginning 537 B.C.
5th (400s)		
4th (300s)	Greece-Macedonia	Conquest by Alexander the Great and upsurge of Hellenization throughout the Middle East
		Death of Alexander the Great in 323 B.C. and the division of his empire
	Egypt	Ptolemies' domination of Palestine, 320-198 B.C.
3rd (200s)		Beginning of the Septuagint with translation of the Pentateuch from Hebrew into Greek
2nd (100s)	Syria	Seleucids' domination of Palestine, 198-167 B.C.
		Development of Hellenistic and Hasidic parties within Jewry
		Failure of Antiochus Epiphanes' attempt to annex Egypt
		Antiochus Epiphanes' violent attempt to force complete Hellenization, or paganization, upon the Jews in 168 B.C.
		Outbreak of the Maccabean Revolt in 167 B.C. and the gaining of Jewish independence under the successive leadership of Mattathias, Judas Maccabeus, Jonathan, and Simon
	Jewish independence	Hasmonean dynasty, 142-37 B.C.
1st (99-1)		Internal strife
		Development of Jewish sects: Sadducees, Pharisees, and Essenes
	Rome	Subjugation of Palestine by the Roman general Pompey in 63 B.C.
		Rise to power in Palestine of Antipater and his son Herod the Great

INTERTESTAMENTAL, AND NEW TESTAMENT HISTORY

CENTURY	DOMINANT POWER	IMPORTANT EVENTS
		Assassination of Julius Caesar
		Augustus' rise to Roman emperorship (27 B.C.-A.D. 14) at the expense of Mark Antony and Cleopatra
		Birth of Jesus c. 6 B.C.
		Death of Herod the Great in 4 B.C.
A.D. 1st (1-99)	Rome	Tiberius' emperorship (A.D. 14-37); Pilate's governorship
		Public ministry, death, and resurrection of Jesus (c. A.D. 27-30)
		Beginnings of the Christian Church under the leadership of Peter, Paul, and others
		Caligula's and Claudius' emperorships (A.D. 37-41 and 41-54 respectively)
		Expansion of the Christian Church
		Beginnings of New Testament literature
		Nero's emperorship (A.D. 54-68)
		Persecution of Christians on limited scale
		Martyrdom of Peter and Paul (A.D. 64-68)
		Short-lived emperorships of Galba, Otho, and Vitellius (A.D. 68-69)
		Vespasian's emperorship (A.D. 69-79)
		First Jewish War (A.D. 66-73)
		Destruction of Jerusalem and the Temple by Titus in A.D. 70
		Titus' emperorship (A.D. 79-81)
		Domitian's emperorship (A.D. 81-96)
		Reconstitution of Judaism at Jamnia with almost total emphasis on the Torah in the wake of the loss of the Temple
		Final production of New Testament literature with the Johannine writings
		Beginnings of further Roman persecution of the Church
2nd (100s)		Nerva's and Trajan's emperorships (A.D. 96-98 and 98-117 respectively)
		Hadrian's emperorship (A.D. 117-138)
		Second Jewish War under the rebel leader Bar Cochba (A.D. 132-135)
		Rebuilding of Jerusalem as a Roman city with a ban against Jewish entrance

A LIST OF ROMAN GOVERNORS OVER JUDEA
From the Banishment of Archelaus in A.D. 6
To the Destruction of Jerusalem in A.D. 70

(The names of those who appear in the New Testament are capitalized.)

A.D.

6———————

           Coponius

10———————

           M. Ambivius

13———————

           Annius Rufus

15———————

           Valerius Gratus

26———————

           PONTIUS PILATE

36———————

           Marcellus

38———————

           Maryllus

                        (From A.D. 41-44 Herod Agrippa I ruled as king over Judea and all Palestine.)

44———————

           Cuspius Fadus

46———————

           Tiberius Alexander

48———————

           Ventidius Cumanus

52———————

           M. Antonius FELIX

59———————

           Porcius FESTUS

61———————

           Albinus

65———————

           Gessius Florus

70———————

A PARTIAL GENEALOGICAL CHART OF THE HERODIAN FAMILY*

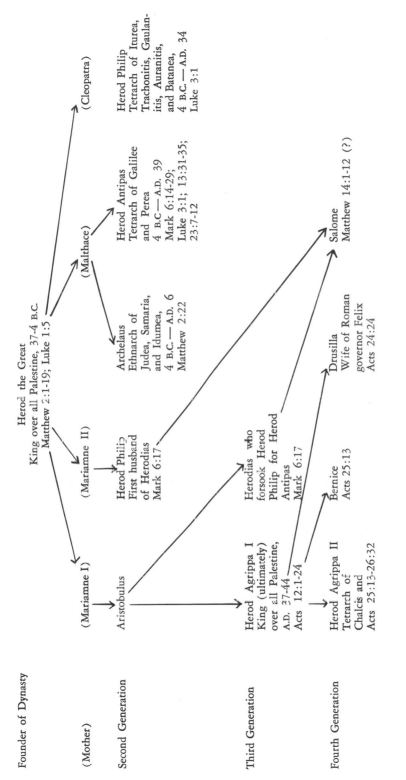

Founder of Dynasty

Herod the Great
King over all Palestine, 37-4 B.C.
Matthew 2:1-19; Luke 1:5

(Mother)

(Mariamne I)

(Mariamne II)

(Malthace)

(Cleopatra)

Second Generation

Aristobulus

Herod Philip
First husband
of Herodias
Mark 6:17

Archelaus
Ethnarch of
Judea, Samaria,
and Idumea,
4 B.C.—A.D. 6
Matthew 2:22

Herod Antipas
Tetrarch of Galilee
and Perea
4 B.C.—A.D. 39
Mark 6:14-29;
Luke 3:1; 13:31-35;
23:7-12

Herod Philip
Tetrarch of Iturea,
Trachonitis, Gaulan-
itis, Auranitis,
and Batanea,
4 B.C.—A.D. 34
Luke 3:1

Third Generation

Herod Agrippa I
King (ultimately)
over all Palestine,
A.D. 37-44
Acts 12:1-24

Herodias who
forsook Herod
Philip for Herod
Antipas
Mark 6:17

Salome
Matthew 14:1-12 (?)

Fourth Generation

Herod Agrippa II
Tetrarch of
Chalcis and
Acts 25:13-26:32

Bernice
Acts 25:13

Drusilla
Wife of Roman
governor Felix
Acts 24:24

*The chart covers only that part of the Herodian family which touches the
New Testament story, and therefore contains numerous omissions. For example, only four of Herod the Great's ten wives appear above.

For further discussion:

In what providential ways did the events of the inter-testamental period constitute preparation for the coming of Christ and the rise of the Church?

What parallels may be validly drawn between the controversy of the Jewish Hellenists and the Hasidim and similar controversy in Church history, especially contemporary?

For further investigation:

(Primary materials)

Barrett, C. K. *The New Testament Background: Selected Documents.* London: S.P.C.K., 1958. Especially pp. 1-21, 105-138, 190-196, 208-216, 223-226.

1 & 2 Maccabees. In *The Oxford Annotated Apocrypha.* Edited by B. M. Metzger. Oxford University Press, 1965.

Josephus. *Antiquitates Judicae.* 2 vols. Loeb Classical Library. Harvard University Press, 1957.

————. *Bellum Judaicum.* 2 vols. Loeb Classical Library. Harvard University Press, 1956.

Polybius. *Histories* xxix. 27. On the meeting between Antiochus Epiphanes and the Roman envoy outside Alexandria.

Yadin, Y. *Herod's Fortress and the Zealots' Last Stand.* New York: Random, 1967. For recent archaeological discoveries confirming Josephus' dramatic account of the Zealots' last stand at Masada at the close of the First Jewish War.

————. *The Finds from the Bar Kokhba Period in the Cave of Letters.* Jerusalem: Israel Exploration Society, 1963. For a technical description of an archaeological dig and discoveries in a cave ˋthat yielded letters from Bar Kokhba during the Second Jewish War.

(Modern treatments)

Pfeiffer, Charles. *Between the Testaments.* Grand Rapids: Baker, 1959.

Russell, D. S. *Between the Testaments.* London: S.C.M., 1960.

Bruce, F. F. *Israel and the Nations.* Grand Rapids: Eerdmans, 1963.

Tenney, M. C. *New Testament Times.* Grand Rapids: Eerdmans, 1956.

CHAPTER 2

The Secular Setting of the New Testament

Leading questions:

How did people in the first century A.D. live, think, speak, work, eat, dress, travel, learn, and entertain themselves?

What differences existed between daily life inside and outside Palestine?

JEWISH POPULATION

It has been estimated that more than 4,000,000 Jews lived in the Roman Empire during New Testament times, perhaps 7 percent of the total population of the Roman world. But scarcely 700,000 of these Jews lived in Palestine. There were more Jews in Alexandria, Egypt, than in Jerusalem; more in Syria than in Palestine! Even in parts of Palestine (Galilee, where Jesus grew up, and Decapolis) Gentiles outnumbered Jews.

LANGUAGES

Latin was the legal language of the Roman Empire, but was used mainly in the West. In the East the *lingua franca* (common language) was Greek. Besides Greek, Palestinians spoke Aramaic and Hebrew, so that Jesus and the first disciples were probably trilingual.[1]

TRANSPORTATION, COMMERCE, AND COMMUNICATION

In transportation, commerce, and communication Palestine was rather poorly developed. The country probably had no paved

---

[1]A common but probably erroneous opinion is that Jesus spoke almost exclusively in Aramaic. But archaeological and literary evidence points to trilingualism. See R. H. Gundry, "The Language Milieu of First-Century Palestine," *Journal of Biblical Literature*, 83 (1964), pp. 404-408.

highways, but there were several main roads. One road led southwest from Jerusalem to Bethlehem and Gaza and northeast from Jerusalem to Bethany, Jericho, and Damascus. Paul was traveling this route when he received his vision of Christ. The second main road branched off the first one in Transjordan and led through Decapolis to Capernaum. Most Jews traveled these two roads in going between Galilee and Judea to avoid Samaria. A third main road went up the Mediterranean coast from Gaza to Tyre. A branch road, on which the risen Jesus conversed with two disciples, went past Emmaus to Jerusalem. The fourth main road led from Jerusalem straight up through Samaria to Capernaum.[2] Along this road Jesus talked with the Samaritan woman by Jacob's well. Finally, the Via Maris (Way of the Sea) went from Damascus through Capernaum by the Sea of Galilee to Nazareth, and on to the coast of the Mediterranean Sea.

Although in Palestine the road system was comparatively poor, throughout much of the Roman Empire the roads were justly famous. They were as straight as possible and durably constructed. Early Christian missionaries used them to full advantage. The imperial post carried governmental dispatches over these highways. Private businesses had their own couriers to

PAVED ROMAN ROADS *throughout much of the empire were straight as possible and durably constructed. Early Christian missionaries used them to full advantage.*

[2]See the map on page 64.

convey messages. People traveled by foot, by donkey, by horse or mule, and by carriage or litter. Because roadside inns were rather dirty, people of better means depended on friends for lodging. One could buy tourist maps in manuscript form, and even guidebooks for tourists.

Water provided the primary means of commercial transportation. Since Egypt was the breadbasket of the Roman Empire, Alexandria was the main port and the outlet for Egyptian grain. Alexandrian ships reached almost two hundred feet in length, had sails, and carried oars for emergencies. One large ship could transport several hundred passengers in addition to cargo. Paul was aboard an Alexandrian ship when he was shipwrecked. Warships were lighter and faster. Galley slaves labored at the oars, of which there were two to five banks, sometimes as many as ten. Barges plied the rivers and canals.

Roads, rivers, and the Mediterranean Sea provided the lines of communication. Papyrus, ostraca (broken bits of pottery), and wax tablets were the writing materials for letters and other documents. For important manuscripts leather or parchment was used. Most news was spread by word of mouth, by town criers, and by public notices posted on bulletin boards.

PUBLIC CONVENIENCES

Alexandria had a well-developed school system. The city library contained well over a half million volumes. Excavations have shown that the city of Antioch, Syria, had two and one-half miles of streets colonnaded and paved with marble and a complete system of night lighting. The major cities of the empire had underground sewage disposal systems. There were public baths for all: admission, one cent. At first people took one bath per day, but later some were taking four to seven baths daily. Shower baths had long since been invented by the Greeks.

HOMES

Houses in the western part of the Roman Empire were built of brick or concrete, at least in the cities. The poorer sections and rural areas had frame houses or huts. In the eastern part of the empire, houses usually consisted of stucco and sun-dried brick. Few windows opened onto the street because the cities lacked proper police forces to prevent thieves from roaming the streets at night and breaking into houses through windows. The more expensive homes had double-door front entrances, sometimes with knockers. A vestibule led to the door, beyond which was a large central court called the *atrium*. Roofs were tile or thatch. In the kitchen an open hearth, or an earthen or stone

TYPICAL PALESTINIAN HOUSING *of Bible times is still common today, such as these houses in Cana of Galilee.*

oven, served for cooking. Oil lamps provided lighting. Plumbing and heating were well developed. Some homes had a central furnace with hot air conveyed by pipes to various parts of the house. Many Roman lavatories had running water, and Pompeiian houses had at least one toilet convenience and sometimes two. Walls were decorated with murals. In larger cities lower and middle class people often rented flats in apartment houses.

Palestinian towns and homes were somewhat different from their Graeco-Roman counterparts and were comparatively backward. One entered a town through a gate in the wall. Inside the gate an open square provided a public place for trade and for social and legal intercourse. Jesus must have preached often in these town squares. The houses were low and flat-roofed, sometimes with a guest chamber perched on top. The building material for these homes was usually bricks made out of mud and straw baked in the sun.

The typical low-class Palestinian had an apartment in a building which contained many apartments, all on ground level. Each apartment had only one room. Part of the room was on a slightly higher level than the other. Beds, chests for clothes, and cooking utensils were located on the higher level. Livestock and other domestic animals inhabited the lower level, or, when the animals were outside, the children played in this lower area. Branches laid across rafters and plastered with mud formed the flat roofs. Rain caused leakage, so that after each rain it was necessary to roll the mud to seal the holes. A parapet around the edge of the roof kept people from falling off, and a flight of stairs on the outside of the house led up to the roof. The housetop was used for sleeping in hot weather, drying vegetables, ripening fruit, and, in devout homes, for praying. The floors consisted of the hard earth or, in better homes, of stone. The beds were merely a mat or coverlet laid on the floor. Only well-to-do homes had bedsteads. People slept in their day garments.

FOOD

The Romans ate four meals a day. The diet of the average person consisted of bread, porridge, lentil soup, goat's milk, cheese, vegetables, fruit, olives, bacon, sausage, fish, and diluted wine. The Jews had only two formal meals, one at noon and another in the evening. The Jewish diet consisted mainly of fruits and vegetables. Meat, roasted or boiled, was usually reserved for festival days. Raisins, figs, honey, and dates supplied sweetening, since sugar was unknown. Fish was a frequent meat substitute. At formal meals people reclined on cushions. For informal meals they sat.

CLOTHING AND STYLES

Men wore tunics, which were shirt-like garments extending from the shoulders to the knees. A belt or sash, called a "gir-

THE PATIO OR COURTYARD of a Palestinian house in Ashdod, a coastal town of Southern Palestine.

dle" in the New Testament, was worn around the waist, coarse shoes or sandals on the feet, and a hat or scarf on the head. In cold weather a mantle or heavy cloak over the tunic provided warmth. These garments were usually white in color. Women wore a short tunic as an undergarment and a sometimes brightly colored outer tunic which extended to the feet. The more fashionable used cosmetics lavishly, including lipstick, eye shadow, and eyebrow paint, and for jewelry wore earrings and nose ornaments. Women's hair styles changed constantly, although Palestinian women wore veils covering the head (not the face). Men wore their hair short and shaved with straight razors. Dandies had their hair curled and applied quantities of hair oil and perfume. Both men and women dyed their hair, often to cover up the gray. False hair added to the coiffure, and both sexes wore wigs. In Palestine men grew beards. Their hair was somewhat longer, but still not so long as portrayed in

THE CLOTHING *of these Palestinian workmen resembles the attire of men living in Palestine in New Testament times.*

the usual pictures of Biblical people. Palestinian styles were generally conservative for both sexes.

SOCIAL CLASSES

In pagan society strata were sharply defined. Aristocratic landowners, government contractors, and others lived in luxury. A strong middle class did not exist because slaves did most of the work. Now dependent on government support, the middle class of previous times had become homeless and foodless mobs in the cities. Less stratification existed in Jewish society because of the leveling influence of Judaism. In general, however, the chief priests and the leading rabbis formed the upper class. Farmers, artisans, and small businessmen comprised most of the population.

Among the Jews, tax collectors (publicans) became special objects of class hatred. Other Jews despised these tax collectors, or more accurately, toll collectors, because of their necessary contact with Gentile superiors. The Romans auctioned the job of collecting tolls to the lowest bidder, that is, to the one who bid the lowest rate of commission for a five-year contract. The toll collector would gather not only the toll and his commission but also whatever he could pocket illegally. For this reason, as well as for his collaboration with foreign overlords, he was generally hated. Bribery of toll collectors by the rich increased the burden of the poor.

Slaves perhaps outnumbered freemen in the Roman empire. It was common to condemn criminals, debtors, and prisoners of war to slavery. Many of Jesus' sayings and parables assume that slavery existed in the Hebrew culture of His time. Paul's letters reflect the presence of slaves in Christian households. Many of the slaves — doctors, accountants, teachers, philosophers, managers, clerks, copyists — were more skilled and educated than their masters. Some slaves bought their freedom or were set free by their masters.

Originally, slaves who had turned criminal were the only ones to be executed by crucifixion. Later, however, freemen who had committed heinous crimes also suffered crucifixion. During the siege of Jerusalem in A.D. 70 Titus crucified as many as five hundred Jews in a day just outside the walls of the city in plain view of the people still inside.[3] Execution by burning at the stake was occasionally practiced. At other times condemned men were forced to fight as gladiators in the arena. Whole groups might kill one another in staged warfare.

---

[3]Josephus, *The Jewish War* V. xi. 1.

THE FAMILY

The basic societal unit was the family. Some factors tended to break down the family, however, such as the numerical preponderance of slaves and the training of children by slaves instead of by parents. The typical Graeco-Roman family had a low birth rate. To encourage larger families, the government offered special concessions to parents of three or more children. Bachelors were probably taxed.

In Palestine large families were common. There was joy at the birth of a boy, sorrow at the birth of a girl. On the eighth day a male child was circumcised and named. The naming of a girl could wait for a month. Families had no surnames, so that people with the same name were distinguished by the mention of their father ("Simon the son of Zebedee"), by political affiliation ("Simon the Zealot"), by occupation ("Simon the tanner"), or by place of residence ("Judas Iscariot," "Iscariot" meaning "the man from Karioth"). At death the family of the deceased performed formal acts of grief, such as rending their garments and fasting, and also hired professional mourners, usually women skilled at wailing. In addition, the family could enlist the services of a professional undertaker.

MORALS

In the exhortations of the New Testament epistles sexual sins usually head the list of prohibitions. Every conceivable type of immorality was attributed to the pagan gods. Temple "virgins" were an integral part of pagan religious rites. Prostitution by both men and women was a well-recognized institution. Slave girls were often the victims of this debauchery. Some men prostituted their own wives and children to gain money. Society accepted pederasty and homosexuality. Obscene pictures often decorated the outside walls of houses, as we know from excavations at Pompeii.

Divorce was easy, frequent, and acceptable. In fact, divorce documents are among the most numerous of the papyrus remains. Murder was common. Parents often "exposed" their infants, that is, abandoned them in the city forum, on a hillside, or in an alley. One letter from a husband to his wife reads, "Should you bear a child, if it is a boy, let it live. If it is a girl, expose it."[4] Often exposed girls were picked up to be reared as prostitutes. It should be added, however, that despite the prevalence of low morality, decent people were not wholly lacking in the Graeco-Roman world.

---

[4]P. Oxy. 744 (1 B.C.). See C. K. Barrett, The New Testament Background, p. 38.

ENTERTAINMENT

Perhaps the most spectacular form of entertainment was the gladiatorial shows. Gladiators were slaves, captives, criminals, and volunteers. Once a whole arena was flooded and a naval battle staged. As many as ten thousand died in a single performance. The sand in the arena became so soaked with blood that it had to be replaced several times during the day. Gladiatorial shows often featured beasts. On one occasion three hundred lions were killed. At the opening of Titus' amphitheater five thousand wild and four thousand tame beasts were slaughtered. Elephants, tigers, panthers, rhinoceri, hippopotami, crocodiles, and snakes fought with one another.

Chariot races corresponded to our automobile races. Betting was common. Naturally, the public idolized winning charioteers.

A risqué stage reflected the immorality of the day. But entertainment was not entirely debauched. The Olympic Games had long been a sports attraction. There was worthy music and literature. Children amused themselves with toys such as baby rattles, dolls with movable limbs, miniature houses and furniture, balls, swings, and games similar to hopscotch, hide and seek, and blind man's buff.

THIS ROMAN STADIUM *near Laodicea was dedicated to Vespasian in* A.D. *79. Remains of some tiers of seats are clearly visible. Ruins at the upper right are probably those of a gymnasium and baths.*

A ROMAN THEATER *in Amman, Jordan. Partially restored, the lower wings are now offices for the Jordanian Department of Antiquities.*

BUSINESS AND LABOR

Trade guilds with patron deities foreshadowed modern labor unions. The trade guilds engaged in politicking, extended aid to members in distress, and gave benefits to widows and orphans of members who had died. In Palestine they regulated days and hours for working.

Industry was limited to small, local shops because the transportation of goods to distant places was prohibitively expensive. Caravans were slow and subject to plunder. Shipping on the Mediterranean Sea could take place only during the calm summer months.

Agriculture was surprisingly advanced in some respects. Farmers were acquainted with different kinds of fertilizer and practiced seed selection according to size and quality. They used pesticides by soaking grain seeds in chemical mixtures to protect them from insect pests. They also practiced crop rotation.

Private companies carried on banking much as it is done today with borrowing, lending, discounting of notes, exchanging of foreign currency, and issuing of letters of credit. The ordinary interest rate varied from four to twelve percent.

SCIENCE AND MEDICINE

Although the Jews were not particularly interested in science during the New Testament period, it did exist. For example, in the third century B.C. Eratosthenes, librarian at Alexandria, taught that the earth was spherical and calculated its size at 24,000 miles in circumference (only eight hundred miles short of the modern estimate) and the earth's distance from the sun at 92,000,000 miles (the modern estimate is 93,000,000). He also conjectured the existence of the American continent.

Medicine, or at least surgery, was more advanced than we might have guessed — a relevant bit of information since one of the New Testament writers, Luke, was Paul's personal physician. Surgeons performed operations on the skull, tracheotomies (incisions into the windpipe), and amputations. Knowledge and use of anesthetics were limited, however, so that the qualifications for a surgeon were given in the following way:

> A surgeon ought to be young, or, at any rate, not very old; his hand should be firm and steady, and never shake; he should be able to use his left hand as readily as his right; . . . he should be so far subject to pity as to make him desirous of the recovery of his patient; but not so far as to suffer himself to be moved by his cries; he should neither hurry the operation more than the case requires, nor cut less than is necessary, but do everything just as if the other's screams made no impression on him.[5]

A variety of medical instruments were used, such as lancets, stitching needles, an elevator for lifting up depressed portions of the skull, various kinds of forceps, catheters, spatulas for examining the throat, and ratchet-worked instruments to dilate passages in the body for internal examination. In the field of dentistry, teeth were filled with gold. False teeth came from the mouths of deceased people or from animals. People sometimes used tooth powder for brushing and polishing the teeth.

Thus, a sampling of first century Graeco-Roman culture shows that although the people of New Testament times lived before the age of science, they were intelligent people whose society and culture in many respects were surprisingly like our own. This was less so in Palestine, where Christianity began, but more so outside Palestine, where Christianity rapidly spread.

For further discussion:

> What cultural preparation for the coming of Christ and the rise of the Church can be seen in the Graeco-Roman world?
>
> Why did Palestinian Jewry tend to be culturally backward? Does the Christian church likewise tend to be culturally backward? If so, is it for similar or different reasons? If not, why not, in view of the fact that Christianity arose out of Judaism?

---

[5]Quoted from A. C. Bouquet, *Everyday Life in New Testament Times* (New York: Scribner's, 1953), p. 171, a book from which much of the material in this chapter has been gleaned.

For further investigation:

Barrett, C. K. *The New Testament Background*: *Selected Documents.* London: S.P.C.K., 1958. Especially pp. 36-44 for quotations from primary sources.

Bouquet, A. C. *Everyday Life in New Testament Times.* New York: Scribner's, 1953.

Daniel-Rops, H. *Daily Life in the Time of Jesus.* New York: Mentor, 1964.

Jones, C. M. *New Testament Illustrations.* Cambridge University Press, 1966.

Everyday Life in Bible Times. Edited by M. B. Grosvenor. National Geographic Society, 1967.

Corswant, W. *A Dictionary of Life in Bible Times.* Completed and illustrated by E. Urech; translated by A. Heathcote. New York: Oxford, 1960.

Bailey, A. E. *Daily Life in Bible Times.* New York: Scribner's, 1943.

Miller, M. S. and J. L. *Encyclopedia of Bible Life.* New York: Harper, 1944.

Wight, F. H. *Manners and Customs of Bible Lands.* Chicago: Moody, 1953.

CHAPTER 3

The Religious Setting of the New Testament

Leading questions:

What were the religious beliefs and practices — esoteric, mythological, superstitious, philosophical — among pagans in the Graeco-Roman period?

How did Jewish religious institutions and beliefs develop from Old Testament to New Testament times?

In what way did the combined pagan and Jewish religious milieu contribute to the birth of Christianity?

PAGANISM

The chief god in the Greek pantheon or hierarchy of gods was Zeus, son of Cronus. Cronus, who had seized the government of the world from his father Uranus, cannibalistically devoured his own children as soon as they were born. But the mother of Zeus saved her infant by giving Cronus a stone wrapped in baby blankets to swallow. Upon reaching adulthood, Zeus overthrew his father and divided his dominion with his two brothers, Poseidon, who ruled the sea, and Hades, who ruled the underworld. Zeus himself ruled the heavens. The gods had access to earth from their capital, Mount Olympus in Greece.

According to the mythology, Zeus had to quell occasional rebellions by the gods, who exhibited very human traits of passion and lust, love and jealousy, anger and hate. The gods were, in fact, superior to men only in power, intelligence, and immortality — certainly not in morality. A very popular god was Apollo, son of Zeus, inspirer of poets, seers, and prophets, and performer of numerous other functions. At Delphi, Greece, a temple to Apollo stood over a cavern, out of which issued vapors

Mythology

33

THE THOLOS (ROUND TEMPLE) OF DELPHI *in Greece was erected early in the fourth century* B.C.

thought to be Apollo's breath. A priestess seated on a tripod over the opening inhaled the fumes and in trance muttered words which were written and vaguely interpreted by priests in answer to enquiring worshipers.

State
Religion

The Roman state religion adopted much of the Greek pantheon and mythology. Roman gods came to be identified with Greek gods (Jupiter with Zeus, Venus with Aphrodite, and so forth). The Romans also added new features such as a priesthood in which the emperor himself acted as *pontifex maximus* (chief priest). The all too human traits of the gods destroyed the faith of many in the Graeco-Roman pantheon. But for others this faith still persisted through the New Testament period.

Emperor
Worship

Following the long established practice of ascribing divinity to rulers, the Roman senate launched the emperor cult by deify-ing, upon their decease, Augustus and subsequent emperors who had served well. Enthusiastic loyalists in the eastern provinces sometimes anticipated the post-mortem deification. The first century emperors who claimed deity for themselves while still alive — Caligula, Nero, and Domitian — failed to receive the honor at death. The insane Caligula (A.D. 37-41) ordered his statue to be erected in the Temple at Jerusalem for worship. Fortunately, the action was delayed by the more sensible Syrian legate since the Jews would surely have revolted. Meanwhile Caligula was assassinated. Domitian (A.D. 81-96) made the first concerted attempt to force worship of himself. The refusal of Christians to participate in what was considered a patriotic duty and unifying pledge of allegiance to the emperor as a god brought increasing persecution.

Much has been written about the widespread popularity and influence of Greek, Egyptian, and Oriental mystery religions in the first Christian century — the cults of Eleusis, Mithra, Isis, Dionysus, Cybele, and numerous local cults. Promising purification and individual immortality, they frequently centered around myths of a goddess whose lover or child was taken from her, usually by death, and subsequently restored. The mysteries also featured secret initiatory and other rites involving ceremonial washing, bloodsprinkling, sacramental meals, intoxication, emotional frenzy, and impressive pageantry by which

Mystery Religions

THE MITHRAS CULT *was carried to Britain by Roman troops, as evidenced by this soldier's mithraeum on Hadrian's wall at Carrowburg near London. Below, a close-up view of the votive inscriptions.*

devotees came into union with the god. Social equality within the mysteries contributed to their appeal. In recent years, however, it has increasingly come to be realized that the absence of early information about these religions probably means that they are not an important factor in New Testament studies.

Not until the second, third, and fourth centuries of the Christian era do we get detailed information concerning the beliefs held by devotees to the mysteries. Therefore, although the pre-Christian existence of mystery religions is undoubted, their pre-Christian beliefs are unknown. Where their later beliefs somewhat paralleled Christian beliefs (the parallels are frequently exaggerated), the direction of borrowing may have been from Christianity to mystery religions[1] rather than vice versa, especially since the pagans were notoriously assimilative (see below on syncretism) and the early Christians exclusive. Moreover, parallels are often more apparent than real, and even where real do not necessarily imply borrowing in either direction.

For example, the myths of dying and rising gods do not really correspond to the New Testament accounts of Jesus' death and resurrection. In the first place, the deaths of the gods are not redemptive. Furthermore, the story of Jesus' death and resurrection had to do with a very recent historical figure; the myths usually had to do with personifications of vegetational processes and thus did not move on the plane of history at all, let alone recent history. Finally, the mythological gods did not rise in full bodily resurrection, but resuscitated only in part or merely revived in the underworld. When the fourteen parts of Osiris' body were reassembled, he became king of the dead in the underworld. All that Cybele could obtain for the corpse of Attis was that it should not decay, that his hair should continue to grow, and that his little finger should move — yet the story of Cybele and Attis (who died by self-castration) is sometimes cited as a parallel to and source for the death and resurrection of Jesus by those who carelessly fail to examine the details of the myth. As a matter of fact, the very thoughts of death by crucifixion and physical resurrection were abhorrent to ancient people, who knew that crucifixion was for criminals and who thought of the body as a prison for the soul and the seat of evil. If Christians had borrowed their concepts from popular mystery religions, one wonders why the pagans widely regarded the Christian Gospel as foolish, incredible, and worthy of persecution.[2]

---

[1]See Gnosticism on next page.

[2]See J. G. Machen, *The Origin of Paul's Religion* (Grand Rapids: Eerdmans, 1947), chapters VI and VII; J. S. Stewart, *A Man in Christ* (New York: Harper, n.d.), pp. 64-80.

THE RELIGIOUS
SETTING
OF THE
NEW TESTAMENT

Superstition
and Syncretism

Superstition had a stranglehold on most people in the Roman Empire. The use of magical formulae, consultation of horoscopes and oracles, augury or prediction of the future by observing the flight of birds, the movement of oil on water, and the markings of a liver, and the hiring of professional exorcists (experts at casting out demons) — all these superstitious practices and many more were a part of everyday life. Jews were among the most sought-after exorcists, partly because it was thought they alone could correctly pronounce the magically potent name *Yahweh* (Hebrew for "LORD"). Correct pronunciation, along with secrecy, was thought necessary to the effectiveness of an incantation. In a practice known as *syncretism* common people simply combined various religious beliefs and superstitious practices. Household idol shelves were filled with images of birds, dogs, bulls, crocodiles, beetles, and other creatures.

Plato's dualistic contrast between the invisible world of ideas and the visible world of matter formed the substratum of first century gnosticism, in which matter was equated with evil and spirit with good. Two opposite modes of conduct resulted: (1) suppression of bodily desires because of their connection with evil matter (asceticism), and (2) indulgence of bodily passions because of the unreality and inconsequentiality of matter (libertinism or sensualism). In both cases Oriental religious notions had corrupted original Platonism. The concept of physical resurrection was abhorrent so long as matter was considered to be evil. Immortality of the soul was desirable, however, and attainable through knowledge of secret doctrines and passwords by which the soul at death could elude hostile demonic guardians of the planets and stars on its flight from earth to heaven. Under this view the religious problem was not human guilt for which forgiveness must be provided, so much as human ignorance for which knowledge must be provided. In fact, *gnosticism* comes from *gnosis*, the Greek word for *knowledge*. To insure the purity of the supreme God, he was separated from the material, and therefore evil, universe by a series of lesser divine beings called "aeons," who emanate from him. Thus, an elaborate angelology developed alongside demonology.

Gnostic ideas seem to stand behind certain heresies attacked in the New Testament. But the contents of a gnostic library discovered in the 1940s at Nag Hammadi, or Chenoboskion, Egypt, seem to confirm that the gnostic concept of a heavenly redeemer did not exist when the Christian movement began. Gnostics apparently borrowed the doctrine of a heavenly redeemer from Christianity at a later date. In the first century, gnosticism was still an aggregate of loosely related religious ideas rather than a highly organized system of doctrine.

The intelligentsia were turning to purer forms of philosophy. *Epicureanism* taught pleasure (not necessarily sensual) as the chief good in life. *Stoicism* taught dutiful acceptance of one's fate as determined by an impersonal Reason which rules the universe and of which all men are a part. The *Cynics*, ancient counterparts to modern hippies, regarded the supreme virtue to be a simple and unconventional life in rejection of the popular pursuits of comfort, affluence, and social prestige. The *Sceptics*, abandoning in their relativism the hope for anything absolute, succumbed to doubt and conformity with prevailing custom. These and other philosophies, however, did not determine the lives of very many people. Generally, superstition and syncretism characterized the masses, so that Christianity entered a religiously and philosophically confused society. The old confidence of the ancient Greeks had gone. The enigmatic universe defied understanding. Philosophy had failed to provide satisfactory answers. So had the traditional religions. Men felt helpless under the fate of the stars, which were considered to be angelic-demonic beings. A mood of despair, at best pessimism, prevailed.

ELEUSIS, *near Athens, was the center of the Eleusinian cult of Demeter, the Earth Goddess. These sculptured fragments are among the ruins of the Temple of Demeter at Eleusis.*

A COMPLETE SCROLL OF ISAIAH *in Hebrew was discovered at Qumran. The parchment scroll measures twenty-four feet in length.*

JUDAISM

More important than the pagan religious and philosophical milieu was the Judaism out of which Christianity arose. Judaism as it was in the first century originated toward the close of the Old Testament period during the Assyro-Babylonian exile. The prophets had predicted exile as punishment for idolatry prac ticed by the Israelite nation. Fulfillment of the prediction permanently cured the nation of idolatry. The temporary loss of the Temple during the exile gave rise to increased study and observance of the Old Testament law (the Torah[3]) and at least ultimately to establishment of the synagogue as an institution. It is debatable whether synagogues originated right during the exile or later during the intertestamental period. But a reasonable conjecture is that since Nebuchadnezzar had destroyed the first Temple (Solomon's) and deported most of the people from Palestine, they established local centers of worship called synagogues ("assemblies") wherever ten adult Jewish men could

The Synagogue

---

[3]The Hebrew word *torah* had a wider meaning than "law." It also connoted instruction, teaching, and divine revelation *in toto,* and referred variously to the ten commandments, the Pentateuch, the whole Old Testament, and the oral law, or traditional interpretations of the rabbis.

THE CAPERNAUM SYNA-
GOGUE *dates back to the
third century* A.D. *Top:
artist's sketch of the restored structure. Center:
floor plan. Bottom: mod-
ern ruins of the excavated
structure.*

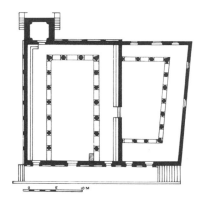

be found. Once established as an institution, synagogues continued after the rebuilding of the Temple under Zerubbabel's leadership.[4]

The typical synagogue was a rectangular auditorium with a raised speaker's platform, behind which rested a portable chest or shrine containing Old Testament scrolls. The congregation sat on stone benches running along two or three walls and on mats and possibly wooden chairs in the center of the room. In front, facing the congregation, sat the rulers or elders of the synagogue. Singing was unaccompanied. To read from an Old Testament scroll, the speaker stood. To preach, he sat down. For prayer, everyone stood. The typical synagogue service consisted of

antiphonal recitation of the Shema (Deuteronomy 6:4 ff., the "golden text" of Judaism[5]) and the Shemone Esreh (a series of praises to God),[6]

prayer,

singing of psalms,

readings from the Hebrew Old Testament law and prophets with a Targum, or loose oral translation into Aramaic (or Greek), which many Jews understood better than Hebrew,

a sermon (if someone competent was present), and

a blessing or benediction. There was freedom in the wording of the liturgy. The whole congregation joined in the "Amen" at the close of prayers. The head of the synagogue selected different members of the congregation to lead the recitations, read the scripture, and preach. Competent visitors were likewise invited to speak, a practice which opened many opportunities for Paul to preach the Gospel in synagogues.

The elected head, or ruler, of the synagogue presided over meetings and introduced strangers. The synagogue attendant (hazzan) took care of the scrolls and furniture, lighted the lamps, blew the trumpet announcing the Sabbath day, stood beside the readers to insure correct pronunciation and accurate reading of the sacred texts, and sometimes taught in the synagogue school. A board of elders exercised spiritual oversight of the congregation. Erring members faced punishment by whipping and excommunication. Alms taken into the synagogue were dispensed to the poor. The early Christians, mainly Jews, naturally adopted the synagogue organization as a basic pattern for their churches.

The synagogue was more than a center for religious wor-

---

[4]See Ezra 3-6; Haggai; Zechariah 1-8 for the rebuilding of the Temple.

[5]"Hear, O Israel: The LORD our God is one LORD" (Deuteronomy 6:4), later expanded by verses 5-9; 11:13-21; Numbers 15:37-41. *Shema* is the Hebrew word behind "Hear."

[6]*Shemone Esreh* means *eighteen,* but in fact the exact number of benedictions has varied from time to time.

ship every Saturday. During the week it became a center for administration of justice, political meetings, funeral services, education of Jewish lads, and study of the Old Testament. The study of the Torah in synagogues tended to obscure the importance of offering sacrifices in the Jewish Temple, so that the rabbi, or teacher of the law, began to upstage the priest.

The Temple

The sacrifices prescribed by the Mosaic law could legitimately be offered only in the central sanctuary. The second Temple continued to be important, therefore, until its destruction by Titus in A.D. 70. The urging of the prophets Haggai and Zechariah had spurred its rebuilding during the Old Testament period of restoration from the exile. Plundered and desecrated by Antiochus Epiphanes in 168 B.C., it had been repaired, cleansed, and rededicated by Judas Maccabeus three years later. Herod the Great launched a beautification program, but that project had hardly been completed, long after his death, than the Temple was again destroyed.

The Temple proper stood in the middle of courts and cloisters covering about twenty-six acres. Gentiles could enter the outer court; but inscriptions in Latin and Greek warned them on pain of death not to enter the inner courts, reserved for Jews alone. Just outside the Temple proper stood the altar of burnt-offering and the laver full of water to be used by the priests for washing. Inside the first room, or holy place, where a seven-branched golden lampstand which burned olive oil, a table with the bread of (God's) presence ("shewbread"), and a small altar for burning incense. A heavy veil curtained off the in-

THE TEMPLE AREA TODAY *with a view through the arches to the Mount of Olives.*

nermost room, the Holy of holies, into which only the high priest entered but once a year on the Day of Atonement. The ark of the covenant, the lone piece of furniture in the Holy of holies during Old Testament times, had long since disappeared in the upheavals of invasion and captivity. Besides private sacrifices, daily burnt-offerings for the whole nation were sacrificed in mid-morning and mid-afternoon in conjunction with the burning of incense, prayers, priestly benedictions, pouring out of wine as a libation (liquid offering), blowing of trumpets, and chanting and singing by choirs of Levites to the accompaniment of harps, lyres, and wind instruments. Sabbaths, festivals, and other holy days required additional ceremonies.

Closely related to the Temple worship were the religious festivals and holy days of the Jews. The Jewish civil year began approximately in September-October, the religious year approximately in March-April. Following is the religious calendar of the Jews:

The Religious Calendar

THE JEWISH RELIGIOUS CALENDAR

FEAST OF		DATES[7]
Passover and Unleavened bread,	commemorating the exodus from Egypt and marking the beginning ("first fruits") of the wheat harvest	Nisan (Mar.-Apr.) 14 15-21
Pentecost, or Weeks,	marking the end of the wheat harvest	Iyar (Apr.-May) Sivan (May-June) 6
		Tammuz (June-July) Ab (July-Aug.) Elul (Aug.-Sept.)
Trumpets, or Rosh Hashanah,	marking the first of the civil year and the end of the grape and olive harvests	Tishri (Sept.-Oct.) 1 & 2
Day of Atonement, or Yom Kippur,	for national repentance, fasting, and atonement (not called a "feast")	10
Tabernacles, or Booths, or Ingathering,	commemorating the living in tents on the way from Egypt to Canaan — a joyous festival, during which the people lived in temporary shelters made of branches	15-22
Lights, or Dedication, or Hanukkah,	commemorating the rededication of the Temple by Judas Maccabeus, with brilliant lights in the Temple precincts and in Jewish homes	Heshvan (Oct.-Nov.) Kislev (Nov.-Dec.) 25- Tebet (Dec.-Jan) 2 or 3
Purim,	commemorating the deliverance of Israel in the time of Esther, with the public reading of the book of Esther in synagogues	Shebet (Jan.-Feb.) Adar (Feb.-Mar.) 14

[7]Because of differences in calendrical systems the equivalents in our months are only approximations.

THE HEBREW TEXT *from Isaiah (47:2 — 48:6). The Old Testament text existed in three linguistic forms in the first century: original Hebrew, the Septuagint (Greek), and the Targums (Aramaic).*

The Mosaic law prescribed the first six items on the calendar (Passover-Tabernacles).[8] The remaining two (Hanukkah and Purim) arose later and apart from scriptural command. Pilgrims thronged to Jerusalem from elsewhere in Palestine and also from foreign countries for the three main festivals of Passover-Unleavened Bread, Pentecost, and Tabernacles.

The Literature of Judaism: Old Testament

The Old Testament existed in three linguistic forms for Jews of the first century: the original Hebrew, the Septuagint (a Greek translation), and the Targums (oral translations into Aramaic, which were beginning to be written down). The Targums also contained traditional material not in the Biblical text.

Apocrypha

Written in Hebrew, Aramaic, and Greek and dating from the intertestamental and New Testament periods, the apocryphal books of the Old Testament contain history, fiction, and wisdom literature. The Jews and later the early Christians did not generally regard these books as sacred scripture, so that *apocrypha*, which originally meant "hidden, secret," and therefore "profound," came to mean "noncanonical." The apocryphal books include the following:

1 Esdras

2 Esdras (or 4 Ezra, apocalyptic in content; see the next paragraph on the nature of apocalyptic)

---

44   [8]See Leviticus 23:4-43 for details.

Tobit
Judith
Additions to the Book of Esther
Wisdom of Solomon
Ecclesiasticus, or the Wisdom of Jesus the Son of Sirach
Baruch
Letter of Jeremiah
Prayer of Azariah
Song of the Three Young Men
Susanna
Bel and the Dragon
Prayer of Manasseh
1 Maccabees
2 Maccabees

Other Jewish books dating from the same era are labeled *pseudepigrapha* ("falsely inscribed"), because some of them were written under the falsely assumed names of long-deceased Old Testament figures to achieve an air of authority. Some of the pseudepigraphal writings also fall into the category of apocalyptic[9] literature, descriptions in highly symbolic and visionary language of the end of present history with the coming of God's kingdom on earth. The purpose of apocalyptists was to encourage the Jewish people to endure persecution until arrival of the Messianic kingdom in the near future. The failure of this hope to materialize eventually stopped the publication of apocalyptic literature.

Pseudepigrapha
and Apocalyptic

The pseudepigraphal literature, which has no generally recognized limits, also contains anonymous books[10] of legendary history, psalms, and wisdom. A list of pseudepigraphal books follows:

1 Enoch
2 Enoch
2 Baruch, or the Apocalypse of Baruch
3 Baruch
Sibylline Oracles
Testaments of the Twelve Patriarchs
Testament of Job
Lives of the Prophets
Assumption of Moses

---

[9]From the Greek word *apokalypsis,* meaning "unveiling, revealing," here with reference to future events.

[10]Roman Catholics designate the pseudepigrapha as the apocrypha and the apocrypha as the deuterocanonical books. Others call the pseudepigrapha "the outside books," since only some of them are pseudonymous and almost no one regards them as canonical. (The Ethiopic canon includes 1 Enoch and Jubilees.)

Martyrdom of Isaiah
Paralipomena of Jeremiah
Jubilees
Life of Adam and Eve
Psalms of Solomon
Letter of Aristeas
3 Maccabees
4 Maccabees

Dead Sea Scrolls

In addition, the Qumran scrolls discovered in caves near the Dead Sea include literature similar to the traditional pseudepigrapha:

Damascus (or Zadokite) Document (fragments of which were known before)
Rule of the Community, or Manual of Discipline
War Between the Children of Light and the Children of Darkness
Description of the New Jerusalem
Thanksgiving Hymns (Hodayoth)
Psalms of Joshua
Pseudo-Jeremianic literature
Apocryphal Danielic literature

QUMRAN CAVES *where the scrolls were discovered, are located a short distance from the Qumran community ruins and the Dead Sea.*

Various commentaries (peshers) on Psalms, Isaiah, Hosea, Micah, Nahum, Habakkuk, and Zephaniah

Various books of laws, liturgies, prayers, beatitudes, mysteries, wisdom, and astronomical and calendrical calculations

Rabbinical case decisions about interpretive questions concerning the Old Testament law formed a memorized oral tradition in New Testament times. This tradition grew during the succeeding centuries until it was enshrined in writing in the Jewish Talmud. A Palestinian edition was produced in the fourth century A.D. and a Babylonian edition about three times longer, making it encyclopedic in length, during the fifth century A.D. Chronologically, the Talmud consists of the Mishnah, or oral law, developed by rabbis up through the second century A.D., plus the Gemarah, containing comments on the Mishnah by rabbis living from the third through the fifth centuries A.D. Topically, the Talmud consists of the halakah, or strictly legal portions, and the haggadah, or nonlegal portions (stories, legends, explanatory narratives). Claiming that the oral law dated back to Moses at Mount Sinai, the rabbis elevated their conflicting interpretations of the Old Testament to a position of even greater importance than the Old Testament itself. Two famous schools of rabbinical interpretation were the moderate school of Hillel and the strict school of Shammai.

Despite its intensely nationalistic spirit, Judaism attracted large numbers of proselytes, who were full converts,[11] and God-fearers, who were Gentiles willing to practice Judaism partially, but unwilling to undergo circumcision and observe the stricter Jewish taboos. These Gentiles found Judaistic theology superior to Gentile polytheism and superstition, for the Jews emphasized their monotheistic belief in one God and opposed idolatry even in their own Temple. Unconverted pagans, on the other hand, could not comprehend a temple without an idol. Why a temple, if not to house an image?

Jewish beliefs sprang from the acts of God in history as recorded in a collection of sacred books (the Old Testament), and not, as in pagan religions, from mythology, mysticism, or philosophic speculation. The Old Testament emphasized the fate of the nation, so that the doctrine of individual resurrection appears infrequently. The intertestamental period saw an increased emphasis on the fate of the individual and therefore

---

[11]Male proselytes had to be circumcised. All had to baptize themselves in the presence of witnesses and (ideally) offer a sacrifice in the Temple at Jerusalem. It may be that self-baptism was a later requirement in lieu of sacrificing, after the destruction of the Temple.

on the doctrine of individual resurrection. However, nationalism and the awareness of being the chosen people by no means had died.

The Jews were looking for the Messiah to come. Indeed, some Jews awaited a variety of messianic figures — prophetic, priestly, and royal. But they did not generally expect the Messiah to be a suffering and dying savior or a divine being. They looked for God to use a human figure in bringing politico-military deliverance from Roman domination. Or God Himself would deliver His people and then introduce the Messiah as ruler.[12] "This present age," evil in character, was to be followed by the utopian "days of the Messiah" or "day of the Lord," indeterminate or variously calculated as to length. Afterwards, "the coming age," or eternity, would begin. Occasionally in Jewish thinking, the messianic kingdom merged with the eternal age to come. In the meantime the Jews followed a rigid system of ethics based on obedience to the Old Testament law and rabbinical interpretations of it, in strong contrast to the immoralities of the Greek and Roman pantheon practiced by the devotees of those pagan gods.

The Sects and Other Groups Within Judaism: Pharisees

The Pharisees ("separated ones," probably in a ritualistic sense) originated shortly after the Maccabean revolt as an outgrowth of the Hasidim, objectors to the Hellenization of Jewish culture.[13] As middle class laymen for the most part, the Pharisees were the largest Jewish religious sect, but still only about six thousand strong in the time of Herod the Great. They scrupulously observed the rabbinical as well as the Mosaic laws. A Pharisee could not eat in the house of a "sinner" (one who did not practice Phariseeism), but might entertain a sinner in his own house. He had to provide clothes, however, lest the sinner's own clothes be ritually impure.

Observance of the Sabbath was similarly scrupulous. Some rabbis of the Pharisees forbade spitting on the bare ground during the Sabbath lest the action by disturbing the dirt constitute plowing and therefore Sabbath-breaking work. A woman should not look in the mirror on the Sabbath lest she see a gray hair, be tempted to pluck it out, yield to the temptation, and thereby work on the Sabbath. It was a moot question whether a Pharisee might lawfully eat an egg laid on a festival

---

[12]It is probable that some of the higher characterizations of the Messiah as a preexistent divinity, as in the "Similitudes" of 1 Enoch and in 2 Esdras, postdate the rise of Christianity and developed out of the Jewish troubles with Rome during A.D. 66-135 and perhaps also in imitation of the high Christian view of Jesus.

[13]See page 5. "Pharisee" may originally have meant "Persianizer," a taunting designation which the Pharisees reinterpreted to mean "separated one."

day. Were such eggs tainted in spite of the fact that hens are unaware of festival days?

But the Pharisees devised legal loopholes for their convenience. Although one could not carry his clothes in his arms out of a burning house on the Sabbath, he could put on several layers of clothing and bring them out by wearing them. A Pharisee was not supposed to travel on the Sabbath more than three-fifths of a mile from the town or city where he lived. But if he wished to go farther, on Friday he deposited food for two meals three-fifths of a mile from his home in the direction he wished to travel. The deposit of food made that place his home away from home, so that on the Sabbath he could travel yet another three-fifths of a mile. Jesus and the Pharisees repeatedly clashed over the artificiality of such legalism. The average Jew nevertheless admired Pharisees as paragons of virtue. Indeed, they were the mainstay of Judaism.

The aristocratic Sadducees were the heirs of the intertestamental Hasmoneans. Although fewer than the Pharisees, they wielded more political influence because they controlled the priesthood.[14] Their contacts with foreign overlords tended to reduce their religious devotion and carry them farther in the direction of Hellenization. Unlike the Pharisees, they regarded only the first five books of the Old Testament (the Pentateuch, Mosaic law, or Torah) as fully authoritative and denied the oral law of the nonpriestly rabbis. They did not believe in divine foreordination, angels, spirits, or the immortality of the soul and resurrection of the body, as did the Pharisees.

Though strict, in one sense the Pharisees were progressive; for they kept applying the Old Testament law to new and changing circumstances of daily life. But the comfortably situated Sadducees wanted to maintain the status quo and therefore resisted any contemporizing of the law lest they lose their favored positions of affluence and wealth. Because the center of priestly power, the Temple, was destroyed in A.D. 70 along with large numbers of the Sadducees themselves, the Sadducean party disintegrated. The Pharisees survived to become the foundation for orthodox Judaism in later centuries.

The Essenes were a smaller sect of about four thousand people. Like the Pharisees, they evolved from the Hasidim (those who became disgruntled with the expanding political aims of the

---

[14]The prevalent view that the Sadducees were the party of the priesthood has been challenged by Victor Eppstein in *Zeitschrift für die Neutestamentliche Wissenschaft*, 55 (1964), pp. 50-54, and *Journal of Biblical Literature*, 85 (1966), pp. 213-224. "Sadducees" may originally have meant "members of the supreme council," reinterpreted by the Sadducees to mean "the righteous ones." Others relate the term to Zadok, priest under David and Solomon.

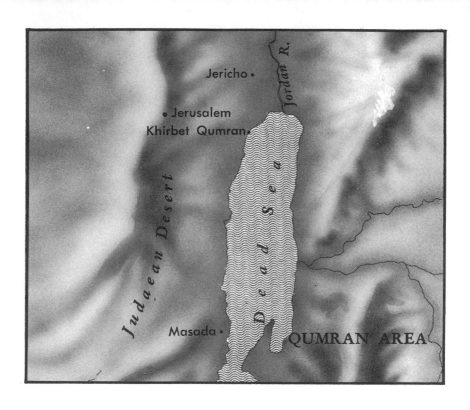

Map showing Jericho, Jerusalem, Khirbet Qumran, Masada, the Judaean Desert, Dead Sea, Jordan R. — QUMRAN AREA

QUMRAN *as viewed south over the ruins from the citadel. The Dead Sea is visible in the background.*

Hasmoneans). Some of them lived in monastic communities, such as the one at Qumran, which produced the Dead Sea Scrolls. Admission required a two or three year probation and relinquishment of private property and wealth into a common treasury. The more strict refrained from marriage. They outperformed the Pharisees in their punctilious legalism. For this reason it is doubtful that they contributed significantly to the rise of Christianity as has been suggested by some modern writers. If Jesus denounced Pharisaical legalism, He certainly could not have owed very much to the even more rigid Essenes. Moreover, Jesus' mingling with sinners contrasted sharply with Essene withdrawal from society.

The Essenes did not offer animal sacrifices in the Jerusalem Temple because they regarded the Temple as polluted by a corrupt priesthood. As symbols of their own purity they wore white robes. The sect regarded itself as the elect remnant living in the last days. They looked for the appearance of several eschatological figures — a great prophet, a military-political messiah, and a priestly messiah — and girded themselves for a forty years' war which was to culminate in the messianic kingdom. A former leader called the "Teacher of Righteousness" exerted a profound influence on their beliefs and practices, but hardly occupied the position of divine and redemptive prominence accorded to Jesus in Christian doctrine.

The Herodians were not a religious sect, but a small minority of influential Jews — mainly the Sadducean aristocracy of priests — who supported the Herodian dynasty and, by implication, the Roman rule, which had put the Herods in power. By contrast, the Zealots were revolutionaries dedicated to the overthrow of Roman power. They refused to pay taxes to Rome, regarded acknowledgment of loyalty to Caesar as sin, and sparked several uprisings, including the Jewish revolt which resulted in the destruction of Jerusalem in A.D. 70. Scholars usually identify the Zealots with the Sicarii ("assassins"), who carried concealed daggers. The Sicarii may have been an extremist branch of Zealotry, however, or a separate group that eventually fused with the Zealot movement. One of Jesus' twelve disciples had been a zealot ("Simon the Zealot," Luke 6:15; Acts 1:13).

Herodians and Zealots

The scribes were neither a religious sect nor a political party, but a professional group. "Lawyer," "scribe," and "teacher (of the law)" are synonymous terms in the New Testament. To these must be added "rabbi," literally, "my great one," or "my master, teacher." Originating with Ezra, according to tradition, the scribes interpreted and taught the Old Testament law and delivered judicial pronouncements on cases brought to them. Application of the law to daily life necessitated their interpre-

Scribes

51

tive function. What, for example, constituted working on the Sabbath? The disciples ("learners") of the scribes followed behind them wherever they went and learned by rote memory the minutiae of the Old Testament and of rabbinical lore. The scribes taught in the Temple precincts and synagogues and occasionally debated in the presence of their disciples.

By the time of Jesus most of the scribes belonged to the sect of the Pharisees, though not all Pharisees possessed the theological expertise required of scribes. Since scribal activity was gratuitous, scribes depended on a trade for financial support. For example, Paul, who had received rabbinical training, was a tentmaker (Acts 18:3). Although he lacked formal theological education, Jesus was called "Rabbi" and gathered disciples around Himself. He frequently taught in easy-to-remember rhythmic structure, sententious sayings, and vivid parables. Always he taught authoritatively (*"verily* I say . . ."; compare Matthew 7:28 f.). In contrast, the scribes endlessly quoted past rabbinical opinions.

Sanhedrin

The Romans allowed the Jews to handle many of their own religious and domestic matters. As a result, numerous local courts existed. The Jewish supreme court was the great Sanhedrin, which met daily, except for Sabbaths and other holy days, in the Temple area. The Sanhedrin even commanded a police force. The high priest presided over the seventy other members of the court, who came from both the Pharisaical and the Sadducean parties. The New Testament refers to the Sanhedrin by the terms "council," "chief priests and elders and scribes," "chief priests and rulers," and simply "rulers."

"People of the Land"

In Palestinian Jewry the masses of common people, called "the people of the land," remained unaffiliated with the sects and political parties. Because of their ignorance of and indifference to the Old Testament law and the rabbinical regulations, the Pharisees held them in contempt and criticized Jesus for mingling with them.

Diaspora

Outside Palestine the Jews of the Diaspora ("Dispersion") fell into two categories: (1) the Hebraists, who retained not only their Judaistic faith, but also their Jewish language and customs, and thereby incurred Gentile hatred for their standoffishness; and (2) the Hellenists, who adopted the Greek language, dress, and customs while retaining their Judaistic faith in varying degrees. An outstanding example of Hellenistic Judaism was Philo, a first century Jewish philosopher and resident of Alexandria. He combined Judaism and Greek philosophy by allegorizing the Old Testament. Doubtless, Judaism outside Palestine tended to be less strict and more influenced by Gentile modes of thinking than Judaism in Palestine. But we must not overdraw the differences; for Hellenistic influences had pervaded Palestine, so that Judaism there was much more variegated than the Talmud, which represents a later and more monolithic stage of Judaism, would lead us to believe. After the failure of the revolts against Rome in A.D. 70 and 135, Palestinian Judaism increasingly consolidated toward uniformity along the lines of a de-apocalypticized Phariseeism; for the Sadducees had lost their base of influence in the Temple and the Romans had defeated the hopes of smaller apocalyptic-minded sects such as the Essenes.

Jewish children received their first lessons in Hebrew history and religion, practical skills, and perhaps also reading and writing from their parents. The Mosaic law and the Proverbs in the Old Testament contain many injunctions concerning this parental responsibility, which included the employment of physical chastisement for failure to learn properly. Jewish lads entered local synagogue schools at about six years of age. There they used the Old Testament as a textbook for reading and writing. Lessons also included simple arithmetic, extrabiblical Jewish tradition, and the complex Judaistic rituals. Besides this very narrow academic training, every Jewish boy learned a trade. To become an advanced scholar in the Old Testament, a Jewish young man attached himself as pupil to a rabbi. For example, Paul, before his conversion, studied under the famous rabbi Gamaliel (Acts 22:3).

Jewish
Education

In contrast, Graeco-Roman education was liberal in its scope. Slaves supervised Graeco-Roman lads in their earlier years by giving them their first lessons and then leading them to and from private schools until they were brought into adulthood with a great deal of ceremony. As young men they could then attend universities at Athens, Rhodes, Tarsus, Alexandria, and other places to study philosophy, rhetoric (oratory), law, mathematics, astronomy, medicine, geography, and botany. Or they could attend the lectures of peripatetic ("walking about") philosophers, so called because they dispensed their wisdom as they strolled. The high degree of literacy, evidenced by papyrus remains, shows that education was widespread. It was common for people to carry small notebooks for jotting down grocery lists, appointments, and other memoranda. Even shorthand was used.

Graeco-Roman
Education

In conclusion, a wide range of literature, including extra-Biblical writings as well as the New Testament, helps us reconstruct the pagan and Jewish backgrounds necessary for a more complete understanding of the New Testament. The Judaism out of which Christianity arose was a monotheistic faith with cross currents of religious and political thought and with various religious and cultural institutions.

For further discussion:

What religious preparation for the coming of Christ and the rise of Christianity is apparent in the times just before the New Testament?

Do modern people hold to mythological, superstitious, and syncretistic beliefs and practices? If not, why not? If so, what are those beliefs and practices — and why has modern scientism failed to banish them?

What parallels (as well as differences) may be drawn between Gnosticism and current philosophy of education?

What counterparts to the Pharisees, Sadducees, Essenes, Herodians, and Zealots might one find in Christendom today? To which of those groups would you have joined yourself, and why? If to none of them, give your reasons.

In what ways has the educational process in Western culture combined characteristic traits of both Jewish and Graeco-Roman educational practice?

For further investigation:

(Primary materials)

Barrett, C. K. *The New Testament Background: Selected Documents.* London: S.P.C.K., 1958. Especially pp. 29-36, 48-104, 124-127, 139-189, 200-205, 216-266.

The Oxford Annotated Apocrypha. Edited by B. M. Metzger. New York: Oxford, 1965.

The Apocrypha and Pseudepigrapha of the Old Testament. Edited by R. H. Charles. 2 vols. Oxford: Clarendon, 1913. With technical introductions and notes.

Vermès, G. *The Dead Sea Scrolls in English.* Baltimore: Penguin, 1962.

(Modern treatments)

Tenney, M. C. *New Testament Times.* Grand Rapids: Eerdmans, 1965. Especially pp. 79-128.

Eastwood, C. C. *Life and Thought in the Ancient World.* Philadelphia: Westminster, 1965.

Glover, T. R. *The Conflict of Religions in the Early Roman Empire.* Boston: Beacon, 1960.

Rose, H. J. *Religion in Greece and Rome.* New York: Harper & Row, 1959.

Jonas, H. *The Gnostic Religion.* 2nd revised edition. Boston: Beacon, 1963.

Grant, R. M. *Gnosticism.* New York: Harper & Row, 1961.

Wilson, R. M. *The Gnostic Problem.* Naperville, Illinois: Allenson, 1958.

Bonsirven, J. *Palestinian Judaism in the Time of Jesus Christ.* New York: Holt, Rinehart & Winston, 1963.

Guignebert, C. *The Jewish World in the Time of Jesus.* New Hyde Park, New York: University Books, 1959.

Coss, T. L. *Secrets from the Caves.* New York: Abingdon, 1963.

Bruce, F. F. *Second Thoughts on the Dead Sea Scrolls.* Revised and enlarged edition. Grand Rapids: Eerdmans, 1961.

Mansoor, M. *The Dead Sea Scrolls.* Grand Rapids: Eerdmans, 1964.

The last three entries are only representative of numerous volumes on the Dead Sea Scrolls. For a full account of their discovery, see J. C. Trever, *The Untold Story of Qumran* (Westwood, New Jersey: Revell, 1965).

CHAPTER 4

The Canon and Text of the New Testament

Leading questions:

How did the early Church at first manage without the New Testament?

How did the New Testament then come to be considered by the Church as an authoritative collection of books?

How do we know that our New Testament represents a substantially accurate version of what its authors originally wrote?

THE CANON

The New Testament canon consists of the books accepted by the early Church as divinely inspired Scripture. The term *canon* originally meant *a measuring reed* but developed the metaphorical meaning *standard*. As applied to the New Testament, it refers to those books accepted by the Church as the authoritative standard for belief and conduct.

At first, Christians did not have any of the books contained in our New Testament. They depended, therefore, on the Old Testament, on oral tradition about Jesus' teaching and redemptive work, and on direct revelation from God through Christian prophets. Even after the writing of the New Testament books, many of them had not been distributed geographically throughout the whole Church. And before they were gathered into the New Testament, Christian writers had produced still other books — some good, some inferior. Books such as Paul's epistles and the gospels received canonical recognition very quickly. Uncertain authorship caused other books, such as Hebrews, to be questioned for a while. The early Church hesitated to adopt 2 Peter because its Greek style differed from that in 1 Peter and thus raised doubts about its claim to authorship

56

by the Apostle Peter. Because of their brevity and limited circulation some books simply did not become known widely enough for rapid acceptance into the canon.

Quotations of New Testament books in an authoritative manner by the early Church fathers help us recognize what books they regarded as canonical. Later, the Church compiled formal lists, or canons. One of the earliest was the canon of Marcion (C. A.D. 144). A Gnostic heretic, Marcion taught that a harsh Old Testament God and a loving New Testament God oppose each other, that Jesus Christ came as a messenger of the loving New Testament God, that He was killed at the instigation of the Old Testament God, that Jesus entrusted the Gospel to the twelve apostles, who failed to keep it from corruption, and that Paul became the sole preacher of the true Gospel. Marcion therefore selected only those books which he considered to be free from and contrary to the Old Testament and Judaism — Luke (with some omissions) and most of Paul's epistles. The violent reaction of orthodox Christians against Marcion's short list shows that the church as a whole had already accepted the New Testament books which Marcion rejected. Otherwise Marcion's canon would not have caused so much disturbance. In the fourth century all our New Testament books were generally recognized and others excluded. Church councils of the fourth and fifth centuries merely formalized existing belief and practice concerning the New Testament canon.

One must believe that God providentially guided the early Church in its evaluation of various books so that those which were truly inspired became accepted and those which were not inspired, though sometimes valued on an unauthoritative level, were rejected from the canon. The process of selection took time, and differences of opinion arose. But we may be grateful that the early Church did not accept books without evaluation and at times debate. Most readers who will compare the sub-apostolic writings[1] and the New Testament apocrypha[2] with the canonical books of the New Testament will heartily endorse the critical judgment of the early Christians.

Various criteria for canonicity have been suggested, such as agreement with the oral apostolic doctrine of the first century and edifying moral effect. However, some books which did

---

[1]So called because they were written in the age immediately following that of the apostles by the "apostolic fathers." Books in this category are 1 and 2 Clement, the Epistles of Ignatius, the Epistle of Polycarp to the Philippians, the Didache or Teaching of the Twelve Apostles, the Epistle of Barnabas, the Shepherd of Hermas, the Martyrdom of Polycarp, the Epistle to Diognetus, and the fragments of Papias.

[2]These fanciful and sometimes heretical books are different from the Old Testament apocrypha and are not accepted as canonical by any branch of the Church.

edify nevertheless failed to achieve canonical status in the Church. The same is true of some books which carried forward the tradition of apostolic doctrine. More important — in fact, crucial — was the criterion of apostolicity, that is, authorship by an apostle or by an apostolic associate and thus also a date of writing within the apostolic period.

Mark was an associate of both the Apostles Peter and Paul. Luke was a companion of Paul. And whoever authored Hebrews exhibits close theological contacts with Paul. James and Jude were half- or stepbrothers of Jesus and associates of the apostles in the early Jerusalem church. Traditionally, all other authors represented in the New Testament were apostles — Matthew, John, Paul, and Peter. Modern criticism casts doubt on some of the traditional ascriptions of authorship. Such questions receive individual attention in later sections of this book. But even under negative critical views it is not usually denied that non-apostolic books were written in the apostolic tradition by followers of the apostles.

Jesus Himself affirmed the full authority of the Old Testament as Scripture.[3] Then He made His own words and deeds equally authoritative,[4] and promised the apostles that the Holy Spirit would remind them of His ministry and teach them its significance (John 14:26; 16:12-15). The canon of the New Testament, then, is the authoritative record and interpretation of God's revelation of Himself through Jesus Christ — an interpretive record predictively authenticated by our Lord Himself, whose view of His own words and deeds, now written and expounded by the apostles and their associates, was certainly no less than His view of the Old Testament as the Word of God.

THE TEXT

Papyrus was the writing material for most, and perhaps all, of our New Testament books. Undoubtedly the authors or their scribes used the ancient scroll form, but some of the books may have been written in codex form with separate pages bound together as in modern books. It was common practice for an author to dictate to a writing secretary, called an *amanuensis*.

---

[3]For example, Matthew 5:17-19a: "Think not that I have come to abolish the law and the prophets; I have come not to abolish them but to fulfil them. For truly, I say to you, till heaven and earth pass away, not an iota, not a dot, will pass from the law until all is accomplished. Whoever then relaxes one of the least of these commandments and teaches men so, shall be called least in the kingdom of heaven"; John 10:35b: "the scripture cannot be broken."

[4]See, for example, the statements, "You have heard that it was said to the men of old, [there follows an Old Testament quotation] . . . But I say to you . . ." in the Sermon on the Mount (Matthew 5:21, 27, 31, 33, 38, 43; compare Mark 1:22, 27; Luke 4:32, 36).

Sometimes the author gave his *amanuensis* a degree of freedom in choice of words.[5]

The original documents, none of which are extant, go by the term *autographs*. At first, when private individuals and churches desired copies, these were made one by one. But as the demand increased, a reader dictated from an exemplar to a roomful of copyists. Gradually errors of sight and sound, inadvertent omissions and repetitions, marginal notes, and deliberate theological and grammatical "improvements" slipped into the text. Concern for the purity of the text led to checking of manuscripts against other manuscripts, sometimes several times. Nevertheless, the number of errors continually grew.

As the sacredness of the New Testament became increasingly felt and the Church grew richer, more durable writing materials, such as vellum (calfskin) and parchment (sheepskin), came into use. Earlier manuscripts were usually written entirely in capital (uncial, or majuscule) letters, later manuscripts in cursive, small (minuscule) letters. Lacking at first, word divisions, punctuation marks, and chapter and verse divisions were later developments.[6] The earliest manuscripts in the possession of modern scholars date from the second century.[7] Most of the variant readings, or differences, in early manuscripts have to do with spelling, word order, the presence or absence of "and" and "the," and other inconsequential matters.

PORTION OF THE SEPTUAGINT *included in Codex B (Codex Vaticanus), one of the oldest Greek manuscripts, from the fourth century* A.D.

---

[5]See pages 257 f.

[6]Stephen Langton (d. 1228) divided the text into chapters, R. Stephanus into verses in his printed edition of 1551.

[7]The earliest, the Rylands Fragment of John, dates from about A.D. 135.

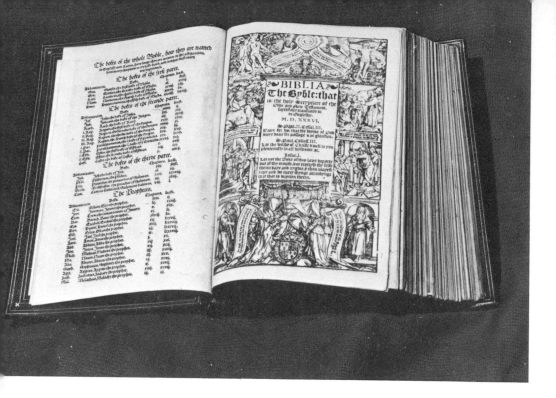

COVERDALE'S BIBLE *was the first complete English Bible to be printed in England, in 1537. Shown here are the contents and title pages.*

The primary sources for determining the original text of the New Testament are Greek manuscripts, early versions (that is, translations, especially Syriac and Latin), and quotations in the writings of the early Church fathers and in lectionaries (readings from the New Testament in ancient liturgies). By comparing these, scholars can usually decide among variant readings with a fair degree of certainty. Among their most important criteria for evaluation are preference for the reading in the oldest and most carefully copied manuscripts and versions, preference for the reading which best explains the development of other readings, preference for the more difficult reading (since it is more probable that a copyist made an expression easier than harder), and preference for the shorter reading (because copyists were more liable to add to the text than to delete). The materials for determining the original text of the New Testament are far more numerous and ancient than those for the study of any of the old classical writings. Thanks to the labors of textual critics, the remaining uncertainties in the text of the Greek New Testament are not serious enough to affect our understanding of what it teaches.

So far as English versions of the New Testament are concerned, John Wycliffe produced his translation from the Latin in 1382 and William Tyndale a translation directly from the Greek in 1525. Following a succession of further English Bibles, the Roman Catholic Douay Version appeared in 1582 and the King James (or Authorized) Version in 1611. But the earliest and best manuscripts of the New Testament had not yet been discovered, and the following centuries saw great advances in scholarly knowledge of the kind of Greek used in the New Testament. A large contribution came from the study of numerous papyri found during the last hundred years. As a result, numerous versions have appeared in recent times: the English Revised Version (1881), the American Standard Version (1901), the Revised Standard Version (1946), the New English Bible (1961), the New American Standard Bible New Testament (1963), and various individual efforts, best known of which is J. B. Phillips' *The New Testament in Modern English.*

For further discussion:

Attempt to reconstruct a typical church service before the formation of the New Testament canon as a basis for preaching and teaching. Also reconstruct an early Christian's private devotional life without the New Testament.

What evidences of continued Marcionism are still apparent?

How and why are Christian classics such as Augustine's *Confessions,* John Bunyan's *Pilgrim's Progress,* and some of Charles Wesley's hymns to be distinguished from the canonical books of the New Testament?

Why did the Church close the canon? Or is it still open?

Does translation of Scripture practically take away its quality of inspiration by removing the reader one step from the original text?

What are the advantages of a single accepted translation of the New Testament versus many different translations?

For further investigation:

(Primary materials containing translations of the subapostolic writings and the New Testament apocrypha)

Grant, R. M. *et al. The Apostolic Fathers.* 6 volumes. New York: Nelson, 1964-   . With extensive introductions and notes.

Lake, K. *The Apostolic Fathers.* 2 volumes. Loeb Classical Library. New York: Putnam's, 1930. With Greek text as well as English translation.

Lightfoot, J. B. *The Apostolic Fathers.* Edited and completed by J. R. Harmer. New York: MacMillan, 1898 (reprinted by Baker Book House in Grand Rapids). With short introductions and Greek text as well as English translation.

James, M. R. *The Apocryphal New Testament.* New York: Oxford, 1924.   61

Hennecke, E. *New Testament Apocrypha.* Edited by W. Schneemelcher and translated by R. M. Wilson. 2 vols. Philadelphia: Westminster, 1963/66. With technical introductions and notes.

(Modern discussions of the canon)

Harris, R. L. *Inspiration and Canonicity of the Bible.* Grand Rapids: Zondervan, 1957.

Ridderbos, H. N. *Authority of the New Testament Scriptures.* Translated by H. De Jongste. Nutley, New Jersey: Presbyterian & Reformed, 1963.

Filson, F. V. *Which Books Belong in the Bible?* Philadelphia: Westminster, 1957. Chapter V.

Cross, F. L. *The Early Christian Fathers.* Naperville, Illinois: Allenson, 1960. Chapter V.

(Modern surveys of textual criticism)

Bruce, F. F. *The Books and the Parchments.* Revised edition. Westwood, New Jersey: Revell, 1953.

Metzger, B. M. *The Text of the New Testament: Its Transmission, Corruption, and Restoration.* 2nd edition. New York: Oxford, 1969. Somewhat more technical, but the best up-to-date treatment.

PART II

The Crucial Event:
Jesus' Career

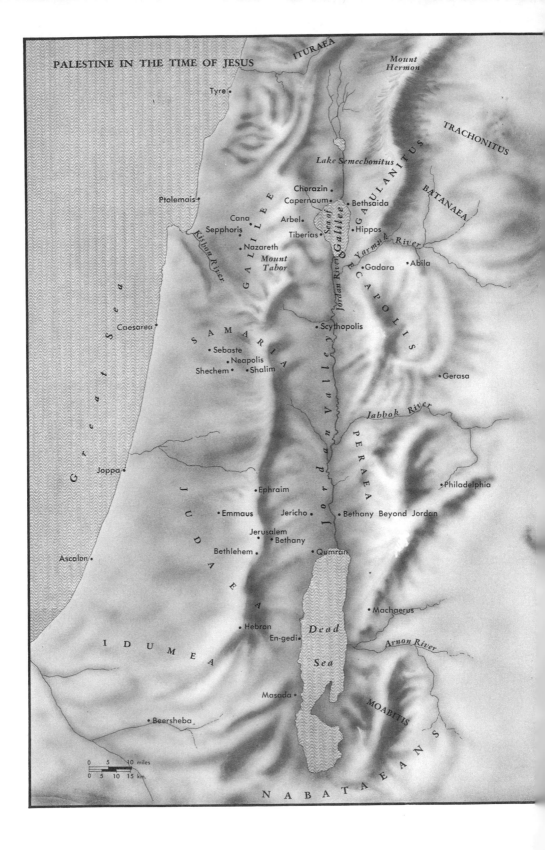

PALESTINE IN THE TIME OF JESUS

CHAPTER 5

The Life of Jesus

Leading questions:

Are there literary sources for the life and teaching of Jesus outside the New Testament, and if so, what is their value?

Are the gospels independent or interdependent? If the latter, what are their relationships?

What sources, if any, lie behind the gospels as we know them?

How reliable is the information about Jesus in the gospels from the standpoint of historical criticism?

How did the gospels come to be written, and what are modern understandings of their portraiture of Jesus?

SOURCES

Although not the first documents of the New Testament to be written (some of the epistles were written first), the four canonical gospels — Matthew, Mark, Luke, and John — fittingly stand first as the main sources for a study of the life of Jesus. The few noncanonical sources — the first century Jewish historian Josephus (with later insertions by Christian copyists), the Babylonian Talmud, and the Roman writers Pliny the Younger, Tacitus, Suetonius, and Lucian — are so brief that they are valueless in attempting to reconstruct Jesus' career. They do confirm, however, that He lived, became a public figure, and died under Pontius Pilate and that within a dozen years of His death worship of Him had spread as far as Rome.

Extrabiblical History

There are sayings of Christ recorded outside the four canonical gospels. Paul, for example, quotes a dominical[1] saying otherwise unknown: "It is more blessed to give than to receive" (Acts 20:35). These *agrapha*, as they are called, differ from

Agrapha

---

[1]From the Latin *dominicus,* "lord, master," and frequently used of that which pertains to the Lord Jesus.

Jesus' sayings in the gospels, but are quoted by early Christian writers and are sometimes placed in the margins of ancient manuscripts of the New Testament. *Agrapha* is Greek for "unwritten." These sayings were of course written down (otherwise we would not know them), but not in the text of the gospels — hence the designation "unwritten."

Other records of Jesus' sayings outside the canonical gospels are the Oxyrhynchus papyri and the Gospel of Thomas. The Gospel of Thomas, discovered in Nag Hammadi, Egypt, about 1945, is not really a gospel, for it does not contain a narrative thread; and the Apostle Thomas was not its author. Both the so-called gospel and the Oxyrhynchus papyri purport to be collections of Jesus' sayings. Some of the sayings are almost exactly like those recorded in the canonical gospels. Others obviously stem from canonical sayings, but have been changed. Still others wholly differ from anything found in the New Testament.[2]

GREEK PAPYRUS FRAGMENTS
*from Oxyrhynchus in
Egypt that contain sayings
ascribed to Jesus.*

---

[2]Here are examples of extracanonical sayings varying in degree of similarity to canonical sayings (from *The Gospel According to Thomas,* Coptic text established and translated by A. Guillaumont *et al.* [New York: Harper, 1959]):

Logion 54: Jesus said: Blessed are the poor, for yours is the Kingdom of Heaven.

Logion 46b: But I have said that whoever among you becomes as a child

Concerning their relationship to the New Testament, three possibilities present themselves: (1) the noncanonical records draw from the canonical gospels; (2) the noncanonical records represent an independent tradition of Jesus' sayings; (3) both relationships hold true in a mixed way. Whatever the relationship, it is generally agreed that the Oxyrhynchus papyri and the Gospel of Thomas reflect a largely corrupted tradition concerning the words of Jesus.

Luke 1:1 mentions numerous written gospel records antedating the third gospel, but none of these except Mark and possibly Matthew has survived. Post-apostolic apocryphal gospels did survive, however, and they present a motley picture of heretical beliefs and pious imagination, especially in filling out the details of Jesus' childhood and the interval between His death and resurrection, about which the canonical gospels are largely silent.[3]

SOURCE CRITICISM OF THE GOSPELS

The student of Jesus' life must go first to the primary sources, the canonical gospels. Immediately the "synoptic problem" confronts him: Why are the first three (or synoptic) gospels so much alike? (*Synoptic* comes from two Greek words meaning, "a seeing together.") One answer is the oral tradition theory that resemblances are due to a rapid crystallization of the tradition about Jesus in a more or less fixed oral form, which later came to be written down. Most modern scholars doubt that word-of-mouth transmission could have retained so many and such minute verbal resemblances as exist among the synoptics, especially in narrative portions, not so likely to be memorized verbatim as (possibly) the words of Jesus.[4]

---

       shall know the Kingdom, and he shall become higher than John.

Logion 82: Jesus said: Whoever is near to me is near to the fire, and whoever is far from me is far from the Kingdom.

See further Joachim Jeremias, *Unknown Sayings of Jesus,* 2nd English edition, translated by R. H. Fuller (London: S.P.C.K., 1964).

[3]See M. R. James, *The Apocryphal New Testament* (Oxford: Clarendon, 1924); or E. Hennecke, *New Testament Apocrypha,* edited by W. Schneemelcher and translated by R. M. Wilson, 2 vols. (Philadelphia: Westminster, 1963/66). The latter work has extensive technical introductions and notes in addition to translations.

[4]Two Scandinavian scholars, H. Riesenfeld (*The Gospel Tradition and Its Beginnings* [London: Mowbray, 1957]) and B. Gerhardsson (*Memory and Manuscript: Oral Tradition and Written Transmission in Rabbinic Judaism and Early Christianity* [Uppsala: Gleerup, 1961], and *Tradition and Transmission in Early Christianity* [Uppsala: Gleerup, 1964]) have revived the oral tradition theory. Their emphasis on the factor of memory in the ancient Jewish culture reinforces our estimate of the gospels as trustworthy, but does not explain the literary interrelationships of the synoptics, particularly in narrative material.

Marcan
Priority

The usual solution is the Mark-Q documentary hypothesis: Matthew and Luke based most of their narrative on Mark, drew most of Jesus' sayings, or teaching, from a lost document designated Q,[5] and added distinctive material of their own. Scholars marshal a number of arguments in favor of the priority of Mark. In Luke 1:1-4 the writer actually states that he utilized other documents, containing eyewitness material, in writing his own gospel. That at least opens the possibility that Mark was one of those documents behind Luke. More specifically, Matthew incorporates nearly all of Mark, Luke about one-half. Both Matthew and Luke often repeat the exact words of Mark, even in minute details. Furthermore, Matthew and Luke usually abide by Mark's sequence of the events in Jesus' life, not departing *together* from that sequence, as one would have expected them to do at least occasionally if they had not both been drawing on Mark.[6] Frequently it appears that Matthew and Luke changed the wording of Mark to clarify his meaning,[7] to omit material the meaning of which might be mistaken,[8] to delete material unnecessary for their own purposes,[9] and to smooth awkward grammar (a mere matter of style, not accuracy)[10] — all phenomena which indicate the utilization of Mark.

Q Hypothesis

Since similarities in narrative material appear to rise from common use of the document Mark by Matthew and Luke, similarities between Matthew and Luke in *teaching* material not contained in Mark have led to the positing of a second document, Q, thought to be an early collection of Jesus' sayings with a minimum of narrative framework. Q would be something like the Gospel of Thomas and the Oxyrhynchus collection of Jesus' sayings, or better yet, like Old Testament prophetical books which contain an account of the prophet's call, extensive records of his preaching, sometimes bits and pieces of narrative, but no account of the prophet's death. Thus Q might be

---

[5]The designation Q is usually connected with the German word *Quelle,* meaning "source."

[6]In other words, it appears that Mark is the anchor which keeps Matthew and Luke from drifting very far away (and never at the same time) from the order of events contained in Mark. Occasional, independent differences in sequence arise because topical considerations sometimes override chronology in the minds of the evangelists (a technical term for the writers of the gospels).

[7]For example, compare Mark 2:15 and Luke 5:29 as to whose house was the scene of the banquet.

[8]For example, Matthew and Luke omit Mark's story that Jesus' family thought He had gone mad, perhaps because *their* readers might place a wrong interpretation on the incident and infer too much.

[9]For example, Matthew 8:14 and Luke 4:38 omit the names of Andrew, James, and John in Mark 1:29 and retain only Peter's name.

[10]For example, Mark 2:7 (literally translated), "Who can forgive sins except one, God?" becomes, "Who can forgive sins except God alone?" in Luke 5:21. Mark has a rough and ready style — forceful, but not elegant.

thought to begin with the baptism and temptation of Jesus
(His "call"), continue with His teaching, but lack any account
of His suffering (passion), death, and resurrection.

Problems remain with the Q-hypothesis, however. For instance, the degree of agreement between Matthew and Luke on
the sayings tradition varies widely. Many scholars therefore
think that Matthew and Luke used or made different Greek
translations of an originally Aramaic Q. Still others, doubting
the very existence of a Q document (why did it not survive?),
adopt for the sayings material the theory of many short documents, or the oral tradition hypothesis (easier to believe for
sayings than for narrative), or a combination of both. Some believe that Luke used Matthew for much of the teaching material, but if so, why did Luke frequently rearrange the Matthaean
order of that material?

Proposing a four-document hypothesis, B. H. Streeter added
M for the sayings of Jesus distinctive to Matthew and L for most
of the matter distinctive to Luke. He also advanced the Proto-
Luke theory: the first edition of Luke's gospel consisted only of
Q + L, to which Luke later added a preface and the birth
stories and interspersed Marcan material. There is no general
agreement on Streeter's proposals.[11]

Marcan priority appears to be established. About Q there is
more uncertainty. Perhaps we are to think of a body of loose
notes on Jesus' teaching taken by Matthew. Documents such as
M and L are doubtful. In his gospel Matthew often arranges and
collects the sayings of Jesus topically instead of chronologically,
as do also the other gospels, but to a lesser degree. In contrast
to Matthew, Luke may have used Mark as a supplement rather
than as the backbone of his narrative (so Streeter); but that is
only a possibility at the present stage of research. It is unnecessary to say that where Matthew and Luke utilized Mark or another common source, their historical testimony is inferior.
Rather, they wanted to preserve the unity of the apostolic tradition about Jesus precisely because it was historically accurate and
deserved a united testimony in its favor. Where they change
Mark, they do so not in ways that falsify the record, but in ways
that combat misinterpretation of Marcan information, add further
details, omit others, and bring out different theological implications.

FORM CRITICISM OF THE GOSPELS

The earliest Christians did not have any of the four gospels,
let alone all four. In the first decades of the twentieth cen-

---

[11]B. H. Streeter, *The Four Gospels* (New York: St. Martin's, 1951),
Part II; compare V. Taylor, *The Formation of the Gospel Tradition* (New
York: St. Martin's, 1960), Appendix A.

tury, therefore, German scholarship set for itself the ambitious task of inferring by literary analysis (*Formgeschichte*, "form history") of the gospels what the *oral* tradition about Jesus was like before it came to be written down. For example, from the beginning of the Christian movement the passion story must have been told and retold at the Lord's Supper and in sermons. Then, as the need for instruction in Christian conduct arose, isolated bits of tradition about the words and deeds of Jesus were recalled as an authoritative pattern. Should Christians marry? Divorce? Pay taxes? The oral tradition about Jesus was kept alive to answer these and similar questions.

Methodology

Form critics try to determine the nature and content of the oral tradition by classifying the individual units of the written gospel material according to literary form[12] and usage in the early Church. The common categories are (1) apothegms, paradigms, or pronouncement stories (stories climaxing in a saying of Jesus) for sermon illustrations, (2) miracle stories as models for the activities of Christian healers, (3) sayings and parables for catechetical instruction, (4) legends designed to magnify the greatness of Jesus (with perhaps a core of historical truth, but greatly exaggerated), and (5) the passion story for celebration of the Lord's Supper and evangelistic preaching. This approach assumes that the early Christians modified the information about Jesus and even invented stories and sayings to meet the needs which arose out of missionary preaching, catechetical instruction, sermonizing, formation of liturgies, doctrinal controversies, and questions of church discipline. As a result, the gospels tell us more about the *Sitz im Leben* ("situation in life") of the early Church than about that of Jesus. To determine the truth about Jesus one must strip away editorial accretions such as geographical and chronological notations, miraculous features, and doctrinal elements supposedly dating from a period later than Jesus.

Results

The Old Testament scholar J. Wellhausen fostered form criticism of the gospels. M. Dibelius popularized it. K. L. Schmidt convinced many that the geographical and chronological framework in Mark was Mark's own invention. And R. Bultmann (best known of the form critics) concluded after detailed analysis that almost all of the gospel tradition was fabricated or highly distorted. A typical line of reasoning is that since Christians believed in the messiahship of Jesus, they justified their belief by concocting stories in which Jesus performed Messianic miracles. We should, thinks Bultmann, "demythologize" the gospels (take

---

[12]A technical designation for an individual unit, or section, of the gospels — such as the story of Jesus' healing a leper or the record of a parable — is the term *pericope* (pĕ rĭk′ō pē).

away the myths) in order to make the Christian message palatable to modern man, who, from his naturalistic viewpoint, can no longer accept the supernatural claims of the gospels in behalf of Jesus.[13]

Form criticism has placed salutary emphasis on literary analysis as a means toward reconstructing the oral gospel tradition and on the continuing relevance of Jesus' words and works for the life of the early Church. The openness of Jesus toward Gentiles, for example, must have helped the entrance of Gentiles into the Church. But utility was not the only factor. Form critics have not allowed enough for purely biographical interest in Jesus on the part of the first Christians. If the early Church really was concerned to appeal to the words and deeds of Jesus for justification of her beliefs and practices — as form critics themselves admit, indeed, assert, then the strongest motives existed for remembering Him. Even Paul, who apparently had not known Jesus, could quote no higher authority (see, for example 1 Corinthians 7:10 ff.).

Nor have form critics allowed for the possibility that the gospel tradition was preserved simply because it was true, as well as because it provided good material for Christian evangelization, teaching, and liturgy. The single generation between Jesus and the writing of the gospels did not allow enough time for extensive proliferation of tradition about Jesus. Mythologies normally do not develop in less than half a century. Yet the early Christians were proclaiming Jesus as a risen and exalted Savior-God almost immediately after His death. Moreover, during the first decades of Church history the hope of Jesus' soon return burned brightly. The early Christians would not therefore have felt very much need for more information about Jesus than was already available.

Form critics seem also to have forgotten that both Christian and anti-Christian eyewitnesses of Jesus' career must have deterred wholesale fabrication and distortion of information. Numerous references throughout the New Testament indicate that the early Christians highly valued the factor of eyewitness in testimony for the sake of reliability. For examples, see Luke 1:1-4; John 1:14; 20:30, 31; 1 Corinthians 15:5-8; 1 John 1:1-4. Not only would both friendly and unfriendly eyewitnesses have provided a restraining influence, but also their recollection of Jesus' teaching and example would have been called upon for solutions to ecclesiastical and doctrinal problems, for answers to

---

[13]See R. Bultmann *et al., Kerygma and Myth,* edited by H. W. Bartsch, revised edition of this translation by R. H. Fuller (New York: Harper, 1961), pp. 1-44; Bultmann, *The History of the Synoptic Tradition,* translated by J. Marsh (New York: Harper & Row, 1963) — very technical; and numerous other writings both by Bultmann and about his methodology and theology.

inquiries from prospective converts, and for apology in the face of malicious charges. There is more than one reason, then, not to underestimate the eyewitness factor behind the gospel tradition.

We must not think that all ancient people gullibly accepted every tale of the supernatural they heard. Scepticism in the Graeco-Roman world was widespread. Even among the disciples evidence had to overcome doubt, as in the case of Thomas, who at first disbelieved the report of Jesus' resurrection. Had Jesus not been the arresting figure portrayed in the gospels, why the great stir about Him? Why was He crucified? Why did people follow Him, and continue to believe on Him and proclaim Him as Savior even after He had died the death of a criminal — indeed, almost immediately after His execution? Would they have been willing to suffer and die, as they did, for a false tradition of their own making? And especially, why did Jews, trained from childhood to worship only the invisible God, feel constrained to worship a man they had known? If the gospels are not reliable, we draw a blank at the beginning of the Christian movement. But the dramatic upsurge of Christianity demands an explanation equal to the phenomenon.

The Church father Papias said in the early second century that Mark wrote down the reminiscences of Peter concerning Jesus. There is not sufficient reason to doubt Papias' statement, or the reliability of the gospels in general. On the contrary, the text of the gospels contains numerous indications of authenticity. Realistic details abound — references to places, names, and customs unnecessary to the overall story — just as one expects in eyewitness accounts. Descriptions of legal practices and social conditions in Palestine *vis à vis* the Hellenistic world exhibit amazing accuracy.[14] Later Christians would have glorified the twelve apostles (as did later Christian literature) rather than unflatteringly portrayed them as bumbling, thickheaded, unbelieving, and cowardly on many occasions. Why would sayings of Jesus embarrassingly difficult to interpret have been invented?[15] Their very difficulty implies authenticity. Also, it is doubtful that distortion and invention would have preserved or produced the distinctively Semitic form of poetry in the teaching of Jesus recorded by the evangelists.[16] The same is true concerning other traits of its Semitic style, which shines

---

[14]See A. N. Sherwin-White, *Roman Society and Roman Law in the New Testament* (Oxford: Clarendon, 1963), chapter 6 and pp. 186 ff.

[15]For examples see Matthew 10:23; Mark 9:1; 13:32.

[16]The poetic form of parallel statements, as in the Hebrew poetry of the Old Testament, is not apparent in most English translations of the gospels. But here is an example of the Semitic poetic parallelism in Jesus' teaching:
Ask, and it will be given to you;
Seek, and you will find;
Knock, and it will be opened to you (Luke 11:9).

through in spite of the fact that the gospels were written in Greek, a non-Semitic language.

The absence of parables from the epistles shows that the early Christians did not use parables as a pedagogical device and therefore must not have created them in the gospels. Similarly, the absence in the epistles of the Christological title "Son of man" (frequent in the gospels) shows it to be distinctive of Jesus and thus authentic. Conversely, the failure of the gospels to say anything about many of the burning issues reflected in Acts and the epistles (such as whether or not Gentile converts should be circumcised) shows that the early Christians carefully protected Jesus' teaching from admixture with their own later developments of doctrine. Paul meticulously separated his own pronouncements on marriage and divorce from the Lord's (1 Corinthians 7:6, 7, 8, 10, 12, 17, 25, 26, 28, 29, 32, 35, 40). Only a' positive assessment of the gospel tradition adequately explains the beginnings of Christianity and the literary features of the gospels and epistles.

THE KERYGMA

The prominent British scholar C. H. Dodd provided an alternative to radical form criticism by distinguishing a common pattern in the sermons in the early chapters of Acts (especially 10:34-43) and in the letters of Paul where Paul occasionally summarizes the Gospel (for example, 1 Corinthians 15:3 ff.; 11:23 ff.; Romans 1:2, 3; 10:9):

Jesus has inaugurated the fulfillment of Messianic prophecy.
He went about doing good and performing miracles.
He was crucified according to God's plan.
He was raised and exalted to heaven.
He will return in judgment.
Therefore, repent, believe, and be baptized.

This pattern Dodd called the *kerygma* (Greek for "proclamation"). Gradually the bare outline of the *kerygma* became filled with stories, sayings, and parables from Jesus' life. As eyewitnesses began to die off, the gospels were written for a permanent record. Also, as the Gospel spread geographically far from Palestine to places where eyewitnesses were not available for confirmation, the need arose for trustworthy written records to be utilized by Christians in their preaching about Jesus' words and deeds. Thus, the gospel of Mark is an expanded *kerygma* in written form.[17]

---

[17]C. H. Dodd, *The Apostolic Preaching and Its Development* (London: Hodder & Stoughton, 1936). In addition, Dodd distinguished *didache,* "teaching" for Christian life and faith, from the evangelistic *kerygma* designed to make converts. It is increasingly recognized that the distinction is hard to maintain. Indeed, the outline of the *kerygma* itself may not have been so rigid as Dodd's reconstruction.

A common idea is that at first the Christians did not even think of writing about the career of Jesus because they expected Him to return in the immediate future. When He failed to do so decade after decade, it dawned on the Christians that more formal and fixed accounts were needed to fill the ever-widening gap. This may be partially true. But the expectation that Jesus would return almost immediately has been overestimated. Closer scrutiny of the relevant texts in the New Testament shows that the early Christians looked for the Second Coming as a *possibility* within their lifetime, but not as a certainty. The books of the New Testament are not products of embarrassment over the delay in the return of Jesus. They exude far too much confidence for us ever to think that.

REDACTION CRITICISM

In reaction against piecemeal treatment of the gospels by form critics, some post-World War II scholars have analyzed the gospels as unified compositions carefully edited (redacted) by their authors to project distinctive theological views. In other words, "redaction criticism" (*Redaktionsgeschicte*) treats the gospels as wholes rather than centering attention on individual sayings and stories. Perhaps the best known and most representative example of this approach is H. Conzelmann's hypothesis that Luke reinterpreted Jesus' ministry to be the midpoint of history with the age of the Church and the Second Coming to follow, not the final stage of history, as Conzelmann alleges the earliest Christians believed.[18] Usually the particular theological viewpoint of the evangelist is attributed to an entire school of thought within the Church. Redaction criticism is really an extension of form critical methodology on a larger scale, so that it too often suffers from the same unjustifiable assumption of historical distortion in the gospels. Nevertheless, value lies in the emphasis on broad theological themes.

THE STUDY OF JESUS' LIFE

Most contemporary scholars agree that a full-scale biography of Jesus is impossible because the gospels are very selective in the amount and kind of information they present about Jesus. But in the nineteenth century, before this restriction was felt so keenly, several outstanding biographies of Jesus appeared. A radical treatment by the German scholar D. F. Strauss (1835) concluded that most of the material in the gospels was mytho-

---

[18]H. Conzelmann, *The Theology of St. Luke,* translated by G. Buswell (London: Faber & Faber, 1960). We must question, however, Conzelmann's conclusion that Luke's view of history represents a *shift* from an expectation that Jesus would return almost immediately.

logical. E. Renan's life of Christ (1863) became famous for its literary beauty. In it this French writer portrayed Jesus as an amiable carpenter who turned into an apocalyptist. In 1883 Alfred Edersheim, a converted Jew, produced his widely used and orthodox *Life and Times of Jesus the Messiah* from a background of acquaintance with rabbinical lore. At the turn of the century the typical liberal view, outstandingly represented by the German scholar A. Harnack, saw in Jesus a good example of sacrificial service to mankind and a teacher of lofty ethical ideals, but not a divine-human redeemer.

In 1906 Albert Schweitzer startled the theological world with his *Quest of the Historical Jesus.* As indicated by the original German title, *Von Reimarus zu Wrede,* it was a critical survey of modern studies of Jesus' life. Schweitzer argued that liberal treatments rested on preconceived notions of modern scholars rather than on the data in the gospels. According to Schweitzer, Jesus thought that God's kingdom on earth was about to arrive and that He would then become the Messiah. In fact, Jesus told the twelve disciples that God would send the Son of man (the superhuman Messiah) to establish the kingdom before they completed a preaching mission throughout Galilee (Matthew 10:23). When His expectation failed to materialize, Jesus became increasingly convinced that He would have to die for the bringing about of the kingdom.

Meanwhile, He revealed the secret of His messiahship to Peter, James, and John at the transfiguration. Peter then betrayed the secret to the rest of the twelve on the occasion of his great confession (Mark 8:27-30; Matthew 16:13-20; Luke 9:18-20). (To achieve this reconstruction Schweitzer had to switch the order of Peter's confession and Jesus' transfiguration as given in the synoptics.) Judas then betrayed the secret to the Jewish authorities, who set in motion the events which culminated in the death of Jesus. Jesus Himself courageously but foolishly thought that God would raise Him from the dead and immediately reveal Him to the world on the clouds of heaven for the establishment of the divine kingdom on earth. That, of course, did not happen — and for Schweitzer Jesus became a tragic and mysterious figure hard for modern men to understand but worthy of imitation in His selfless dedication.

Schweitzer's portrait of Jesus has not received general acceptance. He laid too much stress on Matthew 10:23, which can be interpreted in other ways. He disregarded statements by Jesus that God's kingdom had already arrived. He failed to explain adequately why Jesus gave large amounts of ethical teaching. Someone who believed and proclaimed that the world was going to end in the next few weeks or months would hardly have felt the need for instructing people at length on how to behave in the present evil society. Schweitzer's great contribution, however, was that he forced reconsideration of the eschatological[19] teaching of Jesus and the Messianic implications of His ministry, both of which were being passed over lightly by most liberal scholars.

In the present state of research on the life of Jesus, disparate opinions clamor for recognition. Bultmannians still reject most of the gospel tradition. Some of Bultmann's former students, dubbed 'post-Bultmannians," accept a tiny bit more as authentic, but the amount is insignificant.[20] Mediating scholars accept a larger proportion as authentic; they feel free, however, to reject the rest. Orthodox scholars find good historical and theological reasons for total acceptance of the gospel records. This does not imply that the evangelists always quoted the words of Jesus verbatim. The differences among the gospels imply frequent editorial arrangement and paraphrasing, a perfectly legitimate way to convey someone else's meaning. Nor do orthodox scholars insist on a complete and always chronological account of Jesus' activities. But measured by the purpose for which they were written — to proclaim the good news about Jesus the Christ — the gospels merit full trust.

For further discussion:

> How do literary interrelationships, differences among the gospels in wording and order, and the use and revision of source materials relate to belief in the divine origin and inspiration of the Bible?

> To what extent, if any, should the Gospel be made palatable or acceptable to modern man (a major question raised by Bultmann's program of demythologization)?

> What is a "myth"? What is its relationship to historicity? To universal human experience? Depending on definitions, does the Bible contain myths?

For further investigation consult the books cited in the footnotes to the preceding chapter and the bibliography at the close of the following chapter. For evangelical treatments of some of the issues here discussed, see also

Bruce, F. F. *The New Testament Documents: Are They Reliable?* 5th revised edition. Grand Rapids: Eerdmans, 1960.
Althaus, P. *et al. Jesus of Nazareth, Saviour and Lord.* Edited by C. F. H. Henry. Grand Rapids: Eerdmans, 1966.
Ladd, G. E. *The New Testament and Criticism.* Grand Rapids: Eerdmans, 1966.

---

[19]*Eschatological* means "having to do with the 'end' of history."
[20]See J. M. Robinson, *A New Quest of the Historical Jesus* (Naperville: Allenson, 1959).

In general terms compare *The Life of Apollonius* by Philostratus, parts of which are quoted in C. K. Barrett, *The New Testament Background: Selected Documents* (New York: Harper & Row, 1961), pp. 76-79, with the portraits of Jesus given in the gospels.

To appreciate some of the issues debated by source, form, and redaction critics, carefully compare the Matthaean and Lucan accounts of the Sermon on the Mount (5-7 and 6:20-49 respectively), the different accounts of the Last Supper (Matthew 26:20-35; Mark 14:17-31; Luke 22:14-38; John 13-17), or practically any other part of the gospel tradition, including smaller units.

CHAPTER 6

The Four Gospels

Leading questions:

> Who wrote the gospels?
>
> How do we determine their authorship?
>
> How close did the authors stand to the eyewitness tradition of Jesus' life and teaching?
>
> What are the indications concerning the date of writing?
>
> To what audience, from what perspective, and with what purpose did the evangelists write?
>
> What are the distinctive characteristics and special emphases of the several gospels?
>
> What is the overall plan and movement of each gospel?

The books we call the gospels were a new kind of literature at their time of writing. Unlike true biographies, they lack contemporary historical background, analysis of character and personality, and probing of the inner thoughts of the hero. Nor are the gospels like Hellenistic miracle narratives, in which the real or supposed acts of ancient miracle workers were celebrated — there is much more than narration of miracles in the gospels. Nor do the gospels present us with simple memoirs. Rather, they are written proclamations of redemptive history from theological perspectives.

MARK: THE GOSPEL OF JESUS' REDEMPTIVE ACTIVITY

Marcan Authorship and Petrine Tradition

Since titles were added only later to the gospels, we depend on early tradition and internal evidence for questions of authorship. The first gospel to have been written takes its name from John Mark, who appears as the companion of Paul, Barnabas, and Peter in Acts and the epistles. The early Church father Papias is reported to have said in the first half of the second century that Mark accurately wrote down in his gospel Peter's

78

reminiscences of Jesus' life and teachings, but not always in chronological or rhetorical order since the purpose was spiritual instruction rather than artistic chronicling of events.[1] Irenaeus, Clement of Alexandria, Origen, and Jerome confirm authorship by Mark in association with Peter.

Although the order of Mark's material appears in general to be chronological, key words and similarity of subject matter frequently form the principle of arrangement for individual stories and sayings. For example, Mark 2:1—3:6 contains the following stories: the healing of the paralytic and the forgiving of his sins with the subsequent discussion on the authority of Jesus to forgive sins; the argument about Jesus' eating with publicans after the call of Levi (Matthew); the debate over fasting; the criticism of the disciples for plucking and eating grain on the Sabbath and Jesus' defense of them; and Jesus' healing a man's withered hand over the objections of the Pharisees. Mark strings together these stories apparently because they all deal with Jesus' controversies with the scribes and Pharisees.

With little exception Mark is the gospel of action instead of lengthy discourse. In quick-moving narrative Mark relates Jesus' activities as the mighty and authoritative Son of God, particularly His miracles of healing and exorcisms. The kingdom of God invades the kingdom of evil as Jesus combats Satanic and demonic forces. An adverb usually translated "immediately" or "straightway" (but also "forthwith," "at once," "as soon as," "anon") is the key word. Mark is so fond of it that he does not always mean "immediately" in the strict sense, but uses it simply as a transitional word to convey the thought that Jesus was constantly busy as the servant-worker.

Action

The redemptive activity of Jesus culminates in the account of Jesus' passion, death, and resurrection, to which Mark devotes a disproportionately large amount of space — so much, in fact, that the gospel has been called little more than a passion account with a prologue. Peter's confession of Jesus' messiahship at Caesarea Philippi (8:27-30) forms a turning point in the gospel. From then on Jesus begins to predict His suffering and death as the Son of man, and the narrative moves inexorably to that end. The disciples were used to thinking of the Son of man, Jesus' favorite self-designation taken from Daniel's vision of a human-like figure coming in glory to judge mankind (Daniel 7:13, 14), in terms of majesty, and therefore found it difficult to understand and accept Jesus' statements.

---

[1]Quoted by Eusebius, *Ecclesiastical History* III. xxxix. 15. Compare the special mention of Peter in Mark 16:7: "Go, tell His disciples and Peter, ..."

Modern scholars have suggested a number of different purposes behind the writing of Mark. Some think that Mark wrote to give catechetical instruction to new converts. But his failure to give very much of Jesus' teaching undermines that view. Others think that Mark wrote his gospel for liturgical use in church services. But the arrangement and style lack the smoothness and symmetry one would expect in a liturgical document. Still others think that Mark wrote to cover up a failure by Jesus to proclaim Himself the Messiah. Mark backhandedly removed this embarrassment to Christian theology by inventing the "Messianic secret." That is, he put into Jesus' mouth prohibitions against public revelation of His messiahship (for example, 8:30) in order to make it appear that Jesus really did teach in private that He was the Messiah, though He actually did not.[2] Others think oppositely that by inventing the Messianic secret Mark was attempting to *soften* the offensiveness of a ministry that was overly Messianic. Both views which see Mark's purpose in the Messianic secret depend on an illegitimate scepticism regarding the accuracy of reporting in the gospels; and most readers of Mark will not gain the impression that he was embarrassed either by too little or by too much Messianism in the tradition about Jesus.

Historically, it is quite understandable why Jesus suppressed publicity of His messiahship: (1) the Jews misconceived the Messiah to be a politico-military figure to the practical exclusion of spiritual redemptorship — thus Jesus spoke of His sacrificial suffering and death in terms of the suffering Servant of the Lord depicted in Isaiah (particularly 52:13—53:12); (2) the Jews lacked the dimension of deity in their concept of the Messiah — thus Jesus referred to Himself as the superhuman Son of man who came with the theophanic symbol of clouds for everlasting dominion over the world in one of Daniel's visions (7:13, 14); (3) had Jesus encouraged publicity of His messiahship in spite of the certainty of misunderstandings, He almost certainly would have exposed Himself to quick arrest and trial — thus He gained time and avoided a premature end to His ministry by the suppression. It is not at all necessary or advisable, then, to think that Mark "invented" the Messianic secret.

The true purpose of Mark is evangelistic. He narrates the story of Jesus to win converts to the Christian faith. For the attainment of this purpose, Mark constructs his gospel quite simply. He begins with John the Baptist and the baptism and temptation of Jesus (1:1-13), proceeds to the ministry of Jesus in and around Galilee (1:14—9:50), continues with the ministry

---

[2]W. Wrede, *Das Messiasgeheimnis in den Evangelien: Zugleich ein Beitrag zum Verständnis des Markusevangeliums* (Göttingen: Vandenhoeck und Ruprecht, 1901, 3rd ed., 1963). Wrede attributed this motivation to the predecessors of Mark whose material he used.

on the way to Jerusalem through Transjordan and Judea (10:
1-52), and concludes with the accounts of Jesus' divinely planned
passion, death, and resurrection (11:1—16:8).

But we do not know how the gospel ended. Some of the best
early manuscripts and versions end with 16:8. Others add the
"long ending" (included in the familiar King James Version),
and others a short ending. The long ending appears to be a
scribal attempt to make up an appropriate conclusion by sum-
marizing the resurrection appearances recorded in the other gospels. The short ending likewise appears to lack authenticity.
But it is unknown whether the gospel ends at 16:8 or whether
the true ending is lost.[3]

Early Christian tradition evinces uncertainty whether Mark   Date
wrote his gospel before or after the martyrdom of Peter (A.D.
64), and modern scholars dispute the date of Mark's writing.
Those who regard "the abomination of desolation" in 13:14 as a
reference to the fall of Jerusalem in A.D. 70 after it happened
must necessarily date the book after that event. But a *post
eventum* allusion to the destruction of the Temple would
surely have been clearer, and this method of dating assumes that
the verse in question is a backward historical reference rather
than a genuine prediction by Jesus. Data is lacking to answer
firmly the question of date. But if one accepts the phenomenon
of predictive prophecy, no compelling reasons exist to deny an
early date in the period A.D. 45-70. In fact, if Luke ended Acts
without describing the outcome of Paul's trial in Rome because
the trial had not yet taken place, then Acts must be dated
about A.D. 61, its preceding companion volume, the gospel of
Luke, somewhat earlier, and — since the gospel of Luke utilized
Mark — Mark still earlier in the fifties or late forties.

Mark probably wrote for a Roman reading audience. He   Roman Audience
translated Aramaic expressions for the benefit of his readers   and Place of
(3:17; 5:41; 7:34; 14:36; 15:34). Even more indicatively, he   Writing
explained Greek expressions by their Latin equivalents (12:42;
15:16) and used a number of other Latin terms. Confirmation
comes from the mention in 15:21 of a Rufus, who according to
Romans 16:31 lived in Rome (unless the two texts refer to different men with the same name). In addition, the presence of
Mark in Rome (symbolically called "Babylon") according to 1
Peter 5:13, the combination of Papias' statement that Mark was

---

[3]This textual question does not affect any major doctrine of the Christian
faith. Biblical inspiration is certainly not at issue, only what was the original
text of the Bible as opposed to later additions by copyists. The earliest and
most trustworthy manuscripts of the New Testament had not yet been discovered in 1611, so that the translators of the King James Version could not
have known that the long ending was textually doubtful.

Peter's interpreter with the early tradition of Peter's martyrdom in Rome, the indication in the anti-Marcionite prologue to Mark[4] that Mark wrote his gospel in Italy, and further statements by Clement of Alexandria and Irenaeus add external testimony to the Roman origin and address of the gospel of Mark.

A SUMMARY OUTLINE OF MARK

Theme: the redemptive activity of Jesus

INTRODUCTION:
- A. The ministry of John the Baptist (1:1-8)
- B. The baptism of Jesus (1:9-11)
- C. The temptation of Jesus (1:12, 13)

I. THE REDEMPTIVE ACTIVITY OF JESUS IN AND AROUND GALILEE (1:14—9:50)
- A. The first preaching (1:14, 15)
- B. The call of Simon, Andrew, James, and John (1:16-20)
- C. A group of miracles (1:21-45)
  1. Evorcism in the synagogue at Capernaum (1:21-28)
  2. The healing of Peter's mother-in-law and others (1:29-39)
  3. The cleansing of a leper (1:40-45)
- D. A group of controversies (2:1—3:35)
  1. The forgiveness and healing of a paralytic (2:1-12)
  2. The call of Levi [Matthew] and Jesus' eating with publicans and sinners (2:13-17)
  3. The question about fasting (2:18-22)
  4. The plucking and eating of grain on the Sabbath (2:23-27)
  5. The healing of a withered hand on the Sabbath (3:1-6)
  6. Jesus' withdrawal and choice of The Twelve (3:7-19a)
  7. The charges that Jesus was insane and possessed by Beelzebul (3:19b-35)
- E. A group of parables (4:1-34)
  1. The seed and the soils [more commonly, the sower] (4:1-20)
  2. The lamp (4:21-25)
  3. The growing grain (4:26-29)
  4. The mustard seed and others (4:30-34)
- F. More miracles (4:35—5:43)
  1. The stilling of the storm (4:35-41)
  2. The exorcism of Legion from the Gerasene demoniac (5:1-20)
  3. The healing of the woman with a constant hemorrhage and the raising of Jairus' daughter (5:21-43)
- G. Rejection at Nazareth (6:1-6)
- H. The mission of The Twelve throughout Galilee (6:7-13)
- I. The beheading of John the Baptist (6:14-29)
- J. The feeding of the five thousand (6:30-44)
- K. Jesus' walking on the water (6:45-52)
- L. Ministry at Gennesaret with controversy over ceremonial defilement (6:53—7:23)
- M. More miracles (7:24—8:26)
  1. Exorcism of a demon from the daughter of a Syro-phoenician woman (7:24-30)
  2. The healing of a deaf-mute (7:31-37)
  3. The feeding of the four thousand (8:1-10)
  4. The demand of the Pharisees for a sign in the midst of miracles (8:11-21)
  5. The healing of a blind man (8:22-26)

---

[4]The anti-Marcionite prologues are early manuscript introductions directed against Marcionism, a brand of the Gnostic heresy.

N. Peter's confession of Jesus' messiahship (8:27-30)

O. Peter's concept of Jesus' messiahship and discipleship, corrected by Jesus' prediction of suffering, death, and resurrection (8:31—9:1)

P. The transfiguration (9:2-13)

Q. The exorcising of a demon from a boy (9:14-29)

R. Another prediction by Jesus of His death and resurrection (9:30-32)

S. Jesus' making a child an example of His disciples (9:33-50)

II. THE REDEMPTIVE ACTIVITY OF JESUS ON THE WAY TO JERUSALEM THROUGH TRANSJORDAN AND JUDEA (10:1-52)

A. The question of divorce (10:1-12)

B. Jesus' blessing of children (10:13-16)

C. The rich young ruler (10:17-31)

D. Another prediction by Jesus of His death and resurrection (10:32-34)

E. The request of James and John for places of honor and Jesus' reply concerning self-sacrificial service (10:35-45)

F. The healing of blind Bartimaeus (10:46-52)

III. THE REDEMPTIVE ACTIVITY OF JESUS DURING THE WEEK OF HIS PASSION, DEATH, AND RESURRECTION (11:1—16:8)

A. The triumphal entry (11:1-11)

B. The cursing of the barren fig tree (11:12-14)

C. The cleansing of the Temple (11:15-19)

D. The withering of the fig tree (11:20-26)

E. Debates in the Temple (11:27—12:44)

    1. The demand for a sign from Jesus (11:27-33)

    2. The parable of the vineyard (12:1-12)

    3. The question about paying taxes to Caesar (12:13-17)

    4. The question about the resurrection (12:18-27)

    5. The question about the most important commandment (12:28-34)

    6. Jesus' question about the Messiah's Davidic descent and lordship (12:35-37)

    7. Jesus' warning against the scribes (12:38-40)

    8. The widow's mite versus large gifts from the rich (12:41-44)

F. The Olivet Discourse (13:1-37)

G. The Sanhedrin's plot against Jesus (14:1, 2)

H. The anointing of Jesus by Mary of Bethany (14:3-9)

I. The bargain of Judas Iscariot to betray Jesus (14:10, 11)

J. The Last Supper (14:12-31)

K. Jesus' praying in Gethsemane (14:32-52)

L. The arrest of Jesus (14:43-52)

M. The trial of Jesus (14:53—15:20)

    1. The hearing before the Sanhedrin, with Peter's denials (14:53-72)

    2. The hearing before Pontius Pilate, with the release of Barabbas (15:1-20)

N. The crucifixion, death, and burial of Jesus (15:21-47)

O. The resurrection of Jesus (16:1-8)

MATTHEW: THE GOSPEL OF THE MESSIAH AND THE NEW PEOPLE OF GOD

Authorship

The same Papias who said Mark wrote down Peter's reminiscences also said that Matthew wrote *logia* (Greek for "sayings, oracles") in Hebrew or Aramaic, which others translated as they were able.[5] In context *logia* most naturally refers to a gospel. But we do not possess a gospel from the pen of Matthew in either of the Semitic languages Hebrew and Aramaic, only the present Greek gospel, which appears *not* to be a translation from a Semitic original. For example, why should Matthew

---

[5]Quoted by Eusebius, *Ecclesiastical History* III. xxxix. 16.

have given the Semitic originals and Greek translations of a *few* terms, such as "Immanuel" (1:23), if the *whole* gospel were translation from Hebrew or Aramaic? Some have thought that Papias referred only to a catena of Messianic proof texts in Hebrew or Aramaic drawn up by Matthew and later incorporated in Greek translation into this gospel, or to an earlier Semitic edition of Matthew not directly related to our present Greek edition. Yet another understanding is that Papias referred to our present Greek Matthew as written in the Hebrew *style* (rather than language) and as Matthew's *interpretation* of Jesus' life (alongside Mark's interpretation). If so, there is no reference to *translation* of Matthew from a Semitic original. Finally, it is thought by some that *logia* in Papias refers to Q.[6] Certainty about the meaning of Papias' statement thus eludes us.

Modern scholars usually deny that the Apostle Matthew wrote the gospel bearing his name. Following the equation of Papias' *logia* with Q, some suggest that Matthew did write Q and that his name became mistakenly attached to the first gospel (in the order of our canon) because the unknown writer of the first gospel utilized so much of Q. But if there was a Q, adequate reasons do not exist for denying that Matthew might have written both, especially if Q was a body of loose notes on Jesus' teaching taken by Matthew and incorporated into his formal gospel. It is argued to the contrary that an apostle like Matthew would not have borrowed from a non-apostle like Mark. But Matthew may simply be corroborating the Petrine and therefore apostolic tradition recorded by Mark, while adding his own material. And regardless of stature, ancient authors regularly borrowed from previous writers; and no one thought that by so doing they were plagiarizing, or demeaning themselves. Modern feelings did not apply. Early Church tradition unanimously ascribes the first gospel to Matthew, and false ascription to a relatively obscure apostle such as Matthew seems unlikely until a later date when all the apostles became canonized in Christian imagination.

The organizational skill of the author (see below) agrees with the probable mentality of a tax collector such as the Apostle Matthew had been. So also does the fact that this is the only gospel to contain the story of Jesus' paying the Temple tax (17:24-27). The account of the call of Matthew to discipleship uses the apostolic name "Matthew"[7] rather than the name "Levi" used by Mark and Luke and omits the possessive pronoun "his" used with "house (home)" by Mark and Luke in describing the place where Matthew entertained Jesus at dinner (9:9-13; com-

---

[6]See pages 68 f.
[7]See the lists of the apostles in Matthew 10:2-4; Mark 3:16-19; Luke 6:13-16; Acts 1:13.

pare Mark 2:13-17; Luke 5:27-32). These incidental details may well constitute telltale indications of Matthaean authorship in support of the early Church tradition.

If Matthew utilized Mark and Mark dates from the period A.D. 45-70, Matthew probably dates from slightly later within that same era. Denial of predictive prophecy by Jesus and a generally more negative critical approach will force a later date in the eighties or nineties,[8] although a number of orthodox scholars prefer a late date because of other considerations, such as the argument that Matthew's interest in the Church (he is the only evangelist to use the term, and that twice) betrays a later period when the doctrine of the Church was assuming more importance as a result of the delay in Jesus' return. But the doctrine of the Church already plays an important role in the Pauline epistles, all written before A.D. 70. And if Matthew wrote to evangelize Jews,[9] it seems less likely that he wrote after A.D. 70, when the breach between Church and synagogue widened, than before A.D. 70, when prospects for converting Jews seemed brighter.

The gospel of Matthew is the gospel of the Messiah and of the new people of God, the Church, which at least for the time being has replaced the old covenant nation of Israel. The first gospel begins with the nativity (chapters 1 and 2). In the great middle section, primarily Marcan narrative (usually condensed) and discourses of Jesus alternate. Chapters 26-28 conclude the gospel with accounts of Jesus' passion and resurrection.

The discourses in Matthew are more or less lengthy "sermons," to which isolated sayings of Jesus have been added in appropriate places. Each discourse ends with the formula, "It came to pass that when Jesus had finished these sayings, ..." The discourses and their themes are as follows:

1) The Sermon on the Mount (chapters 5-7): The Meaning of True (Inward) Righteousness
2) The Commission of The Twelve (chapter 10): The Meaning of Witness for Christ (Persecution and Reward)
3) The Parables (chapter 13): The Meaning of the Kingdom
4) [No generally used title] (chapter 18): The Meaning of Humility and Forgiveness

---

[8] Those who balk at predictive prophecy think that the phraseology of 22:7 ("The king . . . sent his troops . . . and burned their city") clearly points back to the destruction of Jerusalem in A.D. 70 from a later vantage point.

[9] The point is disputed, but this is the natural and general impression most readers will gain from the gospel.

5) The Denunciation of the Scribes and Pharisees (chapter 23) and the Olivet Discourse, often called "The Little Apocalypse" (chapters 24, 25): The Meaning of Israel's Rejection [God has rejected Israel because they have rejected Jesus the Messiah; a time lapse will therefore occur, Jerusalem will be destroyed, the nations will be evangelized, and then Christ will return]

The fivefold structure of these discourses suggests that for the benefit of Jewish readers Matthew was portraying Jesus as a new and greater Moses. Like Moses He spoke part of His law from a mountain. Like Moses his teaching is contained in five sections, corresponding to the Pentateuch (Genesis, Exodus, Leviticus, Numbers, and Deuteronomy, together called "The Law of Moses"). By omitting the story of the "widow's mite," Matthew even welds the denunciation of the scribes and Pharisees and the Olivet discourse into a single unit (contrast Mark 12:38 ff.; Luke 20:45 ff.) in order to gain his fivefold arrangement.

His comparison of Jesus to Moses shows itself elsewhere, too, as in the borrowing of phraseology from the story of Moses to describe Jesus' nativity and transfiguration (Exodus 2:15; 4:19, 20; 34:29; Deuteronomy 18:15; with Matthew 2:13, 20, 21; 17:2, 5 respectively). Indeed, in Matthew's (but not Luke's) version of the Sermon on the Mount, Jesus Himself consciously sets His teaching alongside the Mosaic law in a series of statements, "You have heard that it was said to the men of old [there follows a quotation from the Pentateuch] . . . But I say to you . . ." (Matthew 5:21, 27, 31, 33, 38, 43).

Besides the fivefold structure of the discourses, there are many other indications of Matthew's penchant for organization. Groupings of three and seven appear to be favored by Matthew. He divides the genealogy of Jesus into three sections (1:17). He gives from Jesus' teaching three examples of righteous conduct, three prohibitions, and three commandments (6:1—7:20). And there are the further instances of three parables, three questions, three prayers, and three denials. Perhaps Matthew wrote under the impress of the Jewish law that in the mouth of two or three witnesses every word should be established (Deuteronomy 17:6; 19:5; actually quoted in Matthew 18:16). There are seven parables in Matthew 13 and seven woes against the scribes and Pharisees in chapter 23. Even though some of these numerical groupings doubtless go back to Jesus Himself and the events themselves, their frequency in Matthew shows his fondness for them above that of the other evangelists.

The editorial organization of Jesus' teaching, its strongly ethical content, and its emphasis on discipleship have led to the views that the first gospel was intended to be a catechetical manual for new converts or a scholastic manual for Church leaders and that it was designed for liturgical and homiletical reading in the services of the early churches. But the first gospel gives a much clearer impression of having been written to evangelize Jews and to confirm them in their faith after conversion.

Matthew's recurring stress on Jesus' fulfillment of the law and of Messianic prophecy in the Old Testament ("Such and such happened so that what was spoken by so-and-so the prophet might be fulfilled") and his tracing of Jesus' genealogy back to Abraham, father of the Jewish nation, also indicate the Jewish slant of the first gospel. By way of contrast, Mark does not trace the ancestry of Jesus at all. His interest lies in what Jesus *does,* and his Gentile readers (like most modern readers) would have little concern for the genealogy of Jesus. But it is very important for Matthew to demonstrate to his Jewish readers that the genealogy of Jesus their Messiah goes back to Abraham through David.

Still other Jewish features are the typically Jewish designation of God as the "Father in heaven" (fifteen times in Matthew, only once in Mark, and not at all in Luke), reverential substitution of "heaven" for the name of God (especially in the phrase "kingdom of heaven," where the other evangelists have "kingdom of God"), typically Jewish interest in eschatology (Matthew has a whole chapter more of the Olivet Discourse than Mark and Luke), frequent references to Jesus as the "son of David," allusions to Jewish customs without elucidation (23:5, 27; 15:2 in contrast with the explanation in Mark 7:2, 3), the record of Jesus' paying the Temple tax (17:24-27, lacking in the other gospels), and statements of Jesus which have specially Jewish flavor (for example, "I was sent only to the lost sheep of the house of Israel" [15:24]; "Go nowhere among the Gentiles, and enter no town of the Samaritans, but go rather to the lost sheep of the house of Israel" [10:5, 6]; also 5:17-24; 6:16-18; 23:2, 3). Matthew appears to tell the nativity story against Jewish charges that Jesus was born illegitimately, learned magical arts in Egypt, and came from Nazareth instead of the proper place, Bethlehem (chapters 1 and 2). Matthew also counters the Jewish charge that the disciples of Jesus stole away His body (28:11-15).

On the other hand, universalism also characterizes the gospel of Matthew. He closes with the great commission for His followers to make disciples of all nations (28:19, 20). Toward the beginning of the gospel, the Gentile magi worship the infant Messiah in the nativity story (2:1-12). Jesus is quoted as saying that "many will come from the east and west and sit at table with Abraham, Isaac, and Jacob in the kingdom of heaven, while the sons of the kingdom will be thrown into the outer darkness" (8:11, 12). "The field is the *world*" in the parable of the wheat and tares (13:38). According to the parable of the vineyard, God will transfer His kingdom from Israel to others (21:33-43). And Matthew is the only evangelist to use the word "church" in his gospel (16:18; 18:17). We must say, then, that Matthew is a Jewish Christian gospel with a universal outlook.

Place of Writing

The Jewish nature of the first gospel suggests that it was written in Palestine or Syria, particularly Antioch, to which many of the original Palestinian disciples had migrated (Acts 11:19, 27). The remarkable concern for Gentiles may tip the scales in favor of Antioch, the city with the church that sent Paul on his Gentile missions. In agreement with this is the fact that the oldest witness for the knowledge of the gospel of Matthew is the early bishop of the church in Antioch, Ignatius (first quarter of the second century; *Epistle to the Smyrnaeans* 1:1; *Epistle to Polycarp* 1:2, 3).

A SUMMARY OUTLINE OF MATTHEW

Theme: the Messiah and the new people of God

I. THE NATIVITY OF THE MESSIAH (1:1—2:23)
   A. His genealogy (1:1-17)
   B. His birth (1:18-25)
   C. The worship of Him by the Magi (2:1-12)
   D. The flight into Egypt for protection from Herod the Great (2:13-18)
   E. The return and residence in Nazareth (2:19-23)
II. THE MINISTRY OF THE MESSIAH IN WORDS AND WORKS (3:1—25:46)
   A. Narrative (3:1—4:25)
      1. The preparatory ministry of John the Baptist (3:1-17)
         a. His preaching (3:1-12)
         b. His baptism of Jesus (3:13-17)
      2. The temptation of Jesus by Satan (4:1-11)
      3. Beginnings of Messianic preaching and miracle-working in Galilee, with the call of Simon Peter, Andrew, James, and John (4:12-25)
   B. First discourse: the Sermon on the Mount (5:1—7:29)
   C. Narrative (8:1—9:34)
      1. The cleansing of a leper (8:1-4)
      2. The healing of a centurion's servant (8:5-13)
      3. The healing of Peter's mother-in-law and others (8:14-17)
      4. The cost and urgency of discipleship (8:18-22)
      5. The stilling of the storm (8:23-27)
      6. The deliverance of two Gadarene demoniacs (8:28-34)
      7. The forgiveness and healing of a paralytic (9:1-8)
      8. The call of Matthew and Jesus' eating with publicans and sinners (9:9-13)
      9. The question about fasting (9:14-17)
      10. The healing of a woman with constant hemorrhaging and the raising of a ruler's deceased daughter (9:18-26)
      11. The healing of two blind men (9:27-31)
      12. The deliverance of a dumb demoniac (9:32-34)
   D. Second discourse: the commission and instruction of the twelve disciples for their mission throughout Galilee (9:35—11:1)

E. Narrative (11:2—12:50)
   1. The testimony of Jesus to John the Baptist (11:2-15)
   2. Jesus' condemnation of the unrepentant (11:16-24)
   3. His thanksgiving to the Father and invitation to the weary (11:25-30)
   4. His lordship over the Sabbath (12:1-14)
     a. His defense of the disciples' plucking and eating grain on the Sabbath (12:1-8)
     b. His healing a withered hand on the Sabbath (12:9-14)
   5. His withdrawal and further healings (12:15-21)
   6. His delivering a blind and dumb demoniac and defense of His exorcisms (12:22-37)
   7. His refusal to give any sign except that of Jonah, condemnation of self-righteousness, and identification of His true spiritual kindred (12:38-50)
F. Third discourse: seven parables about the kingdom (13:1-52)
   1. The seed and the soils [more commonly, the sower] (13:1-9)
   2. The reasons for parabolic teaching: baffling of unbelievers and illumination of believers (13:10-17)
   3. The interpretation of the seed and the soils (13:18-23)
   4. The wheat and the tares (13:24-30)
   5. The grain of mustard seed (13:31,32)
   6. The leaven and the fulfillment of Scripture by the parabolic method (13:33-35)
   7. The interpretation of the wheat and the tares (13:36-43)
   8. The buried treasure (13:44)
   9. The costly pearl (13:45, 46)
  10. The dragnet with good and bad fish and a final statement about understanding the parables (13:47-52)
G. Narrative (13:53—17:27)
   1. The rejection of Jesus at Nazareth (13:53-58)
   2. The death of John the Baptist (14:1-12)
   3. The feeding of the five thousand (14:13-21)
   4. Jesus' and Peter's walking on the water (14:22-36)
   5. Ceremonial versus moral and ethical defilement (15:1-20)
   6. The deliverance of the demonized daughter of a Canaanite woman and other healings (15:21-28)
   7. The feeding of the four thousand (15:32-39)
   8. Another refusal to give any sign except that of Jonah (16:1-4)
   9. A warning against Phariseeism and Sadduceeism (16:5-12)
  10. Peter's confession of Jesus' messiahship and the blessing of Peter (16:13-20)
  11. Prediction by Jesus of His suffering, death, and resurrection; a rebuke of Peter for trying to dissuade Jesus; and a call to cross-bearing discipleship (16:24-28)
  12. The transfiguration of Jesus (17:1-13)
  13. The healing of a demonized boy (17:14-21)
  14. Another prediction by Jesus of His death and resurrection (17:22, 23)
  15. The paying of the Temple tax, or "Peter's Penny" (17:24-27)
H. Fourth discourse: humility and forgiveness, with the parable about the two servant debtors (18:1-35)
I. Narrative (19:1—22:46)
   1. The questions of divorce and marriage (19:1-12)
   2. Jesus' blessing the children (19:13-15)
   3. The rich young ruler and the cost and reward of discipleship (19:16-30)
   4. The parable of the employer and the laborers (20:1-16)
   5. Another prediction by Jesus of His death and resurrection (20:17-19)
   6. The request for positions of honor by the mother of James and John for her sons (20:20-28)
   7. The healing of two blind men near Jericho (20:29-34)

8. The triumphal entry (21:1-11)
9. The cleansing of the Temple (21:12-17)
10. The cursing and withering of the fig tree (21:18-22)
11. The challenge to Jesus' authority (21:23-27)
12. The parable of the obedient and disobedient sons (21:28-32)
13. The parable of the wicked tenants (21:33-46)
14. The parable of the royal marriage feast and wedding garment (22:1-14)
15. The question about paying taxes to Caesar (22:15-22)
16. The question of the Sadducees about the resurrection (22:23-33)
17. The question about the identity of the greatest commandment (12:34-40)
18. Jesus' question about the Messiah's Davidic descent and lordship (22:41-46)

J. Fifth discourse (23:1—25:46)
1. Woes against the scribes and Pharisees (23:1-39)
2. The Olivet Discourse (24:1—25:46)
   a. A preview of events leading up to and including the return of Christ (24:1-31)
   b. Exhortations to watchfulness, with the parables of the fig tree, the thief, the faithful and unfaithful servants, the ten virgins, and the talents (24:32—25:30)
   c. The judgment of the sheep and the goats (25:31-46)

III. THE DEATH AND RESURRECTION OF THE MESSIAH (26:1—28:20)
A. Another prediction by Jesus of His death, the plot of the Sanhedrin, and the anointing of Jesus in Bethany, with the resultant bargain by Judas Iscariot to betray Jesus (26:1-16)
B. The Last Supper (26:17-35)
C. Jesus' praying in Gethsemane (26:36-46)
D. The arrest (26:47-56)
E. The trial (26:57—27:26)
1. The hearing before Caiaphas, with Peter's denials (26:57-75)
2. The condemnatory decision of the Sanhedrin (27:1, 2)
3. The hearing before Pontius Pilate, with the suicide of Judas and the release of Barabbas (27:3-26)
F. The crucifixion and death of Jesus (27:27-56)
G. The burial (27:57-66)
H. The resurrection (28:1-15)
I. The great commission (28:16-20)

EXCURSUS ON NEW TESTAMENT QUOTATIONS OF FULFILLED OLD TESTAMENT PASSAGES

Matthew's emphasis on fulfilled Messianic prophecy makes appropriate here a consideration of the fulfillment motif throughout the New Testament. The writers of the New Testament and Jesus Himself saw in the new age the fulfillment of both conscious predictions and unconscious typology in the Old Testament. (Typology refers to historical events, persons, and institutions divinely intended to be prefigurative, quite apart from whether or not the Old Testament authors were aware of the predictive symbolism.)

Fulfillment Themes

Here is a summary of the main themes of both direct and typological fulfillment in Matthew and the rest of the New Testament. Jesus fulfilled the activities of the LORD Himself as described and predicted in the Old Testament (Matthew 1:21;

3:3, 4 par. [10]; 11:5 par.; 13:41; 24:31 par.; 27:9, 10). Jesus is the foretold Messianic king (Matthew 1:23; 2:6, 23; 3:17 par.; 4:15, 16; 21:5; 22:44 par.; 26:64 par.), the Isaianic Servant of the LORD (Matthew 3:17 par.; 8:17; 11:5 par.; 12:18-21; 1 Peter 2:22 ff.), and the Danielic Son of man (Matthew 24:30 par.; 26:64 par.; 28:18). He climaxes the line of prophets (Matthew 12:39, 40 par.; 13:13-15 par., 35; 17:5 par.; 1 Corinthians 10: 2; 2 Corinthians 3:7 ff.; Hebrews 3:1 ff.), the succession of righteous sufferers since Old Testament times (Matthew 21:42 par.; 27:34, 35 par., 39 par., 43, 46 par., 48 par.), and the Davidic dynasty (Matthew 12:42 par.). He reversed the work of Adam, who plunged the human race into sin (Matthew 4:1 ff. par.; Romans 5:12; 1 Corinthians 15:21, 22, 45 ff.; Hebrews 2:6 ff.; compare Luke 3:38). He fulfilled the promise to Abraham (Galatians 3:16). Since He was the ideal Israelite, His own personal history recapitulated the national history of Israel (Matthew 2:15, 18; 4:4, 7, 10 par.).

Melchizedek prefigured the priesthood of Christ, as did also, in an inferior and sometimes contrasting way, the Aaronic priesthood (Hebrews 7-10). The paschal lamb and other sacrifices symbolized His redemptive death (1 Corinthians 5:7; Ephesians 5:2; Hebrews 9, 10; Romans 3:25; 1 Peter 1:19 ff.; Revelation 5:6 ff.), as well as Christian devotion and service (Romans 12:1; 15:16; Philippians 2:17). Jesus is life-giving bread like the manna (John 6:35; 1 Corinthians 10:3), the source of living water like the rock in the desert during Israel's journey from Egypt to Canaan (1 Corinthians 10:4; compare John 7:37), the serpent lifted up in the wilderness (John 3:14), and the tabernacle and temple of God's abode among men (John 1:14; 2: 19 ff.; compare Colossians 1:19).

John the Baptist was the predicted prophetic forerunner of Jesus (Mark 1:2, 3). Jesus inaugurated the foretold eschatological period of salvation (John 6:45) and established the new covenant (Hebrews 8:8-12; 10:16, 17). Judas Iscariot fulfilled the role of the wicked opponents of Old Testament righteous sufferers (Acts 1:20). The Church is, or individual Christians are, the new creation (2 Corinthians 5:17; Galatians 6:15; Colossians 3:10), the spiritual seed of Abraham by incorporation into Christ (Galatians 3:29; 4:24 ff.; Romans 4:1 ff.; 9:6 ff.; Philippians 3:3), the new Israel (Romans 9:6 ff.; 11:17 ff.; 2 Corinthians 6:16; 1 Peter 2:9, 10), and the new temple (1 Corinthians 3:16; 6:19; 2 Corinthians 6:16; Ephesians 2:20 ff.). The Mosaic law prefigured divine grace both positively and negatively (John 1:17; Colossians 2:17; Galatians). The Deluge

---

[10]The abbreviation *par.* means *parallel(s)* and refers to parallel passages in the other gospels. For the Old Testament passages quoted or alluded to, see marginal references in a good cross-reference Bible.

stands for the last judgment (Matthew 24:34 ff.) and for baptism (1 Peter 3:20, 21). The passage through the Red Sea and the rite of circumcision foreshadowed baptism (1 Corinthians 10:2; Colossians 2:11, 12). Jerusalem stands for the celestial city (Hebrews 12:22; Revelation 21:2 ff.; Galatians 4:26). Entrance into Canaan prefigures the entrance of Christians into spiritual rest (Hebrews 3:18—4:13). And proclamation of the Gospel to all men fulfills the promise to Abraham and prophetic predictions of universal salvation (Acts 2:17 ff.; 3:25; 13:47; 15:16 ff.; Romans 15:9 ff., 21).

Text-Plots and Testimony Books

C. H. Dodd called attention to the fact that the New Testament writers tended to draw fulfillment-quotations from a rather limited set of Old Testament passages ("text-plots") considered especially relevant for the new age.[11] Perhaps the early Christians also drew up manuals of Old Testament proof texts, called "testimony books" by modern scholars. Something like a testimony book did appear among the Dead Sea Scrolls, but of course it is not Christian in orientation.

Interpretive Method

It is also worth noting that the New Testament writers did not distort the original meaning of the Old Testament texts, not even in typological applications (although the point is disputed by negative critics), in sharp contrast to the impudent disregard of original intent by other Jewish writers of the New Testament period. Apparently the early Church learned the new and proper way of interpreting the eschatological significance of the Old Testament from Jesus Himself (compare Luke 24:27).

Text-Forms

The Septuagint forms the textual basis for most of the Old Testament quotations, but variations frequently occur. Matthew in particular appears to have utilized the Hebrew text of the Old Testament, the Targums, and other textual traditions in addition to the Septuagint.[12]

Historicity

Sometimes it is charged that the early Christians distorted and even invented incidents in the life of Jesus to obtain "fulfillment" of a supposed Messianic prophecy. It is true that the writers of the gospels frequently borrowed Old Testament phraseology to describe the events of Jesus' career. But the allusions to Old Testament texts are frequently far too fleeting for those texts to have formed the basis of free invention and distortion of tradition. Some of the quoted Old Testament passages are so obscure that they could hardly have been the source for corruption of the tradition about Jesus. The Old Testament quota-

---

[11]C. H. Dodd, *According to the Scriptures* (London: Nisbet, 1961).
[12]See K. Stendahl, *The School of St. Matthew and Its Use of the Old Testament* (Philadelphia: Fortress, 1968); R. H. Gundry, *The Use of the Old Testament in St. Matthew's Gospel* (Leiden: Brill, 1967), for technical studies.

tions appear to be later additions to the information concerning Jesus. The gospel tradition came first, the recognition of correspondences to ancient Messianic predictions later.

LUKE: THE GOSPEL OF HISTORICAL CERTAINTY

The author of the third gospel begins with a reference to previous narratives of Christian beginnings based on reports of "eyewitnesses and ministers of the word" (1:1, 2). He then defines his project, which is "an orderly account" of that reliable tradition, and states his purpose, which is to convince his readers of the historical certainty of the Christian tradition (1:3, 4).

The gospel of Luke and the Acts of the Apostles must come from the same author, for they both begin with dedications to Theophilus and share common interests and a common style of writing. Moreover, Acts refers back to the "first book" (Acts 1:1). Since the third gospel and Acts must come from the same author, we deduce Luke's authorship of Luke-Acts from the fact that he is the only one of Paul's traveling companions mentioned in the epistles who could have written the "we"-sections of Acts. All the others are excluded by their being mentioned in the third person in Acts or by the impossibility of harmonizing their geographical movements according to the epistles with the geographical movements in the "we"-sections of Acts.[13] Moreover, early tradition confirms Lucan authorship.[14]

Luke was probably a Gentile (or at least a Hellenistic Jew) and may have been converted at Antioch in Syria.[15] His name is Greek. In the farewells in Colossians 4:10-14 Paul seems to distinguish him from (Hebraistic?) Jews and links him with Gentiles. His facility in using the Greek language also suggests that he was a Gentile (or Hellenistic Jew) more at home in the Greek language than most Jews would have been. The Greek style of Luke, together with that in the Epistle to the Hebrews, is the most refined in the New Testament. Exceptions occur where he appears to have been following Semitic oral or written sources, or adopting a Semitic style of Greek to sound "Biblical,"

---

[13]See pages 217 f.

[14]The Muratorian Canon; the anti-Marcionite prologue to Luke; Irenaeus, *Against Heresies* III. i. 1; and later writers.

[15]Compare the anti-Marcionite prologue to the third gospel and the "we" reading of Codex D in Acts 11:28, an Antioch context. The majority of scholars regard Luke as a Gentile. For recent defenses of his Jewishness, see E. E. Ellis, *The Gospel of Luke* (London: Nelson, 1966), pp. 52, 53; W. F. Albright, in Johannes Munck's *The Acts of the Apostles* (Garden City: Doubleday, 1967), pp. 264-267; B. Reicke, *The Gospel of Luke,* translated by R. MacKenzie (Richmond: Knox, 1964), pp. 12-23.

or Septuagintal. On the other hand, both of the books authored by Luke begin with a formal dedication in Graeco-Roman literary style — the only New Testament books to do so. Paul calls Luke "the beloved physician" in Colossians 4:14, a description confirmed by Luke's more than usual interest in sickness and by his frequent use of medical terms[16] — although this feature of his writings may be overstressed.

Luke dedicates his work to Theophilus, perhaps a potential or recent convert or a patron who sponsored the circulation of the third gospel (and Acts), and slants both of his books toward Gentiles, especially those who have open-minded interest in the historical origins of Christianity. Thus Luke is concerned to establish the political innocence of Jesus under Roman law.[17] He shows that the Gospel is universal, that Jesus has broken down the barrier between Jews and Gentiles and inaugurated a world-wide community in which the old inequalities between slaves and freemen, men and women no longer exist. Because Luke addresses a Gentile audience, he does not exhibit Jewish interest in fulfilled Messianic prophecy to the degree that Matthew does. He also modifies peculiarly Jewish expressions and allusions to Jewish customs so that Gentile readers may better understand.[18]

There are many specific indications of this universalism that includes Gentiles, indications that are largely missing in the other gospels. Special interest attaches to dating Jesus' career by events of secular history (1:5; 2:1; 3:1, 2). Jesus is "a light . . . to the Gentiles" (2:32). The quotation of Isaiah 40 includes "all flesh shall see the salvation of God" (3:6). The genealogy of Jesus goes back, not just to Abraham, father of the Jewish nation (as in Matthew), but to Adam, father of the whole human race (3:23-38). Jesus calls attention to Elijah's staying with a Phoenician widow instead of an Israelite and to Elisha's healing a Syrian leper (Naaman) rather than an Israelite (4:25-27). In common with Matthew, Luke contains the great commission to evangelize "all nations" (24:47; compare Matthew 28:19, 20). But Matthew's is a universalism in which Jewish Christianity has

---

[16]See, for example, Luke's comment that the woman with the constant hemorrhage had spent all her money on doctors (Luke 8:43 according to some ancient manuscripts).

[17]See especially Luke's narration of the trial scene before Pilate, where the Roman governor repeatedly absolves Jesus of guilt (23:1-25).

[18]For example, "Woe to you, scribes and Pharisees, hypocrites! For you are like whitewashed tombs" (Matthew 23:27) refers to the Jewish custom of whitewashing gravestones to make them clearly visible so that no one would unintentionally contract ceremonial defilement by brushing against them. Luke paraphrases in order to get rid of the distinctive custom, but keeps the essential thought: "Woe to you! For you are like concealed tombs, and the people who walk over them are unaware of it" (Luke 11:44).

shed its parochialism. Luke's is a Hellenistic universalism which never knew Jewish narrowness.

Lucan universalism includes not only Gentiles in general, but also social outcasts such as the immoral woman who anointed Jesus' feet (7:36-50), Zacchaeus the publican (19:1-10), the repentant criminal who died alongside Jesus (23:39-43), the prodigal son (15:11-32, parabolic), the repentant publican (18:9-14, parabolic), Samaritans, and poor people. James and John draw rebuke for wanting to call down fire from heaven on a Samaritan village (9:51-56). The good Samaritan in the parable appears in a favorable light (10:29-37). The one leper out of ten who returns to thank Jesus for healing is a Samaritan, designated "this foreigner" (17:11-19). At Nazareth Jesus preaches "good news to the poor" (4:16-22). In the Magnificat, Mary says that God "has exalted those of low degree . . . filled the hungry with good things, and sent away the rich empty" (1:52b, 53). The beatitude upon the poor lacks Matthew's qualification "in spirit" (6:20; compare Matthew 5:3), as also the beatitude upon the hungry lacks Matthew's qualification "for righteousness" (6:21; compare Matthew 5:6). And Luke balances the beatitudes upon the poor and hungry with woes against the rich and full (6:24, 25). He is the only evangelist to include Jesus' words: "When you give a dinner or a banquet, do not invite your friends or your brothers or your kinsmen or rich neighbors, . . . But when you give a feast, invite the poor, the maimed, the lame, the blind" (14:12, 13). It is Luke who calls the Pharisees "lovers of money" (16:14) and gives us the parables of the rich fool, the unjust steward who acted charitably (and therefore shrewdly), and the rich man and Lazarus (12:13-21; 16:1-13, 19-31).

Lucan universalism shows itself also in the special attention paid to women: Mary, Elizabeth, and Anna in the nativity story (1, 2), the widow of Nain (7:11-17), the women who supported Jesus (8:1-3), the immoral woman (7:36-50), Mary and Martha (10:38-42), the poor widow (21:1-4), the women who lamented Jesus (23:27-31), watched the crucifixion (23:49), and intended to embalm Jesus, but witnessed the empty tomb and reported the resurrection (23:55—24:11).

Luke thus portrays Jesus as a cosmopolitan Savior with broad sympathies, one who mingles with all sorts of people, socializes with both Pharisees and publicans (7:36 ff.; 11:37 ff.; 14:1 ff.; 19:1-10), and concerns Himself with victims of personal calamity (7:11-17; 8:40-56; 9:37-43). Where Matthew concentrates on Jesus and the kingdom, Luke concentrates on Jesus and people, with resultant character sketches which are quite vivid.

Prayer

On numerous occasions Jesus appears as a man of prayer: at His baptism (3:21), after ministering to the crowds (5:16), before choosing The Twelve (6:12), before Peter's confession and the prediction of His own death and resurrection (9:18), at the time of His transfiguration (9:28, 29), upon the return of the seventy from their mission (10:21), before teaching the disciples to pray (11:1), in Gethsemane (22:39-46), and twice on the cross (23:34, 46). Almost all of these references to Jesus' prayers are distinctive to Luke. Only Luke records two parables of Jesus about prayer (11:5-13; 18:1-8) and informs us that Jesus had prayed especially for Peter (22:31, 32).

The Holy
Spirit

Luke similarly emphasizes the work of the Holy Spirit. He tells us that John the Baptist is to be filled with the Holy Spirit even from his mother's womb (1:15). The Holy Spirit comes upon Mary so that she can miraculously give birth to the Son of God (1:35). When Mary visits Elizabeth, Elizabeth is filled with the Holy Spirit to say, "Blessed are you among women, and blessed is the fruit of your womb" (1:41, 42). When John the Baptist is born and then named, his father Zechariah (Zacharias) is filled with the Holy Spirit and prophesies (1: 67). The Holy Spirit rests upon Simeon, informing him that he will behold the Messiah before death, and leads him to the Temple to see the Christ child (2:25-27). After the reception of the Spirit at His baptism, Jesus is "full of the Holy Spirit" and "led by the Spirit" in the wilderness (4:1). Following His temptation He returns to Galilee "in the power of the Spirit" (4:14). Upon the return of the seventy disciples from their successful mission, He "rejoiced in the Holy Spirit" (10:21). And before His ascension He promises that the Spirit will clothe the disciples "with power from on high" (24:49). As a

The Success of
the Gospel

result, the gospel of Luke (as later the book of Acts) throbs with the joy of success, the thrill of an irresistible movement of divine grace in human history.[19] It is for this reason above all that we must reject recent attempts to interpret Luke's view of history as an adjustment to the ever lengthening delay of the Parousia.[20] Luke writes not out of embarrassment, but out of supreme confidence in the inevitably successful advance of the Gospel inaugurated by Jesus the "Lord" (a favorite designation of Jesus in Luke) and carried on by His disciples in the energy of the Spirit.

Date

Nothing prevents a fairly early date for the third gospel, slightly after that of Mark under the assumption that Luke uti-

---

[19]See the references to joy in 1:14, 44, 47; 6:21, 23; 10:21; 15:5-7, 9, 10, 23-25; 24:52, 53.

[20]See page 74.

lized Mark. Many scholars feel that Luke's changing "the abomination of desolation" in Mark to a description of a siege of Jerusalem (21:20) proves that Luke wrote after A.D. 70. But this line of reasoning again overlooks or denies the possibility that Jesus really did predict the siege and destruction of Jerusalem. Luke may have omitted to mention "the abomination of desolation" simply because he knew that this phrase from Daniel 9:27; 11:31; 12:11 would convey no meaning to his Gentile reading audience. If Luke were conforming Jesus' words to the events in and around A.D. 70, why did he retain the command, "Flee to the mountains" (21:21), in spite of the fact that during the siege of Jerusalem Christians fled to Pella in the *non*mountainous region of Transjordan?

Acts closes with Paul's awaiting trial in Rome probably because events had progressed no farther at the time of writing.[21] If so, Acts dates from some time before A.D. 64, the traditional and generally accepted date of the martyrdom of Paul (and Peter). Then if Luke wrote his gospel before Acts, as would seem logical, the gospel must likewise date from a slightly earlier time before A.D. 64.[22] The place of writing might be

Place

RUINS OF PELLA, *located east of the Sea of Galilee. Pella was described by Josephus as a flat valley surrounded by a higher plain, or plateau.*

Rome, where Luke was staying with Paul during his imprisonment (although the early tradition is divided between Greece and Rome for the place of writing).

The gospel of Luke is the most comprehensive of the synoptics. Indeed, it is the longest book in the New Testament. In the first two chapters Luke begins with a prologue and the birth and childhood stories of Jesus. The baptism, genealogy, and temptation of Jesus follow in 3:1—4:13, the Galilean ministry (parallel to Mark) in 4:14—9:50, the last journey to Jerusalem in 9:51—19:27, and finally passion week, the crucifixion, the resurrection, the postresurrection ministry, and the ascension in 19:28—24:53. The last journey to Jerusalem is the most distinctive contribution of Luke to our knowledge of Jesus' career. In that section he presents Jesus' ministry in Perea, gives many of the most famous parables not elsewhere recorded (the good Samaritan, the rich fool, the prodigal son, Dives and Lazarus, the Pharisee and the publican, and others), and emphasizes the significance of Jerusalem as the goal of Jesus' ministry. (Later, in Acts, Jerusalem will become the place from which Christian witnesses go out to evangelize the world.) The nativity story in Luke contains very much information not found in Matthew, including several hymns and an account of John the Baptist's birth. Finally, Luke gives material in his resurrection narrative quite different from that in the other gospels, and becomes the only evangelist to describe the ascension of Jesus.

SUMMARY OUTLINE OF LUKE

Theme: the historical certainty of the Gospel

Prologue: Dedication to Theophilus and statement of purpose to write an orderly account of historical trustworthiness (1:1-4)

I. THE NATIVITY AND CHILDHOOD OF JOHN THE BAPTIST AND JESUS (1:5—2:52)
   A. The annunciation of John the Baptist's birth to Zechariah and Elizabeth (1:5—2:25)
   B. The annunciation of Jesus' birth to Mary (1:26-38)
   C. The visit of Mary to Elizabeth and the Magnificat (1:39-56)
   D. The birth, circumcision, and naming of John the Baptist, and the Benedictus (1:67-79)
   E. John the Baptist's growing up in the wilderness (1:80)
   F. The birth of Jesus (2:1-7)
   G. The visit of the shepherds (2:8-20)
   H. The circumcision and naming of Jesus (2:21)
   I. The presentation in the Temple, with the Nunc Dimittis of Simeon and the adoration of Anna (2:22-40)
   J. Jesus' visit to the Temple at the age of twelve (2:41-52)
II. THE BEGINNINGS OF JESUS' MINISTRY (3:1—4:13)
   A. The preparatory ministry of John the Baptist (3:1-20)
   B. The baptism of Jesus (3:21, 22)
   C. The genealogy of Jesus (3:23-38)
   D. The temptation of Jesus (4:1-13)

III. THE GALILEAN MINISTRY (4:14—9:50)
   A. The rejection of Jesus in Nazareth (4:14-30)
   B. An exorcism in the synagogue at Capernaum (4:31-37)
   C. The healing of Peter's mother-in-law and further miracles and preaching (4:38-44)
   D. A miraculous catch of fish and the call of Simon Peter, James, and John to discipleship (5:1-11)
   E. The cleansing of a leper (5:12-16)
   F. The forgiveness and healing of a paralytic (5:17-26)
   G. The call of Levi [Matthew] and Jesus' eating with publicans and sinners (5:27-32)
   H. Remarks about fasting (5:33-39)
   I. Jesus' defense of His disciples' plucking and eating grain on the Sabbath (6:1-5)
   J. The healing of a withered hand on the Sabbath (6:6-11)
   K. The choice of the twelve (6:12-16)
   L. The Sermon on "a level place" [on the Mount] (6:17-49)
   M. The healing of a centurion's servant (7:1-10)
   N. The raising from the dead of a widow's son (7:11-17)
   O. The question of John the Baptist and Jesus' answer and tribute to him (7:18-35)
   P. Jesus' anointing by and forgiveness of the sinful woman (7:36-50)
   Q. Preaching with financial support from certain women (8:1-3)
   R. The parable of the seed and the soils [more commonly, the sower] and of the lamp (8:4-18)
   S. The attempt by the family of Jesus to see Him, and His remark about His true spiritual kin (8:19-21)
   T. The stilling of the storm (8:22-25)
   U. The deliverance of the Gerasene demoniac (8:26-39)
   V. The healing of the woman with the constant hemorrhage and the raising of Jairus' daughter from the dead (8:40-56)
   W. The mission of The Twelve (9:1-6)
   X. The guilty fear of Herod Antipas over the death of John the Baptist (9:7-9)
   Y. The feeding of the five thousand (9:10-17)
   Z. Peter's confession of Jesus' messiahship and the prediction by Jesus of His death and resurrection, with a call to cross-bearing discipleship (9:18-27)
   AA. The transfiguration (9:28-36)
   BB. The deliverance of a demonized boy (9:37-45)
   CC. Remarks on humility (with a child as an example) and tolerance (9:46-50)
IV. THE LAST JOURNEY TO JERUSALEM (9:51—19:27)
   A. Jesus' determination to go to Jerusalem and the inhospitality of a Samaritan village (9:51-56)
   B. Remarks on discipleship to would-be disciples (9:57-62)
   C. The mission of the seventy (10:1-24)
   D. The parable of the good Samaritan (10:25-37)
   E. Entertainment of Jesus by Mary and Martha (10:38-42)
   F. Teaching about prayer, including the Lord's prayer and the parable of the host whose guest arrived at midnight (11:1-13)
   G. Polemical episodes (11:36—12:12)
      1. Defense against the charge of Satanic empowerment, refusal to give any sign except that of Jonah, and the parable of the lamp (11:33-36)
      2. Exposé of the Pharisees and lawyers [scribes] (11:37-54)
      3. Warning against Phariseeism (12:1-12)
   H. Remarks on covetousness, anxiety, trust, and eschatological watchfulness, including the parable of the rich fool (12:13-59)
   I. A call to repentance, including the parable of the fig tree (13:1-9)
   J. The healing on a Sabbath of a woman bent over (13:10-17)
   K. The parables of the mustard seed, leaven, and narrow door (13:18-30)

L. Jesus' refusal to panic in the face of Herod Antipas and the lamentation over Jerusalem (13:31-35)
M. The Sabbath healing of a man with dropsy (14:1-6)
N. The parable about invitations to a marriage feast (14:7-14)
O. The parable of the great banquet (14:15-24)
P. The parables of the tower-builder and the king who goes to war (14:25-35)
Q. Three parables in defense of welcoming sinners (15:1-32)
   1. The parable of the lost sheep (15:1-7)
   2. The parable of the lost coin (15:8-10)
   3. The parable of the prodigal son and the elder brother (15:11-32)
R. Two parables about the use of money (16:1-31)
   1. The parable of the unjust steward, with further comments to the Pharisees (16:1-18)
   2. The parable of the rich man and Lazarus (16:19-31)
S. Remarks on forgiveness, faith, and sense of duty (17:1-10)
T. The healing of ten lepers and the gratitude of one, a Samaritan (17:11-19)
U. The coming of God's kingdom and the Son of man, including the parable of the widow and the unjust judge (17:20—18:8)
V. The parable of the Pharisee and the publican (18:9-14)
W. Jesus' welcoming little children (18:15-17)
X. The rich young ruler (18:18-30)
Y. Prediction by Jesus of His death and resurrection (18:31-34)
Z. The healing of a blind man near Jericho (18:35-43)
AA. The conversion of Zacchaeus (19:1-10)
BB. The parable of the pounds (19:11-27)

V. PASSION WEEK AND THE DEATH, RESURRECTION, POSTRESURRECTION MINISTRY, AND ASCENSION OF JESUS IN AND AROUND JERUSALEM (19:28—24:53)
A. Passion week and the death of Jesus (19:28—23:56)
   1. The triumphal entry, including the cleansing of the Temple (19:28-48)
   2. Theological debate in the Temple precincts (20:1—21:4)
      a. The challenge of Jesus' authority (20:1-8)
      b. The parable of the wicked tenants of the vineyard (20:9-18)
      c. The question about paying taxes to Caesar (20:19-26)
      d. The Sadducees' question about the resurrection (20:27-40)
      e. Jesus' question about the Messiah's Davidic ancestry and lordship (20:41-44)
      f. Warning against the scribes (20:45-47)
      g. The widow's two copper coins (21:1-4)
      h. The Olivet Discourse (21:5-38)
   3. The Sanhedrin's plot to kill Jesus and the bargain with Judas Iscariot (22:1-6)
   4. The Last Supper (22:7-38)
   5. Jesus' praying in Gethsemane (22:39-46)
   6. The arrest (22:47-53)
   7. The trial (22:54—23:25)
      a. The nighttime hearing in the high priest's house, with Peter's denials of Jesus (22:54-65)
      b. The early morning condemnation by the Sanhedrin (22:66-71)
      c. The first hearing before Pilate (23:1-5)
      d. The hearing before Herod Antipas (23:6-12)
      e. The second hearing before Pilate, with Pilate's grudging release of Barabbas and delivering up of Jesus for crucifixion (23:13-25)
   8. The crucifixion (23:26-49)
      a. The carrying of Jesus' cross by Simon of Cyrene and the lament of the women (23:26-31)
      b. The crucifixion and mocking of Jesus (23:32-38)
      c. The repentant criminal (23:39-43)

      d. The death of Jesus (23:44-49)
    9. The burial (23:50-56)
B. The resurrection (24:1-12)
C. The postresurrection ministry (24:13-49)
    1. The walk to Emmaus with Cleopas and another disciple (24:13-35)
    2. The appearance in Jerusalem (24:36-43)
    3. Jesus' teaching about Himself from the Old Testament and the great commission (24:44-49)
D. The ascension (24:50-53)

JOHN: THE GOSPEL OF BELIEVING IN JESUS FOR ETERNAL LIFE

Written in simple style, the last of the gospels exhibits a theological profundity beyond that of the synoptics. Early Church tradition indicates that the Apostle John wrote the fourth gospel toward the close of the first century in Ephesus, a city of Asia Minor. Particularly important is the testimony of Irenaeus, a disciple of Polycarp, who was in turn a disciple of the Apostle John — a direct line of tradition with only one link between Irenaeus and John himself.[23]

Authorship

In the past some scholars insisted that this gospel was not written until the mid-second century, and therefore certainly not by the Apostle John. But discovery of the Rylands Fragment of John forced abandonment of that view. The papyrus fragment dates from about A.D. 135 and necessarily implies several previous decades for the writing, copying, and circulation of the fourth gospel as far as the Egyptian hinterland, where the fragment was discovered. Other very early papyri containing the text of John confirm the implication of the Rylands Fragment.

But many scholars still are not convinced that the Apostle John wrote the gospel. Some suggest that a disciple of the Apostle John, perhaps the Elder John mentioned by Papias[24] (c. A.D. 125), wrote it and was later confused with the apostle of the same name. Closer inspection of Papias' statement shows, however, that Papias probably used the term "elder" in an apostolic sense, and so becomes a very early witness for authorship by the *Apostle* John.[25]

---

[23]*Against Heresies* II. xxii. 5; III i. 1; iii. 4; and the reports in Eusebius, *Ecclesiastical History* III. xxiii. 1-4; IV. xiv. 3-8; V. viii. 4; xx. 4-8.

[24]Quoted by Eusebius, *Ecclesiastical History* III. xxxix. 4.

[25]"If, then, any one came who had been a follower of the elders, I questioned him in regard to the words of the elders, — what Andrew or what Peter said, or what was said by Philip, or by Thomas, or by James, or by John, or by Matthew, or by any other of the disciples of the Lord, and what things Aristion and the presbyter [elder] John, the disciples of the Lord, say" (Papias, as quoted by Eusebius, according to the translation in *A Select Library of Nicene and Post-Nicene Fathers of the Christian Church*, Second Series, edited by P. Schaff and H. Wace, translated by A. C. McGiffert [New York: Scribner's, 1904], vol. I, p. 171). Both times the name John appears in Papias' statement, it appears with *both* the designations "elder"

THE PAPYRUS RYLANDS GRK. *457, a fragment of John's gospel, dates back to the first half of the second century* A.D.

The writer of the fourth gospel claims to be an eyewitness of Jesus' ministry (1:14; compare 19:35; 21:24, 25) and exhibits a Semitic style of writing[26] and an accurate knowledge of Jewish customs (for example, the customs of water-pouring and illumination of candelabra during the Festival of Tabernacles, presupposed in 7:37-39; 8:12) and of Palestinian topography as it was before the holocaust of A.D. 70 (for example, the pool with five porches near the Sheep Gate [5:2] and the paved area outside the Praetorium [19:13], both in Jerusalem and both archaeologically confirmed in recent times).[27] In addition, vivid details such as one would expect from an eyewitness, yet incidental to the story, appear everywhere — numbers (*six* water jars [2:6], *three* or *four* miles [5:19], *one hundred* yards [21:8], *153* fish [21:11]), names (Nathanael [1:45 ff.], Nicodemus

and "disciple." By contrast, Aristion, even though designated a disciple, lacks the title "elder" when mentioned alongside John. This fact points toward a single individual named John. Papias wanted to make plain the single identity of John by repeating the designation "elder" just used for the apostles but omitted with Aristion. Papias mentioned John a *second* time because he was the only one of the apostles still alive and speaking. Admittedly, Eusebius interpreted Papias to refer to two different men named John and even claimed a tradition of two Johns with different tombs in Ephesus; but Eusebius wished to find a way around apostolic authorship of the book of Revelation, which he disliked. It would appear, then, that from Papias' statement he may have conjured up an Elder John allegedly distinct from the Apostle John in order to attribute Revelation to the elder rather than the apostle.

[26]Seen especially in parallel statements. This has led to the theory, not popular, that John originally wrote his gospel in Aramaic.

[27]Some scholars therefore date the fourth gospel three decades or so earlier than the closing years of the first century, against the early tradition.

[3:1 ff.], Lazarus [11:1 ff.], Malchus [18:10], etc.), and many other vivid touches. These facts substantiate both the early tradition of apostolic authorship and its corollary that the gospel represents trustworthy historical tradition.

Moreover, the author writes as "the disciple whom Jesus loved," not out of egotism — he never identifies himself by name! — but to emphasize that the contents of the gospel merit belief since they come from the man in whom Jesus confided. Still further, the beloved disciple repeatedly appears in close association with Peter (13:23, 24; 20:2-10; 21:2, 7, 20 ff.). The synoptists tell us that James and John the sons of Zebedee worked at fishing with Peter and with him formed the inner circle of The Twelve. Since James had long since died as a martyr (Acts 12:1-5) and since Peter appears as a different person from the beloved disciple, only John is left to be the beloved disciple and author of the fourth gospel. For if someone other than the beloved disciple wrote the fourth gospel, why did he not attach the name of John to the "disciple whom Jesus loved"? The anonymity of the beloved disciple can hardly be explained unless he himself wrote the gospel, and the process of elimination identifies him with John the Apostle.

Supplementation of the Synoptics

John consciously supplements the synoptics.[28] He emphasizes the Judean ministry and largely omits parables and the theme of God's kingdom. Apparently John thought that the synoptists had presented enough information about the Galilean ministry and the kingdom. John also supplements the synoptics by making clear that Jesus' public ministry lasted considerably longer than a reading of the synoptics alone would indicate. Unconcerned with giving a complete chronology of Jesus' life, the synoptists mention only the last Passover when Jesus died. But John lets us know that there were at least three and probably four Passovers during the public career of Jesus, so that it lasted at least more than two years and probably from three to three and a half years.[29]

Jesus' Speech in John

With the possible exception of Matthew, the fourth gospel contains more extended discourses by Jesus than do the synoptics. The discourses tend to cut down on narrative material. Questions and objections from the audiences frequently punctuate the discourses, and John regularly reports Jesus as speaking in a style different in many respects from that which the synoptists report. The differences stem partly from John's own way of translating into Greek dominical teaching which was originally

---

[28]Others feel that the fourth evangelist did not know the synoptics, or that he reworked the synoptic tradition at a number of points.

[29]See A. T. Robertson, *A Harmony of the Gospels* (New York: Harper & Row, 1950), pp. 267-270.

spoken in Aramaic and Hebrew (as well as Greek) and partly from John's habit of paraphrasing, with the result that the vocabulary and style of the evangelist frequently appear in his record of Jesus' teaching. In the synoptics the translation is apparently more literal and the paraphrasing less extensive.[30] Often loose translation and paraphrasing can communicate the intended meaning of a speaker even more effectively than direct quotation, so that John's procedure is not at all illegitimate. On the other hand, we must not overestimate the degree of Johannine paraphrasing or looseness in translation, for the two famous parallel passages in Matthew 11:25-27 and Luke 10:21, 22 prove that Jesus could and did speak in the style represented by the fourth gospel. Prominent in those passages are the Father-Son relationship and emphasis on divine revelation, knowledge, and election — all typical of the gospel of John. It is also possible that John preserved the more formal aspects of Jesus' teaching such as sermons in synagogues and disputes with Jewish theologians.

Johannine Theology

Running through the fourth gospel, many important theological themes appear and reappear in different combinations and sometimes continue into 1-3 John and Revelation. John expounds these themes by skillfully alternating narratives and discourses, so that the words of Jesus bring out the inner meaning of His works. Much of the action in the gospel thus becomes symbolic. For example, the washing of the disciples' feet by Jesus represents the cleansing effect of His redemptive work. There is also frequent irony, such as that which tinges the question of Jesus, "I have shown you many good works from the Father; for which of these do you stone me?" (10:32). And just as the works of Jesus bear a symbolic meaning, so also His words often carry second and even third meanings. "Born again (or anew)" also means "born from above" (3:3 ff.), and the reference to Jesus' being "lifted up" points not only to the method of His execution, but also to His resurrection and exaltation back to heaven (12:20-36, especially 32).

**Word
Truth**

The Johannine theological themes begin under the category of revelation. Jesus is the revelatory *Word* (Logos) of God. As such he reveals the *truth,* which is more than veracity. It is the ultimate reality of God's own person and character, as *witnessed*

**Witness
Light and
Darkness**

to by Jesus, the Father himself, the Spirit, Scripture, and others. The *light* thus illuminates those who believe and drives back

---

[30]The vocabulary and style of John himself are recognizable from those parts of the fourth gospel where Jesus is *not* speaking and from 1-3 John. Revelation, also Johannine, is somewhat different for various possible reasons (see pages 363 f.).

the *darkness* of evil. The repulsion of darkness is the *judgment* of the world. Not that Jesus came to condemn the world, but He did come to discriminate between those who belong to the light and those who belong to the darkness — and the latter already stand self-condemned by their unbelief. The *world*, human society dominated by Satan, opposes the light and thus becomes the object of divine wrath. That makes it all the more remarkable that God "loved the world" (3:16). The *love* of God came through Jesus Christ and continues to manifest itself through the love of Jesus' disciples for one another. To demonstrate the divine love, Jesus descended from the Father and worked toward His "*hour*," the time of His suffering and death on behalf of the world. For revealing the Father's *glory* in this way, the Father in turn glorified the Son by heavenly exaltation. By *election* and *belief* (John lets stand the antinomy between divine choice and human response) some men experience the *regeneration* of the Holy Spirit so that they come into the saving *knowledge* of God through Christ. But although election and actual belief characterize only some, *universality* characterizes the invitation. Those who do accept receive *eternal life* (not only quantitatively everlasting but also qualitatively divine), an *abiding* place in Christ, and the *Paraclete*, or Holy Spirit in His roles of Comforter, Counsellor, and Advocate. All of this is but to skim the surface of Johannine theology; each theme has nuances left unmentioned above.

THE
FOUR GOSPELS

Judgment

The World

Love

The Hour

Glory

Election

Belief

Regeneration

Knowledge

Universality

Eternal Life

Abiding

The Paraclete

Preeminently, however, John is the gospel of believing. Indeed, the verb *believe* is the key word of the gospel:

> Many other signs therefore Jesus also performed in the presence of the disciples, which are not written in this book; but these have been written that you may believe that Jesus is the Christ, the Son of God; and that believing you may have life in His name (20:30, 31).

Christological in content, this believing highlights the *deity* of Jesus as the unique and preexistent Son of God who in obedience to His Father became *a real human being* in order to die sacrificially for the redemption of mankind. Such an emphasis went against the denial of His humanity and death by Gnostics, early Christian heretics who thought that anything material or physical was inherently evil.[31] Thus, not only does the deity of Jesus receive emphasis (beginning with "the Word was God" [1:1] and many times throughout the gospel); so also His humanity: "the Word became flesh" (1:14), grew tired and thirsty (4:6, 7; 19:28) wept (11:35), and physically died and rose again (19:30-42; 20:12, 17, 20, 27, 28). (Note the fourfold gospel portraiture of Jesus: the royal Jewish Messiah in Matthew; the

---

[31]See pages 358 f.

divine Servant-Worker in Mark; the sympathetic Savior in Luke; the incarnate Son of God in John.) Jesus Himself demands this Christological belief by making a series of "I am . . ." claims in the fourth gospel:

"I am the bread of life" (6:35, 48; compare verses 41, 51).
"I am the light of the world" (8:12).
"I am the door" (10:7, 9).
"I am the good shepherd" (10:11, 14).
"I am the resurrection and the life" (11:25).
"I am the way, and the truth, and the life" (14:6).
"I am the true vine" (15:1, 5).

Besides these are "I am" statements not followed by a complement which suggest the claim to be the I AM-YAHWEH of the Old Testament (4:25, 26; 8:24, 28, 58; 13:19; compare 6:20; 7:34, 36; 14:3; 17:24; Exodus 3:13 ff.).

Realized Eschatology

When a person believes, he immediately receives eternal life — therefore C. H. Dodd's phrase: *"realized eschatology."*[32] Full enjoyment awaits in the future, but every believer also savors a foretaste in the present. Perhaps some Christians were perturbed and some non-Christians incredulous over the delay in Jesus' return — thus the Johannine emphasis on salvation *now*. Along these lines John seeks to evangelize unbelievers with the Gospel and/or to establish Christians in their faith. (It is difficult to decide whether John wrote for unbelievers, believers, or both.)

Anti-Baptist Polemic

It is possible that a subsidiary purpose of John was the correction of a cult that had grown up around the figure of John the Baptist. Acts 19:1-7 shows that there had been followers of John the Baptist in Ephesus some decades earlier during the time of Paul, and according to early tradition Ephesus is the place where John the Apostle wrote his gospel. Moreover, John takes great pains to show that Jesus is superior to the Baptist, that the Baptist had to decrease and Jesus increase, that through His disciples Jesus baptized more followers than the Baptist, and that Jesus had testimony even greater than that from the Baptist (1:15-37; 3:25-30; 4:1, 2; 5:33-40). The matter hangs in doubt, however, because these phenomena may instead reflect the Apostle John's own experience of conversion from the Baptist to Jesus.

Anti-Jewish Polemic

It is unlikely that John wrote his gospel as a polemic against Judaism; for although the unbelieving Jews appear in a bad light because of their unbelief, the "world" as a whole does also (for

---

[32]But against a thoroughgoing realized eschatology in which the future Christian hope is lost, compare the references to the final resurrection and judgment in 5:25-29 and the Second Coming in 14:1-3. The phrase "inaugurated (or proleptic) eschatology" would be better.

example, see 15:18, 19). During the last part of the first century, the Jews incorporated into the liturgy of their synagogue services the Benediction against Heretics to root out all Jewish Christians who might still be participating in those services.[33] Some have thought that that benediction provided the occasion for the fourth gospel as an encouragement to Jewish Christians to endure ostracism from the synagogue without recanting their Christian profession. But although the Benediction against Heretics may have given special point to the references in 9:22 and 16:2, which mention the putting of Jesus' disciples out of synagogues, the fourth gospel, in contrast to Matthew, Hebrews, and James, does not give the impression of having been written to an audience so narrow as to include only Jewish Christians. Jewish features do not predominate, and those which do appear stem merely from the Jewish milieu of Jesus' life rather than from deliberate accent.

On the other hand, there is no conscious suppression of the Jewishness of Jesus' career. We must therefore reject the hypothesis that the fourth gospel represents a Hellenistic portrait of Jesus in which He is played up as a divine man, in contrast to the historically realistic portrayal of Him as an eschatological prophet. As a matter of fact, Jesus' deity appears clearly and early already in the synoptics. Furthermore, the Dead Sea Scrolls have shown that the religious vocabulary of John's gospel is characteristic of first century Judaism, so that no need exists to search for Hellenistic models farther afield.[34]

Theories of literary sources behind the fourth gospel stumble against the unity of style which pervades the entire book. Theories of disarrangement of the original text solve problems of interpretation only to create new ones; and with one minor exception they lack manuscript evidence.

In several respects John 1:11, 12 presents a summary of the kinds of material included in the fourth gospel. "Those who were His own did not receive him" — the somber backdrop of the gospel is the repeated Jewish rejections of Jesus: when He cleansed the Temple (chapter 2); after He healed the paralytic (chapter 5); after He fed the five thousand (chapter 6); when His half brothers taunted Him (chapter 7); when He attended the Festival of Tabernacles (chapter 7); when He claimed to be the

---

[33]"For the excommunicate let there be no hope, and the kingdom of pride do Thou quickly root out in our days. And let the Christians and the heretics perish as in a moment. Let them be blotted out of the book of life, and with the righteous let them not be written. Blessed art Thou, O Lord, who subdueth the proud."

[34]Against C. H. Dodd, *The Interpretation of the Fourth Gospel* (Cambridge University Press, 1960).

light of the world (chapter 8); when He asserted His oneness with God the Father (chapter 10); and after He raised Lazarus (chapter 11).

"But as many as received Him" — in contrast to the general Jewish rejection, some individuals did receive Jesus through personal encounter with Him: Andrew, John (unnamed in the text), Peter, Philip, Nathanael (chapter 1); Nicodemus (chapter 3); the Samaritan woman (chapter 4); the man born blind (chapter 9); Mary and Martha (chapter 11); the eleven in the upper room (chapters 13-16); and Mary Magdalene (chapter 20).

"To them He gave the right to become children of God" — John describes in detail a number of miracles performed by Jesus, but calls them "signs" because of their value in symbolizing the transforming power of belief in Jesus: the changing of water to wine illustrates the transformation from the ritual of Judaism to the better reality of the Gospel (chapter 2); the healing of the nobleman's son pictures the transformation from spiritual sickness to health (chapter 4); the healing of the paralytic, from impotence to strength (chapter 5); the feeding of the five thousand, from emptiness to fullness (chapter 6); the walking on the water, from fear to assurance (chapter 6); the giving of sight to the blind man, from darkness to light (chapter 9); the raising of Lazarus, from death to life (chapter 11); and the miraculous catch of fish, from failure to almost unmanageable success (chapter 21).

All three lines of thought converge in the passion story: "Those who were His own did not receive Him" — the trial and crucifixion; "but as many as received Him" — the three Marys and the beloved disciple standing beside the cross; "to them He gave the right to become children of God" — the transforming power of Christ's resurrection.[35]

SUMMARY OUTLINE OF JOHN

Theme: believing in Jesus as the Christ and Son of God for eternal life

PROLOGUE: Jesus Christ the revelatory Word [Logos] of God (1:1-18)

I. THE FAITH-PRODUCING IMPACT OF JESUS' INITIAL MINISTRY (1:19—4:42)
  A. Narrative (1:19—2:25)
    1. The testimony of John the Baptist and the making of the first disciples (1:19-51)
    2. The turning of water to wine at a wedding in Cana (2:1-12)
    3. The cleansing of the Temple and the performing of miraculous signs in Jerusalem (2:13-25)
  B. Discourse[36] (3:1—4:42)

---

[35]See further J. S. Baxter, *Explore the Book* (London: Marshall, Morgan & Scott, 1955), vol. V, pp. 291 ff.

[36]"Discourse" frequently includes a degree of dialogue.

      1. The new birth, in conversation with Nicodemus (3:1-21)
      2. The superiority of Jesus, as testified by John the Baptist during their concurrent baptizing ministries (3:22-36)
      3. The water of life, in conversation with the Samaritan woman, with her resultant conversion and that of her fellow townspeople (4:1-42)

II. THE AUTHORITY OF JESUS' LIFE-GIVING WORDS (4:43—5:47)
  A. Narrative (4:43—5:18)
      1. The healing of an official's son (4:43-54)
      2. The healing on a Sabbath of the invalid by a pool in Jerusalem (5:1-9a)
  B. Discourse: the authority of Jesus' words (5:9b-47)

III. THE GIVING OF JESUS' BODY AND BLOOD FOR THE LIFE OF THE WORLD (6:1-71)
  A. Narrative: the feeding of the five thousand and the walking on the water (6:1-21)
  B. Discourse: the bread of life (6:22-71)

IV. THE ILLUMINATION OF MANKIND BY JESUS, WITH THEIR RESULTANT DIVISION INTO UNBELIEVERS, DESTINED FOR JUDGMENT, AND BELIEVERS, DESTINED FOR ETERNAL LIFE (7:1—8:59)
  A. Narrative: the attendance of Jesus at the Festival of Tabernacles and division of opinion about Him (7:1-52)
  B. Discourse: the light of the world and the true children of Abraham (8:12-59)

V. THE TENDER CONCERN OF JESUS, IN CONTRAST TO THE CRUELTY OF THE JEWISH RELIGIOUS AUTHORITIES (9:1—10:39)
  A. Narrative: the healing of the blind man and his excommunication from the synagogue (9:1-41)
  B. Discourse: the good shepherd, hirelings, thieves, and robbers (10:1-39)

VI. THE GIFT OF LIFE THROUGH THE DEATH OF JESUS (10:40—12:50)
  A. Narrative (10:40—12:19)
      1. The raising of Lazarus, with the consequent plot of the Sanhedrin to kill Jesus (10:40-11:57)
      2. The anointing of Jesus by Mary of Bethany, and the plot of the Sanhedrin to kill Lazarus (12:1-11)
      3. The triumphal entry (12:12-19)
  B. Discourse: the dying grain of wheat which springs to fruitful life (12:20-50)

VII. THE DEPARTURE AND RETURN OF JESUS (13:1—20:29)
  A. Discourse (13:1—17:26)
      1. The cleansing of the disciples and their menial service toward one another, as signified by Jesus' washing of their feet (13:1-20)
      2. The announcement of betrayal and dismissal of Judas Iscariot (13:21-30)
      3. The advantages to the disciples of Jesus' departure and the coming of the Paraclete (Comforter, Counsellor) [the Upper Room Discourse] (13:31—16:33)
      4. The high priestly prayer of Jesus for His disciples (17:1-26)
  B. Narrative (18:1—20:29)
      1. The arrest (18:1-11)
      2. The hearings before Annas and Caiaphas, with Peter's denials (18:12-27)
      3. The hearing before Pilate (18:28—19:16)
      4. The crucifixion and burial (19:17-42)
      5. The empty tomb and two resurrection appearances, first to Mary Magdalene and then to the disciples (20:1-29)

CONCLUSION: the purpose in the writing of the fourth gospel, inspiration of life-bringing faith in Jesus as the Christ, the Son of God (20:30, 31)

EPILOGUE (21:1-25)

A. Narrative: a third resurrection appearance to the disciples, with a miraculous catch of fish and breakfast on the shore of the Sea of Tiberias [Galilee] (21:1-14)
B. Discourse: the recommission of Peter (21:15-23)

FINAL AUTHENTICATION (21:24, 25)

A COMPARATIVE CHART OF THE FOUR GOSPELS				
THE GOSPELS	MARK	MATTHEW	LUKE	JOHN
Probable date of writing	50s	60s	60s	80s or 90s
Probable place of writing	Rome	Antioch in Syria	Rome	Ephesus
First intended reading audience	Gentiles in Rome	Jews in Syria (and Palestine?)	Interested Gentile enquirers	General population of Asia Minor
Thematic emphasis	Jesus' redemptive activity	Jesus the Jewish Messiah and His disciples, the new people of God	The historical certainty of the Gospel	Believing in Jesus for eternal life

For further discussion:

What are the advantages and disadvantages of having a fourfold, as opposed to single, portrait of Jesus in the New Testament?

Which of the gospels is best suited to the following modern audiences, and why? (a) white middle class Americans (b) minority groups (c) intellectuals (d) children (e) young people (f) elderly people (g) those who have never heard the gospel

Is there a difference among the gospels in the clarity and earliness with which Jesus' messiahship comes into view? If so, how is the difference to be explained?

How much editing of Jesus' deeds and words by the evangelists is consonant with an accurate account?

To what extent is Christian faith dependent on history and historical research? Compare the Lucan perspective on Jesus' life.

For further investigation (the literature is so extensive it is best to give only several general treatments, which will in turn refer interested readers to the numerous primary sources):

(From a conservative standpoint)

Harrison, E. F. *Introduction to the New Testament.* Grand Rapids: Eerdmans, 1964. Chapters 5-9.

Guthrie, D. *New Testament Introduction: The Gospels and Acts.* Chicago: Inter-Varsity, 1965.

(From a liberal standpoint)

Fuller, R. H. *A Critical Introduction to the New Testament.* London: Duckworth, 1966.

Grant, R. M. *A Historical Introduction to the New Testament.* New York: Harper & Row, 1963.

Feine, P., J. Behm, and W. G. Kümmel. *Introduction to the New Testament.* Translated by A. J. Mattill. New York: Abingdon, 1966.

(From the standpoint of modern Roman Catholic scholarship, sometimes liberal)

Wikenhauser, A. *New Testament Introduction.* Translated by J. Cunningham. New York: Herder and Herder, 1958.

Feuillet, A., and A. Robert. *Introduction to the New Testament.* Translated by P. W. Skehan *et al.* New York: Desclee, 1965.

See also Moule, C. F. D. *The Birth of the New Testament.* 2nd edition. New York: Harper & Row, 1966.

CHAPTER 7

Introductory Overview of Jesus' Public Life and Teachings

Leading questions:

What are the dates of the public career of Jesus?

What are the general developments and the ultimate outcome of His ministry?

Where are the origins of His teaching and how does He go beyond them?

What are the framework and primary motifs of His doctrine?

Dates

The dates of Jesus' public ministry remain somewhat uncertain, largely because we do not know how Luke figured the beginning of Tiberius' reign (Luke 3:1; see the commentaries). But the three-year period from A.D. 27 to 30 is as likely as any. Traditionally this span of time has been divided into a year of obscurity, a year of popularity, and a year of rejection.

Obscurity

The year of obscurity began with the heralding ministry of John the Baptist, his baptism of Jesus, and the Satanic temptation of Jesus. It continued with the making of the first disciples, the first miracle of turning the water to wine at Cana in Galilee, the initial cleansing of the Temple, the conversation with Nicodemus, the return via Samaria to Galilee, and the beginning of extensive preaching and miracle-working tours throughout Galilee.

Popularity

The preaching and performing of miracles continued during the year of popularity with large crowds in attendance. His popularity reached its peak at the feeding of the five thousand, but suddenly began to wane when Jesus refused to become a bread-king and militaristic warlord.

In the year of rejection Jesus withdrew northwest into Phoenicia, turned eastward north of the Sea of Galilee and then southward to Decapolis ("ten cities"), a Gentile region southeast of Galilee. Avoiding the crowds as much as possible, He concentrated on teaching the twelve disciples in private. During this period Peter confessed the messiahship of Jesus. The disciples had recognized Jesus as the Messiah before, but the significance of the confession lay in the fact that the disciples were loyal to Jesus as the Messiah while the populace were turning away. Jesus began to predict His death and resurrection. The transfiguration occurred. The last journey to Jerusalem began. It was really a rather roundabout, back and forth itineration in Perea (southern Transjordan) and Judea, as well as in Galilee. During this time Jesus spoke several of His most famous parables, such as those about the good Samaritan and the prodigal son. The raising of Lazarus convinced the Sanhedrin that they should eliminate Jesus and with Him the threat of a Messianic revolt.

Passion week began with the triumphal entry on Palm Sunday. On Monday Jesus cursed the fig tree and cleansed the Temple again. The cleansing of the Temple hardened the Sanhedrin in their determination to get rid of Him. On Tuesday Jesus debated with the Pharisees and Sadducees in the Temple courtyards and spoke His prophetic discourse to the disciples on Mount Olivet. Also, Judas arranged to betray Jesus. Wednesday is silent in the gospel records, unless Jesus and the disciples ate the Passover meal Wednesday evening (Tuesday evening is also possible), earlier than most of the Jews. Otherwise, the last supper took place Thursday evening, the trials Thursday night and early Friday morning, and the crucifixion and burial Friday during the day. The Roman guard watched the tomb throughout Saturday. The resurrection occurred early Sunday morning, and Jesus appeared to His disciples a number of times during forty days of postresurrection ministry. Finally He ascended little more than a week before the outpouring of the Holy Spirit on the Day of Pentecost.[1]

The style of Jesus' teaching was colorful and picturesque. Figures of speech abounded. He frequently created epigrammatic sayings not easily forgotten, and delighted in puns, which usually fail to come through in translation. Many sayings are cast in the parallelistic forms of statement characteristic of Semitic poetry. His use of parables was masterful.

In the content of His teaching Jesus built upon the Old Testament foundation of ethical monotheism, that is, the belief in one God of love and righteousness who acts redemptively and judg-

---

[1]For a more detailed outline of the life of Christ, see pages 208 ff.

mentally in history according to His covenantal relationships with men. By declaring sins forgiven, claiming to be the judge of all men's eternal destinies, demanding utter allegiance to Himself, making extravagant "I am . . ." statements, and introducing many sayings with *amen* (translated "verily" or "truly") in a tone of ultimate authority, Jesus obviously considered Himself a unique person. But He reluctantly used and accepted the term "Messiah" because of its dominantly political and nationalistic overtones in first century Judaism. He preferred to speak of Himself as "the Son of man" whom Daniel saw in a vision as a superhuman figure coming from heaven to judge and rule the whole world (Daniel 7:9-14). But Jesus also associated the suffering of the Servant of the Lord (Isaiah 52:13—53:12) with Himself as the Son of man. Significantly, the designation "Son of man" for Jesus occurs almost exclusively on the lips of Jesus Himself. Among the Jews it was largely unused in a Messianic sense and was therefore a neutral term. Consequently, Jesus could build up His own definition. The term "Son (of God)" occurs both in Jesus' claims for Himself and in the words of others about Him.

Jesus' consciousness of uniquely divine sonship expressed itself in the use of the Aramaic word *abba*, "Father," in the childlike and affectionate sense of "Dadda," or "Daddy," but without oversentimentality. The rabbis dared to speak of God only as *abbi*, "my Father," a more formal address in Aramaic. Jesus even taught His disciples to address God as *abba* because of their relationship to God through Him. In previous times God was viewed largely as father of the Israelite nation as a whole, so that the frequency, warmth, and individualistic emphasis with which Jesus spoke of the divine fatherhood mark a distinctive feature of His teaching.

Loving God and neighbor comprise the two main ethical imperatives, according to Jesus. His view of righteous living emphasized inward motivation in opposition to outward show. He put the golden rule, which had been stated negatively many times before, into a positive form.

Framing all that Jesus taught was His proclamation that the time of God's kingdom had dawned. He Himself represented that kingdom. But He foresaw His rejection and redemptive death and resurrection. Beyond those events lay the age when His disciples would evangelize the world. Then He would return to judge mankind and to establish the divine kingdom fully and forever.[2]

---

[2]See pages 144 f., for greater detail about the kingdom of God.

For further discussion:

How would a modern biographer have differed from the evangelists in presenting the life of Jesus? What might he omit, add, emphasize, and deemphasize? Why do the evangelists in some respects not write as a modern biographer would have written?

What aspects of Jesus' life and teachings do modern people tend to find unacceptable — intellectually, esthetically, and socially — in comparison with ancient people, and why?

How do the startling claims of Jesus for Himself square with His teaching about humility, His demand for personal allegiance with His teaching about unselfish service toward others, and (in general) His egocentricity with His very sanity? Or is it right to speak of His egocentricity (some would even say megalomania)?

For further investigation:

(From a conservative standpoint)

Harrison, E. F. *A Short Life of Christ.* Grand Rapids: Eerdmans, 1968.
Stewart, J. S. *The Life and Teaching of Jesus Christ.* Nashville: Abingdon, 1958.
Ridderbos, H. *The Coming of the Kingdom.* Philadelphia: Presbyterian and Reformed, 1962.
Vos, G. *The Self-Disclosure of Jesus.* Grand Rapids: Eerdmans, 1954.
Andrews, S. J. *The Life of Our Lord.* Revised edition. Edinburgh: T. & T. Clark, 1891.
Morgan, G. C. *The Crises of the Christ.* New York: Revell, 1903.
Stalker, J. *The Life of Jesus Christ.* New York: Revell, 1912.

(From a fairly conservative standpoint)

Hunter, A. M. *The Work and Words of Jesus.* Philadelphia: Westminster, 1950.
Barclay, W. *Jesus as They Saw Him.* New York: Harper, 1963.
————. *The Mind of Jesus.* New York: Harper, 1961.
Turner, H. E. W. *Jesus, Master and Lord.* 2nd edition. Naperville, Illinois: Allenson, 1954.

(From a liberal standpoint)

Bultmann, R. *Jesus and the Word.* New York: Scribner's, 1960.
Bornkamm, G. *Jesus of Nazareth.* New York: Harper, 1960.
Stauffer, E. *Jesus and His Story.* New York: Knopf, 1960. (In some respects conservative)
Taylor, V. *The Life and Ministry of Jesus.* Nashville: Abingdon, 1955. (In some respects conservative)

(Nontechnical commentaries from a conservative standpoint)

Tasker, R. V. G. *The Gospel According to St. Matthew.* Grand Rapids: Eerdmans, 1961.
Cole, R. A. *The Gospel According to St. Mark.* Grand Rapids: Eerdmans, 1961.
Geldenhuys, J. N. *Commentary on the Gospel of Luke.* Grand Rapids: Eerdmans, 1954.
Ellis, E. E. *The Gospel of Luke. The Century Bible.* New Edition. London: Nelson, 1966.

Tasker, R. V. G. *The Gospel According to St. John.* Grand Rapids: Eerdmans, 1960.

Barclay, W. *Gospel of Matthew,* two volumes, *Gospel of Mark, Gospel of Luke, Gospel of John,* two volumes. Philadelphia: Westminster, 1957-1959. (Somewhat less conservative than the above)

CHAPTER 8

A Harmonistic Study of the Gospels:
The Beginnings

Leading questions:

How do the evangelists differently introduce their accounts of Jesus' life and ministry?

What are the details and order of the events concerning the nativity and childhood of Jesus?

In what manner did Jesus step into public life, and how did He go about gathering a following? What was the nature of His activities?

In the prologue to the third gospel Luke states his purpose in utilizing previously compiled eyewitness materials to write an orderly account of Jesus' career. That purpose was to convince Theophilus of the historical certitude of the Gospel. "In order" implies careful arrangement, but not necessarily chronological at every point. *Read Luke 1:1-4* (§1).[1]

The Lucan Prologue

Read John 1:1-18 (§2). The prologue of John is highly theological. Some scholars think that originally it was a hymn, now incorporated into the fourth gospel with editorial insertions and revisions. The first phrase, "In the beginning," recalls Genesis

The Johannine Prologue

---

[1]Paragraph numbers here and following refer to A. T. Robertson, *A Harmony of the Gospels* (New York: Harper & Row, 1950). Harmonies of the gospels set the texts of the gospels in parallel columns where the editor considers the contents to be parallel. The editor also arranges the pericopes in what he thinks is the most probable chronological order. Robertson's harmony is probably the most widely used. The harmonistic approach has suffered from those who see the evangelists as purveyors of unreliable information, for under that view the differences among the gospels stem from falsification of the data. It becomes pointless to harmonize untrustworthy reports. If the gospels are reliable, however, the harmonistic approach follows naturally; for then the differences are due to complementary perspectives within the reporting. To achieve as complete a picture as possible, combine reports (but without straining for harmonization where sufficient information is lacking).

1:1. The application of the term "Word" (Greek: *Logos*) to Jesus indicates that He is God's speech, or mode of communication, to us, in contrast to the Hellenistic divine title, "Silence." The phrase "the word of the Lord" in the Old Testament, the use of "word" for the Gospel in the New Testament, the personification of wisdom in the Old Testament and intertestamental Jewish literature, the use of "word" in the Targums as a surrogate for God, and the technical use of Logos for the Reason which governs the universe by philosophers such as the Stoics and the Alexandrian Jew Philo — some or all of these usages provide background for the Johannine use of Logos.[2] But only John identifies the Logos absolutely with God and then dares to identify the Logos with a human being who lived in history, Jesus.

The Word is in communion with God the Father ("with God") and therefore comes from Him. Yet He is the same as God ("the Word was God"). He is the Creator, and by coming into the world He becomes the source of spiritual life and illumination for all men. Those who receive Him by believing in Him — in contrast with most of His own people, the Jews — become the children of God, not by human powers of procreation ("blood . . . the will of the flesh . . . the will of man," verse 13) — that is, not by virtue of physical ancestry, Jewish or otherwise — but by the action of God Himself.

The Word's becoming a human being ("the Word became flesh") and dwelling (literally, "tabernacled, pitched his tent") among other human beings is the doctrine of the incarnation (verse 14). His glory is not external glitter, but the moral excellence of God's character ("grace and truth"), which He fully reveals to mankind as only a unique ("only begotten") son can possibly do. John the Baptist (verses 6-8, 15) testifies to Jesus' superiority ("he . . . is become before me" in rank) because of His pre-existence as the Logos ("he was before me" in time and eternity). In the incarnation of the Logos the invisible God becomes visible (verse 18).

Tables of Descent

Scholars have suggested various explanations for the differences between the genealogies of Jesus in Matthew and Luke.[3] The most probable solution is that Luke gives Jesus' real descent through His mother Mary, but substitutes the name of Mary's husband ("Being the son [as was supposed] of Joseph," Luke 3:23) because it was not customary to include the names of

---

[2]See representative selections from extra-Biblical literature in C. K. Barrett, *The New Testament Background: Selected Documents* (New York: Harper & Row, 1956), pp. 54, 55, 61, 62, 67, 68, 183-185, 216-221.

[3]For a survey see the extended note in the back of Robertson's *Harmony*, pages 259-262.

women in ancestral lists. On the other hand, Matthew gives the descent of Jesus' foster father because in Jewish society (and Matthew wrote for Jews) legal rights, such as the claim to the Messianic throne of David, passed through the father even though he be only a foster father. It turns out, however, that both Joseph and Mary traced their ancestry back to David, and of course to Abraham.

Contrary to custom, the Matthaean genealogy includes four women: Tamar, an adulteress; Rahab, a harlot; Ruth, a Moabitess, the propriety of whose midnight appeal to Boaz might easily be questioned (Ruth 3:1-14); and the wife of Uriah, Bathsheba, whom David seduced. Matthew apparently wanted to disarm in advance arrogant prejudice against the circumstances of Mary's giving birth to Jesus by reminding Jewish readers of incidents involving women in their own cherished history which might well raise eyebrows among outsiders. Furthermore, all four women were Gentiles. Their inclusion in this genealogy points to the motif of universal salvation in the rest of the gospel. In the statement of Matthew 1:16, "Jacob begat Joseph the husband of Mary, of whom was born Jesus," the Greek word for "whom" is feminine and can refer only to Mary, in keeping with the doctrine of the virgin birth. Matthew artistically arranges his genealogy into three sets of fourteen generations apiece. But to do so he deliberately omits three generations listed in the Old Testament and counts David twice to emphasize for his Jewish audience that Jesus is the Davidic Messiah. It is possible that Matthew stresses the point even further by intending the number fourteen to be a subtle reference to David, for in Hebrew the numerical value of the name David is fourteen. *Read Matthew 1:1-17; Luke 3:23-38 (§3).*

THE NATIVITY AND CHILDHOOD OF JESUS

Read Luke 1:5-25 (§4). Twenty-four different platoons of priests served in the Temple, each for approximately two separate weeks out of the year. Zacharias was filling his assignment in "the course of Abijah." The casting of lots determined which priest gained the privilege of burning incense in the Temple; and once privileged to do this, the priest was disqualified from then on to give other priests a chance. During this once in a lifetime experience, an angel of the Lord announced to Zacharias that he and his wife Elisabeth (or Elizabeth) were going to have a son, who should live like a Nazirite ("no wine or strong drink") and who would prepare the Jews for the Messianic times. The angel made Zacharias dumb for his unbelief.

Luke tells the nativity story from the standpoint of Mary. The angel Gabriel announced to Mary that in the near future she was to give birth to Jesus, the Son of God and Davidic king. She was to do so, moreover, in a state of virginity through the miraculous power of the Holy Spirit. After Gabriel's departure Mary visited her relative Elisabeth in Judea to share her secret. There she burst into a hymn of praise, called "The Magnificat of Mary," drawn largely from the Old Testament song of Hannah (1 Samuel 2:1-10). Ultimately Elisabeth gave birth to her son.

At the ceremony of circumcision and name-giving on the eighth day after the birth, friends and relatives suggested that the child be named after his father. But the parents insisted on the name "John," which means "The LORD is gracious," appropriate because of the parents' old age. When the dumbness of Zacharias left, he burst into a joyful hymn known as "The Benedictus." *Read Luke 1:26-80* (§§5-8).

Read Matthew 1:18-25 (§9). The purpose of Matthew in his nativity account is apologetic. He wants to counteract Jewish slander that Jesus was illegitimately born by giving from Joseph's standpoint a detailed explanation of the circumstances surrounding Jesus' birth. In Jewish society betrothal was as binding as marriage. Only divorce or death could break it. In the event of death, the surviving partner became a widow or widower. Joseph and Mary were betrothed. When Joseph discovered that Mary was pregnant, he determined to divorce her as privately as possible (that is, with a minimum of legal witnesses) to avoid a public spectacle. Joseph may have suspected unfaithfulness on Mary's part; or, if Mary had already informed him of what had happened, he may have feared to intrude himself as a husband into the sacred situation. Or perhaps he did not want to pass himself off as father of the divine child. Whatever his feelings and state of knowledge, an angel of the Lord instructed him to proceed with the wedding and to call the name of the son "Jesus" ("the LORD is salvation") because of the deliverance from sin he would bring.

Matthew adds that these events fulfilled Isaiah's prophecy of the virgin birth. The statement that Joseph refrained from intercourse with his wife "*till* she had brought forth a son" (verse 25) implies that Mary did not remain perpetually virgin. The frequently cited mythological parallels to the story of Jesus' virgin birth are not true parallels, for in them the gods have physical intercourse with the human mothers-to-be. It is therefore wrong to speak of virgin births in those myths.[4]

---

[4]See J. G. Machen, *The Virgin Birth of Christ,* 2nd edition (New York: Harper, 1932), especially chapter XIV; J. Orr, *The Virgin Birth of Christ* (London: Hodder & Stoughton, 1970), especially chapter VI.

Read Luke 2:1-38 (§§10-13). Luke places Jesus' birth in the context of a census during the administration of Quirinius in Syria. It used to be charged confidently that Luke put Quirinius' governorship too early. But further investigations, including archaeological discoveries, suggest that Luke was not wrong after all. (The secular historical picture is not entirely clear even yet.) Joseph and Mary were required to enroll in Bethlehem, their ancestral town. There Mary gave birth in a manger. Probably the manger was well-trodden clay in a cave. Angels announced the Messianic birth to shepherds near Bethlehem in a song, "Gloria in excelsis (Glory in the highest; that is, Praise in heaven). . . ." The shepherds were the forerunners of the humble folk who later flocked around Jesus. But even more importantly, they provided the appropriate setting for the presentation of Jesus as another shepherd king like David.

After forty days of ritual purification for Mary, she and Joseph took Jesus to the Temple. There Simeon and Anna, two aged and godly Jews, happily recognized in the infant Jesus the long-awaited Messiah. But Simeon darkly warned that many Israelites would "fall" as well as "rise" because of Jesus and that something would happen to pierce Mary's motherly heart like a sword. The enigmatic statements pointed forward to Jesus' public min-

The Birth
of Jesus
and Visit of
The Shepherds

Presentation
in the Temple

BETHLEHEM *as viewed south to Manger Square and the Church of the Nativity. This was the ancestral town of both Joseph and Mary.*

istry and crucifixion, which were to evoke among the Jews both unbelief, leading to downfall under divine judgment, and faith, leading to ascent in divine favor. The fate of Jesus was also to bring sorrow upon Mary.

The Adoration of the Magi

Matthew now tells his version of Jesus' birth. His purpose is still apologetic. If Jesus was acknowledged as the royal Messiah by Gentiles (the wise men), then Jews should also do so. Growing up in Nazareth did not disqualify Jesus from messiahship, as the Jews charged; for although political circumstances caused Nazareth to become His home town, He was born in Bethlehem, exactly as prophesied concerning the Messiah.

The wise men, or Magi, may have been Persian astrologers. The three kinds of gifts they brought do not necessarily imply that they were three in number. We do not know what star they saw "at its rising" (a better translation than "in the east," Matthew 2:2, 9). It may have been a conjunction of Saturn and Jupiter, which had well-known symbolic meanings. Or it might have been a comet, or a miraculous luminary for this special occasion alone. When the wise men arrived, Jesus was no longer in a stable, but in a house. The fact that Herod the Great had infants in Bethlehem up to two years old slaughtered, a deed quite in keeping with his character as known from extra-Biblical records, need not imply that Jesus was nearly two years old. Herod may have simply been leaving a margin for error. Since Herod died in 4 B.C., the birth of Jesus must have taken place before that year.[5]

The Flight to Egypt

Significantly, the personal history of the Messiah repeated certain aspects of the national history of Israel: the going to Egypt and coming back under divine protection (Hosea 11:1), and the sorrowing of mothers over their slaughtered infants in Bethlehem and over their exiled children at the time of the Babylonian captivity (Jeremiah 31:15). *Read Matthew 2:1-23; Luke 2:39 (§§14-16).*

The Return and Residence in Nazareth

"He shall be called a Nazarene" (Matthew 2:23) occurs no place in the Old Testament, but probably refers to Jesus' residence in Nazareth as a fulfillment of Isaiah 11:1 and related passages. Isaiah calls the Messiah a "shoot," or "branch" (Hebrew: *netzer*, from which "Nazareth" is probably derived), who will grow to greatness from the obscurity of the Davidic dynasty, which is compared to the cutoff stump of a tree. Certainly the "Branch-Town" Nazareth was an obscure, unlikely place for the upbringing of the Branch-Messiah!

---

[5]See the extended note in Robertson's *Harmony*, pages 262-267, on the probable time of the Savior's birth.

Luke alone tells us anything about the boyhood of Jesus, and that is very little. At the age of thirteen, Jewish boys became full-fledged members of Judaism. Apparently the parents of Jesus took Him to the Temple at twelve years of age to familiarize Him with the Temple and the festivals celebrated there. *Read Luke 2:40-52* (§§17-19). Jesus' statement, "Did you not know that I had to be in my Father's house?" reveals an early awareness of unique relationship to God the Father. Luke concludes with the summary statement that Jesus grew intellectually ("in wisdom"), physically ("in stature"), spiritually ("in favor with God"), and socially ("in favor with men").

THE BEGINNINGS OF JESUS' MINISTRY THROUGHOUT PALESTINE

John the Baptist appeared on the public scene some time during the years shortly before A.D. 30. He probably had no connection with the Essene community at Qumran on the northwest shore of the Dead Sea. Some scholars think otherwise, but John seems to have been a lone, hermit-like prophet rather than a former member of a monastic group. He preached repentance for the Jews as preparation for the imminent arrival of God's kingdom. This preparatory ministry ful-

NAZARETH, *located in lower Galilee, was the hometown of Joseph and Mary. Here Jesus spent His childhood and grew up to manhood.*

filled prophecies by Malachi and Isaiah. (Mark mentions by name only Isaiah, the more prominent of the two prophets.) By the time of John it was probably required of Gentile proselytes that they baptize themselves as a rite of initiation into Judaism; but John required baptism *for Jews* as a sign of repentance from sins. Or, if proselyte baptism had not yet come into Judaism (the evidence is disputed), John may have borrowed the practice of ritual self-washings from the Essenes and endowed it with new significance.[6] Under either theory of origin, John innovated by administering the rite himself — therefore the phrase, "baptism *of John*." Hypocritical Pharisees and Sadducees came to be baptized only because they wanted to maintain their reputation for religiosity. John compared them to snakes fleeing from a grass fire.

Exhibiting his interest in social problems, Luke quotes John's admonition to the crowds that repentance meant sharing with those in need, to the tax collectors that repentance meant honesty, and to the soldiers that repentance required gentleness and contentment. But the overarching eschatological message of John was that a greater person was coming, one who would baptize the repentant, comparable to wheat, with the Holy Spirit, and the unrepentant, comparable to chaff, with the fire of judgment. Wheat was trodden on a threshing floor to separate the kernels from the chaff and then was thrown into the air so that the wind might blow the chaff to one side for gathering and burning. The kernels remained for storage in a granary. *Read Mark 1:1-8; Matthew 3:1-12; Luke 3:1-18* (§§20-23).

**Jesus'
Baptism**

The baptism of Jesus marked His entrance into public life. Baptism by John ordinarily symbolized repentance from sin. Since Jesus had no sin, His baptism posed a problem. John protested that the roles should be reversed, so that Jesus might baptize him with the Holy Spirit. But Jesus insisted on being baptized, for at least two reasons: (1) He needed to identify Himself with the sinful humanity He came to save; and (2) His baptismal burial in the water and coming up out of it

---

[6]See the note by C. S. Mann in J. Munck, *The Acts of the Apostles*, revised by W. F. Albright and C. S. Mann (Garden City: Doubleday, 1967), pp. 281-283, and C. H. H. Scobie, *John the Baptist* (Philadelphia: Fortress, 1964), pp. 95 ff. For an opposite view, see H. H. Rowley, "The Baptism of John and the Qumran Sect," *New Testament Essays: Studies in Memory of T. W. Manson*, edited by A. J. B. Higgins (Manchester University Press, 1959), pp. 218-229. We know that in the second century A.D. the Gentile who offered himself for baptism was asked why he did so, in view of antisemitism. If he answered with a sense of unworthiness to share in the sufferings of Israel, he was instructed in some aspects of the Mosaic law. Then he dipped himself into the water as two scholars of the Torah recited commandments from the Old Testament. See G. F. Moore, *Judaism* (Cambridge: Harvard, 1950), vol. I, pp. 332-335.

would dramatize His coming death, burial, and resurrection.
Read Mark 1:9-11; Matthew 3:13-17; Luke 3:21-23 (§24).

All three members of the Trinity figure in the baptismal narrative: the Son submitted Himself to baptism; the Father assured Him; and the Spirit anointed Him for His official role. The words of the Father came from the Old Testament, identifying Jesus both with the Davidic Messiah ("You are my beloved Son," from Psalm 2:7, a royal psalm) and with the Servant of the LORD ("in you I am well pleased," from Isaiah 42:1, one of the "Servant songs" in the latter half of Isaiah).

Read Mark 1:12, 13; Matthew 4:1-11; Luke 4:1-13 (§25). The temptation of Jesus constituted a probationary test through which He qualified to bear the sins of others by resisting sin Himself. The first Adam succumbed in the best of conditions. Christ the last Adam withstood under the worst conditions. As in the story of the Fall, Satan was the tempter.[7] The temptations may have been inward and mental, outward and literal, or a combination of both.

The introduction to the first two temptations, "If you be the

THE JORDAN RIVER *near the Jericho area just north of the Dead Sea.*

---

[7]"Satan" is a Hebrew term equivalent to the Greek term "Devil" (*Diabolos*). Both terms mean "accuser."

TYPICAL JUDEAN WILDER-NESS *area east of Bethle-hem.*

Son of God," was an attempt to make Jesus *doubt* the voice of assurance at His baptism: "You *are* my beloved Son." The suggestions that He make bread from the stones and that He jump over the cliff at the edge of the Temple area (or from the pinnacle or balcony of the Temple) to see whether God would send angels to catch Him in midair were aimed at prompting Jesus to *test* that word of assurance at His baptism. In the third temptation, "All these things [the kingdoms of the world and their glory] I will give you, if you fall down and worship me," Satan aimed at persuading Jesus to gain His destiny as Messianic ruler of the world by avoiding the cross. Each time Jesus parried the temptation with a quotation from Deuteronomy having to do with the testing of Israel in the wilderness. It is worth noting, however, that Satan also quoted scripture for his own ends. And where Israel the nation failed her test, Jesus the ideal Israelite passed.

Luke reverses the order of the second and third temptations apparently to make the temptation which took place in Jerusalem climactic; for throughout Luke-Acts Jerusalem appears as the center stage of redemptive history, the goal toward which Jesus moves in the gospel of Luke and the base from which Christians carry the Gospel in Acts. Matthew's order of temptations is chronological, then, and Luke's order topical.

126

Jewish leaders sent a delegation to ask John the Baptist whether he were the Christ, or Elijah (returned to prepare Israel for the day of the Lord in accordance with Malachi 4:5), or another great prophet expected to appear in the last times. (The Jews awaited a variety of eschatological figures.) John denied all the proposed identifications, but he claimed to be the voice calling for preparation of the way of the LORD (Isaiah 40: 3). He also indicated that a greater figure was already in his audience. *Read John 1:19-34* (§§26, 27). John could proclaim Jesus as God's sacrificial lamb to remove the sin of the world because of the divine identification of Jesus by the descent of the Holy Spirit at the baptism. Matthew's account has previously indicated that *before* the baptism John recognized the identity of Jesus as the Messiah, who did not need to be baptized as a sign of repentance from sin. The fourth gospel merely indicates that John had not known Jesus before this occasion and that the descent of the Spirit confirmed John's intuition that Jesus was the Messianic baptizer in the Holy Spirit (1:31-34).

The Baptist's Witness to Jesus

In the subsequent narrative two of John's disciples begin to follow Jesus. They are Andrew and an unnamed disciple, probably the Apostle John, who as author refrains from mentioning his own name. Andrew brought his brother Simon to Jesus. Jesus said that Simon was to be called "Cephas" (Aramaic) or "Peter" (Greek). The English translation for both is "rock," or "stone." Jesus then summoned Philip. Philip brought Nathanael, who as a native of Cana in Galilee voiced scepticism that anything good could come from the rival, neighboring town of Nazareth. But Jesus complimented Nathanael for his honesty and assured him that ultimately he would see Jesus as the exalted Son of man in heaven waited upon by angels.[8] *Read John 1:35-51* (§28).

The First Disciples

John presents the changing of water to wine at Cana as a sign which symbolizes that the redemptive message and activity of Jesus, represented by the wine Jesus produced, supersedes Judaism, represented by the "holy water" used in Jewish rituals of purification. The original supply of wine had run out during the week-long wedding festival. Upon being informed of the lack by His mother, Jesus courteously ("Woman" is not a rude address, as it sounds in English translation) but decisively intimated that although He might remedy the situation, He would not do so because of her suggestion. The only valid reason for performing a miracle was that it fitted into the Father's plan of action leading to the "hour" of Jesus, the climactic week of His

The First Miracle

---

[8]Alternative interpretations of John 1:51 are that Jesus was to become the line of communication between heaven and earth, like Jacob's ladder, or staircase (Genesis 28:12), or that the Father in heaven was going to communicate with the Son of man on earth.

death and resurrection.[9] The six stone waterpots contained about twenty gallons apiece. The master of ceremonies ("ruler of the feast") half in amazement and half in jest somewhat crudely remarked that although most hosts served inferior wine after the guests had become drunk and could not tell any difference in wines, the present host had saved the good wine till last. *Read John 2:1-12* (§§29, 30).

EXCURSUS ON GOSPEL MIRACLES

The first miracle of Jesus raises the question of the supernatural, to which modern "scientific" man often objects. But if there is a God who has acted in history, especially revealing Himself through Jesus Christ, how else may we expect Him to have acted than supernaturally? If He had not, we could point to a lack of historical evidence that it really was *God* acting. Nothing is more natural for a God who reveals Himself than that He do so in extraordinary ways in order to be recognized. The very fact that other religions often claim what is supernatural proves that men really do expect the divine to show itself in this way.

A truly scientific attitude will keep open the possibility of the supernatural and test claimed extraordinary events in past history by searching questions: Were there eyewitnesses? If so, was their number sufficient and their character and intelligence trustworthy? How tenaciously did they hold to their testimony under pressure? Are there early written records, or only late records written long after mythology could have invaded oral tradition? Questions like these put the claims of other religions to supernatural events in a poor light, the claims of Christianity in a favorable light. In the case of Jesus' career there were many eyewitnesses. Those who allied themselves with Jesus willingly suffered ostracism, torture, and even death for what they proclaimed concerning Him — and they felt constrained to make proclamation even at such cost. They could have saved themselves by admitting falsehood in their testimony about Jesus or simply by ceasing to witness.

Furthermore, the records of Jesus' ministry began to be written well within half a century after Jesus lived. The interim was too short for mythological development, especially with the restraining influence of both friendly and unfriendly eyewitnesses. The very extravagance of the stories from a naturalistic point of view makes it unlikely that they were invented and accepted during the period when eyewitnesses were still

[9]See John 7:30; 8:20; 12:23, 27; 13:1; 17:1.

living.[10] Thus the claims of other religions to the miraculous do not at all undercut Christianity's similar claims when both are tested by the tools of historical research in an openminded way. Instead, they show that men do expect and have a right to expect God to reveal Himself in ways that are unusual.[11]

Read John 2:13-22 (§31).[12] The background of Jesus' cleansing the Temple is that sacrificial animals and fowl were sold in the Temple area for the benefit of pilgrims who could not bring their sacrifices because of long distances. The money changers exchanged foreign currency into Jewish currency so that pilgrims from other countries could buy the animals. Jesus objected to commercialism in the sacred cloisters. It also appears that both the prices and the rates of exchange were exorbitantly high. Annas, high priest emeritus, controlled the business. The general populace probably sympathized with the action of Jesus against the greedy Temple authorities. His statement about raising up the destroyed Temple in three days cryptically referred to the resurrection of His body and implied that now the true Temple, or center of worship, was Jesus Himself. His presence outmoded the building in Jerusalem just as His driving out of the sacrificial animals symbolized their coming uselessness because of His approaching death as God's final sacrifice.

The Cleansing
of the
Temple

Still in Jerusalem for the Passover, Jesus gained disciples by performing miracles. As usual John calls them "signs." But recognizing the superficiality of faith which progresses no further than observance of miracles, Jesus refused to become caught up in a popular Messianic movement. *Read John 2:23—3:21* (§32).

The description of Nicodemus as "a ruler of the Jews" means that he was a member of the Sanhedrin. He came to Jesus at night instead of in the daytime probably for fear of damaging his reputation. His statement that Jesus must be "a teacher come from God" (3:2) contrasts Jesus as a miracle worker with the purely academic theologians who came from rabbinical

Nicodemus and
The New Birth

---

[10]Concerning apostolic miracles, Paul would not have dared appeal argumentatively to the miracles he had performed among the Galatians if they had never seen him do any (see Galatians 3:4).

[11]See further C. S. Lewis, *Miracles* (New York: Macmillan, 1947); and for more technical discussions, E. L. Mascall, *The Secularization of Christianity* (New York: Holt, Rinehart & Winston, 1966); H. van der Loos, *The Miracles of Jesus* (Leiden: Brill, 1965), pp. 3-113.

[12]The synoptics put a Temple cleansing toward the close of Jesus' ministry. Many scholars feel that either the synoptists or John has changed the chronological order for topical reasons. On the other hand, it is not inconceivable that Jesus began His ministry with a protest against the corrupt officialdom of the Temple as a challenge to repentance, and made another, final protest before His passion as a preview of the divinely punitive destruction which was to come in A.D. 70.

schools. Jesus' reply that a person has to be "born anew and
from above" means that faith in His miracles alone is not enough.
Saving faith must involve a moral and spiritual commitment so
deep that it effects a renewal comparable to starting life all
over again with a new nature from heaven above. Only then
can one see or enter the future kingdom of God. In a preliminary way, however, the believer even now begins to enjoy the
eternal life of the divine rule.

Faith by itself does not produce spiritual renewal. Rather, at
the moment of genuine faith in Jesus Christ, the Holy Spirit
cleanses the heart.[13] Jesus compares the invisible work of the
Spirit to wind. Wind itself cannot be seen, but its effects are
quite apparent. In making the comparison, Jesus was playing
on the double meaning of a word which meant both "spirit" and
"wind." The renewing work of the Spirit finds its basis in the descent of Jesus from heaven and His ascent back to heaven via
the cross. Jesus here compares His coming crucifixion to Moses'
lifting up the serpent in the wilderness (3:13, 14; see Numbers
21:8, 9).

**The Baptist
and Jesus**

For a while Jesus carried on a ministry of baptism through His
disciples. He Himself did not administer the rite. When John
the Baptist heard about this seemingly rival activity, he issued a
glowing tribute to Jesus in which he compared Jesus to a bridegroom and himself to the best man ("friend of the bridegroom").
In Jewish custom the best man made wedding preparations
for the groom. John also contrasted his own earthly origin with
the heavenly origin of Jesus. *Read John 3:22–4:4; Luke 3:19,
20; Mark 1:14; Matthew 4:12; Luke 4:14* (§§33, 34).

**The Samaritan
Woman**

Read John 4:5-42 (§35). Some say that in the story of Jesus'
conversation with the Samaritan woman the "sixth hour" (verse
6) was noon (the Jewish reckoning, counting from dawn and
from sunset). But John probably used the Roman (and modern) method of counting from midnight and from noon. If
so, the time was 6 P.M.[14] The Samaritan woman was astonished

---

[13]"Born of water and the Spirit" simply refers to the cleansing work of
the Spirit in regeneration. Compare Titus 3:5; Ezekiel 36:25-27. It is from
the passage in Ezekiel as well as from the rabbinical comparison of a
proselyte to a newborn child that Jesus expected Nicodemus to understand
His words. See commentaries for other interpretations, which equate the
water with baptism, natural birth, the Spirit Himself, or the Word.

[14]John 1:39 then means that the first disciples met Jesus at 10:00 A.M.,
a more natural basis for the statement that "they stayed with him that day"
than if they did not meet Him until 4:00 P.M. Here in John 4 six o'clock is
better than noon because women customarily drew water in the evening rather
than in the midday heat. The woman was too shameless to have avoided
other women by coming to the well at an irregular time. Likewise in
4:52 "the seventh hour" as 7:00 P.M. rather than 1:00 P.M. better fits the
circumstance that the nobleman had made a twenty mile trek, or full day's
journey, from Capernaum to Cana. In John 19:14 treating "the sixth hour"

that Jesus, a Jew, asked for a drink from a Samaritan, "for the Jews do not use the same vessels with Samaritans" (the meaning of verse 9). Jesus said that He could give her "living water." She thought He referred to the flowing water of a stream or an artesian spring, as opposed to static water in a well. Jesus explained that the thirst-quenching water He gave resulted in eternal life (verse 14). Still understanding Him materialistically, she thought that He spoke of literal water with magical potency to quench physical thirst.

Jesus shifted the topic of conversation to her sordid life. Immediately recognizing His prophetic insight, she asked whether nearby Mount Gerizim, where the Samaritan Temple lay in ruins, or Jerusalem, where the Jewish Temple still stood, was the proper place to worship. Jesus indicated that the Jews had been correct up to that time, but now the time had come for true worshipers of God to dispense with the outward forms of

IN SAMARIA, *a view from Jacob's well toward Mount Ebal.*

---

as 6:00 A.M. (Roman reckoning) rather than noon (Jewish reckoning) harmonizes with synoptic indications concerning the time of Jesus' crucifixion. And when in 20:19 John writes about the evening of the first Easter Sunday as the evening of "the first day of the week," he most certainly uses the Roman method; for according to Jewish reckoning that evening was the beginning of the *next,* or *second,* day of the week (new days beginning at sunset).

Temple rituals. They must now worship "in spirit and in truth." The phrase has nothing to do with sincerity, but rather is a veiled way of saying that men can approach God only through Jesus Himself, the giver of the Spirit (symbolized by the life-giving water; compare 7:37-39) and Himself the Truth, who perfectly reveals God (compare 14:6). Jesus then identified Himself to the Samaritan woman as the Messiah. The woman believed and influenced her fellow townspeople also to believe.

For further discussion:

What modern terms instead of "Word" might John have used to designate Jesus as God's communication to man?

From what sources might Matthew and Luke have gleaned their information about Jesus' birth? How did they come to know the details of Jesus' temptation?

Compare John the Baptist and his message with the Qumran sect of Essenes and their beliefs (see pages 123, 124).

How was it possible for the divine Son of God genuinely to be tempted?

Analyze the psychology of Jesus' dealings with the woman of Samaria.

Can the scientific method afford to relax the uniformity of nature and the analogy of events in order to make room for miracles?

For further investigation:

See the works listed on pages 115 f., and those appearing in the footnotes to this chapter.

CHAPTER 9

The Great Galilean Ministry

Leading questions:

How did Jesus gain popularity with the crowds, and then lose it?

Why did tensions develop between Jesus and the Jewish leaders, and at what points?

What were the reactions of Jesus to His fame and to the later decline in His popularity?

How did he develop the main lines of His teaching as His ministry progressed?

Read Mark 1:14, 15; Matthew 4:13-17; Luke 4:14, 15; John 4:43-54 (§§36-38, 40[1]). As the Jewish Messiah, Jesus should have received His greatest honor in Jerusalem, the religious center of Judaism. But "a prophet has no honor in his own country." Consequently, Jesus returned to Galilee and made Capernaum His base of activities. In Cana He healed the son of a nobleman from a distance by His mere word. It took great faith for the nobleman to approach Jesus for such a favor and even greater faith to leave believing that his son had been healed.

To Galilee and a Healing

Read Mark 1:16-20; Matthew 4:18-22; Luke 5:1-11 (§41). The Lucan story differs from that in the other two synoptics and may well portray a later, third step toward full-time discipleship. John 1 has already indicated a preliminary acquaintance with Jesus on the part of Andrew, John (by inference), and Simon Peter, an acquaintance which explains why they were now willing to forsake their fishing occupation to follow Jesus. To this must be added the fact that James and John were half cousins of

The First Disciples

---

[1]§39 in Robertson's *Harmony* should probably be equated with §69. Luke brought forward Jesus' rejection in Nazareth as a prototype of the rejection of Jesus elsewhere. Thus Luke here arranged his material topically rather than chronologically.

THE SITE OF CAPERNAUM, *on the northwest side of the Sea of Galilee.*

Jesus (compare Mark 15:40; 16:1; Matthew 27:56; and John 19:25, together with commentaries).

Teaching, Healings, and Exorcisms

The scribes constantly appealed to rabbinical tradition. By contrast, the authoritative tone of Jesus' teaching and His powerful expulsion of demons greatly impressed the crowds. *Read Mark 1:21-39; Luke 4:31-44; Matthew 4:23-25; 8:14-17* (§§42-44). After healing Peter's mother-in-law, Jesus healed many other sick people and expelled demons — after sunset, because the Sabbath ended then and people could carry their afflicted relatives and friends to Jesus without breaking the prohibition against working on the Sabbath. The general characterizations of Jesus' Galilean ministry emphasize not only teaching and preaching, but also miracle working and exorcism (a technical term for the expulsion of demons). Healings, resuscitations, and exorcisms represented an invasion and preliminary overthrow by God's kingdom of Satan's kingdom as represented by disease, death, and demonism.

The Cleansing of a Leper

As outcasts from society, lepers were unable to enter any walled city and had to shout "Unclean!" lest others draw near them. *Read Mark 1:40-45; Matthew 8:2-4; Luke 5:12-16* (§45). The Mosaic law prohibited touching a leper; but when Jesus touched this leper, He did not contract uncleanness. Rather,

134

the purity of Jesus cleansed the leper. Jesus then commanded the leper to perform the prescribed ritual so that he might be certified as fit to reenter society. Perhaps Jesus also meant to demonstrate that He did not really oppose the Mosaic law.

Another healing story emphasizes the power of Jesus to forgive sins as well as to heal. *Read Mark 2:1-12; Matthew 9:1-8; Luke 5:17-26* (§46). Since the roofs were made of mud plastered over a network of rafters and branches, it was a simple matter to dig a hole over the spot where Jesus was. It appears from Luke either that tiles had to be removed first or that for the benefit of his readers Luke makes a "cultural translation" of the typical mud roof of Palestinian homes into the tiled roof more common elsewhere in the Roman Empire.

Levi and Matthew were alternate names borne by the same individual. *Read Mark 2:13-17; Matthew 9:9-13; Luke 5:27-32* (§47). At the dinner given by Levi, Jesus' socializing with despised toll collectors and "sinners" who were lax in their observance of Mosaic and rabbinical regulations contrasted sharply with the self-righteous aloofness of the Pharisees, as well as with the isolationism of the Qumran sectaries, who produced the Dead Sea Scrolls.

Read Mark 2:18-22; Matthew 9:14-17; Luke 5:33-39 (§48). In defending His disciples' failure to fast, Jesus compared His ministry to the Messianic wedding feast expected by the Jews. Weddings are joyous occasions. It is inappropriate for wedding guests to go without food as a sign of sorrow. Then Jesus compared the incompatibility of His new message and Judaism both to the incompatibility of a patch of unshrunken cloth and an old garment (taking a patch from a new garment spoils the new garment and also causes a worse rent in the old garment when the patch shrinks after its first washing!) and to the incompatibility of new wine and old wineskins, which have already stretched as much as possible and will therefore burst from the expanding pressure of new wine.

Read John 5:1-47 (§49). The unnamed festival which is the setting for Jesus' Sabbath cure of the lame man may have been the Passover (see the commentaries). Archaeologists have excavated what was almost certainly the Pool of Bethesda[2] with five porticoes. The earliest manuscripts omit the explanation in verses 3b, 4 about an angel's periodically stirring the water. Rabbinical law allowed a doctor to treat sickness on the Sabbath only if the person's life was in danger, so that the healing of lameness as well as the carrying of a mat ("bed") consti-

The Forgiveness and Healing of a Paralytic

The Call of Matthew-Levi

The Question of Fasting

The Healing of a Lame Man at the Pool of Bethesda

---

[2]Or Bethzatha or Bethsaida.

tuted a serious breach of rabbinical law. Jesus defended His action by associating His work of healing with God the Father's work of sustaining creation, a work which, unlike creation, had never ceased even on the Sabbath (verse 17). This close self-association with God sounded blasphemous to the Jews (verse 18). But rather than yield, Jesus proceeded to claim full knowledge of the Father's activities and full authority from the Father for giving eternal life and for judging mankind. Jesus both gives life to the spiritually dead (verses 24, 25) and will raise the physically dead at the last day (verses 28, 29). In claiming authority as the Son of man to judge the human race, Jesus drew on the vision of Daniel 7 to identify Himself with the superhuman Son of man from heaven to whom the Ancient of Days (God) gave authority to judge all men. Jesus admitted that according to Jewish and Roman law His own word would be inadmissible in court to support His claims (verse 31). But

THE POOL OF BETHESDA *excavation in Jerusalem reveals the depth of deposit since the time of Christ.*

A WHEAT FIELD *ready for harvesting in Dothan Valley, about thirteen miles north of Shechem.*

John the Baptist had testified in His behalf. Even more convincing was the evidence of the miracles God enabled Jesus to perform and the witness of the Father Himself, probably His inner voice of assurance to the believer (verses 32-37). Moreover, had the Jews heeded their own Scriptures, in which they trusted, they would have recognized Jesus as the fulfiller of Messianic prophecy.

Read Mark 2:23-28; Matthew 12:1-8; Luke 6:1-5 (§50). The disciples were plucking grain while going through the fields, not because they wished to antagonize the Pharisees, but because they were genuinely hungry. Deuteronomy 23:25 permitted the practice. Stealing was not the charge, therefore, but working on the Sabbath by rubbing the grain in their hands to separate the kernels from the chaff (threshing!). Defending His disciples again, Jesus appealed to the unlawful eating of the sacred shewbread by David and his men (I Samuel 21:1-6). This proved that human necessities might take precedence over

Sabbath Controversies

legal technicalities. The illustration was all the more pertinent in that David ate the shewbread *on the Sabbath* according to rabbinical tradition. Jesus also appealed to the fact that the law itself commanded priests to break the Sabbath by burning incense, changing the shewbread, and offering a double burnt offering (Numbers 28:9, 10). If David and the priests could guiltlessly overlook Sabbath prohibitions for the sake of more important matters, how much more could the greater Son of man and those associated with Him!

Yet another Sabbath controversy ended with the Pharisees and the Herodians joining together to scheme for Jesus' removal. Normally the Pharisees opposed these mainly Sadducean supporters of the Herodian family in political power, but their common hatred of Jesus brought them together. *Read Mark 3:1-6; Matthew 12:9-14; Luke 6:6-11* (§51).

Withdrawal

Read Mark 3:7-12; Matthew 12:15-21 (§52). Mark indicates that people came to Jesus from as far south as Idumea and from as far north as Tyre and Sidon (see the map on page 64). Matthew relates the withdrawal of Jesus from the crowds and His dampening of publicity to Isaiah's prophecy that the Servant of the LORD would not seek popularity.

The Choice of the Twelve

Read Mark 3:13-19; Luke 6:12-16 (§53). The twelve disciples whom Jesus chose after a night of prayer became the nucleus of a new people of God, the Church. Their number corresponded to the twelve patriarchs (Jacob's sons) from whom the tribes of Israel descended. The term *apostle*, used by Luke, connotes someone who is sent with delegated authority to represent the sender.

The Sermon on the Mount

In his account of the Sermon on the Mount, Matthew pictures Jesus as the new Moses going up to a mountain for the promulgation of a new law, much as Moses delivered the Old Testament law from Mount Sinai. In the Sermon on the Mount Jesus spiritually interpreted the unchanging principles of divine law already embodied in the Mosaic legislation. Most of the ceremonial features of the Mosaic law He omitted, although mention of "the gift at the altar" (Matthew 5:23, 24) betrays the transitional nature of the period during which He spoke the sermon. The old age was dying; distinctively Mosaic features are therefore generally absent. The new age was dawning; Jesus therefore repromulgated God's righteous demands for the new people of God, His disciples.

Luke indicates that Jesus spoke at "a level place" on the mountain slope where crowds were able to gather around. Alternatively, Luke anticipates what happened *after* the speaking of the sermon in writing that Jesus came down and stood on a level place (6:17-19), and then steps back to record the sermon Jesus spoke *before* His descent. (Chronological sequence is not always the main consideration in any of the gospels.) Luke omits some of the distinctively Jewish subject matter which appears in Matthew. And Matthew has inserted sayings of Jesus spoken on other occasions at appropriate places in the sermon.[3]

"Blessed (happy) are . . ." means "Congratulations to . . . !" This form of statement is known as a "beatitude." Luke also records a series of woes, which balance the beatitudes. *Read Matthew 5:1-20; Luke 6:17-26* (§54, introduction and subsections 1, 2). It is usually thought that in calling His disciples "the salt of the earth" Jesus was referring to the preservative and therefore life-giving qualities of salt. But He may have had in mind the use of certain types of salt as fertilizer. By enriching the earth, Christians produce spiritual fruit pleasing to God. Mixture of qualities foreign to discipleship, however, reduces fertilizing, or life-giving, effectiveness. Jesus went on to affirm the full authority of the Old Testament as Scripture, even to the last jot, the smallest letter in the Hebrew alphabet, and tittle, the short extension of a stroke which differentiates some very

HORNS OF HATTIN *(Jebel Hattin) looking out toward the Sea of Galilee. This traditional site of the Sermon on the Mount is generally known as the Mount of Beatitudes.*

---

[3]See further the note in Robertson's *Harmony*, pp. 273-276.

similar letters in the Hebrew alphabet. He then put His own teaching on the same level of authority.

In the next part of the Sermon on the Mount Jesus did not audaciously set aside the Old Testament commandments. He had just affirmed their full authority! He did, however, contrast His own interior interpretation of the Old Testament with the superficially external interpretations of the Pharisaical rabbis. And He indicated that the new eschatological situation in some instances required new commandments to transcend the old. *Read Matthew 5:21-48; Luke 6:27-30, 32-36* (§54, subsection 3).

The prohibitions against calling a "brother" abusive terms underline the necessity of mutual love among disciples. The instructions to pluck out an eye or cut off a hand prone to evil exhibit the use of hyperbole, deliberate exaggeration for the sake of emphasis. Jesus meant that disciples must rigorously exercise moral self-discipline. To "forswear" (Matthew 5:33) is to break an oath. Rabbis taught that an oath which omitted God's name might be broken without guilt. Jesus argued that since all things — heaven, earth, Jerusalem, and all else — have connection with God, an oath in the name of anything is binding. The use of oaths is therefore wrong. The "yes" and "no" of a person should really mean yes and no so consistently that an oath is not needed to convince people the person is telling the truth.

Being compelled to go a mile (Matthew 5:41) alluded to being forced by Roman soldiers and governmental agents to carry supplies. Jesus denied that the *lex talionis* (law of retaliation: "an eye for an eye . . .") should be used for personal vengeance. But He did not deny its validity as a principle of legal justice (Matthew 5:38). Against modern popular misunderstanding, the *lex talionis* safeguarded justice by not allowing *excessive* punishment, as well as by insisting on adequate punishment. "Thou shalt love thy neighbor" (Matthew 5:43) came from the Old Testament, "and hate thine enemy" from rabbinical teaching. Another obvious example of hyperbole occurs in Luke 6:29: "from him who taketh away thy cloke [outer garment] withhold not thy coat [inner garment] also."

Read Matthew 6:1-18 (§54, subsection 4). Hypocrites receive all the reward they will ever obtain when other men admire their religiosity. Certainly God will give them no recognition. In the model Lord's Prayer a sense of divine nearness ("Our Father") balances a sense of divine transcendence ("who art in heaven"). "Hallowed be thy name" asks that the reputation of God be held high. "Thy kingdom come. Thy will be done on earth as it is in heaven" expresses a longing for the establishment of God's kingdom on earth. "Give us this day our daily bread" asks for the necessities of physical life. In the petition for forgiveness, debts are a figure of speech for sins. The petition does not imply that our forgiving other people merits God's forgiveness of us. Rather, forgiving others proves the genuineness of the repentance from our own sins: "Forgive us our debts *as* [not *because*] we forgive our debtors." "And lead us not into temptaton" means, "Do not let us succumb to testing [whether by trial through hardship or by enticement to evil]," and represents the opposite of the self-confident attitude which later characterized Peter. The final petition is for deliverance from evil as personified in Satan, "the evil one." The earliest and best manuscripts lack the familiar doxology, "For thine is the kingdom and the power and the glory forever."

A healthy eye sparkles with light as though it were a lamp. Illness dulls the sparkle. An "evil [unhealthy] eye" stands for spiritual illness as a result of coveting "mammon [money]." *Read Matthew 6:19-34* (§54, subsection 5). "Be not anxious" means "Do not worry." Covetousness and anxiety, then, lie behind men's lust for money. But Jesus did not prohibit making plans and provision for the future.

Read Matthew 7:1—8:1; Luke 6:37-42, 31, 43-49 (§54, subsections 6-8). Jesus prohibited captious criticism which delights in faultfinding ("Judge not, that ye be not judged"). But He was not denying the right, indeed the necessity, of making moral and spiritual judgments (compare 1 Corinthians 2:15). A "mote" is a speck of dust, a "beam" a large piece of timber. "Give not that which is holy to the dogs" prohibits indiscriminate broadcasting of Christian truth to those who are adamant in their hostility to the Gospel. Truth must be kept from desecration by ridicule. The gate to life is narrow because the false teachers about whom Jesus warns obscure it and because a person may be self-deceived into thinking that lip service brings the benefits of discipleship. Jesus concluded the Sermon on the Mount with a portrait of Himself as the judge of the eternal destinies of all men according to whether or not they have obeyed His words — a stupendous claim indeed!

Read Matthew 8:5-13; Luke 7:1-10 (§55). Matthew's condensed narrative makes it appear that the centurion approached Jesus in person. But Luke's greater detail relates that the centurion sent word to Jesus through two successive delegations of Jews and friends respectively. The centurion thought himself unworthy as a Gentile to entertain Jesus in his home. But he believed that a word of command from Jesus would dispel the disease from his servant as easily as though he himself were issuing orders to his soldiers. Remarking on the great faith of the centurion, Jesus intimated that many Gentiles would enter the kingdom of heaven, while the Jews ("sons of the kingdom"), who had enjoyed superior spiritual advantages, would be cast into outer darkness with weeping and gnashing of teeth (figures of speech for despairing remorse).

The Widow of Nain

In the raising of the widow's son at Nain, the primary concern was not for the deceased son, but for the bereaved mother. *Read Luke 7:11-17* (§56).

The Baptist and His Doubts

Discouraged by his imprisonment, John the Baptist sent two of his followers to ask Jesus whether He really was the Messiah, as John himself had previously announced. *Read Matthew 11:2-19; Luke 7:18-35* (§57). In response to the question, Jesus pointed to His miracles and preaching in fulfillment of Isaiah 35:5, 6; 61:1 as adequate proof that He was indeed the Messiah. He also pronounced a blessing upon those who did not stumble at the fact that He was not turning out to be a military hero. Jesus then eulogized John by saying that among those "born of women" none has been greater than he. "Yet he who is least in the kingdom of heaven is greater than he." Why? Because John was prior to and outside the kingdom? Hardly, because in Christ the kingdom had already come (Matthew 12:28; Luke 11:20; 17:20, 21) and even the Old Testament patriarchs Abraham, Isaac, and Jacob belong to it (Matthew 8:11). Perhaps Jesus was contrasting purely human greatness (with emphasis on "*born of women*") with the spiritual privilege of citizenship in the kingdom. More intriguing is the possibility that "he who is least in the kingdom of heaven" is Jesus Himself — in His role as the suffering Servant of the Lord and as the junior of John the Baptist in physical age. Jesus went on to scold the Jews for being so stubborn in their unbelief that they accepted neither the ascetic John nor the affable Jesus. He compared the stern message of the Baptist to a child's game of mock funeral with wailing and mourning and his own gracious message to a game of mock wedding with fluting and dancing. Like fickle children the Jews could not be pleased. But all who know wisdom because they know God recognize the truth no matter how or by whom it is presented.

Woes and an Invitation

Read Matthew 11:20-30 (§58). After the woes against the Galilean "cities of opportunity," Jesus thanked God for revealing all things to Him and for choosing humble, receptive people ("babes") rather than those who are wise in their own opinion. Then follows an invitation in which Jesus claims to be a gentle and patient teacher who does not burden His followers with numerous picayunish regulations, as did the rabbis.

It was customary for uninvited people to enter and watch a dinner party. The prostitute who did so in the following story could stand behind Jesus perfuming His feet because in usual fashion Jesus was reclining horizontally on a cushion, His head toward the table, His feet stretched out behind with sandals off. *Read Luke 7:3-50* (§59).

THE GREAT
GALILEAN
MINISTRY

The Anointing
of Jesus by
a Prostitute

Read Luke 8:1-3 (§60). The women mentioned in this passage financially supported Jesus and The Twelve during their itineration.

Read Mark 3:19-30; Matthew 12:22-37 (§61). In answer to the charge that He exorcised demons by Satanic power, Jesus ridiculed the notion that Satan opposes his own forces. But if Jesus exorcised by the power of the Holy Spirit, this was a sign the kingdom of God had arrived. To reject this evidence in a deliberate and final manner, as the scribes and Pharisees were doing, constituted the unpardonable sin.

Read Matthew 12:38-45 (§62). Since Jesus had already performed numerous miracles, the request by scribes and Pharisees for an authenticating sign came from closed rather than open minds. In answer, Jesus compared the coming sign of His death, burial, and resurrection to Jonah's stay of three days and three nights in the belly of the sea monster. But if Jesus died on Good Friday and rose Easter Sunday morning, He did not spend three full twenty-four hour periods in the tomb. To the Jews, however, any part of a twenty-four hour day-night period counted for the whole, and Jesus lay in the tomb a whole twenty-four hour period plus parts of two others. Alternatively, "three days and three nights" is an imprecise expression for a short period of time and is not intended to be taken with exactitude. In verse forty-two "the queen of the south" is the Queen of Sheba. The parable of the man who "swept and garnished" himself after an inhabiting demon had left, only to have that demon return with seven others who were worse, points to the scribes and Pharisees: their well-scrubbed self-righteousness invited a fate worse than if they had been unvarnished sinners like the common people they despised.

The family of Jesus tried to approach Him, but could not because of the crowd. The omission of Joseph may imply that Jesus' foster father had died by that time. The report that the mother and brothers of Jesus wanted to speak with Him gave Jesus the opportunity to say that His spiritual kin are those who obey God's will. *Read Mark 3:31-35; Matthew 12:46-50; Luke 8:19-21* (§63).

EXCURSUS ON THE KINGDOM IN THE
TEACHING OF JESUS

With the partial exception of Luke, the gospels fail to accent
the terms *gospel* ("good news") and *preach the gospel* (or
evangelize), but do stress the theme of the *kingdom*. Just the
opposite is true of Acts and the epistles.

**"Heaven"
and "God"**

The initial message of both John the Baptist and Jesus focused
on the kingdom. Frequently the two phrases "of God" and
"of heaven" modify the term "kingdom." The phrases are synonymous. Parallel usage occurs within the same passage. For example, Jesus says in Matthew 19:23, 24 that it is difficult for a
rich man to enter the kingdom *of heaven;* so difficult, in fact, that
it is easier for a camel to go through the eye of a needle than for
a rich man to enter the kingdom *of God.* The phrases also alternate in parallel accounts in different gospels. For example,
"to such [children] belongs the kingdom *of God*" (Mark 10:
14) becomes ". . . *of heaven*" in Matthew 19:14. Only the gospel
of Matthew has "kingdom of heaven," because Matthew, writing for Jews, reflects the growing Jewish custom of avoiding
divine names for fear of desecrating them. "Heaven," then, was
a substitute for "God," just as the prodigal son said, "I have
sinned against heaven," meaning "God," and just as some people
today say, "For heaven's sake" instead of "For God's sake."
Either Matthew's "kingdom of heaven" represents Jesus' phrase,
which the other evangelists translated into "kingdom of God"
for Gentiles who might not understand the use of "heaven" for
"God"; or Jesus regularly used "kingdom of God," and Matthew
substituted "heaven" in deference to his Jewish readers. Or possibly Jesus used both phrases, His choice depending on the audience and on the emphasis He wished to give. The use of the
term "heaven" slightly accented divine sovereignty.

Definition

The term *kingdom* carries two primary meanings: (1) the
sphere of dominion; and (2) the activity of reigning. Because of the verbal idea in the second meaning, many scholars
prefer the translation, "the rule, or reign, of God." Both ideas
are present in the New Testament usage of *kingdom*. The con-
textual flow of thought determines which of the two connotations
predominates. The general concept of reigning includes delivering the subjects and bringing blessing upon them, as well
as exercising authority over them.

**Realized
Eschatology**

John the Baptist and Jesus (at first) said that the kingdom was
"at hand [near]" and that people must prepare for it by repentance (Matthew 3:2; 4:17; Mark 1:14, 15). His ministry under way, Jesus began to say that the kingdom had already come.
"If I cast out demons by the Spirit of God, then the kingdom of

God has come upon you" (Matthew 12:28 = Luke 11:20; compare Matthew 11:12, 13 = Luke 16:16; 17:20, 21). In other words, God's rule was invading the world in the person and activity of Jesus. One must therefore enter the kingdom by faith in Him (John 3:3). Emphasis on the arrival of the kingdom with Jesus' first advent and ministry is called "realized eschatology" and is associated with C. H. Dodd.

Jesus also spoke in another vein about the kingdom's arrival yet in the future at the end of the present age: ". . . until that day when I drink it new in the kingdom of God" (Mark 14:25); "many shall come . . . and recline . . . in the kingdom of heaven" (Matthew 8:11 = Luke 13:28, 29). The petition Jesus taught His disciples to pray, "Thy kingdom come," also implies that the kingdom is yet to come. Exclusive emphasis on the futurity of the kingdom is called "consistent eschatology" and is associated especially with Albert Schweitzer. Schweitzer himself, of course, did not believe in consistent eschatology, but argued that Jesus so believed and taught.[4]

Consistent Eschatology

Both realized and consistent eschatology receive support from convincing proof texts. The evidence is strong that Jesus taught both present and future forms of the kingdom. Therefore the "mystery" of the kingdom is that before its full manifestation on earth at the Second Coming of Christ, believers presently enjoy the future blessings of eternal life in anticipatory fashion.

The Mystery of The Kingdom

In His preaching, Jesus offered the kingdom of God to the Jews, but on the spiritual basis of individual repentance and faith rather than on a politico-nationalistic basis. By rejecting Jesus, the majority of Jews, including their official leaders, rejected God's rule through the Messiah. Consequently, God has transferred His kingdom to the Church (Matthew 21:42, 43; compare Colossians 1:13; Romans 14:17; Acts 8:12; 28:23, 28-31) until the restoration of Israel (Matthew 19:28).[5]

The Kingdom, Israel and the Church

Jesus put much of His teaching about the kingdom into parabolic form. The parables were more or less extended figures of speech, often in story form. In the past, interpreters assigned allegorical meanings to every detail in the parables. The scholarly world then veered toward Adolf Jülicher's insistence that each parable contains one didactic point alone and that other

Parables

---

[4]A. Schweitzer, *The Quest of the Historical Jesus,* 3rd edition, translated by W. Montgomery (London: Adam & Charles Black, 1954), especially chapters XVff.

[5]See further the three books by G. E. Ladd, *The Gospel of the Kingdom* (Grand Rapids: Eerdmans, 1959); *Jesus and the Kingdom* (New York: Harper & Row, 1964); and *Crucial Questions about the Kingdom of God* (Grand Rapids: Eerdmans, 1952); and A. J. McClain, *The Greatness of the Kingdom* (Grand Rapids: Zondervan, 1959), for a broader perspective.

details are solely for realism.[6] Currently it is coming to be realized that the distinction between a parable with a single point and a multifaceted allegory is artificial. Allowance must be made for some allegorism in parables, especially in the longer ones.

Jesus designed the parables of the kingdom to obscure the truth in figurative language from non-disciples who had refused to heed His plain talk, as well as to illustrate the truth for disciples, to whom He explained at least the more elaborate parables. The parables were distinctive to Jesus' style of teaching. Only He uses them in the New Testament — a strong indication of authenticity, since parables would have appeared in other parts of the New Testament if they had been a didactic form used by the early Church and then read back into the mouth of Jesus.

Seed and Soils

"The Parable of the Sower" (Matthew 13:18) can be a misleading title if wrongly used for interpretation. The sower is not even identified in the interpretation. All the emphasis lies on the seed, which represents the word, or message, of the kingdom, and the different types of soil, which stand for different receptions of the word by men. It may seem strange that the sower wasted seed among the thorns, on rocky ground, and especially on the hard path. But villagers beat pathways through the middle of fields for lack of a road system, and a Palestinian farmer appears not to have plowed just before sowing, but afterward. Moreover, he could hardly tell where the seeds of thorns lay hidden in the soil, and a thin layer of soil also prevented his seeing the rocks underneath other parts of the field. The birds swooped down to gobble up the seeds lying exposed on the hard ground of the path. After the plowing, the seed in the thin soil sprouted first because it had only one direction to develop and the heat absorbed by the rocks underneath had caused rapid germination. But the lack of depth in the soil made the plants wither and die. In other areas the seeds from the dried up thorns and weeds of the previous year had been plowed in with the good seed. They sprouted up and smothered the tender shoots of grain. Finally, the good soil produced a bumper crop.

The point of all this is that the rule of God brought by Jesus does not at first coerce men into submission as though it were a sword. That will happen at the return of Christ after men have had their chance to believe voluntarily. Rather, God now sees fit to introduce His kingdom by mere words, the preaching of the Gospel, or (figuratively) the sowing of seed. Everything de-

---

[6]A. Jülicher, *Die Gleichnisreden Jesu,* 2 vols. (Tübingen, 1910). For a wealth of information concerning the background of the parables, see J. Jeremias, *The Parables of Jesus,* revised edition (New York: Scribner's, 1963).

pends on the kind of reception men give to this message. Some, like the hard ground, do not let the word penetrate. The result is that Satan quickly snatches it away. Others, like the thin, rocky ground, receive the word enthusiastically but superficially. As a result, they give up their profession of discipleship at the advent of hardship and persecution. Still others allow worldly pursuits to crowd out the word. Finally, some receive the word seriously, deeply, and unreservedly. The results are very gratifying, "thirtyfold, sixtyfold, and a hundredfold," meaning that many times more seeds of grain are harvested than sown. A thirtyfold yield was average. Sixtyfold was excellent. A hundredfold was extraordinary (compare Genesis 26: 12). Jesus wanted to teach that in the end, at the harvest which is His return, the word of the kingdom will produce favorable results far beyond expectation.[7] *Read Mark 4:1-25; Matthew 13:1-23; Luke 8:4-18* (§64, introduction and subsection 1[a]).

PALESTINIAN FARMER PLOWING *his field, in Samaria.*

---

[7]For a fantastic estimate of agricultural fruitfulness in the Messianic age, see Syriac Baruch 29:5, where it is said that the yield will be ten thousand-fold. Each vine will grow one thousand branches, each branch one thousand clusters, each cluster one thousand grapes; and each grape will produce a cor of wine. (The cor is an uncertain measurement of quantity, probably falling with the range of 35-60 gallons.)

Read Mark 4:26-29 (§64, subsection 1[b]). In the parable of the growing seed, the seed springs up and develops through no creative power of the farmer and in a way that baffles his understanding. Thus Jesus denies that the kingdom will come by human effort or achievement. God alone will bring it about, apart from the attempt of Zealots to precipitate the kingdom by revolution or the attempt of rabbis and others to induce it by perfect observance of the Mosaic law. In view is the full manifestation and establishment of the kingdom at the return of Christ, as indicated by the reference to the harvest. The order of words in the phrase "sleep and rise night and day" reflects the Jewish conception of the twenty-four hour day as beginning at nightfall.

Read Matthew 13:24-53; Mark 4:30-34 (§64, subsections 1[c]-2[e]). The Jews expected the kingdom of God to arrive in a blaze of glory with military victories over the Gentile powers. The supposed beginning of the kingdom in the ministry of Jesus seemed singularly unimpressive to them. The parable of the almost invisible mustard seed which grows large enough for birds to nest in its branches indicates that although the kingdom may have begun small during the first advent of Christ, yet in the end it will be very imposing. The parable of the leaven carries a similar point. Three measures of meal is about fifty pounds of flour, an immense quantity making a huge lump of dough! Thus Jesus underscored the lesson of the parable: the kingdom may now be only a pinch of yeast in a very large mass of dough, but ultimately it will dominate the whole earth. Of course, Jesus did not mean that His disciples would succeed in converting all men. Rather, at His return the kingdom will encompass the entire world.[8]

The twin parables of the discovered treasure and the valuable pearl do not urge heroic self-sacrifice so much as joyful abandonment to the kingdom of God through a sense of its ultimate worth in the age to come. No deprivation is really a sacrifice

---

[8]Others interpret the leaven as symbolic of the evil which corrupts Christendom. It is true that elsewhere leaven regularly stands for evil, but the association with the parable of the mustard seed and the growing Jewish disenchantment with Jesus at the time He spoke the parable favor the above interpretation, in which Jesus declared that the kingdom was present despite its current unimpressiveness. Other figures of speech occur with clearly different meanings in different passages. For example, salt variously represents incorruption, fidelity, and judgment (Matthew 5:13; Mark 9:49, 50; Luke 14:34; compare Colossians 4:6). Jesus may here have purposefully chosen a figure which usually has an evil connotation to drive home the point that the kingdom of God is more active and powerful than the evil kingdom of Satan. Some have also thought that the birds in the parable of the mustard seed represent false teachers who invade the Church. But the phraseology comes from Nebuchadnezzar's dream (Daniel 4:12, 21), where the nesting of birds in the branches of a tree indubitably points to the large size of the tree.

FISHERMEN *of Galilee with their nets.*

in view of that. Repeated invasions of Palestine caused fearful people to bury their treasures for safekeeping. Here the one who buried his treasure apparently had died or had been killed, so that the treasure was ownerless. Under the law of those times it was quite ethical for the discoverer of the treasure to hide it again and purchase the field so as to obtain the treasure legally.

The twin parables of the wheat and tares (or darnels, a kind of weed) and of the good and bad fish caught in the same net teach that until the kingdom of God becomes completely dominant at the return of Christ (the harvest), it will coexist in the world with the kingdom of Satan. In other words, the judgmental separation was not to occur immediately, as the Jews were hoping in nationalistic terms. Ordinarily darnels were weeded out. But here they were so numerous that their roots were intertwined with those of the wheat. Seine nets were either dragged between two boats or laid out by one boat and drawn to shore with two long ropes. The bad fish were fish ceremonially unclean according to the Mosaic law because they lacked scales or fins, and other marine creatures considered inedible by the Jews.

The parable of "the householder who brings out of his treasure things new and old" concludes the collection of parables in Matthew 13 with a picture of the disciple who knows how to draw spiritual truths from the parables.

In the story of the storm and its stilling, the humanity and deity of Jesus stand strikingly side by side. Through physical weariness He slept during the storm. Yet with divine power He

The Wheat and Tares; The Good and Bad Fish

The Householder

The Stilling of the Storm

149

quieted the storm by a mere word of command. *Read Mark 4:35-41; Matthew 8:18, 23-27; Luke 8:22-25* (§65).

Read Mark 5:1-20; Matthew 8:28-34; Luke 8:26-39 (§66). Mark and Luke mention only the spokesman of the pair of demoniacs who approached Jesus. The demons called themselves "Legion" because they were many. A Roman army legion usually had six thousand men, but the term is figurative here. The demons felt a premonition of approaching catastrophe. They were surprised, however, that it was arriving so soon for them: "Have you come here to torment us before the time [that is, before the last judgment]?" They asked not to be cast into the abyss (hell), but to be allowed to enter a nearby herd of pigs. Here, as elsewhere, demons appear as vagabond evil spirits who desire bodily habitation. These demons did not foresee that their entering the pigs would cause the herd to rush madly over the precipice into the lake.

Freed from the demons, the men were no longer restless, but clothed, sensible, and sociable. Jesus could urge them to tell about their deliverance because the Decapolis region was Gentile. The two important reasons for keeping His messiahship comparatively secret — the Jewish misconception of messiahship

GERASA, *modern Jerash, was one of the leading cities of the Decapolis. The Roman ruins (foreground) are the Forum and Street of the Columns.*

as political and the danger of premature arrest — did not exist outside Jewish territory. Some object to the destruction of private property by Jesus' exorcism. But it shows that the work of God's kingdom overrules property rights, both because the kingdom represents divine sovereignty in action and because it meets human needs which are more important than property rights. Those who wailed over the loss of the pigs should have rejoiced at the display of grace and power in behalf of oppressed human beings.

In the next story, the woman with the constant hemorrhage was an outcast from society, unable to take part in the Jewish religion, to enter the Temple, or to touch other people. Separation even from her husband was required by law according to Leviticus 15. The Oriental custom of calling all the physicians available with the hope that at least one might cure her had exhausted her financial resources. Jesus made her healing public, at least partially to remove the public stigma and thus facilitate her reentry into normal social life. *Read Mark 5:21-43, Matthew 9:18-26; Luke 8:40-56* (§67).

Mark and Luke represent Jairus as saying his daughter is about to die. Matthew represents him as saying she had just died. But Matthew has simply telescoped the account, so that in his shortened version the news of the daughter's death has to appear quickly, whereas it can be saved until later in the longer and more detailed accounts of Mark and Luke. The professional mourners in the house of Jairus ridiculed Jesus' statement that the girl was only sleeping. But Jesus knew he would raise her from the dead, and so spoke of her death as mere sleep. In addition, the comparison between death and sleep was common in the ancient world even apart from the prospect of being raised from the dead. "Talitha cumi" is Aramaic for "Little girl, arise." Her eating proved the reality of her resuscitation.

Read Matthew 9:27-34; Mark 6:1-6; Matthew 13:54-58; Luke 4:16-31[9] (§§68, 69, 39). The people of Nazareth failed to understand how the boy they had seen grow up in their town could have become a rabbi with supernatural power. Their unbelief prevented Jesus from performing very many miracles there. In the synagogue He followed the custom of standing to read the Scripture and sitting to preach. Several items in His sermon enraged the audience: (1) His implicit claim to be the Servant of the Lord speaking in the scriptural passage from Isaiah; (2) His stopping the reading just short of a reference to "the day of vengeance" (Isaiah 61:2), the central theme in the nationalistic messianism of first century Jews, who interpreted

[9]See the note on page 133.

the phrase in terms of their revenge on the Gentile nations; and (3) the hint that ultimately His ministry would include Gentiles, as had Elijah's and Elisha's. Jesus escaped their attempt to throw Him over a cliff by slipping through the turbulent crowd — whether miraculously or not is not indicated.

The Mission of the Twelve

Read Mark 6:6-13; Matthew 9:35—11:1; Luke 9:1-6 (§70). Jesus commanded prayer for the sending of laborers into the harvest, then proceeded to send The Twelve in pairs to preach and to heal throughout Galilee. Haste was the primary consideration in the first part of Jesus' instructions. Not having time to minister to Gentiles and Samaritans, the disciples must limit their activities to the Jews as God's covenant people with the first claim. To travel swiftly the disciples had to travel lightly. Jesus therefore prohibited needless baggage.[10] They were not to waste time hunting for the best places to stay or trying to convince those who did not quickly accept their message.

The mention of "the day of judgment" in Matthew 10:15 triggers a set of eschatological instructions for the far future (verses 16-42). Jesus intended this section not for the immediate occasion, but for the Jewish remnant in the period of tribulation before His return. In the immediate future the disciples were not to speak to Gentiles (verses 5, 6). But now testimony to the Gentiles comes into view (verse 18). In spite of persecution during the tribulation the Jewish remnant is to witness boldly, fearing only God, who alone has power to destroy soul as well as body (verse 28).

The Baptist's Beheading and Antipas' Fear

The story of John the Baptist's death provides the background for Herod Antipas' guilty fear that Jesus was John returned from the dead. John's relationship to Herod and Herodias remarkably parallels Elijah's relationship to Ahab and Jezebel, especially when it is recalled that John the Baptist came "in the spirit and power of Elijah." *Read Mark 6:14-29; Matthew 14:1-12; Luke 9:7-9* (§71).

Feeding the Five Thousand: Turning Point in Jesus' Career

For several reasons all four gospels narrate the feeding of the five thousand. It was perhaps the most impressive of Jesus' miracles. In retrospect the multiplied bread had associations with the Lord's Supper. And the incident was the turning point

---

[10]The "purse" was a beggar's pouch. The disciples were not to beg alms. Mark 6:8 allows a staff, but Matthew 10:10 and Luke 9:3 prohibit it. It may be doubted that we have the correct text of Mark, since Matthew and Luke seldom depart from Mark together and probably never in a case of clear contradiction. An early scribe might well have thought that the prohibition of a staff was too harsh, and therefore modified the original text of Mark. The same possibility exists for Mark's allowance of sandals in relation to Matthew's prohibition of them. Alternatively, Matthew and Luke prohibit an *extra* staff, as well as an extra coat, extra shoes, and other unneeded items.

in the career of Jesus. He performed the miracle during the springtime season of Passover, exactly the time of year when the Jews expected the Messiah to manifest Himself. Furthermore, the Jews expected the Messiah to repeat the Old Testament miracle of manna by feeding them as a second Moses at a great apocalyptic feast. The Dead Sea Scrolls even contain instructions for the table arrangements at this feast. Consequently, when Jesus miraculously fed the crowd (precisely what they expected the Messiah to do), at the Passover season (precisely when they expected the Messiah to show Himself openly as the Messiah), they surged forward to make Jesus their king. But He refused. Jesus insisted on becoming the spiritual monarch over their hearts before accepting a politico-military crown. He dismissed the crowd, sent His disciples across the lake, and withdrew to a mountain for private prayer. By His own decision His peak of popularity had become the downturn in His fortunes. *Read Mark 6:30-46; Matthew 14:13-23; Luke 9:10-17; John 6:1-15* (§§72, 73).

"The fourth watch of the night," during which Jesus came **Walking on Water** walking on the water to the storm-tossed disciples, was approximately 3:00-6:00 A.M. The story neither glorifies Peter's faith in walking on the water as Jesus did nor criticizes Peter's faltering and sinking. Rather, it magnifies the grace and power of Jesus. *Read Mark 6:47-56; Matthew 14:24-36; John 6:16-21* (§§74, 75).

The day after the feeding of the five thousand, Jesus charged **The Bread of Life Discourse** the crowds with failure to perceive the significance of His miracle. The Jews believed that God had given the manna through the merits of Moses. Jesus indicated that the real bread was not the manna of Moses, but Jesus Himself sent from God the Father. Those whom God has chosen will come to Christ and never be lost. The words of Jesus about eating His flesh and drinking His blood refer to appropriating by faith the benefits of His violent, sacrificial death. The phraseology resembles the words of institution at the last supper. *Read John 6:22-71* (§76).

Since Jesus seems not to have appeared in Jerusalem at this **Ritual and Real Purity** Passover season, the Jewish leaders there sent a delegation to investigate His activities. Upon arrival they criticized the disciples of Jesus for breaking rabbinical tradition by eating with ceremonially unclean hands. (Hygiene was not at all the issue.) In reply, Jesus asked why they transgressed the law of God by their rabbinic traditions. He cited an example: a son who wanted to avoid the obligation of giving something useful to his needy parents might, according to the rabbis, dedicate it to God for future offering, so that giving it to anyone else was prohibited. In the meantime the son retained possession and use of the item for himself. Jesus then declared inward, spiritual defilement to be far more important than outward, ceremonial defilement. By thus repealing the dietary restrictions of the Old Testament, He anticipated the abrogation of the Mosaic law as a result of His death. *Read Mark 7:1-23; Matthew 15:1-20; John 7:1* (§77).

A Syro-
Phoenician
Woman's Faith

Jesus then went to the region of Tyre and Sidon (Phoenicia, or modern Lebanon) to avoid the crowds in Galilee. *Read Mark 7:24-30; Matthew 15:21-28* (§78). Jesus tested the Syro-Phoenician woman's faith. In the dialogue "children" refers to the Jewish people, "dogs" to Gentiles. Jews regularly spoke of Gentiles as "dogs." But the form of the word Jesus used means "little dogs," household pets. The woman believingly seized this expression to argue that even Gentiles may expect a crumb of God's grace from the Messianic banquet table. It took great faith for her to conceive that the deliverance of her daughter would be only a crumb for Christ to give.

Feeding the
Four Thousand

Appropriately after the dialogue on Jews and Gentiles, Jesus performed another miracle of feeding — this time for a crowd of four thousand people, including many Gentiles. As the Jews more and more rejected Jesus, Gentiles increasingly came into view. *Read Mark 7:31-8:9; Matthew 15:29-38* (§79).

Messianic
Signs

Read Mark 8:10-12; Matthew 15:39-16:4 (§80). In this passage Jesus charged the Pharisees and Sadducees with being intelligent enough as weather forecasters to know that the same phenomenon in the sky can portend different things at different times. Yet they did not recognize the obvious sign that the Messianic times had begun. That sign was His miraculous ministry as a whole.

Sadducean and
Pharisaic Leaven

Read Mark 8:13-26; Matthew 16:5-12 (§81). The leaven of Herod and that of the Sadducees (Mark and Matthew respectively) are the same, for the political supporters of the Herodian family were Sadducees by religious conviction. The leaven of the Sadducees (or Herod) consisted of their materialism and antisupernaturalism. The leaven of the Pharisees was their rigid legalism. The last part of this section records the only known instance of a gradual healing by Jesus. It is barely possible that Mark intended the hazy sight of the blind man in the first stage of healing to symbolize the hazy concept of messiahship exhibited by Peter in the next section.

Peter's
Confession
of Jesus'
Messiahship

Read Mark 8:27-30; Matthew 16:13-20; Luke 9:18-21 (§82). This was not the first recognition of Jesus' messiahship by the disciples. But it was significant because of the waning of Jesus' popularity, which the disciples had doubtless detected. When Jesus told Peter, "Flesh and blood has not revealed it to you," He meant that no human being had done so.

The name "Peter" means "rock," or "stone." The statement,
"Upon this rock I will build my church," uses a related Greek
word *petra* ("rock"). If Jesus was speaking Aramaic, however,
the words were identical. The main possible interpretations are
that the foundational rock of the Church is (1) Jesus, the bed-
rock, as distinct from Peter, a mere stone; (2) the truth of Peter's
confession, that is, Jesus' messiahship and deity (3) Peter as
the leader and representative of the whole apostolic band (not
necessarily as the "first pope"). The statement that the gates of
Hades will not prevail against the Church means that because
of the resurrection to life eternal, death will not be able to
conquer the Church.

The keys of the kingdom and the binding and loosing have
been variously explained as references to authority for establishing rules of Church order and discipline, authority to open the
door of the Church first to Jews and then to Gentiles (as Peter
did on the Day of Pentecost and later in Cornelius' house),
authority to forgive sins (a Roman Catholic view), and — most
probably — authority to admit or to refuse admittance into the
Church on the basis of people's response to the Gospel. In receiving this authority, Peter represented the entire apostolic
band; for the power of binding and loosing belongs to all the
apostles according to Matthew 18:18. Indeed, if binding and
loosing refers to declaring the terms of forgiveness in the Gospel,
the authority belongs to all Christians; for all Christians are
to proclaim the Gospel.

Peter, however, shared the common Jewish misconception of
messiahship. When Jesus began to predict His own approaching
death and resurrection, Peter objected. In harsh tones Jesus told
Peter that he did not understand God's plan. Jesus then urged
all the disciples to take up their crosses and follow Him. A man
condemned to crucifixion carried the horizontal piece of his
cross to the place of execution through jeering, spitting, cursing
crowds. Taking up one's cross to follow Jesus means, therefore,
to expose oneself to the hostility of the unbelieving world even
at the risk of life itself. *Read Mark 8:31-37; Matthew 16:21-
26; Luke 9:22-25 (§83).*

The account of Jesus' transfiguration immediately follows the
prediction that "some" of the disciples will see the glorious
coming and kingdom of Christ. A notation of time, "after six
days," joins the transfiguration to the prediction. (Luke has
"after *eight* days" because he inclusively counts the day of the
statement and the day of the transfiguration, in addition to the
days in-between.) It is logical to conclude that the transfiguration fulfilled Jesus' promise. "Some" of the disciples — Peter,
James, and John — witnessed the event. And it was a private

preview of the glory of God's kingdom on earth at the return of Christ. *Read Mark 8:38—9:8; Matthew 16:27—17:8; Luke 9:26-36* (§§84, 85).

The shining face, the cloud, and the voice all recall the experience of Moses on Mount Sinai and indicate that Jesus is here being portrayed as "greater than Moses." The appearance of Moses and Elijah indicated that Jesus was the fulfillment of the law and the prophets respectively. The topic of conversation was Jesus' decease (literally: "exodus," or "going out"), which He was to accomplish at Jerusalem. The verb "accomplish" implies that Jesus' death was purposeful rather than accidental. Peter wanted to pitch tents for an extended stay on the mountain. But Jesus must continue on the path to the cross. The divine intent behind the transfiguration was to bolster the faith of the disciples. Their belief in Jesus stood in danger of ruin by the increasing Jewish opposition to and rejection of Him.

The Baptist and Elijah

On the way down from the Mount of Transfiguration Jesus told His bewildered disciples that in one sense Elijah had already reappeared, as Malachi predicted, in the person of John the Baptist. But in another sense Elijah would yet come to prepare Israel by repentance for the Second Advent of Christ. *Read Mark 9:9-13; Matthew 17:9-13; Luke 9:36* (§86).

Faith

Jesus then cast out a demon which the disciples had failed to exorcise through lack of believing prayer. *Read Mark 9:14-32; Matthew 17:14-20, 22, 23; Luke 9:37-45* (§§87, 88). The statement, "When Jesus saw that a multitude came running together, he rebuked the unclean spirit" (Mark 9:25), implies that Jesus hurried His action to escape the gathering crowd. During the last phase of His ministry Jesus constantly sought privacy for the teaching of His disciples. "This mountain" (which can be removed by faith, Matthew 17:20) was the nearby Mount of Transfiguration, probably Mount Hermon north of Galilee, and stood for any humanly impossible task or problem. Since the exorcism re-excited hopes that Jesus would prove to be a conquering Messiah, Jesus repeated the prediction of His death and resurrection.

Peter's Penny, or the Temple Tax

The story of "Peter's Penny," as it is commonly known, has to do with the annual tax on every male Jew above nineteen years old for the upkeep of the Temple services. That Matthew alone narrates this story corresponds to his once having been a tax gatherer. *Read Matthew 17:24-27* (§89). The argument of Jesus was that the new age of God's kingdom had dawned, so that the Temple was outmoded by the presence of Jesus. And since a king does not tax his own sons, Jesus and His disciples were not obliged to pay the Temple tax. But following the law of love — avoidance of offending people unnecessarily — Jesus

THE SILVER DENARIUS OF
TIBERIUS, *a coin current
throughout the empire in
the time of Christ, was
commonly used in the
payment of taxes to Rome.*

had Peter pay the tax with a coin which had been dropped
into the lake and swallowed by a fish.

Read Mark 9:33-50; Matthew 18:1-14; Luke 9:46-50 (§§90,
91). The little child Jesus took in His arms represents the believing disciple (see Mark 9:42) in all of his childlike weakness,
defenselessness, persecution, and humility in contrast with The
Twelve's misconception of discipleship as self-advancement. Receiving a little child in the name of Christ means accepting and
believing the witness of a Christian disciple (the "little child").
"Cause to stumble" means "cause to sin." Matters such as cutting
off a hand which causes one to sin again illustrate Jesus' use of
hyperbole. But the command is not to be taken any less seriously because of the exaggeration! Mark 9:49, 50 contains a
play on a double symbolism of salt: salt stands for (1) the
seasoning of eternal punishment ("salted with fire"); and (2)
the incorruptible qualities of discipleship, such as holiness and
graciousness, which in turn produce peacefulness ("Salt is good;
. . . be at peace with one another"). The reference in Matthew
18:10 to the angels of the "little ones" stands behind the doctrine
of guardian angels for those who are destined to salvation.

*Childlikeness
and Discipleship*

Read Matthew 18:15-35 (§92). The Qumran community,
which produced the Dead Sea Scrolls, had rules similar to those
laid down by Jesus for ruptures in fellowship between disciples.[11]
The four steps in Jesus' instructions are (1) a private conference;
(2) a conference in the presence of two or three witnesses;
(3) consideration of the matter by the entire church; and (4)
ostracism of the obstinate party. The wronged person is not to
wait for apologies from the person in the wrong, but is to
initiate the movement toward reconciliation. Hopefully the
parties will settle their differences before all four steps are
taken. The "seventy times seven" in verse twenty-two should

*Reconciliation
and Forgiveness*

[11]Damascus Document 9:2; Manual of Discipline 6:1.

probably be translated "seventy-seven times." It denotes forgiveness an indefinite number of times, in contrast to the bloodthirsty seventy-sevenfold vengeance about which Lamech boasted in Genesis 4:24.

The Unmerciful Servant

In the parable of the unmerciful servant, the debt of ten thousand talents owed to the king by the first servant amounted to about $10,000,000 in silver content, much more than that in buying power, a fantastically unrealistic figure designed to point up the magnitude of our debt of sin to God. The king commanded that the servant and his wife and children be sold into slavery as partial payment, but mainly as punishment. Since Jews prohibited sale of wives, Jesus was trying to shock His Jewish listeners with an inhuman Gentile practice. The servant's plea for patience, "I will pay you all," strikes another unrealistic note. How could he pay a debt so vast? His appeal for more time was just as absurd as any thought on the part of sinful man that he can pay his debt of sin to God. What we need from God is not more time to work off our debt, but immediate mercy. That is what the king proffered. The magnitude of the debt was matched by the magnitude of royal forgiveness.

But God's forgiveness is not the main point of the parable; it is rather the necessity for human forgiveness in imitation of God's. As the servant was going out with his own forgiveness fresh in mind, he refused his fellow servant's plea for more time to pay back a very manageable debt of eighteen dollars. There was no need for cruelty then, but the first servant had his fellow servant thrown into debtor's prison. Doubtless he would have sold his fellow servant into slavery. But because the law forbade a man to be sold for less than his own value in a slave market (and a man brought more than eighteen dollars), the next cruelest measure was taken — imprisonment. The reaction of other servants led to a reversal of the king's initial verdict. "Till he should pay all" indicates eternal punishment, since he could never hope to pay all. Thus, since God forgives us so very much, we ought to forgive the little others do against us. We do not merit divine mercy by forgiving others. But a person is not really sorry for his own sins if he is not willing to forgive the sins of others against himself. The "society of the forgiven" cannot exist if its members are unforgiving, for then they have no fellowship either with the forgiving God or with one another. Forgiveness has to be *worked out* as well as received. Failure to do so indicates not only failure to appreciate God's mercy, but also failure to appropriate it.

The Nature of Discipleship

Read Matthew 8:19-22; Luke 9:57-62 (§93). In this section the first man who volunteered to follow Jesus exuded overconfidence. He lacked awareness that discipleship involves suffering. The second man lacked a sense of urgency. Going home to bury his father would have cost days of mourning and ceremonial purification and probably also meant staying at home *until* his father died. But discipleship is more important than devotion to parents. The third man, who wanted first to say good-by to his household, lacked single-minded purpose. Jesus' answers give three qualities necessary for discipleship: a sacrificial spirit, immediacy of obedience, and determination. Discipleship demands intelligent and unconditional commitment.

The unbelieving half brothers of Jesus sarcastically suggested that as a public figure He should seek publicity by displaying His miracles in Jerusalem at the Festival of Tabernacles, the most popular and therefore most heavily attended of the pilgrim feasts. Jesus answered that, unlike others, He regulated His movements by God's timetable, not according to considerations of popularity. Besides, His destiny was the world's hatred, not public acclaim. He therefore waited awhile before going privately to Jerusalem. *Read John 7:2-10; Luke 9:51-56* (§§94, 95).[12]

For further discussion:

Did Jesus break the Sabbath?

What was the purpose behind the choosing of twelve special disciples?

How should we apply Jesus' teaching about non-retaliation? Is His teaching in the Sermon on the Mount pacifistic, idealistic, realistic, practical?

What are moderns to think of demon possession and Jesus' exorcisms? Why might demon possession be less apparent in Western culture?

Drawing on modern urban life, compose a parable to illustrate one of the points made in Jesus' parables; then compare it for naturalness and impact with the corresponding parable by Jesus.

For further investigation:

See the works listed on pages 115f. and those appearing in the footnotes to this chapter.

---

[12]See the extended note in Robertson's *Harmony,* pages 276-279, for discussion of Jesus' last journey to Jerusalem as narrated by Luke.

CHAPTER 10

The Later Judean and Perean Ministry

Leading questions:

> In what ways does the later teaching of Jesus reflect the deteriorating relationship between Himself and Jewry?
>
> How does Jesus defend the style and content of His ministry?
>
> Along what theological lines does the later teaching of Jesus lay the groundwork for even later apostolic doctrine?

Debate at the Festival of Tabernacles

When Jesus did not at first appear at the Festival of Tabernacles, the people engaged in debate about Him. But the debate was subdued through fear of what the Jewish leaders might do. When Jesus finally arrived, He heard some Jews wondering how He was able to participate in theological debate without previous training in a rabbinical school. ("How knoweth this man letters?" does not refer to the ability to read and write, but to theological training.) In answer, Jesus claimed that His teaching came from God, who sent Him. When Jesus suggested that they were seeking to kill Him, the people scoffed. Perhaps they were pretending ignorance of their leaders' schemes. They must have known since they had been afraid to speak openly about Jesus and later wondered why their leaders did not immediately arrest Him. Jesus then defended His healing of the paralytic by the pool of Bethesda (John 5) by noting that the Mosaic law itself made circumcision, affecting only one member of the body, more important than the Sabbath by requiring it to be performed on the eighth day even though that day be the Sabbath. How much more should the *healing* of a *whole* man override the Sabbath law!

But the Jews insisted that Jesus could not be the Messiah because they knew He came from Nazareth. They thought the Messiah's origin would be unknown. When Jesus announced that He was going away, the Jews conjectured a mission to the Diaspora Jews outside Palestine or perhaps even to the Gentiles

("Greeks"). During the first seven days of the Festival of Tabernacles, priests brought water in a golden vessel from the Pool of Siloam to the Temple for a water-pouring ceremony.[1] On the climactic eighth (or seventh) day of the festival, Jesus shouted to the crowd in the Temple courts that He was the source of the true spiritual water, the life-giving Spirit. But most of the Jews, unaware that Jesus was born in Bethlehem, objected that Jesus could not be the Messiah because He came from Galilee instead of from Bethlehem (see Micah 5:2). Thus in this one passage are reflected the apparently contradictory views of the Jews that the origin of the Messiah would be unknown and that His birth in Bethlehem would be known. *Read John 7:11-52* (§96).

The story of the woman taken in adultery does not belong in canonical scripture. The earliest and best manuscripts, undiscovered when the King James Version was produced in 1611, omit it entirely. Later, inferior manuscripts have it inserted in various places. The very principles of textual criticism which assure the reliability of the rest of the New Testament rule out this passage. Conversely, to insist on the originality of this passage in the text of the New Testament is to undermine the bases of our assurance that we have a substantially accurate text elsewhere in the New Testament. The story itself may be historically true, however, having been preserved in Christian oral tradition before interpolation into the canonical text. *Read John 7:53—8:11* (§97).

The accusers tried to put Jesus on the horns of a dilemma. If He recommended the death penalty in accordance with the Mosaic law, they could accuse Him of going against Roman authority, which forbade the Jews to impose the death penalty. If He did not recommend the death penalty, they could destroy Jesus' reputation by telling the people that Jesus did not hold to the Mosaic law. It was customary for the eldest accuser to throw the first stone. The center of attention, therefore, shifted to the eldest when Jesus challenged, "He that is without sin among you, let him first cast a stone at her." Each accuser left as he became the eldest in the group through the exit of someone older. Various suggestions concerning what Jesus wrote on the ground are inconclusive. The final "sin no more" exempts Jesus from teaching an easygoing attitude toward sexual immorality.

Throughout the week-long Festival of Tabernacles the Jews kept four huge candelabra burning in the Temple area to commemorate the pillar of fire which led and guarded Israel in

---

[1]See the Mishnaic quotation from *Sukkah* 4.1,5ff.; 9.5ff., in C. K. Barrett, *The New Testament Background*, pp. 157-159.

the wilderness.[2] That custom formed the background for Jesus' claim to be the true spiritual light. But light brings judgment on darkness. So Jesus played on several possible meanings of the verb *to judge*: (1) to form an opinion about, here in a superficial, human way; (2) to condemn; (3) to discriminate between. When the Jews asked, "Where is thy Father?", they were not only challenging Jesus to produce His father as a witness. They were also insinuating that He was born out of wedlock. *Read John 8:12-20* (§98).

Abrahamic Descent

Read John 8:21-59 (§99). In the statement by Jesus that the unbelieving Jews were from beneath, He from above (verse 23), "beneath" and "above" are "earth" and "heaven." The claim of the Jews to be free overlooked their political servitude to Rome and to preceding world powers, but was perhaps intended to refer to inward spiritual freedom. To their boast of descent from Abraham Jesus replied that spiritual descent is more important than physical descent. The Jews had in fact subjected themselves to the slavery of sin, so that they were more like the slave-born Ishmael than the freeborn Isaac. The statement, "Before Abraham was, I am," was a claim to be the eternal God of redemption, Yahweh, I AM WHO I AM (Exodus 3:14).

A Blind Man Healed and Excommunicated

Some Jews thought that a man could sin in a previous existence or in his mother's womb and be punished for it in this life. Others thought that children suffered for the sins of their parents. The disciples considered these possibilities when they saw the blind man whom Jesus proceeded to heal. *Read John 9:1-41* (§100). Jesus made clay with spittle and applied it to the blind man's eyes to elicit faith because spittle was popularly thought to have curative power, and also to set the stage for the washing, which had the symbolic value of cleansing. The meaning of Siloam, "Sent," points to Jesus, the one God sent to be the Savior. Once again Jesus broke the rabbinical rule that cures were not to be performed on the Sabbath unless life was in danger. In addition, the making of clay constituted kneading and therefore work. The casting out in verse thirty-four refers to excommunication of the former blind man from the synagogue. Counteracting this action of the Pharisees, Jesus pronounced judgment on them by saying that if they were blind, they would realize their need, repent, believe, and have their sins removed. But since they see, they feel self-sufficient and therefore remain unrepentant and unforgiven.

The Good Shepherd

The allegory of the good shepherd is a commentary on the blind man (a sheep), Jesus (the good shepherd), and the Pharisees (thieves and robbers). Shepherds left their sheep over-

[2]*Ibid.*

night in a walled enclosure (fold) in charge of a porter. In the morning the shepherds came to the porter and called out their sheep, who recognized the shepherd's voice and their own names. In contrast, thieves and robbers climbed over the wall of the sheepfold and thereby caused the sheep to panic. The shepherd was known, in other words, by his gentleness and by the favorable response of the sheep, as in the story of the blind man and Jesus. Thieves and robbers were known by their savage treatment of the sheep and by the unfavorable response of the sheep, as in the altercation between the blind man and the Pharisees. *Read John 10:1-21* (§101). When Jesus claimed to be the door of the sheep, He changed the metaphor slightly, in accordance with the necessity for shepherds themselves to guard the opening of the sheepfold with their sleeping bodies when a porter was unavailable. The "other sheep" of verse sixteen are Gentiles, who were to come into the one flock, the Church.

The mission of the seventy disciples probably took place for the most part in Perea (southern Transjordan) rather than in Judea, against the paragraph headings in Robertson's *Harmony*. The number seventy may correspond to the rabbinical reckoning of the Gentile nations as seventy in number. The mission, then, previewed the later worldwide mission of the Church to the Gentiles. As in the mission of The Twelve throughout Galilee, haste was important. No time for long-winded Oriental salutations or inquiries about the ceremonial purity of the food in this Gentile area. *Read Luke 10:1-24* (§102). Jesus' statement, "I beheld Satan fallen as lightning from heaven," probably means that Jesus saw in the disciples' exorcisms a preview of Satan's downfall at the end of this age.

The Mission of the Seventy

The parable of the good Samaritan explained the Old Testament command, "Thou shalt love thy neighbor as thyself" (Leviticus 19:18). The question of the scribe, "Who is my neighbor?" attempted to draw Jesus into the rabbinical debate over whether the term "neighbor" included non-Pharisees and personal enemies. But the parable did not quite answer the question. "Who is my neighbor?" was the wrong question anyway, for it implied that the crux lay in a legal definition. The right question is, "To whom can I be a neighbor?" for it arises out of an attitude which recognizes anyone in need as a neighbor, without quibbling over definitions. In the parable the emphasis obviously rests on the figure of the Samaritan because of his shock value to a Jewish audience. We would have expected him to be the injured man. Yet he is the *helper*, not the man in need of help. The point, therefore, is not that we should help *even* a Samaritan or *even* anyone. Genuine love does not notice such distinctions. *Read Luke 10:25-37* (§103).

The Good Samaritan

The road from Jerusalem to Jericho descended over three thousand feet in less than fifteen miles through gorges and ravines infested with bandits. The priest and the Levite feared ceremonial defilement from what might have been a corpse for all they knew. This would have cost them the purchase of ashes of a red heifer for purification, the loss of Temple privileges such as eating from the Temple sacrifices during a week of defilement, the arrangement of burial for the corpse, and the rending of a perfectly good garment as a sign of grief. The priest and the Levite quite clearly saw in the victim a threat of personal loss and inconvenience.

The Samaritan had equal reason to pass by the injured and possibly dead man, however, for Samaritans likewise avoided defilement from the dead — and perhaps even more reason, because chances were the victim was a detestable Jew. But not only did the Samaritan stop to investigate. When he discovered the man was an injured Jew, he treated the wounds with wine to disinfect them and with olive oil to soothe them, tore bandages from his own turban or linen undergarments to wrap up the lesions, went on foot as the Jew rode the donkey (the slower pace exposing them to greater danger of further attack by bandits), paid enough money to an innkeeper for two weeks of

ROAD FROM JERUSALEM TO JERICHO *where folds of earth reveal the tortuous structure of the land through which the road passes.*

convalescence, and pledged unlimited credit for any additional expenses — all without hope of reimbursement since Samaritans had no legal rights in Jewish courts. *That*, implied Jesus, is loving your neighbor as yourself. When asked to identify the true neighbor in the parable, the scribe could not bring himself to say, "the Samaritan," but used a circumlocution, "The one who showed mercy on him."

THE LATER JUDEAN AND PEREAN MINISTRY

Mary "also" sat at the Lord's feet. That is, she conversed with Jesus *as well as* served Him; whereas overly busy Martha *only* served. *Read Luke 10:38-42* (§104).

Mary and Martha

Read Luke 11:1-13 (§105). The traveler in this parable about prayer had journeyed during the evening to avoid the afternoon heat and so arrived at midnight, very late by the standards of ancient orientals, who retired early. The oriental "law of hospitality" caused the traveler's host to wake a neighbor at midnight for provisions of food. The three small loaves of bread for which he asked were considered a meal for one person. The neighbor's reluctance was aggravated by the fact that Palestinian families slept close together on mats in the same room, so that to rise and unbolt the door would wake up the whole family. The absence in his reply of a polite address, such as "Friend" in the request to him, shows his annoyance. But if persistence triumphed in a situation like that, how much more effective will persistence be in prayer to the gracious God, who is not at all reluctant to grant our requests.

The Importunate Host

Read Luke 11:14-36 (§106). For comments see the notes to §§61, 62 on page 143. In Jesus' statement, "When thine eye is single, thy whole body also is full of light," the word "single" means "healthy." Speaking figuratively, Jesus meant that healthy spiritual perception illumines a person's whole life and being.

Healthy Vision

In his remarks about Phariseeism, Jesus noted that the Pharisees scrupulously observed minute religious regulations at the expense of the important principles. In fact, the rabbis "built a hedge around the law," that is, went farther than Moses required just to be on the safe side. The result was a rigid legalism (not to be confused with commendable obedience to divine commands) which spawned hypocrisy and pride. *Read Luke 11:37-54* (§107). The way to keep the inside of the cup and platter clean is to give their contents to the needy (verse 41). In other words, charity is better than ceremonial purity. In verse forty-nine "the wisdom of God" is a personification of a divine attribute and thence a title for God Himself. When Jesus said, "From the blood of Abel unto the blood of Zachariah" (verse 51), He meant, "From the first martyr in the Old

Phariseeism

Testament to the last," because in the Hebrew arrangement of the Old Testament books Genesis, where we read about Abel, came first and 2 Chronicles, where we read about Zachariah, last. Zachariah was the son of Jehoiada, the high priest during the reign of Joash of Judah, and is not to be confused with the postexilic minor prophet of the same name.

Messianic Crisis

Again Jesus cautioned against the hypocrisy of the Pharisees. *Read Luke 12:1-59* (§108). When called on to settle a dispute over inheritance, Jesus refused. Instead, He warned against the covetousness which caused the dispute and exhorted men to watch for His Second Coming rather than expend all their energies on material concerns. At the final judgment the "few" and "many stripes" according to degrees of knowledge (verses 47, 48) indicate degrees of punishment in eternity. Jesus spoke of His approaching death as a baptism and noted the fact that differing responses to His ministry had caused divisions within families. Perhaps He meant that the older generation and the younger generation were at odds because the younger was more willing to accept Him than was the hidebound older generation. The section closes with a comparison between Israel and a debtor who is in danger of being cast into debtor's prison, where there is no way to earn money and no prospect of release till the debt is paid. Israel had better quickly plead for divine mercy by repenting and accepting Jesus as the Messiah before it is too late and all hope for the nation is lost.

The Fruitless Fig Tree

Galilean zealots were notoriously turbulent. Pilate had had some of them slaughtered as they were offering sacrifices to God. The Jews tried to prompt Jesus into a statement sympathetic toward the Galilean zealot-martyrs so that they might accuse Jesus Himself of zealotry before the Roman authorities. *Read Luke 13:1-9* (§109). In the parable of the fruitless fig tree, the tree represents Israel.[3] Since it took three years before the fruit was considered ceremonially clean and since the owner had for three more years sought in vain for fruit, the tree must have been six years old. Fig trees deprived surrounding vines and other plants by absorbing an extraordinary amount of nourishment from the ground. The owner therefore allowed only one more year, a seventh, for bearing fruit. Likewise, Israel was to have one more chance to bear spiritual fruit pleasing to God. That chance came to an end in A.D. 70, when God permitted the Romans to cut down the Jewish nation.

Sabbath Healing

In another Sabbath healing controversy Jesus argued that the Sabbath was the most appropriate day of the week for acts of mercy since it was a weekly release from the bondage of labor

---

166   [3]Compare Jeremiah 24; Hosea 9:10; Joel 1:7).

and a foretaste of final and complete release from all the effects of sin. *Read Luke 13:10-21* (§110).

The contrast between the present preview of God's kingdom and its future perfected form is like the contrast between the smallness of a mustard seed and the largeness of the tree which comes from it. It is also like the contrast between a pinch of yeast and the huge lump of dough the yeast permeates. See the treatment of §64 on page 148.

Read John 10:22-39 (§111). The feast of Dedication occurred in December and commemorated the rededication of the Temple by Judas Maccabeus after its desecration by Antiochus Epiphanes. When the Jews at the Feast objected to Jesus' making Himself equal with God, Jesus argued that since Jewish rulers were called "gods" in a representative sense in Psalm 82:6, the audience should hardly take exception to His claim as the Messiah to be the Son of God. Besides, His miracles authenticated the claim. In His statement that He had been "sanctified" by the Father (verse 36), there is no implication that the Father had cleansed Him from sin. Rather, the Father had *consecrated* Him for His redemptive mission.

In reply to someone's question whether many or few will be saved, Jesus told the people not to bother about such speculation, but to make sure they themselves would be among the saved, whether they be few or many. The exhortation was especially necessary for the Jews who tended to think that their Jewishness would automatically include them in God's kingdom. Against this feeling of superiority Jesus predicted widespread Gentile salvation. The "last" who will be "first" are Gentiles. The "first" who will be "last" are Jews who fritter away their opportunity. *Read John 10:40-42; Luke 13:22-35* (§§112, 113).

The Herod of verse thirty-one in Luke is Herod Antipas. The enemies of Jesus were trying to frighten Jesus from Herod's territory into Judea, where they might seize Him in the absence of sympathetic crowds. Jesus contemptuously referred to Herod as a female fox (vixen) not to be feared, in contrast, say, to a lion. Perhaps the feminine form of "fox" hinted that Herod was dominated by his unlawful wife Herodias, who had demanded the head of John the Baptist. Jesus went on to indicate that He still had an indefinitely short period of time in which to work His way deliberately toward Jerusalem. With bitter irony He stated that Herod could not rob Jerusalem of the privilege of killing Him. Jerusalem was the proper place for prophets to be martyred! God had forsaken His Temple ("house") in Jerusalem; it would therefore be destroyed. In A.D. 70 it was.

The Messianic
Banquet

Read Luke 14:1-24 (§114). The reference to banquets in Jesus' exhortation to humility and charity prompted someone, thinking of the great Messianic banquet to come, to exclaim, "Blessed is he that shall eat bread in the kingdom of God!" as if it were a privilege reserved for super-religious Pharisees. In the following parable the first invited guests, who made excuses for not coming to the banquet, stand for the hypocritical Pharisees and their kind. The poor, maimed, blind, and lame stand for the Jewish publicans and sinners whom God was bringing into His kingdom. Those brought in from the highways and hedges represent the Gentiles.

Discipleship

Read Luke 14:25-35 (§115). Jesus warned the crowds that to follow Him they had to renounce all other priorities. Love for family must look like hatred by comparison with devotion to Christ. Salt again represents the preservative or fertilizing, and therefore life-giving, qualities of disciples in the world.

"Sinners"

Luke 15 contains three parables which defend Jesus' welcome of irreligious people into His presence in behalf of God. All three show divine joy over sinners who repent. The term "sinners" in Jewish vocabulary included Gentiles (as a matter of course) and Jews who were careless in observing the Mosaic law and rabbinical interpretations of it. These people included adulterers, swindlers, and those in occupations notorious for dishonesty, such as publicans and peddlers, and in occupations causing ritual impurity, such as tanners, who continually had to touch dead animals. *Read Luke 15:1-32* (§116).

The Lost
Sheep

In the parable of the lost sheep the "ninety-nine righteous persons who need no repentance" do not really exist. Jesus was speaking with sarcastic irony about the self-righteous, who think they do not need to repent.[4]

The Lost
Coin

The lost coin belonged to a coin-bedecked headdress of the kind frequently worn by Palestinian wives as part of the dowry given to them at marriage. The woman in this parable lit a candle, not because it was nighttime, but because the typical Palestinian house lacked windows and had only one low door, which let in very little light. The coin apparently had fallen on the lower level of the one room house. There it lay hidden somewhere underneath the straw scattered over the lower level because of the domestic animals. The housewife swept with a broom, probably a small palm branch, not to uncover the coin, but to make it tinkle on the hard earthen floor so that she could determine its whereabouts. Her joy upon discovering the coin represents "joy in the presence of the angels of God over

[4]Alternatively, they are already righteous by divine grace.

one sinner who repents." Jesus was not referring to the joy of angels, but to the joy of *God Himself* in the presence of the angels. A rabbinic saying forms a stark contrast: "There is joy before God when those who provoke him perish from the world."[5]

BRONZE COIN *of Palestine issued by Herod the Great who was king of Judea at the time of Christ's birth.*

The Prodigal Son

In the parable of the prodigal son, the prodigal demanded his hereditary share of the family property, one-third since there were just two sons and the elder or eldest always received a double portion. Giving inheritances in advance of the father's death was not unknown, but this ordinarily carried only the right to possess the property, not the right to sell it. For if all the family property were sold, the aged parents would be left without a place to live in their declining years. Here, however, the younger son must have brashly turned his part of the property into cash by sale, for he "gathered all together" and went to a distant land. The wasteful spending of his fortune depicts the futility and final ruin of the sinful life. To feed swine was unspeakable degradation for a Jew, to whom pigs were repulsively unclean in a ceremonial as well as a literal sense.

Repentance grew out of the prodigal's sense of misery and need and made him resolve to return home with the confession, "Father [a respectful address], I have sinned against heaven [a reverential Jewish substitute for the sacrosanct title *God*] and in your sight [an admission of guilt first in relation to God and then in relation to his father]," and with the plea to be restored only as a hired servant. Denying any claim on his father, he would ask for mercy.

[5]Siphre Numbers 18:8, §117 (37a); cited by A Edersheim, *The Life and Times of Jesus the Messiah* (New York: Longmans, Green, & Co., 1899), vol. II, p. 256; and H. L. Strack-P. Billerbeck, *Kommentar zum Neuen Testament aus Talmud und Midrasch* (Munich: C. H. Beck, 1924), vol. II, p. 209.

But he underestimated his father's love, just as we all underestimate the love of God. When the father saw his son returning, he ran to meet him. Running was unusual and undignified for an aged oriental man, but the father's love and joy overpowered his sense of decorum, as if to say that God also forgets His dignity in a burst of joy when a sinner turns in repentance to Him. The father's kiss signified forgiveness. The son began to blurt out his prepared confession, but before he came to the part about being taken back as a hired servant, the father interrupted with commands to clothe him with the best robe as a sign of honor, to place on his finger a signet ring for sealing legal documents as a sign of restored filial authority, to put shoes (a luxury worn only by freemen) on his feet as a sign that he was no longer a hired laborer, and to kill the fatted calf for a banquet of celebration. Since meat did not form part of the daily diet, its use here denotes festivity.

The Elder Brother

The parable of the prodigal son might have ended with the representation of repentant sinners restored to God's family through the ministry of Jesus. But the parable is double-edged. The elder brother, who criticized the restoration of the returned prodigal, stands for the scribes and Pharisees who criticized Jesus' acceptance of publicans and sinners. The words of the elder brother to his father (verses 29, 30) are revealing. He rudely omitted the respectful address, "Father." He avoided calling the prodigal his brother, but referred to him as "your son." He complained that his father had never given him so much as a young goat, let alone a fatted calf for a party with his friends. (One wonders how many friends a man like this had.) It is obvious that like the Pharisees the elder brother followed a sense of duty with no balancing sense of freedom, served his father without fellowship, and prided himself on his own merits. No wonder he felt resentful of the father's grace toward the prodigal.

Similarly, the scribes and Pharisees wanted God to discriminate between the deserving (themselves) and the undeserving (publicans and sinners). No parties for prodigals! Discipline would be better. In fact, there is a rabbinical parable in which a son is redeemed from bondage, but is brought back as a slave rather than as a son so that obedience may be forced from him.[6]

The father's reply to the elder brother graciously begins with an affectionate "Son," reminds him that all the family property is now deeded to him, and explains that festivity is appropriate

---

[6]Cited by Edersheim, *Life and Times,* vol. II, p. 262; quoted in Barrett, *The New Testament Background,* p. 152 (from *Siphre Numbers, Shelah,* §115, 35a).

because *"your brother"* (not "my son") was (as good as) dead and lost, but now is alive and found. What was the elder brother's response? We do not know. Jesus left the parable open-ended because the scribes and Pharisees and all others who trust in their own merits finish the parable according to whether they renounce their self-righteousness to join in the Messianic feast of salvation or shut themselves out by retaining their self-righteousness.

The elder brother finally shows that a person does not have to *feel* lost to *be* lost. One can be estranged from God right on home territory. But everyone is invited — both flagrant sinner and decent elder brother — on the same terms, God's forgiving grace.

Read Luke 16:1—17:10 (§117). In the parable of the unjust steward, the steward (a household business manager) first of all sets a negative example of unfaithfulness by wasting his master's goods and of resultant punishment by losing his job (compare verses 1, 2 with 10-13). One cannot serve both his master and money. The steward tried, and lost his position. Men will be unfaithful like the steward unless they work for eternal reward as something more to be desired than earthly wealth. Money should not be despised, but it should be used to gain abiding spiritual riches. Serve God, therefore, and make money subordinate.

In the further part of the parable the steward becomes a positive example of prudent foresight. He had the debtors to his master dispose of their old bills and write new, smaller ones in their own handwriting. In that way the steward hoped that if the ruse were discovered, the absence of his handwriting would exonerate him from blame. A debt of nine hundred gallons of olive oil was reduced to four hundred and fifty gallons, another debt of one thousand bushels of wheat to eight hundred bushels. The dishonesty in cheating the master by reducing the debts is irrelevant. Jesus elsewhere compared God to an unjust judge and His own return to the housebreaking of a thief, so that the dishonesty of the steward does not destroy the positive point of the comparison here. Specifically, the steward used money to help other people and thus to make friends for the period of his unemployment. Similarly, disciples of Jesus must use money in charitable enterprises, for such action will be to their own advantage in the eternal future.

The Pharisees, who loved money, resembled the rich man in the next parable, who selfishly and shortsightedly disregarded Lazarus, a helpless, poor man who sat at his gate in need of charity. The rich man is therefore the obverse of the foresighted steward in the preceding parable. "Lazarus" is Greek for the

Hebrew "Eleazar," which means "God is (his) help." No one else helped him. The crumbs from the rich man's table, which Lazarus would like to have eaten, were pieces of bread used as napkins to wipe the hands and then discarded underneath the table. The phrase "Abraham's bosom" implies a heavenly banquet scene with Lazarus as a recently arrived guest reclining on a cushion immediately in front of Abraham. The banquet scene makes appropriate the rich man's request that Lazarus dip his finger in water. The address of the rich man, "Father Abraham," appeals to his Jewish descent from Abraham. But Abraham's response, beginning with "Son," indicates that although as a Jew the rich man had enjoyed every advantage, Hebrew ancestry in itself did not guarantee heavenly bliss.

Jesus' reference in Luke 17:6 to the rooting up of the sycamine (or mulberry or sycamore) tree by faith, grows out of the fact that the roots of that tree were considered extraordinarily strong and deep.

The Raising of Lazarus

As Jesus went into Judea to raise His friend Lazarus[7] from the dead, the disciples objected that the Jews there would seize Him. However, Jesus indicated that His sunset hour of death was fixed by God. While it was still daylight, that is, before His divinely appointed time to die arrived, He did not need to fear Jewish plots. *Read John 11:1-44* (§118).

In verses 25, 26 Jesus' assurance to Martha in her sorrow over the death of her brother Lazarus, that whoever lives and believes on Him will never die, may carry a double meaning: (1) believers will never suffer spiritual death, which is eternal separation from God; and (2) believers alive at the second coming will not have to die even physically, since they will be caught up to meet Christ as He descends (compare 1 Thessalonians 4:16-18).

The Jews thought that Lazarus was hopelessly dead, for in their view the spirit hovered over the body for three days and then departed. Lazarus had been dead *four* days. In the weeping of Jesus over the death of His friend, even though He was about to raise him, and in the calling of Lazarus from the dead, the human feelings and divine power of Jesus mysteriously stand side by side. But Jesus not only wept. He boiled with anger over the deadly effects of sin (verse 33 in the meaning of the Greek text). Then He reversed those effects.

The Plot of the Sanhedrin

The Sanhedrin was afraid that by reviving His popularity this latest miracle of Jesus would bring about a Messianic revolt which would bring down harsh Roman reprisal. Later, the Romans did crush a Jewish revolt, but ironically, one which arose out of

[7]This Lazarus is to be distinguished from "Lazarus" in the above parable.

rejection rather than acceptance of Jesus as the Messiah. The high priest Caiaphas brushed aside the hesitancy of the Sanhedrin by recommending the death penalty for Jesus, so that the death of one man might save the whole nation from destruction at the hands of Rome. His words carried a deeper meaning than he himself understood; for he was unconsciously predicting the death of Jesus to bring salvation *from sin* — and that not only for the Jewish nation, but also for all God's people, both Jews and Gentiles in the one Church. *Read John 11: 45-54* (§119).

Read Luke 17:11-37 (§120). Jesus denied that the kingdom of God would come when the Jews observed the law completely, a common Jewish belief, or that it would come with a spectacular display of easily observed glory (verse 20). Rather, it was already among them in the person and ministry of Jesus (or within them, at least potentially). See further the comments on §139, pages 187 ff.

The Presence of the Kingdom

Read Luke 18:1-14 (§121). In Jewish society the early marriageable age for girls of thirteen or fourteen years resulted in many young widows. Since the "importunate widow" brought her case to one judge instead of to a tribunal, it must have concerned a matter of money, such as an unpaid debt or a part of an inheritance withheld from her. The judge "did not fear God" — he was corrupt; and he "did not regard man" — he lacked sympathy. The rich and influential opponent of the widow had bribed the judge, but she was too poor to do so. Her only weapon was a tenacious faith that justice would be done. Finally, the judge, exasperated at her persistence, awarded her the case. If then a corrupt and unpitying judge will rule in favor of an oppressed widow because she does not give up asking for a favorable and just decision, how much more will God, who is both righteous and gracious, vindicate His persecuted people suddenly (the meaning of "speedily" in verse 8, since the parable as a whole implies delay) at the return of Christ?

The Widow and the Judge

In the well-known parable of the Pharisee and the publican, the prayer of the Pharisee may be paralleled by the following excerpt from the Jewish Prayer Book: "Blessed art thou, O Lord our God, King of the Universe, who hast not made me a Gentile . . . who hast not made me a slave . . . who hast not made me a woman." The publican stood in an obscure corner where no one would notice him. But modern stereotyping of the figures of the Pharisee and the publican has taken away the force of the parable. Pharisees seriously served God by fasting twice a week (Mondays and Thursdays), tithing all their possessions, and keeping the moral, ethical, and ceremonial command-

The Pharisee and the Publican

ments of the law. The common people greatly admired them. Publicans, on the other hand, collaborated with the hated Roman oppressors, fleeced their fellow Jews, and practiced all sorts of fraud; the common people detested them. The audience must have been shocked to hear Jesus put the Pharisee in such a bad light, the publican in such a good light. But the very unexpectedness in the reversal of good and bad roles underscored the nature of forgiveness as an unmerited gift from God solely on the basis of repentant faith.

Divorce

Jewish rabbis agreed among themselves that the Mosaic law allowed divorce with the right to remarry (see Deuteronomy 24:1). But they disagreed on what constituted valid grounds for divorce. According to the followers of the famous rabbi Hillel, almost anything displeasing to the husband made divorce permissible. In contrast, the followers of Shammai regarded immorality by the wife as the only valid reason for divorce. The Pharisees now attempted to draw Jesus into the rabbinical debate. *Read Mark 10:1-12; Matthew 19:1-12 (§122).*

Circumventing the Mosaic provision for divorce, Jesus went back to the very beginning, the creation of Adam and Eve. He stated that God's ideal is no divorce at all. In Matthew's account the Jews proceeded to ask why Moses commanded divorce, if it was against God's will. Jesus answered that Moses did not *command* divorce so much as *allow* it because of human wickedness ("hardness of heart"). That is, the Mosaic law was necessarily conditioned by the corruption of human society and therefore did not represent God's ideal in this respect. Then Jesus (still in Matthew's account) stated the only valid ground for divorce — fornication.

Many critics argue that since Mark does not contain the phrase "except for fornication," Jesus really did not speak it, but that Matthew has inserted the phrase to soften a total prohibiton of divorce by Jesus. On the other hand, accepting Matthew's report of Jesus' words, we may understand "fornication" in any one of several ways: (1) immorality in general, whether premarital or postmarital (the Greek word behind "fornication" occurs regularly in this general sense throughout Greek literature); (2) premarital unchastity (then Jesus allowed divorce only during the betrothal period, betrothal being so binding in Jewish society that only divorce could break it); (3) incest, that is, marrying relatives closer than allowed by the Mosaic law (then Jesus taught that divorce is legitimate only in incestuous marriages, which should not have been made in the first place).

Marriage

The disciples responded that if marriage is as binding as indicated in Jesus' ruling, it is safest not to marry at all, lest one choose the wrong mate and be unable to divorce her. Jesus answered that only a minority should refrain from marriage, those who are physically incapable by birth or by castration and those who voluntarily refrain so that they may devote themselves more fully to preaching the Gospel.

After the subject of marriage, the subject of children quite naturally arose. Once again the low position of little children in society illustrates the humility necessary for entrance into the kingdom of God. *Read Mark 10:13-16; Matthew 19:13-15; Luke 18:15-17* (§123).

Children

A rich young ruler seemed to think that he could gain eternal life by a single heroic act. When Jesus remonstrated that no one is good except God, he was not avoiding the application of the term "good" to Himself, but trying to lead the man to see that if Jesus really was good, He must be divine. Jesus then quoted several of the ten commandments to the rich young ruler, but stopped before "Thou shalt not covet." The ruler said that he had kept the commandments mentioned. However, his guilty conscience pointed to the unmentioned tenth commandment; he knew he had coveted. Jesus therefore told him to give away his riches and become a disciple. But his chronic love of money overpowered his desire for eternal life.

The Rich
Young Ruler

When Jesus mentioned the difficulty of entrance into the kingdom by wealthy people, the disciples were shocked. The Jews equated riches with divine favor. Jesus went on to say that what is humanly impossible, the salvation of the wealthy, is nevertheless possible with God. When Peter reminded Jesus how much the disciples had given up to follow Him, Jesus assured them of a reward in "the regeneration" when He will return to restore the nation of Israel under divine blessing. *Read Mark 10:17-31; Matthew 19:16—20:16; Luke 18:18-30* (§124).

In the parable which closes the Matthaean passage, the vineyard owner ("householder") hired workers from the village marketplace at sunrise ("early in the morning") for a full day's work at the normal wage scale of about twenty cents per day. In the meantime, unemployed laborers whiled away the hours in the marketplace waiting for a job to turn up. At 9:00 A.M., noon, 3:00 P.M., and 5:00 P.M. (the third, sixth, ninth, and eleventh hours respectively from dawn) the employer, giving assurance of a fair wage, hired more workers. It must have been sheer pity which caused him to hire workers at 5:00 P.M. for only one hour's labor. Since every day was payday, the owner instructed his foreman to give the men their money — but to every man a *full* day's wage and in reverse order, the last being paid first. Ordinarily those who had worked all day would have been paid first and would have left before they saw that the latecomers were receiving an equal amount. But Jesus introduced

The Laborers
in the
Vineyard

the unrealistic feature to bring out the point of the parable in the argument which ensued. It is this: just as the employer was not being unfair to those who had worked all day (they received a full wage according to contract), but only being generous to the latecomers *so that they might receive a liveable wage* (any less would have been below subsistence), so also God grants His grace to the undeserving out of sheer generosity. In response, then, to Peter's "We have left all and followed thee; what then shall we have?" Jesus first assured Peter that they would receive plenty, but proceeded to tell the parable as a warning that eternal life is still a gift even though it may look like a paycheck. Although from another standpoint rewards will differ according to degrees of service, *salvation itself* has nothing to do with the amount of work done. Therefore, we should not pharisaically begrudge God's graciousness to others. All of us are undeserving late-comers. The deserving early-comers exist only in the parable, not in real life.

No Special Privilege

Read Mark 10:32-45; Matthew 20:17-28; Luke 18:31-34 (§125). The disciples were amazed at Jesus' determination to go to Jerusalem although He predicted His death would occur there. When James and John with their mother asked for favored positions in the kingdom, the other disciples were "moved with indignation" because they entertained similar ambitions. Jesus answered that like Him the disciples were destined for suffering and martyrdom, symbolized by "the cup [of suffering]" and "the baptism [of death]," before glory.

Blind Bartimaeus

Usually the crowds wanted to see Jesus perform a miracle, but in the story of blind Bartimaeus in Jericho they were eager for Jesus to arrive in Jerusalem so that He might inaugurate the kingdom of God according to their political conception of it. Surely His determination to go to Jerusalem in spite of opposition from the authorities meant that He was about to declare war, crush His enemies, and establish the visible kingdom. *Read Mark 10:46-52; Matthew 20:29-34; Luke 18:35-43* (§126). As in the story of the Gerasene demoniacs, Mark and Luke mention only the spokesman (Bartimaeus) in the pair mentioned by Matthew. The suggestion that the healing occurred on the way out from old Jericho and into the new Jericho built by Herod the Great resolves the seeming discrepancy between Mark and Matthew ("as he went out") and Luke ("as he drew near").

Zacchaeus The Publican;

Read Luke 19:1-28 (§127). Zacchaeus' promise to restore four times as much as he had defrauded far exceeded what the Mosaic law required in most cases such as this. The practice of local leaders in going to Rome to gain imperial support for their claims to local rulership forms the background for the parable of the pounds (one pound = c. $17). The nobleman's trip to a distant country, the time he spent there, and his return and calling his servants to account represent Jesus' return to heaven, the present age of the Church, and the Second Coming and judgment of our works. The parable teaches that, contrary to the expectations of the crowd accompanying Jesus, the kingdom of God in its outward political form would not appear immediately. Instead, there was to be an interval during which Jesus would be absent. Meanwhile disciples are to work faithfully. When Jesus does return, there will not be a triumph for the Jewish nation in which every Jew will automatically have part. Rather, Jesus will reward or punish people *individually*. Perhaps we feel sorry for the harshly treated servant who instead of investing the money entrusted to him carefully preserved it. The point is, however, that no such condition as "safe" discipleship exists. To follow Jesus truly entails the risk of life-investment, as opposed to the security of life-preserving.

NEW TESTAMENT JERICHO *with a view of the mound of the citadel (beyond the palm tree) built by Herod the Great.*

For further discussion:

Relate the teaching of Jesus on loving one's neighbor to proper Christian attitudes toward modern social problems.

How far should the Church enter into debatable, or even clear-cut, social issues?

How does Jesus' teaching about the proper use of money apply to an affluent society and to the ideological war between capitalism and communism?

Apply Jesus' strictures on divorce to marital and divorce problems today.

In what ways does Jesus' style of interpersonal relationships present an example worthy of imitation?

Why should the Pharisees and the Sanhedrin have opposed Jesus so strenuously? Why should Jesus have antagonized them?

For further investigation:

See the works listed on pages 115 f.

CHAPTER 11

The Denouement

Leading questions:

What were the immediate occasions for the plot against Jesus and the bargain to betray Him?

What were the actions and words of Jesus in the week immediately preceding His death — to the crowds and Jewish leaders in public and to His disciples in private?

How did the Lord's Supper relate to the Passover meal, and what was its significance?

How was the trial of Jesus conducted, and under what charge(s) was He crucified?

What are the historical evidences and theological meaning of Jesus' resurrection?

What were the varying reactions of the disciples to the fast-paced and sharply turning events in the last week of Jesus' public ministry?

PASSION WEEK

Pilgrims were arriving in Jerusalem from Galilee and elsewhere for the Passover festival. The Sanhedrin therefore issued a decree seeking information on the whereabouts of Jesus so that they might arrest and execute Him. They also plotted for the death of Lazarus because of the convincing force of his being brought back to life by Jesus. *Read John 11:55—12:1, 9-11* (§128a).

In his harmony, A. T. Robertson postpones Mary's anointing of Jesus till Tuesday of passion week in seeming agreement with Mark and Matthew. The chronological notations in John, however, require the placing of the event on the Saturday evening before Palm Sunday, just after the end of the Sabbath at sunset (John 12:1, 12). Mark and Matthew delay recounting the

Mary's Anointing of Jesus

story to show the relationship between the incident and Judas' bargain for betrayal. The many differences in detail between this anointing and a similar anointing by a sinful woman narrated in Luke 7:36-50 (§59) prevent an equation between the two.[1] *Read Mark 14:3-9; Matthew 26:6-13; John 12:2-8* (§141).

If present at this meal, Simon must have been a cured leper. Otherwise, because of uncleanness he was absent and the house is simply identified by his name. Perhaps he was the father of Lazarus, Mary, and Martha. John complements the account of Mark and Matthew by adding that the perfume was poured on the feet of Jesus as well as on His head. The perfume had cost at least three hundred denarii, or the equivalent of a whole year's wages for the average working man, since one denarius (about twenty cents or slightly less) constituted a day's pay. Judas Iscariot expressed the feeling of some of the disciples, and especially his own, that the perfume should have been sold for money. The Apostle John editorializes that Judas Iscariot was not concerned about giving alms to the poor, but wanted to pilfer from the apostolic treasury, of which he had charge. Jesus replied to Judas that the act of worship had not at all been wasteful, for Mary had begun to embalm His body in anticipation of His burial. Maybe Mary really did understand that Jesus would have to die. On the other hand, she may have intended her act to be an anointing for kingly rule. If so, Jesus was indicating that whether she realized it or not, she had anointed Him for burial. Judas' loss of face because of public rebuke by Jesus embittered him to the extent that a few days later he offered his services to betray Jesus for a price.

The Triumphal Entry

Read Mark 11:1-11; Matthew 21:1-11, 14-17; Luke 19:29-44; John 12:12-19 (§128b). Several aspects of the triumphal entry on Palm Sunday excited the Messianic hopes of the Jews. The recent raising of Lazarus had reactivated their hope that Jesus would prove to be a power-displaying Messiah after all. Once again, as when Jesus fed the five thousand, it was the Passover season, exactly the time the Jews expected the Messiah to make Himself known. And Jesus began His triumphal entry into Jerusalem from the Mount of Olives, the place from which Zechariah had predicted the Messianic kingdom would be established (Zechariah 14).

Jesus rode an unbroken young donkey never before employed for any other purpose and therefore suitable for this sacred use. We may infer from Matthew that to keep the unbroken donkey in line, the mother was led alongside. The palm branches which the crowds spread on the roadway symbolized Jewish nationalism, as shown by the imprint of palm branches on Jewish coins

---

[1]See Robertson's note, p. 187.

VIEW OF JERUSALEM (*Old City*) *southeast from the Mount of Olives across the Kidron Valley.*

from that period. Their utilization here shows that the crowds still had in mind a nationalistic, political Messiah. But instead of riding into Jerusalem on a war-horse in keeping with the idea of the crowd, Jesus rode on a donkey as a meek and peaceful spiritual monarch (a positive sign of messiahship, however, as the prophetic reference from Zechariah 9:9 shows). The shout "Hosanna!" was roughly equivalent to "God save the King!" When the Pharisees asked Jesus to silence the shouting of His disciples, He replied that if His disciples did not proclaim His messiahship, the very stones would cry out. Jesus may have been hinting that from A.D. 70 onward the tumbled stones of Jerusalem and the Temple would eloquently testify to His messiahship. Certainly He was no longer attempting to keep it secret; the crisis had come. As throughout most of passion week, Jesus went back to Bethany for the night and returned to Jerusalem the next day.

Read Mark 11:12-18; Matthew 21:18, 19, 12, 13; Luke 19:45-48 (§129). Jesus' cursing the barren fig tree on the way into Jerusalem was not a fit of temper, but a symbolic act (see below). It may be wondered why Jesus expected to find figs when they were out of season. Palestinian fig trees, however, normally retained some green (or winter) figs which had not ripened

The Cursing
of the
Fig Tree
and
The Cleansing
of the Temple

181

during the autumnal harvest. When Jesus once more cleansed the Temple upon entering the city, the Sanhedrin was enraged. But they dared not arrest Jesus in the presence of Galilean crowds sympathetic to him.

The Greeks

In the Temple some Greeks, apparently Gentile proselytes or God-fearers[2] who had made a pilgrimage for the Passover, asked Philip (a Greek name) for an audience with Jesus. Philip told Andrew (another Greek name), and together they approached Jesus. *Read John 12:20-50* (§130). Jesus responded — whether to the Greeks or to Philip and Andrew we are not told — that His hour of suffering and exaltation had finally come. He compared His death, burial, and resurrection, and the resultant eternal life for all who believe to a seed which falls into the earth, germinates, and springs up into multiplied life. When Jesus talked about dying, the Jews objected that He could not then be the Messiah. According to their view the Messiah would not die. They therefore concluded that the dying Son of man of whom Jesus spoke must be different from the immortal Messiah and that Jesus must have been claiming to be the Son of man rather than the Messiah.

**The Withering
of the
Fig Tree**

The next morning on the way into Jerusalem the disciples noticed that the fig tree had withered. As elsewhere, Matthew has telescoped his account so that it appears in his gospel as though the whole incident happened on one day. But Matthew expects his readers to know better from Mark; for comparison with Mark shows that the word "immediately" in Matthew 21: 19 should be taken broadly as a reference to the very next day. *Read Mark 11:19-25; Matthew 21:19-22; Luke 21:37, 38* (§131). Many scholars feel that the cursing of the fig tree symbolized divine judgment on Israel (compare Luke 13:1-9). But all that Jesus made out of the incident was a lesson of faith, probably to bolster the disciples for His impending death and His return to heaven.

**Theological
Debate**

Since the presence of sympathetic fellow Galilean pilgrims kept Jesus from being arrested in public by the Sanhedrin, the Jewish rulers tried to destroy His influence by discrediting Him in theological debate. Thus a battle of wits developed in the Temple courtyards. *Read Mark 11:27—12:12; Matthew 21:23— 22:14; Luke 20:1-19* (§132).

**Jesus'
Authority**

When the Jews asked by what authority Jesus did "these things," they were referring specifically to His cleansing of the Temple. Jesus' counter question asked whether they thought the ministry of John the Baptist had possessed divine authority

---

[2]See page 47.

("heaven" stands for God) or merely human authority. The representatives of the Sanhedrin recognized the dilemma into which Jesus was putting them. If they said that John the Baptist's authority came from God, Jesus could ask them why they did not believe John the Baptist's testimony concerning the messiahship of Jesus. On the other horn of the dilemma, if they said that John the Baptist's authority was merely human, they would lose their own influence over the crowds, for the Jewish populace recognized a true prophet in John the Baptist. The rulers therefore refused to answer the question.

The initiative in the theological debate passed over to Jesus. He told three parables. In each the theme is divine displeasure with the official representatives of the Jewish nation. In the first parable the father represents God. The son who said he would not obey his father (the lack of the address, "Sir," in his impudent refusal is glaring), but afterward repented and did obey, stands for the irreligious Jews who were repenting and entering the kingdom of God as a result of Jesus' ministry. The son who said he would obey (he politely addressed his father as "Sir"), but did not, stands for the self-righteous Jewish leaders who refused to accept the rule of God in the person of Jesus the Messiah.

The second parable has as its background the many large farming estates in Palestine owned by foreigners who rented them out to poor Jewish farmers. Times of depression tempted these tenant farmers to withhold payment from the long-absent landlords. In the parable the owner of the vineyard represents God. The vineyard itself is the Jewish nation (compare Isaiah 5:1, 2). The "husbandmen" to whom the vineyard was rented stand for the Jewish leaders. This vineyard-nation was supposed to yield spiritual fruit pleasing to God. The servants who were beaten and killed by the husbandmen represent the Old Testament prophets, and the son who was killed is Jesus. The destruction of the husbandmen prefigures the overthrow of the Jewish hierarchy at the destruction of Jerusalem in A.D. 70. The giving of the vineyard to others represents the transfer of God's kingdom to the new people of God, the international Church. The quotation from Psalm 118 about the corner- or capstone stresses God's vindication of the rejected Messiah.

In the parable of the marriage feast the first invited guests are the Jews who rejected Jesus. The destruction of their city again portrays the events of A.D. 70. Those who finally are brought into the feast are the publicans, sinners, and Gentiles. But this third parable closes with an appendix about a man at the wedding feast who lacked a wedding garment. Some have supposed that hosts provided special garments for weddings, so that the man had no excuse. Probably, however, a wedding garment was simply a newly washed garment. A soiled garment constituted an insult to the host. The man in the parable without a washed garment, then, stands for false disciples, such as Judas Iscariot. The term "Friend," by which the king addressed this man, is the same as that by which Jesus addressed Judas Iscariot in the Garden of Gethsemane at the time of the betrayal and arrest. The conclusion of the parable, "For many are called, but few chosen," means that many (frequently equivalent to "all" in Jewish idiom) are invited into God's kingdom, but only those with truly repentant hearts are chosen to eat at the Messianic banquet table.

The Tax to Caesar

The Herodians (Sadducean supporters of Herod's family in political power) and the anti-Herodian Pharisees again teamed together against Jesus in spite of their antipathy in religion and politics. To trap Jesus into saying something of which they might accuse Him, they sent some of their younger men, who could more easily pretend sincerity than could elders. Beginning with sheer flattery, they asked Jesus whether Jews should pay the annual poll tax which the Romans began to levy about A.D. 6. When imposed for the first time, this tax provoked a rebellion under Judas the Galilean (Acts 5:37). The tax still antagonized the Jews, especially because the Romans required it to be paid with a silver coin stamped with the image of the emperor's head, contrary to Jewish scruples against images. (For general circulation in Palestine the Romans minted copper coins without the imperial image.) *Read Mark 12:13-17; Matthew 22:15-22; Luke 20:20-26* (§133).

The dilemma into which the questioners tried to put Jesus was this: if Jesus said that Jews should pay the tax, He would lose His popularity with the crowds, who hated the tax. If He advised the Jews not to pay the tax, the Jewish officials could accuse Him before the Romans of political subversion, perhaps even zealotry. But a dilemma existed only if the kingdom of Christ were political and therefore cut across the political au-

THE DENARIUS OF CAESAR AUGUSTUS *was possibly the tribute money used to challenge Jesus. Both sides of the coin glorify Caesar.*

thority of Caesar. On the contrary, the spiritual nature of Christ's kingdom did not contradict Caesar's authority to tax. Jesus' asking for the kind of coin with which the tax was paid embarrassed the Jews: by producing it they demonstrated their tacit acceptance of Caesar's dominion, since it was generally acknowledged that a king's domain extended as far as his coins circulated. Jesus then indicated that both Caesar and God have their rights; and what is given to them is not a gift, but the payment of a debt.

The Sadducees, who did not believe in a future, physical resurrection, tried now to abash Jesus by showing what they felt is the absurdity of such a doctrine. Their hypothetical case had to do with the law of levirate marriage, according to which an unmarried surviving brother should produce an heir for his deceased brother by marrying the widow (see Deuteronomy 25: 5, 6). The Sadducees presented the situation of a woman who married seven successive brothers under the levirate law without having any children. Then they triumphantly asked whose wife the woman would be at the resurrection. *Read Mark 12:18-27; Matthew 22:23-33; Luke 20:27-40 (§134).*

Jesus ridiculed the Sadducees for comprehending neither the Scriptures nor the power of God. The resurrection will not merely restore physical life. It will also change the *mode* of life, so that the institution of marriage will no longer exist. The reason is that the abolition of death will do away with the need for propagating the human race. The Sadducees were in error in supposing that resurrection would simply perpetuate earthly life. Later books of the Old Testament contain several clear proof texts for the doctrine of resurrection, but the Sadducees accepted only the Pentateuch as fully authoritative. Jesus therefore appealed to God's statement to Moses at the burning bush, "I am the God of Abraham, Isaac, and Jacob." The argument was that the present tense "I am"[3] implied that Abraham, Isaac, and Jacob were still related to God and therefore alive in spirit as late as the time of Moses. Moreover, since God originally created man a body-soul unity, eternal half existence in spiritual form alone is unthinkable. If then God keeps the dead alive in spiritual form, He must intend to reunite their bodies and spirits at a resurrection.

A Pharisee then asked Jesus to identify the most important commandment in the Old Testament and was answered by Jesus that to love God wholly and your neighbor as yourself are first and second in priority. The sincerity of this Pharisee is a dra-

---

[3]The present tense of the verb *to be* in the statement "I am" is not stated in Mark or in the Hebrew of Exodus 3:6, but is understood in both places and is necessary to the flow of Jesus' argument.

matic foil to highlight the insincerity of the previous questioners of Jesus. *Read Mark 12:28-34; Matthew 22:34-40* (§135).

The Divine, Davidic Messiah

The initiative in the theological debate again passed to Jesus. *Read Mark 12:35-37; Matthew 22:41-46; Luke 20:41-44* (§136). Psalm 110:1 is the Old Testament text most often quoted in the New Testament. Both Jesus and the Pharisees recognized it as a Messianic prophecy by David under the influence of the Holy Spirit. The Jews did not generally believe that the Messiah would be a divine being. In asking why David spoke of the Messiah as "My Lord," Jesus was implying that the Messiah must be divine as well as human.

Denunciation of the Scribes and Pharisees

Read Mark 12:38-40; Matthew 23:1-39; Luke 20:45-47 (§137). The Matthaean version of Jesus' scathing denunciation of the scribes and Pharisees is by far the most detailed. In verse two of his account, Moses' seat refers to the chair on synagogue platforms from which the rabbis of the Pharisees interpreted the Mosaic law to congregations. Jesus told His listeners to obey the Mosaic law when it was taught by the Pharisees, but not to follow their example. He proceeded to compare the rabbis, who added their own rulings to the Mosaic law, to a merciless camel driver who overloads his camel and then will not raise even a finger to adjust the load so that there will be an equal distribution of weight on both sides. "Phylacteries" (verse 5) refers to leather wallets which contained copied portions of the law and were fastened to the left arm and forehead. The Pharisees made them especially large to parade their piety. The display also included the lengthening of the blue borders or tassels at the corners of their garments, worn in accordance with Numbers 15:37-41.

Verse nine in Matthew does not prohibit the family use of the term "father," but it does forbid the religious use of the term "father" in a way which gives men authority properly belonging to God alone. In verses 16 ff. Jesus castigates the Pharisees for their loss of perspective in failing to give priority to the most important parts of the law. Instead, they magnified minute details to give the impression of greater spirituality. "Mint and anise and cummin" were small herbs used for seasoning and medicine. The gnat was a small unclean insect, the camel a large unclean animal. The Pharisees strained wine through a piece of cloth or a fine wicker basket to make sure they would not swallow an unclean insect in drinking the wine. The section concludes with Jesus' lament over the coming destruction of Jerusalem.

The Widow's Offering

186

The story of the "widow's mite" (actually she gave two mites) happened in the treasury, a place in the Temple area where the Jews deposited their money offerings. *Read Mark 12: 41-44; Luke 21:1-4* (§138).

To an exclamation over the beauty of the Temple Jesus responded with a dark prediction of its coming destruction. Some of the disciples then asked when that would take place and how they could tell that the end of the age and Parousia[4] were near. The extensive answer of Jesus is known as "the Little Apocalypse," or "the Olivet Discourse," after the Mount of Olives, where it was given. He foretold false teaching, warfare, earthquakes, famines, plagues, and persecution. But in the midst of all these calamities the Gospel will finally reach all nations. The distress will reach climactic intensity in the tribulation, the last few years before the return of Christ in power and majesty.

The instructions of Jesus to His followers seem to be directed especially toward those who will be living in Palestine during the tribulation. They are to watch for "the abomination of desolation" predicted by Daniel (9:27; 11:31; 12:11). The phrase refers to a desecration of the Temple which will cause it to be forsaken by pious Jews, as in the Maccabean period when Antiochus Epiphanes had an altar to Zeus erected in the Temple and an unclean animal sacrificed upon it, with the result that orthodox Jews refused to worship there until Judas Maccabeus cleansed and rededicated the Temple. Some maintain that Jesus was pointing forward to the desecration of the Temple by the image of the Roman emperor portrayed on the ensigns of the Roman army which captured and destroyed Jerusalem in A.D. 70. But comparison with Daniel 9:27; 2 Thessalonians 2:4; and Revelation 13:11 ff. favors the view that Jesus was referring to an action by a wicked ruler known as the Antichrist, or Man of Sin, or Beast, who will dominate the yet future tribulation period. That action will break an agreement with the Jews by forcing them to stop offering sacrifices to God in their (rebuilt) Temple and by demanding that the Jews worship his own image erected there.

At that time, said Jesus, His followers in Jerusalem and Judea must flee to the mountains. Once again, some have seen fulfillment in the flight of Jewish Christians from Jerusalem to Pella in Transjordan just before the siege of Jerusalem in the first century. But although the route led through mountains, Pella itself was not situated on mountainous terrain. And Jesus went on to say that "immediately after the tribulation of those days" He would return in connection with certain celestial phenomena.

---

[4]*Parousia* is a Greek word commonly used for the Second Advent of Christ and means *presence, arrival, coming,* especially the arrival of a king or emperor, a royal visit, and therefore is very suitable for the coming of Christ in kingly glory.

Yet Jesus has not returned, and by now A.D. 70 is ancient history. The events in and around A.D. 70 may have prefigured what Jesus was talking about, but they hardly fulfilled His predictions. For the benefit of His non-Jewish readers, Luke changes the difficult Jewish phrase, "abomination of desolation," into a description of Jerusalem's siege, capture, and trampling by the Gentiles. But even Luke probably does not refer to A.D. 70 and the following long period of Gentile control over Jerusalem, for he retains the command to flee *to the mountains*, contrary to what the Jewish Christians did. Rather, the references in Luke, as in Mark and Matthew, point forward to the Gentile domination of Jerusalem during the last part of the tribulation.

The Second Coming

The end of the age will come with cosmic disturbances. The conflagration of war and the smoke of burning cities and battlefields will darken the light of sun and moon. Meteorites (falling stars) will streak through the nighttime sky. Then Jesus will return as the Son of man from heaven. "This generation" — that is, the generation which begins to see the portents of the tribulation[5] — can be certain that the end is very near, even though the specific day and hour will stay uncertain. Not even Jesus knew the exact time. This seems to imply that although Jesus always had the capability to draw upon His divine omniscience (and omnipotence), He did so only as warranted by His Messianic ministry. Thus, for example, He really learned as a child and here remained willingly uninformed while displaying superhuman knowledge as occasion demanded. So also He grew tired and thirsty although He exercised power to heal the sick and raise the dead. *Read Mark 13:1-37; Matthew 24, 25; Luke 21:5-36* (§139).

In emphasizing the unexpectedness of His return for the wicked, Jesus drew a comparison with the generation of Noah. The flood took them by surprise in the course of normal human activities — "eating and drinking, marrying and giving in marriage," not at all to be understood with bad connotations. So also the return of Christ in judgment will surprise the spiritually unprepared, whether they be outright unbelievers or, like the wicked servant in the parable here told, false professors of discipleship. All true followers of Jesus will watch, live righteously, and as a result be ready for His return.

The Ten Virgins

The parable of the ten virgins further illustrates the contrast between preparedness and unpreparedness. The bridegroom and his friends had gone to the bride's home to escort her to the groom's home, where the wedding festivities were to take

[5]The ambiguity of "this generation" leaves the possibility open for each generation from Christ's own onward to be the one to experience the final events of the age.

LAMPS OF PALESTINE *from New Testament times. Note the hole at the top for adding oil.*

place. But they were delayed until midnight, probably because the family of the bride insisted on larger dowry presents from the groom and his family. This showed the reluctance of the bride's family to give up their daughter and also complimented the groom for his choice of such an outstanding girl, one who deserved a larger dowry. Finally the groom and his attendants brought the bride in procession to the groom's home.[6]

Meanwhile the ten virgins (the exact nature of their relationship to the bride or groom is unclear) had been waiting with lamps, which were either torches wrapped with rags that had to be soaked repeatedly in oil, or copper fire vases filled with pitch, oil, and rags for burning, or clay bowls with spouts, a wick, and olive oil for fuel. They kept their lamps burning because it would not be easy to kindle them in a hurry when the procession arrived. Five of the young women foolishly overlooked the possibility of delay and ran out of fuel. The extra supply of the five wise virgins represents preparedness for the coming of Christ. When the groom arrived, the five foolish maidens had gone to buy more olive oil. But where? It was midnight. This unrealistic feature dramatizes the warning fact that after the Parousia it will be too late to prepare.

The parable of the talents teaches that preparedness is not only an attitude of mind, but also an investment of one's life in

The Talents

---

[6]Alternatively, the groom had already conducted his bride to the house, had retired to spend the evening with his male friends, and delayed his return beyond expectation.

service for Christ — with risks. One talent was about $1,000 in silver content, but had much greater buying power. See further the comments on the Lucan parable of the pounds, page 176 f.

The Sheep and Goats

The judgment of the nations under the figures of sheep and goats (Matthew 25:31-46) has received various interpretations. Some regard it as the determining of who shall enter the earthly kingdom of Christ immediately upon His return. The qualification for entrance may then be viewed as proper treatment of the Jews, the "brethren" of Christ by nationality. Others, however, interpret the kind treatment of the brethren of Christ to be acceptance of His persecuted witnesses and their Gospel, or love of fellow disciples as a criterion of salvation, so that the brethren are the sheep themselves in their relationship to Christ and one another. Then the scene may portray the final judgment having to do with the eternal destinies of all men rather than with entrance into the temporary earthly kingdom.

The Betrayal Bargain

Read Mark 14:1, 2; Matthew 26:1-5; Luke 22:1, 2 (§140). Jesus predicted His arrest and crucifixion two days hence at the Passover. The Sanhedrin was already seeking an opportunity to arrest Him in the absence of sympathetic Galilean crowds. Their desire and Jesus' prediction were fulfilled in that the betrayal offer of Judas Iscariot provided the Sanhedrin an opportunity to seize Jesus secretly during the festival.

Some have whitewashed the motives of Judas Iscariot by saying that he was trying to force Jesus into a situation where Jesus would have to crush the political power of His enemies to establish His own kingdom. But the New Testament consistently portrays Judas as a man who, disappointed in the spiritual nature of Jesus' messiahship, decided to salvage what he could for the time he had wasted in following Jesus. This he did by stealing from the apostolic treasury and, at Satanic instigation, by betraying Jesus for a price. *Read Mark 14:10, 11; Matthew 26:14-16; Luke 22:3-6* (§142).

Preparations for the Last Supper

Read Mark 14:12-16; Matthew 26:17-19; Luke 22:7-13 (§143). Jesus told two of His disciples to enter Jerusalem, look for a man carrying a water jar, follow him into a house, and there prepare the Passover. Ordinarily men carried waterskins, women water jars. A man carrying a water jar, therefore, was very noticeable. The absence of names and the preparedness of the upper room suggest that Jesus had made prearrangements with an acquaintance in the city of Jerusalem. Probably Jesus did not want Judas Iscariot to know where they were going to celebrate the Passover meal lest Judas inform the Jewish authorities too soon and Jesus not have time for the Passover meal, the institution of the Lord's Supper, and the Upper Room discourse.

The synoptists flatly state that on Thursday evening of passion week Jesus and the twelve ate the Passover meal (Mark 14: 12, 17; Matthew 26:17, 20; Luke 22:7, 14). According to many scholars John contradicts the synoptists by indicating that the Jews did not eat the Passover meal till Friday evening after the death and burial of Jesus. John 18:28 does state, "They themselves [the Jews] did not enter the praetorium, so that they might not be defiled, but might eat the passover" — this *after* John's report of the upper room, where the synoptists place the Passover meal. On the surface it would appear that according to John either Jesus and The Twelve ate the Passover earlier than the main body of Jews, or they did not eat it at all. Elsewhere in the fourth gospel, however, the term "Passover" refers to the whole weeklong festival, not just to the meal involving the Passover lamb. John may therefore be implying that the Jews, although they had eaten the Passover lamb the previous evening as Jesus and His disciples had done, did not want to make themselves ceremonially unfit to participate in the further observance of the festival.

It is also argued that the statement, "Now it was the Preparation of the Passover" (John 19:14), within the account of Jesus' trial implies that the Passover was the next day. But "Preparation" was the name of the day of the week which we call "Friday," and (as just noted) "Passover" in John refers to the whole festival. "The Preparation of the Passover" may simply mean "the Friday during the Passover week" with no implication that the Passover lamb was yet to be killed, roasted, and eaten. A closer look at Johannine usage, then, shows that the fourth gospel does not necessarily deny that Jesus ate the Passover lamb with His disciples at the regular time.[7]

An alternative explanation reconciles John and the synoptists by supposing that Jesus and The Twelve ate the Passover meal earlier than most of the Jews. Thus the synoptists are correct in stating that the Last Supper was a Passover meal, and John is correct in implying that the other Jews did not eat the Passover meal till the evening of Good Friday. Possibly Jesus and the disciples, like the Qumran community, followed a calendar slightly different from the calendar of mainstream Judaism; or Jesus may have arranged for an early Passover meal because He foresaw His death before the regular time for the meal.

Read Mark 14:17; Matthew 26:20; Luke 22:14-16, 24-30; John 13:1-20 (§§144, 145). The ambitious scurrying of the disciples

[7]See Robertson's *Harmony*, pages 279-284, for greater detail and other arguments.

for the honored seats nearest Jesus, the host at the meal, contrasts sharply with the humble service of Jesus in washing the disciples' feet, the duty of a slave. According to Jewish custom, the pupils of a rabbi were expected to perform the duties of slaves for him, except for washing his feet, which was too menial. Here the rabbi did for His pupils what not even they were expected to do for Him. Jesus indicated to Peter that the washing was symbolic of cleansing from sin. He then said to all the disciples that it also represented the way in which they should perform humble service toward one another.

The Exit of Judas

Jesus now warned that one of the disciples was going to betray Him. The disciples immediately began to ask who it was. Jesus replied that the betrayer was close enough to be dipping into the same dish with Him. Still the disciples did not know exactly to whom Jesus referred. In the confusion John, who was reclining on a cushion with his back toward Jesus, asked privately who it was and received the answer that the betrayer was the person about to receive the sop, traditionally given to the honored guest at the meal. The sop was a piece of bread dipped in the common dish of broth. Jesus gave it to Judas Iscariot. When Judas went from the room into the night, it was dark in more ways than one. *Read Mark 14:18-21; Matthew 26:21-25; Luke 22:21-23; John 13:21-30* (§146).

Remarks in the Upper Room

After a command to love one another, Jesus predicted Peter's denials and called him by his old name Simon since he would not be acting like a strong "Rock-man." *Read John 13:31-38; Mark 14:27-31; Matthew 26:31-35; Luke 22:31-38* (§147). In the last few verses of the passage in Luke, Jesus relaxed the urgency of the previous missions so that His disciples might now return to normal living. When Jesus talked about buying a sword, the disciples, thinking that Jesus wanted them to fight lest He be arrested, produced two swords. Jesus' statement, "It is enough," sadly dismissed the topic because of their thickheadedness. Two swords would not have been enough to defend Him! How then could they imagine He wanted them to fight?

The Lord's Supper Instituted During the Passover Meal

The Passover liturgy included a blessing, several cups of wine passed around the table, recital of the Exodus story by the host at the meal, eating of the roasted lamb, unleavened bread and bitter herbs, and singing of psalms.[8] In line with the Jewish expectation of a Messianic banquet Jesus had already compared the kingdom of God to a supper. He had also described His sufferings as a cup to be drunk. Furthermore, the Passover commemorated God's redemption of the nation of Israel from slav-

---

[8]See the Mishnaic quotation from *Pesahim* 10:1, 3 ff., in C. K. Barrett, *The New Testament Background*, pp. 155-157.

ery in Egypt in connection with the sacrifice of a Passover lamb. But Jesus had intimated that Israel was now rejected. He therefore instituted the Lord's Supper to commemorate the redemption of a new people of God, the Church, from spiritual slavery to sin through His own sacrificial death on the cross. *Read Mark 14:22-25; Matthew 26:26-29; Luke 22:17-20; 1 Corinthians 11:23-26* (§148).

It should be noted that Jesus did not bless *the bread*. "He blessed" is synonymous with "he gave thanks" and means that He praised *God*. The earliest manuscripts omit the word "broken" in the Words of Institution concerning Jesus' body, represented by the bread. We should therefore read, "This is my body, which is (given) for you." Jesus broke the bread so that each disciple could have a piece, but He did not draw any symbolic meaning from that action. As a matter of fact, Jesus' body was not broken on the cross, as John later makes clear in his account of the crucifixion. That Luke mentions the cup both first and last shows that his narrative is not intended to be taken as a strictly chronological account. In the statement that Jesus' blood was shed "for many," "many" is either a Semitic idiom for "all," or an expression for the totality of the elect as in the sectarian writings among the Dead Sea Scrolls. In "Drink ye all of it," the word "all" goes with "ye": "All of you, drink it" (not "Drink all of it"). The red wine in the cup represented the blood of Jesus as the basis of the new covenant, in contrast to the Mosaic covenant based on the blood of animal sacrifices, which could only cover up sins provisionally and temporarily. Jesus' blood remits sins, that is, takes them clean away. At the conclusion of the Institution, Jesus vowed to abstain from drinking "the fruit of the vine" until the great Messianic banquet at His return.

In His farewell discourse in the upper room Jesus promised to return someday. During His absence the disciples could pray in His name. In other words, as His followers they would attach the authority of His name to their prayers and thereby receive answers. Meanwhile the Holy Spirit would take the place of Jesus (Jesus calls Him "*another* Comforter," John 14:16) and enable the disciples to perform greater works than Jesus had done — greater in geographical extent through the mission to all nations. The term "Comforter" (from the Greek word *Paraclete*) for the Holy Spirit also means "helper, encourager, representative, and lawyer (both defending and prosecuting)." "Mansions" literally means "abodes" and probably refers not only to heavenly dwellings, but also to present spiritual abiding places located in the very person of Christ and prepared by His redemptive work for each believer. *Read John 14* (§149).

Read John 15, 16 (§150). In the Old Testament the vine symbolized Israel. But since God had rejected Israel, the new and

The Upper Room Discourse

true vine was Christ Himself, including all those united to Him by faith. Christ is not just the stem, but the whole vine. As branches, therefore, believers are more than connected with Christ — they are part of Him. Jesus exhorted the disciples to abide in Him, that is, to live in communion with Him through obedience to His commandments and particularly through love toward one another. Jesus also warned of coming persecution. But in 16:7 He said that it was expedient, or advantageous, to the disciples that He go away and the Holy Spirit come, for place and time would not limit the Spirit's activity as they had His. But the Holy Spirit was not only going to minister comfort, encouragement, and instruction to Jesus' disciples. Like a prosecuting lawyer He would also minister conviction to the world concerning its great sin of unbelief in Christ, concerning the vindication of Christ by God the Father through Christ's exaltation back to heaven, and concerning the coming judgment of the sinful world as previewed by the defeat of Satan at the cross (16:8-11).

The High Priestly Prayer

In His great intercessory prayer Jesus asked for the safekeeping, sanctification, and unity of His disciples. *Read John 17 (§151)*.

Gethsemane

The antiphonal singing of Psalms 113-118 concluded the

THE GARDEN OF GETHSE-MANE *includes aged olive trees that easily reach back to early Roman times in Palestine.*

Passover liturgy. Jesus and the disciples then proceeded to the Garden of Gethsemane on the slopes of Mount Olivet, a favorite place of prayer for Jesus. *Read Mark 14:26, 32-42; Matthew 26:30, 36-46; Luke 22:39-46; John 18:1* (§152). In the prayer of Jesus we see clearly His humanity. As it would for any normal human being, the prospect of imminent pain and death caused emotional turmoil, so intense that Jesus dripped sweat as profusely as though He were bleeding. (Luke only draws a comparison; he does not say that Jesus sweat blood.[9]) But Jesus wanted the will of God more than He wanted to escape death. He therefore resolved to drink His cup of suffering and death.

The Roman soldiers, Levitical Temple police, and personal servants of the Jewish rulers who came to arrest Jesus in Gethsemane had prepared themselves for armed resistance by His disciples. When Jesus identified Himself as the one they wanted, the stunning force of His divine personality temporarily threw them backward to the ground. Kissing was the customary way to greet a venerable rabbi, but here the identifying kiss of Judas was shameless hypocrisy. In trying to defend Jesus, Peter cut off the ear of the high priest's servant named Malchus. Only John mentions the names of Peter and Malchus. Perhaps the earlier, synoptic writers refrained from mentioning Peter to protect him from retaliation during his lifetime, whereas Peter had died by the time John wrote. John may have known the name of the servant Malchus because the servant had later become a Christian, or because the unnamed disciple who was acquainted with the high priest (John 18:15, 16) was also acquainted with Malchus.[10]

Luke shows his medical interest by telling us that Jesus healed Malchus' ear. In submitting to arrest, Jesus insisted that His disciples be released. But Peter's impetuosity tensed the situation, so that they had to flee. Running away with them, a young man from outside the circle of The Twelve left his clothing in the clutches of his would-be captors. Very possibly this curious incident is the subtle signature of John Mark to his gospel. If so, he had accompanied Jesus and the others to Gethsemane probably because the last supper had taken place in his home. According to Acts 12:12 the house of John Mark's

---

[9]It must be noted, however, that the comparison to blood is textually uncertain.

[10]It is possible that the unnamed disciple and acquaintance of the high priest was John himself, since he fails to name himself throughout the gospel. However, he also fails to name other disciples (see, for example, 21:1, 2). And in 18:15, 16 the acquaintance of the high priest is not designated the beloved disciple (John). Moreover, there is some problem in thinking that a young Galilean fisherman who still worked for his father knew the high priest in Jerusalem.

mother became a meeting place for the Jerusalem church. *Read Mark 14:43-52; Matthew 26:47-56; Luke 22:47-53; John 18: 2-12* (§153).

TRIAL AND CRUCIFIXION

Jesus' trial had two parts, Jewish and Roman. In each there were three hearings. The Jewish part of the trial consisted of a preliminary examination by Annas, a former high priest and dominant figure in Jewish leadership; a hearing before the Sanhedrin during the night — and therefore illegal — at which Jesus was condemned; and after dawn a formalization of the verdict to cover up the illegality of its having been reached during the night.[11] The Roman part of the trial consisted of a hearing before the Roman governor, Pontius Pilate, a hearing before

Herod Antipas, and another hearing before Pontius Pilate. *Read John 18:12-14, 19-23* (§154), according to which Jesus denied the charge that He was leading an underground movement of political sedition.

Read Mark 14:53, 55-65; Matthew 26:57, 59-68; Luke 22:54, 63-65; John 18:24 (§155). Usually the examining judge sat down while the accused stood, but here the judge tried to browbeat the accused into a confession instead of protecting his rights and maintaining the presumption of his innocence. Standing up dramatically, Caiaphas tried to make Jesus lose His composure by asking whether He did not have a single word of defense against the incriminating evidence of His cryptic claim that He would rebuild the Temple in three days if they destroyed it. The Jews had not understood that He was referring to His body under the figure of the Temple. But knowing that the witnesses had given conflicting testimony against Him, Jesus refused to be intimidated. Caiaphas then played his trump card by asking bluntly whether Jesus claimed to be the Messiah and Son of God. Jesus affirmed that He was, but suggested that He was a different kind of Messiah from what Caiaphas had in mind.

---

[11] In capital cases later (and possibly earlier) Jewish trial procedure required that a trial begin during the daytime, that it be adjourned during nighttime if unfinished, that a majority of only one sufficed for acquittal but that a majority of at least two was necessary for conviction, that a verdict of acquittal might be given on the day the trial began but that a verdict of guilty must be delayed until the next day so that the judges might weigh carefully a condemnatory decision overnight, that therefore no trial could be held on the eve of a Sabbath or a festival day, and that the accused was not to be forced to witness against himself or convicted on his own testimony (the Babylonian Talmud, *Sanhedrin* 4.1, 3-5a; 5.1, quoted in Barrett, *The New Testament Background*, pp. 169, 170). Although there were legal loopholes, in condemning Jesus the Sanhedrin violated all these regulations. Moreover, the members of the Sanhedrin were supposed to be impartial judges, yet at least some of them had participated in the arrest of

Jesus.

The blasphemy probably did not consist in the Messianic claim alone — the Jews apparently felt that history would prove the truth or falsity of a claim to messiahship — but in the further claim to be the Son of God in spite of His seeming lack of divine power at the moment. Caiaphas' rending his garments signified horror at having heard blasphemy. The Sanhedrin passed a sentence of death, but were unable to carry it out because the Romans reserved the right of capital punishment. In fact, Annas himself had been deposed from the high priesthood because he had exercised capital punishment during the absence of a Roman governor. There is some question whether the Jews could execute by means other than crucifixion. Possibly the Sanhedrin wanted to have the Romans crucify Jesus to avoid full blame for Jesus' death from the Jewish, especially Galilean, populace.

Sandwiched in between the two hearings of Jesus before the Sanhedrin is the story of Peter's denying Jesus three times. The Sanhedrin was meeting in the high priest's palace. Peter was able to enter the courtyard through the influence of an unnamed disciple "known to the high priest." Peter's Galilean accent caused the others to suspect that he was a disciple of Jesus, since Jesus was known to be popular in Galilee. *Read Mark 14:54, 66-72; 15:1; Matthew 26:58, 69-75; 27:1; Luke 22:54-62, 66-71; John 18:15-18, 25-27* (§§156, 157).

The ratification of the condemnatory verdict after dawn satis- fied the letter of part of the Jewish legal procedure, according to which trials should take place only in the daytime, and thus lent a semblance of legality to outsiders; but it violated the prohibition against holding trials on festival days, for it was the Passover.

Judas regretted what he had done, but lacked faith for pardon. The accounts of his suicide are somewhat different in Matthew and Acts. Possibly the body of Judas fell from the place where he had hanged himself. It is ironic that the chief priests were careful not to defile the Temple treasury with the price of blood at the very time they were trying to shed the blood of an innocent man. *Read Matthew 27:3-10; Acts 1:18, 19* (§158).

Read Mark 15:1-5; Matthew 27:2, 11-14; Luke 23:1-5; John 18:28-38 (§159). Again it is ironic that the Jews were so concerned about ritual purity they would not enter the palace of a Gentile governor, yet they were condemning their own Messiah. The accusation which the Jews brought against Jesus had nothing to do with the supposed blasphemy for which the Sanhedrin had condemned Him. Blasphemy would have meant nothing to Pilate, a Roman and a pagan. The charges before Pilate, therefore, were trumped-up political accusations according to which Jesus was a rebel and a rival emperor to Tiberius Caesar. Yet the whole ministry of Jesus was calculated to teach that His messiahship was not primarily political. When Pilate told the Jews to judge Jesus according to their own law, he was rubbing in the fact that the Jews lacked authority to inflict capital punishment. Jesus assured Pilate that His kingdom was spiritual, as proved by the fact that His servants did not fight.

Before Antipas

Herod Antipas had come to Jerusalem to observe the Passover festival, not because he was especially pious, but because he wished to maintain popularity with his Jewish subjects. Pilate did not want to assume responsibility for the fate of Jesus. He therefore sent Jesus to Herod for trial. As a Galilean, Jesus properly belonged to Herod's jurisdiction anyway. *Read Luke 23:6-12* (§160). Had Jesus fulfilled Herod's desire to see a miracle performed, Herod probably would have interceded in His behalf. But Jesus refused even to speak to Herod, let alone perform a miracle.

Before Pilate

Read Mark 15:6-19; Matthew 27:15-30; Luke 23:13-25; John 18:39—19:16 (§§161, 162). Faced with Jesus the second time, Pilate delivered a verdict of not guilty. He supported his decision by the fact that Herod Antipas had also failed to find anything blameworthy in Jesus. But instead of letting the decision stand, Pilate began to bargain with the Jews over whether they would rather have Barabbas or Jesus released according to the annual custom of freeing a prisoner as a sign of good will. Ironically, the Jews preferred Barabbas precisely because he was a revolutionist, the very charge they had falsely leveled against Jesus before Pilate.

The Condemnation

Brutal whipping, or scourging, was both a means of extracting information and a prelude to execution. It was also customary for Roman soldiers to enjoy the sport of mocking a condemned man. The crown of thorns may have been an instrument of torture shaped like an emperor's laurel wreath with some of the spikes pointing inward toward Jesus' head. But more probably it was an instrument of mockery with the spikes pointing outward in a radiate crown, such as Roman emperors of that time were pictured as wearing in imitation of the rays of the sun. Having allowed Jesus to be mocked and beaten, Pilate tried to draw out the Jews' sympathy by presenting Him in His sorry condition as someone who had already suffered enough. But the Jews thirsted for blood. Inadvertently they revealed the real reason they had condemned Jesus: He claimed to be the Son of God. Since that title belonged to emperors (among others), Pilate's fear that Jesus really was a political rival to Caésar revived. The possibility of Jesus' divinity may also have troubled him. However, further questioning allayed the fear that Jesus was a political threat. But the Jews shouted that if Pilate released Jesus, he was not a friend of Caesar. Afraid he might lose his governorship if the Jews lodged a complaint against him at Rome, Pilate succumbed to their threat of blackmail. Trying to rid himself of the responsibility by the symbolic act of washing his hands, he gave the order for Jesus' crucifixion.

Crucifixion was a method of execution reserved mainly for criminals and slaves. It had all the associations of the gas chamber or electric chair today. *Read Mark 15:20-23; Matthew 27:31-34; Luke 23:26-33; John 19:16, 17* (§163). The cross

The Crucifixion

GORDON'S CALVARY, *outside the present city wall, is one of the traditional claims as the site of the crucifixion of Christ.*

which Jesus carried was probably only the crossbar, the vertical part of the cross being a permanent fixture on Golgotha, for a whole cross would have been too heavy for one man to carry. The names of Simon of Cyrene, Alexander, and Rufus are known doubtless because they became Christians. Simon, who carried Jesus' cross part of the way, was a Jewish immigrant from Cyrene, a city in North Africa. As women along the way wept over the fate of Jesus, He warned them about the coming destruction of Jerusalem. The Jews had called down His blood on their own heads and upon the heads of their children. God was to take them at their word. "Blessed are the barren" was an appalling beatitude, because childlessness was thought to be a terrible curse. How great must be the judgment which makes even barrenness a blessing! "For if they do these things in the green tree, what shall be done in the dry?" (Luke 23:31) was a figurative way of saying that future distress would make the present distress over which they were weeping seem negligible. The upper-class women of Jerusalem customarily provided those about to be executed with a narcotic drink to relieve their

A SURVEY
OF THE
NEW TESTAMENT

The Super-
scription

The Seven
Last Words

pain. But the bitter wine offered to Jesus apparently was a further piece of cruel mockery.

Read Mark 15:24-32; Matthew 27:35-44; Luke 23:33-43; John 19:18-27 (§164). It was usual to write a description of the crime of a condemned man on a notice board and hang it around his neck or attach it to the cross. Pilate wrote the charge against Jesus as a jibe against the Jews: *This* is your king, this man being crucified like a criminal! Jesus hung on the cross for three hours in the light (9:00 A.M.[12]-noon) and then for three hours in midday darkness (noon-3:00 P.M.).

The evangelists record seven sayings of Christ from the cross, known as the "Seven Last Words":

1) The first was a prayer for the forgiveness of His enemies: "Father, forgive them; for they know not what they do" (Luke 23:34).

2) The second assured the repentant thief that he would be with Jesus in Heaven that very day: "Today shalt thou be with me in Paradise" (Luke 23:43). The emphasis falls on the word "Today," for the thief had spoken of Christ's kingdom as though it were in the distant future.

3) The third saying is a committal of Jesus' mother into the care of the Apostle John. By standing near the cross with some of the disciples, Mary was confessing her own

THE CHURCH OF THE HOLY SEPULCHRE *could also be the site of the crucifixion of Christ since archaeological evidence indicates that this location probably was outside the city wall in New Testament times.*

[12]Using the Jewish method of counting hours from sunrise (and sunset), Mark puts the crucifixion at "the third hour" (15:25), that is, 9:00 A.M. Using the Roman method of counting from midnight (and noon), John puts Jesus' hearing before Pilate at "about the sixth hour" (19:14), that is, somewhere in the early morning. The use of different methods of counting the hours explains the apparent contradiction. See footnote, page 130 f. Others think that John's "sixth hour" puts the crucifixion at noon and that "the third hour" was not in Mark's original text since Matthew and Luke lack it.

loyalty to Jesus. Since the half brothers of Jesus still did not believe on Him, Mary was severing herself from her other sons, upon whom she would be dependent in her old age. As a last will and testament, therefore, Jesus gave the responsibility of caring for His desolate and lonely mother to John: "Woman, behold, thy son! . . . Behold, thy mother!" (John 19:27).

4) The cry of dereliction, "My God, my God, why hast thou forsaken me?" expressed a feeling of abandonment by God (Mark 15:34; Matthew 27:46, deriving from Psalm 22:1). Yet Jesus' faith was still clinging, for He said, "*My* God." The abandonment to death was occasioned by Jesus' bearing our sin.

5) "I thirst" arose from physical anguish (John 19:28).

6) "It is finished!" (John 19:30) was a shout of victory. The Greek has here a single word which was sometimes used on receipts to mean, "Paid in full." Not only was Jesus dying. By dying He had also accomplished redemption. He had paid the debt for sin.

7) The final cry from the cross anticipated the restoration of fellowship with God immediately upon Jesus' expiration: "Father, into thy hands I commend my spirit" (Luke 23:46). *Read Mark 15:33-37; Matthew 27:45-50; Luke 23:44-46; John 19:28-30* (§165).

The veil of the Temple is said to have been sixty feet by thirty feet with the thickness of the palm of the hand (about five inches). The rending of the veil from the *top* to the bottom represented divine action. Its symbolic meaning is that the death of Jesus opened the way into God's holy presence. *Read Mark 15:38-41; Matthew 27:51-56; Luke 23:45, 47-49* (§166).

Read Mark 15:42-46; Matthew 27:57-60; Luke 23:50-54; John 19:31-42 (§167). Yet again it is ironic that the Jews were concerned about punctilious observance of the law in asking that the bodies of the crucified men not be allowed to remain on the crosses during the Sabbath day, which began at sunset Friday evening. The rapid approach of sunset made the burial of Jesus necessarily hasty and temporary. The tomb of Joseph of Arimathea was especially suited for sacred use because it had never been used before. *Read Mark 15:47; Matthew 27:61-66; Luke 23:55, 56* (§168).

THE RESURRECTION, POSTRESURRECTION
MINISTRY, AND ASCENSION

Read Mark 16:1; Matthew 28:1-4 (§§169, 170). On Sunday the women arrived at the tomb to prepare the body of Jesus for permanent burial. But he had risen! An angel had rolled aside

THIS TOMB WITH A ROUND STONE *for closing its entrance was found on the back (eastern) slopes of the Mount of Olives. The tomb is still in operating condition.*

the stone from the mouth of the tomb, not so that Jesus could come out — He had already departed — but so that the women and later the disciples could see the emptiness of the tomb.

The Women

Read Mark 16:2-8; Matthew 28:5-8; Luke 24:1-8; John 20:1 (§171). The apparent discrepancy between Mark and Luke, who say that the women came just after the sun had risen, and John, who says that Mary Magdalene came while it was still dark, is exactly what one would expect from independent accounts of the same event and proves that the story of Jesus' resurrection is not the result of collusion. It may be resolved by supposing that Mary came a little in advance of the other women, or that in John the women began their journey while it was still dark, whereas in Mark and Luke they arrived at the tomb just as the sun rose. Two angels in human form announced the resurrection to the women. Mark and Matthew mention only the spokesman of the pair.

The women still did not believe Jesus had risen from the dead, but thought His body had been stolen. Their report of an empty tomb seemed to the male disciples to be women's idle chatter. In running to investigate, the disciple who outran Peter to the tomb was John. *Read Luke 24:9-12; John 20:2-10* (§172).

Read Mark 16:9-11; John 20:11-18; Matthew 28:9, 10 (§§173, 174). In this reading section, the Marcan passage lacks authenticity, for the oldest and best manuscripts omit it. The words of Jesus to Mary, "Touch me not; for I am not yet ascended unto the Father," sound as though Mary was wrong in touching Him. In Matthew 28:9, 10, however, other women disciples touched Jesus without rebuke. In the evening of the same day Jesus invited the eleven disciples to touch Him for proof of His corporeality. And a week later Jesus invited Thomas to touch Him. It appears that Mary was clinging to Jesus never to let Him go again. With that in mind, the simplest explanation of Jesus' words to Mary lies in the fact that the form of the Greek verb with its negative means, "Stop touching me." Jesus was saying that Mary had received enough tangible proof of His resurrection. She must now come to learn that because He was shortly to ascend to the Father, her relationship to Him must no longer depend on His physical presence.

The Sanhedrin bribed the soldiers who had guarded the tomb to spread the rumor that the disciples of Jesus had stolen away His body while they slept. Since failure at guard duty could carry the death penalty for Roman soldiers, the Sanhedrin also promised to bribe the governor to exercise leniency should he hear that the soldiers had slept on guard duty. *Read Matthew 28: 11-15* (§175).

The village of Emmaus, on the road to which Jesus appeared to two disciples, lay about seven and a half miles west of Jerusalem. *Read Mark 16:12, 13; Luke 24:13-35; I Corinthians 15:5a* (§§176, 177).

That first Easter Sunday evening Jesus appeared to the eleven disciples (actually ten since Thomas was absent and Judas Iscariot was dead[13]) and invited them to handle Him for the purpose of satisfying themselves that His body was real, not apparitional. As further proof He ate food. The next Sunday He again appeared to them, Thomas being present, and satisfied the

[13]With the dropping of Judas Iscariot "the eleven" became a stereotyped designation just as "The Twelve" had been, so that the synoptists can speak of the eleven even though, according to John, Thomas was absent. Compare Paul's use of "The Twelve" in I Corinthians 15:5 and similar stereotyped occurrences in E. Hennecke, *New Testament Apocrypha*, edited by W. Scheemelcher and translated by R. M. Wilson (Philadelphia: Westminster, 1966), vol. II, p. 35.

doubts of Thomas. *Read Mark 16:14; Luke 24:36-43; John 20:19-31; I Corinthians 15:5b* (§§178, 179). Jesus' breathing on the disciples and saying, "Receive the Holy Spirit," anticipated the outpouring of the Spirit on the Day of Pentecost. There is a play on the words "breathed" and "Spirit" (or "Ghost"), for both go back to the same Greek root. The power of forgiving and retaining sins is either apostolic authority to establish precedent in the early Church for discipline, or the authority of all Christian witnesses to declare the terms under which sins may be forgiven, repentance and faith in Christ, and to declare the reason for retention of sins, failure to repent and believe in Christ.

The Fishermen

The Sea of Tiberias was another name for the Sea of Galilee. Having gone back to Galilee, Peter and six other disciples decided to fish all night. Their efforts failed. When Jesus instructed them early the next morning to cast their net on the right side of the boat, John recognized Him. Peter immediately put on his outer cloak over his inner cloak (wearing only an inner cloak was considered nakedness), and plunging into the water, he swam about a hundred yards to shore. There Jesus was already

THIS ROAD TO EMMAUS, *of Roman construction, is where Christ would have walked with the two disciples.*

cooking fish on a fire of coals, and also had a supply of bread. *Read John 21* (§180).

Jesus gently coerced Peter to affirm his love three times to make up for Peter's three denials. When Jesus asked Peter, "Lovest thou me more than these?" the term "these" probably referred both to the fish and fishing gear on one hand and to the rest of the disciples on the other hand. That is, do you love me more than your occupation of fishing? And, do you love me more than these other disciples love me? Before the crucifixion Peter had boasted that although all others might forsake Jesus, he would die with Jesus if necessary. As a result of his denials, however, Peter had learned humility and therefore no longer boasted of love superior to that of the other disciples. Instead, he simply affirmed, "I love thee." Jesus responded by recommissioning Peter as an apostolic pastor to shepherd other disciples: "Feed my sheep."

When Jesus predicted that Peter would die in old age (there is nothing here about death by crucifixion *upside down*, as is sometimes thought[14]), Peter asked what would be the fate of the Apostle John. Jesus brushed aside the question. But John indicates that Jesus' statement was misunderstood in the early Church to mean that he would not die at all, but would live right up to the Second Coming. Verse twenty-four seems to be an authentication of the fourth gospel by the church where John wrote, probably at Ephesus.

Read Mark 16:15-20; Matthew 28:16-20; Luke 24:44-53; I Corinthians 15:6, 7; Acts 1:3-12 (§§181-184). From Mark 16:9 onward (§§173-184) the Marcan column in Robertson's *Harmony* cannot be considered authentic. The earliest and best manuscripts end with Mark 16:8, and the rest hopelessly disagree concerning what follows. We do not know whether Mark intended his gospel to end at 16:8, or whether the true ending was lost.

In the promise of Jesus to be with His disciples "to the end of the world" (Matthew 28:20) the phrase properly means "to the end of the *age*" and points to the Second Advent. "I am with you" reflects "Immanuel . . . God with us" (1:23). The command to evangelize the nations is known as the Great Commission.

After a postresurrection ministry of forty days, Jesus ascended back to heaven with hands upraised in a priestly benediction.

---

[14]Origen (as reported by Eusebius, *Ecclesiastical History,* III. i. 2) in the third century is the first to mention this probably legendary detail of Peter's martyrdom. However, Jesus' prediction that Peter would stretch out his hands and that another would gird him and carry him where he would not want to go may euphemistically describe the preparation of a condemned man for crucifixion.

EXCURSUS ON THE RESURRECTION OF JESUS

That Jesus really did rise from the dead is best seen by considering the shortcomings of alternate possibilities. One is that Jesus only appeared to die, that He lapsed into a coma and later revived temporarily. But His death is indicated by the brutal beating He endured, by the six hours' hanging on the cross, by the thrusting through of His abdomen with a spear and the resultant gushing out of watery fluid and blood, by His partial embalming and being wrapped up in grave clothes, and finally by His being sealed in a tomb. It would require about as much faith to believe that Jesus did not die as to believe that He rose from the dead.

Others suggest that the disciples stole the corpse of Jesus. But to do that they would have had to overpower the Roman guards, an unlikely event, or bribed them, equally unlikely, since the guards knew they would be subject to capital punishment for failing to protect Jesus' body from theft. That the graveclothes lay undisturbed (not even unwrapped!) and the turban still twirled up and set to one side militates against a hasty removal of the corpse by theft. Thieves do not usually take time to tidy up. Here they would probably have taken the body *with* its wrappings.

The surprise, even unbelief, of the disciples at the resurrection of Jesus further show that they did not steal His corpse, unless their surprise and unbelief are fabricated to make the story look convincing. But that would have been a little too clever on the part of the early Christians. Besides, it is unlikely that stories would have been invented in which the apostles are pictured as unbelievers in the resurrection, for the early Church soon began to revere them.

Yet others think that the disciples experienced hallucinations. But the New Testament gives evidence of Jesus' appearances in different places at different times to different parties numbering from one to over five hundred. In 1 Corinthians 15 Paul challenges doubters to ask the eyewitnesses! The appearances were too many and too varied to have been hallucinations. Furthermore, the disciples were psychologically unprepared for hallucinations, since they did not expect Jesus to rise and actually disbelieved the first reports that He had risen. All the unbelieving Jews would have had to do when the report of Jesus' resurrection began to be circulated was to produce the body. But they never did!

The same objection militates against the suggestion that the disciples came to the wrong tomb. Why did the Jews fail to

produce the corpse of Jesus from the right tomb? They must

have known where it was, for they had induced Pilate to put a guard there.

Still others explain that the disciples modeled the account of Jesus' resurrection after the dying and rising of gods in pagan mythology. But the differences are far greater than the similarities. The framework of the myths is not at all historical, as is the framework of the resurrection accounts in the New Testament. In the New Testament there is no connection with the yearly dying and reviving of nature as in the pagan fertility myths. The matter-of-fact style of reporting in the gospels contrasts sharply with the fantasies which abound in the myths. And fullblown resurrection accounts appear *immediately* in the early Church without the lengthy interim required for evolution of detailed mythology. Paul's triumphant statement that most of the more than five hundred people who saw Jesus at the same time and place were still alive, and therefore could be asked, is unbelievably audacious if the whole story were the result of mythological development.[15]

Something unique must have made the first Jewish disciples change their day of worship from the Sabbath to Sunday. Either they were deceived — then the unbelieving Jews could have squelched the Christian movement by producing Jesus' corpse — or they foisted a hoax on the world — then it is psychologically incredible that they willingly suffered torture and death for what they knew to be false. It is also inconceivable for the ancient world that fabricators of such a story would have made *women* the first witnesses of the risen Christ. One does not have to treat the New Testament as inspired by God to feel the force of the historical evidences for the resurrection of Jesus. The gospel accounts must be explained even when they are not regarded as divinely authoritative. Making up one's mind beforehand that such a thing could not have happened is the real obstacle to faith in the resurrection of Jesus Christ.[16]

Since Jesus did rise, there is a man in heaven interceding for those who believe in Him as their sacrificial substitute. His resurrection also guarantees that He will come back again and that those who believe will live with Him forever.

---

[15]See pages 35 f.

[16]For the historicity of the resurrection and a critique of alternative theories, see J. N. D. Anderson, "The Resurrection of Jesus Christ," *Christianity Today,* XII, 13 (March 29, 1968), pp. 4[628]-9[633], with the dialogue and overcomment in the next number (14 [April 12, 1968]), pp. 5[677]-12[684]; F. Morison, *Who Moved the Stone?* (London: Faber & Faber, 1944); J. Orr, *The Resurrection of Jesus* (London: Hodder & Stoughton, 1908); D. P. Fuller, *Easter Faith and History* (Grand Rapids: Eerdmans, 1965).

For further discussion:

In the Olivet Discourse, does Jesus seem to have implied a short delay or a long delay before His return?

From the farewell discourse of Jesus in the upper room and His high priestly prayer, what does Jesus appear to have thought most important for His disciples in His coming absence?

How could Jesus have drawn the acclamation of the crowds on Palm Sunday and incurred their "Crucify him!" less than a week later?

Who was responsible for the unjust death of Jesus?

Is the account of Jesus' trial and crucifixion anti-Semitic in tone?

What parties would play which roles if the passion story were re-enacted today?

Why did Jesus appear after His resurrection only to His disciples? Or did He appear only to His disciples?

For further investigation:

See the works listed on pages 115 f. and those appearing in the footnotes to this chapter, and the following:

Isaiah 53, with the comments of G. L. Archer, *In the Shadow of the Cross* (Grand Rapids: Zondervan, 1957); E. J. Young, *Isaiah 53* (Grand Rapids: Eerdmans, 1952); and D. Baron, *The Servant of Jehovah* (London: Marshall, Morgan, & Scott, 1922).
Psalms 22 and 69.
Morris, Leon. *The Cross in the New Testament.* Grand Rapids: Eerdmans, 1965.
_____. *The Apostolic Preaching of the Cross.* 3rd edition. London: Tyndale, 1965.
Künneth, W. *The Theology of the Resurrection.* St. Louis: Concordia, 1965.

SUMMARY OUTLINE OF A
HARMONISTIC STUDY OF THE GOSPELS

INTRODUCTION

    A. The Lucan prologue (Luke 1:1-4)
    B. The Johannine prologue (John 1:1-18)
    C. The tables of descent (Matthew 1:1-17; Luke 3:23-38)

I. THE NATIVITY AND CHILDHOOD OF JESUS

    A. The annunciation to Zacharias of the birth of John the Baptist (Luke 1:5-25)
    B. The annunciation to Mary of the birth of Jesus and her visit to Elisabeth, with the Magnificat (Luke 1:26-56)
    C. The birth, naming, and childhood of John the Baptist, with the Benedictus of Zacharias (Luke 1:57-80)
    D. The annunciation to Joseph of the birth of Jesus (Matthew 1:18-25)
    E. The birth of Jesus and visit of the shepherds (Luke 2:8-20)

F. The circumcision, naming, and presentation of Jesus in the Temple, with the homage of Simeon and Anna, including Simeon's Nunc Dimittis (Luke 2:21-38)

G. The adoration of the Magi, flight of the Holy Family to Egypt, and return and residence in Nazareth (Matthew 2:1-23)

H. The visit to the Temple (Luke 2:40-52)

II. THE BEGINNINGS OF JESUS' MINISTRY THROUGHOUT PALESTINE

A. The ministry of John the Baptist (Mark 1:1-8; Matthew 3:1-12; Luke 3:1-18)

B. The baptism of Jesus (Mark 1:9-11; Matthew 3:13-17; Luke 3:21-33)

C. The temptation of Jesus (Mark 1:12, 13; Matthew 4:1-11; Luke 4:1-13)

D. The witness of John the Baptist to Jesus (John 1:19-34)

E. The first disciples (John 1:35-51)

F. The first miracle, turning water to wine at a wedding in Cana of Galilee (John 2:1-12)

G. The cleansing of the Temple (John 2:13-22)

H. Nicodemus and the new birth (John 2:23—3:21)

I. The concurrent baptizing ministries of John the Baptist and Jesus, with further testimony from John (John 3:22-36)

J. The imprisonment of John the Baptist and the departure of Jesus into Galilee (John 4:1-4; Luke 3:19, 20; Mark 1:14; Matthew 4:12; Luke 4:14)

K. The Samaritan woman (John 4:5-42)

III. THE GREAT GALILEAN MINISTRY

A. The arrival in Galilee, a general description of Jesus' preaching and healing, the healing of the son of a nobleman, and Jesus' new home in Capernaum (Mark 1:14, 15; Matthew 4:13-17; Luke 4:14, 15; John 4:43-54)

B. The further calling of the first disciples (Mark 1:16-20; Matthew 4:18-22; Luke 5:1-11)

C. Teaching, healings, and exorcisms, including deliverance of the demoniac in the synagogue at Capernaum and the cure of Peter's mother-in-law (Mark 1:21-39; Luke 4:31-44; Matthew 8:14-17, 23-25)

D. The cleansing of a leper (Mark 1:40-45; Matthew 8:2-4; Luke 5:12-16)

E. The forgiveness and healing of a paralytic (Mark 2:1-12; Matthew 9:1-8; Luke 5:17-26)

F. The call of Matthew-Levi (Mark 2:13-17; Matthew 9:9-13; Luke 5:27-32)

G. The question about fasting (Mark 2:18-22; Matthew 9:14-17; Luke 5:33-39)

H. The Sabbath healing of a lame man at the Pool of Bethesda with an apology for Jesus' authority (John 5:1-47)

I. The disciples' plucking and eating grain on the Sabbath (Mark 2:23-28; Matthew 12:1-8; Luke 6:1-5)

J. The Sabbath healing of a withered hand (Mark 3:1-6; Matthew 12:9-14; Luke 6:6-11)

K. Withdrawal from the crowds (Mark 3:7-12; Matthew 12:15-21)

L. The choice of The Twelve (Mark 3:13-19; Luke 6:12-16)

M. The Sermon on the Mount (Matthew 5:1—8:1; Luke 6:17-49)

N. The faith of a centurion and the healing of his servant (Matthew 8:5-13; Luke 7:1-10)

O. The raising of the only son of a widow in Nain (Luke 7:11-17)

P. John the Baptist and his doubts (Matthew 11:2-19; Luke 7:18-35)

Q. Woes on the Galilean "cities of opportunity" and an invitation (Matthew 11:20-30)

209

R. The anointing of Jesus by a prostitute (Luke 7:36-50)

S. The women who supported Jesus and His disciples (Luke 8:1-3)

T. The defense of Jesus against the charge of empowerment by Satan, including the unpardonable sin (Mark 3:19-30; Matthew 12:22-37)

U. The sign of Jonah (Matthew 12:38-45)

V. Jesus' spiritual kin (Mark 3:31-35; Matthew 12:46-50; Luke 8:19-21)

W. The parables of the kingdom, including the seed and the soils [more commonly called the sower], the growing seed, the mustard seed, the leaven, the treasure, the pearl, the wheat and the tares, the good and bad fish, and the householder (Mark 4:1-34; Matthew 13:1-53; Luke 8:4-18)

X. The stilling of the storm (Mark 4:35-41; Matthew 8:18, 23-27; Luke 8:22-25)

Y. The Gerasene (or Gadarene) demoniacs (Mark 5:1-20; Matthew 8:28-34; Luke 8:26-39)

Z. The healing of the woman with a constant hemorrhage and the raising of Jairus' daughter (Mark 5:21-43; Matthew 9:18-26; Luke 8:40-56)

AA. The healing of two blind men and a dumb demoniac (Matthew 9:27-34)

BB. The rejection at Nazareth (Mark 6:1-6; Matthew 13:54-58; Luke 4:16-31)

CC. The mission of The Twelve (Mark 6:6-13; Matthew 9:35—11:1; Luke 9:1-6)

DD. The beheading of John the Baptist and the guilty fear of Herod Antipas (Mark 6:14-29; Matthew 14:1-12; Luke 9:7-9)

EE. The feeding of the five thousand (Mark 6:30-46; Matthew 14:13-23; Luke 9:10-17; John 6:1-15)

FF. The walking on the water (Mark 6:47-56; Matthew 14:24-36; John 6:16-21)

GG. The discourse on the bread of life (John 6:22-71)

HH. Ritual and real purity (Mark 7:1-23; Matthew 15:1-20; John 7:1)

II. The faith of a Syro-Phoenician woman and the healing of her daughter (Mark 7:24-30; Matthew 15:21-28)

JJ. The feeding of the four thousand (Mark 7:31—8:9; Matthew 15:29-38)

KK. A discussion of Messianic signs (Mark 8:10-12; Matthew 15:39—16:4)

LL. Sadducean and Pharisaic leaven (Mark 8:13-26; Matthew 16:5-12)

MM. Peter's confession of Jesus' messiahship, the beatitude upon Peter, the rock-foundation of the church, the keys of the kingdom, binding and loosing (Mark 8:27-30; Matthew 16:13-20; Luke 9:18-21)

NN. Prediction of the passion, with rebuke of Peter and words about cross-bearing discipleship (Mark 8:31-37; Matthew 16:21-26; Luke 9:22-25)

OO. The transfiguration (Mark 8:38—9:8; Matthew 16:27—17:8; Luke 9:26-36)

PP. John the Baptist and Elijah (Mark 9:9-13; Matthew 17:9-13; Luke 9:36)

QQ. The deliverance of a demonized boy and remarks on faith (Mark 9:14-29; Matthew 17:14-20; Luke 9:37-42)

RR. Prediction of the passion (Mark 9:30-32; Matthew 17:22, 23; Luke 9:43-45)

SS. The Temple-tax (Matthew 17:24-27)

TT. Childlikeness and discipleship (Mark 9:33-50; Matthew 18:1-14; Luke 9:46-50)

UU. Reconciliation and forgiveness, including the parable of the unmerciful servant (Matthew 18:15-35)

VV. The nature of discipleship, in response to volunteers (Matthew 8:19-22; Luke 9:57-62)

WW. Journey to the Festival of Tabernacles (John 7:2-10; Luke 9:51-56)

IV. THE LATER JUDEAN AND PEREAN MINISTRY

A. Debate at the Festival of Tabernacles, including Jesus' claim to be the dispenser of living water and the light of the world and a discussion of Abrahamic descent (John 7:11-52; 8:12-59)

B. The healing and excommunication of a blind man (John 9:1-41)

C. The discourse on the good shepherd (John 10:1-21)

D. The mission of the seventy (Luke 10:1-24)

E. The parable of the good Samaritan (Luke 10:25-37)

F. Mary and Martha (Luke 10:38-42)

G. The Lord's Prayer and the parable of the importunate host (Luke 11:1-13)

H. The defense of Jesus against the charge of empowerment by Satan including the parable of the empty house, the sign of Jonah, and remarks on healthy spiritual vision (Luke 11:14-36)

I. Phariseeism (Luke 11:37-54)

J Remarks on hypocrisy, trust in God, covetousness (including the parable of the rich fool), watchfulness (including the parable of the wise and foolish servants), and Messianic crisis (Luke 12:1-59)

K. Repentance and the parable of the fruitless fig tree (Luke 13:1-9)

L. The Sabbath healing of a woman bent over, with the parables of the mustard seed and leaven (Luke 13:10-21)

M. Jesus' claim to deity (John 10:22-42)

N. The number of the saved and Jesus' coming death in Jerusalem (Luke 13:22-35)

O. The Sabbath healing of a man with dropsy, remarks on humility, and the parable of the Messianic banquet (Luke 14:1-24)

P. Remarks on discipleship (Luke 14:25-35)

Q. The parables of the lost sheep, the lost coin, and the prodigal son and elder brother, in defense of Jesus' ministry to sinners (Luke 15:1-32)

R. The parables of the unjust steward and the rich man and Lazarus, on the right and wrong uses of money (Luke 16:1-31)

S. Remarks on giving offense, forgiveness, faith, and obedience (Luke 17:1-10)

T. The raising of Lazarus (John 11:1-44)

U. The plot of the Sanhedrin against Jesus (John 11:45-54)

V. The healing of the ten lepers (Luke 17:11-19)

W. The presence and coming of the kingdom (Luke 17:20-37)

X. Two parables on prayer, the widow and the judge and the Pharisee and the publican (Luke 18:1-14)

Y. Teaching on divorce and marriage (Mark 10:1-12; Matthew 19:1-12)

Z. Children and the kingdom of God (Mark 10:13-16; Matthew 19:13-15; Luke 18:15-17)

AA. The rich young ruler (Mark 10:17-31; Matthew 19:16-30; Luke 18:18-30)

BB. The parable of the laborers in the vineyard (Matthew 20:1-16)

CC. Prediction of the passion with the request of James, John, and their mother for places of honor in the kingdom (Mark 10:32-45; Matthew 20:17-28; Luke 18:31-34)

DD. The healing of blind Bartimaeus and his companion (Mark 10:46-52; Matthew 20:29-34; Luke 18:35-43)

EE. Zacchaeus (Luke 19:1-10)

FF. The parable of the pounds (Luke 19:11-28)

V. PASSION WEEK

    A. The arrival of Passover pilgrims in Jerusalem and the plot of the Sanhedrin against Jesus and Lazarus (John 11:55—12:1, 9-11)

    B. The anointing of Jesus by Mary of Bethany (Mark 14:3-9; Matthew 26:6-13; John 12:2-8)

    C. The triumphal entry (Mark 11:1-11; Matthew 21:1-11, 14-17; Luke 19:29-44; John 12:12-19)

    D. The cursing of the fig tree and the cleansing of the Temple (Mark 11:12-18; Matthew 21:12, 13, 18, 19; Luke 19:45-48)

    E. The Greeks who came to see Jesus, and Jesus' response concerning His death and its significance (John 12:20-50)

    F. The withering of the fig tree (Mark 11:19-25; Matthew 21:19-22; Luke 21:37, 38)

    G. Debate over Jesus' authority (Mark 11:27-33; Matthew 21:23-27; Luke 20:1-8)

    H. The parable of the obedient and disobedient sons (Matthew 21:28-32)

    I. The parable of the vineyard (Mark 12:1-12; Matthew 21:33-46; Luke 20:9-19)

    J. The parable of the marriage feast (Matthew 22:1-14)

    K. The question of paying taxes to Caesar (Mark 12:13-17; Matthew 22:15-22; Luke 20:20-26)

    L. The Sadducees' question about the resurrection (Mark 12:18-27; Matthew 22:23-33; Luke 20:27-40)

    M. The most important commandments (Mark 12:28-34; Matthew 22:34-40)

    N. The divine, Davidic Messiah (Mark 12:35-37; Matthew 22:41-46; Luke 20:41-44)

    O. Denunciation of the scribes and Pharisees (Mark 12:38-40; Matthew 23:1-39; Luke 20:45-47)

    P. The widow's offering of two mites (Mark 12:41-44; Luke 21:1-4)

    Q. The Olivet Discourse, including the tribulation, the abomination of desolation, the Parousia, the parables of the houseowner, the faithful and unfaithful servants, the ten virgins, and the talents, and the judgment of the sheep and goats (Mark 13:1-37; Matthew 24, 25; Luke 21:5-36)

    R. The betrayal bargain between Judas Iscariot and the Sanhedrin (Mark 14:1, 2, 10, 11; Matthew 26:1-5, 14-16; Luke 22:1-6)

    S. Preparations for the Last Supper (Mark 14:12-16; Matthew 26:17-19; Luke 22:7-13)

    T. The Last Supper

        1. Jesus' washing the disciples' feet (Mark 14:17; Matthew 26:20; Luke 22:14-16, 24-30; John 13:1-20)

        2. The exit of Judas Iscariot (Mark 14:18-21; Matthew 26:21-25; Luke 22:21-23; John 13:21-30)

        3. Remarks on loving one another, Peter's coming denials, and return to normal living (John 13:31-38; Mark 14:27-31; Matthew 26:31-35; Luke 22:31-38)

        4. The institution of the Lord's Supper during the Passover meal (Mark 14:22-25; Matthew 26:26-29; Luke 22:17-20; 1 Corinthians 11:23-26)

        5. The discourse in the upper room (John 14-16)

        6. The high priestly prayer of Jesus (John 17)

    U. Jesus' praying in Gethsemane (Mark 14:26, 32-42; Matthew 26:30, 36-46; Luke 22:39-46; John 18:1)

    V. The arrest of Jesus (Mark 14:43-52; Matthew 26:47-56; Luke 22:47-53; John 18:2-12)

VI. THE TRIAL AND CRUCIFIXION

    A. The Jewish part of the trial

        1. The hearing before Annas (John 18:12-14, 19-23)

2. The hearing before Caiaphas and the Sanhedrin (Mark 14:53, 55-65; Matthew 26:57, 59-68; Luke 22:54, 63-65; John 18:24)
3. Interlude: Peter's denials (Mark 14:54, 66-72; Matthew 26:58, 69-75; Luke 22:54-62; John 18:15-18, 25-27)
4. The Sanhedrin's formal condemnation of Jesus after dawn (Mark 15:1; Matthew 27:1; Luke 22:66-71)

B. The suicide of Judas Iscariot (Matthew 27:3-10; Acts 1:18, 19)
C. The Roman part of the trial
1. The first hearing before Pilate (Mark 15:1-5; Matthew 27:2, 11-14; Luke 23:1-5; John 18:28-38)
2. The hearing before Herod Antipas (Luke 23:6-12)
3. The second hearing before Pilate and condemnation (Mark 15: 6-19; Matthew 27:15-30; Luke 23:13-25; John 18:39—19:16)

D. The crucifixion (Mark 15:20-25; Matthew 27:31-36; Luke 23: 26-33; John 19:16-18)
E. The parting of the garments, the superscription, the two criminals, the mockery, the vinegar, and the seven last words (Mark 15:26-37; Matthew 27:37-50; Luke 23:34-46; John 19:19-30)
F. The rending of the veil and other phenomena (Mark 15:38-41; Matthew 27:51-56; Luke 23:45, 47-49)
G. The burial (Mark 15:42-47; Matthew 27:57-66; Luke 23:50-56; John 19:31-42)

VII. THE RESURRECTION, POSTRESURRECTION MINISTRY, AND ASCENSION
A. The empty tomb (Mark 16:1; Matthew 28:1-4)
B. The women at the tomb (Mark 16:2-8; Matthew 28:5-8; Luke 24:1-8; John 20:1)
C. Peter and John at the tomb (Luke 24:9-12; John 20:2-10)
D. The appearance to Mary Magdalene in the garden (John 20:11-18)
E. The appearance to the other women (Matthew 28:9, 10)
F. The Sanhedrin's bribe of the Roman guards at the tomb (Matthew 28:11-15)
G. The appearances to two disciples (including Cleopas) on the way to Emmaus and the appearance of Peter (Luke 24:13-35; 1 Corinthians 15:5a)
H. The appearance to the eleven except for Thomas (Luke 24:36-43; John 20:19-25; 1 Corinthians 15:5b)
I. The appearance one week later to the eleven, Thomas being present (John 20:26-31)
J. The appearance beside the Sea of Galilee to the fishermen disciples, and Peter's restoration (John 21)
K. The further appearances to the eleven, the five hundred, and James, and the great commission (Matthew 28:16-20; 1 Corinthians 15:6, 7)
L. The ascension (Luke 24:44-53; Acts 1:3-12)

PART III

The Triumphant Aftermath: From Jerusalem to Rome

THE CILICIAN GATES, *a main mountain pass through the Taurus range in Asia Minor. Through this corridor Alexander the Great and his army passed eastward for conquest, and later Paul and his companions passed westward to begin the second missionary journey.*

CHAPTER 12

The Acts of the Spirit of Christ Through the Apostles In and Around Jerusalem

Leading questions:

What is the relationship of Acts to the gospel of Luke as to authorship, style, date, and purpose of writing?

Where did Luke get the historical information he recorded in Acts, and of what historical value is it?

Why does Acts end very abruptly?

In what geographical and theological directions did Christianity develop — in relation to the Roman Empire, Judaism, and pagan religions — and under what leaders?

How did Christianity separate from Judaism?

What was the legal status of Christianity and from what source(s) did the first persecutions come?

How and why was Paul very important to the history of the early Church?

According to early Church tradition Luke wrote the book of Acts. If so, the book is a sequel to the gospel of Luke. Evidence within Acts supports Lucan authorship. The book opens with a dedication to Theophilus, as does the gospel of Luke. Vocabulary and style are very similar in the two books. Frequent use of medical terms agrees with Luke's being a physician (Colossians 4:14).[1] By his use of "we" in describing many of Paul's trips, the author of Acts implies he was a traveling companion of Paul. Other traveling companions do not fit the data of the text. For example, Timothy and several others are

Authorship by Luke

---

[1]This argument is not so decisive as once was thought by some, but is still valid.

mentioned apart from the "we" and "us" of Acts 20:4-6. According to the epistles of Paul, neither Titus nor Silas accompanied him to Rome or were with him there. Yet the narrative of his voyage to Rome is one of the "we"-sections. By such processes of elimination Luke is the only likely candidate for the authorship of Acts.

**Literary
Technique**

Acts, together with the gospel of Luke and Hebrews, contains some of the most cultured Greek writing in the New Testament. On the other hand, where Luke appears to be following Semitic sources the Greek style is often rough. Some scholars claim that the speeches and sermons in Acts are literary devices improvised by Luke himself to fill out the stories. That some ancient historians followed such a procedure is true, but not nearly to the extent that has sometimes been claimed. And although Luke does not necessarily give *verbatim* reports of speeches and sermons, he does accurately give the gist of what was said. This is proved by the parallelism of expressions in Peter's sermons in Acts and in 1 Peter, and in Paul's sermons in Acts and in his epistles. These parallelisms can hardly be accidental, and there is no other evidence to indicate that Luke imitated or used in any other way the epistles, or that Peter and Paul imitated Acts when writing their epistles. The only adequate explanation is that Luke did not make up the speeches and sermons, but summarized their contents with accuracy, so that the characteristic phraseology of Peter and Paul is evident in Luke's reporting as well as in their epistles.

**Source
Materials**

For the material in Acts Luke drew on his own recollections where possible. He may have put some of these in a diary at the time of the events. In addition, he doubtless gained information from Paul, from Christians in Jerusalem, Syrian Antioch, and other places which he visited with and without Paul, from other traveling companions of Paul, such as Silas and Timothy, and from Philip the deacon and evangelist and an early disciple named Mnason, in whose homes he stayed (Acts 21: 8, 16). Also available were written sources, such as the decree of the Jerusalem Council (Acts 15:23-29), and perhaps Aramaic or Hebrew documents relating the early events of Christianity in and around Jerusalem.

**Historical
Accuracy**

Archaeological discoveries have confirmed Luke's historical accuracy in remarkable fashion. For example, we now know that the Lucan use of titles for various kinds of local and provincial governmental officials — procurators, consuls, praetors, politarchs, Asiarchs, and others — was exactly correct for the times and localities about which Luke was writing. The accuracy is doubly remarkable in that the usage of these terms was in a constant state of flux because of the changing political status of various communities.[2]

The abrupt ending of Acts is almost astonishing. Luke brings the story of Paul to the point where Paul, imprisoned in Rome, has been waiting for two years to be tried before Caesar. The book closes. What happened to Paul? Did he ever appear before Caesar? If so, was he condemned? Martyred? Acquitted? Released? Luke does not tell. Many suggestions are offered to explain the abrupt ending. Perhaps Luke intended a third volume which would answer these questions. But his first volume, the gospel of Luke, closes with a sense of completeness even though doubtless he already intended to write Acts. Or maybe Luke came to the end of his papyrus scroll. But he would have seen that space was running out and formed an appropriate conclusion. Personal catastrophe may have prevented Luke from finishing the book. But the book already is long enough to fill a lengthy papyrus scroll. Perhaps Luke had accomplished his purpose, which was to show the progress of Christianity from Jerusalem, the place of origin, to Rome, the capital of the empire. But Paul's prison ministry in Rome was hardly climactic; a Christian community already existed there, and the problem remains why Luke did not write of what happened to Paul, the dominant character in Acts 13-28.

The best solution is that Luke wrote up to the events as far as they had happened. That is, at the time of writing Paul was still awaiting trial. Surely it would have been irrelevant for Luke to prove the political innocence of Christianity (see below) if he were writing Acts *after* Nero the emperor had turned against the Christians (A.D. 64). Too late *then* to appeal to the favorable decisions of lesser officials! Luke wrote Acts, therefore, when Paul had been in Rome for two years (c. A.D. 61).[3] The very abruptness of the end of Acts appropriately suggests the unfinished task of worldwide evangelization. What the early Church began, we are to finish.

---

[2]The confirmation of the historical accuracy of Acts has outmoded the "Tübingen hypothesis" of the nineteenth century that a second century author wrote Acts to reconcile the supposedly conflicting viewpoints of Petrine and Pauline Christianity. Evidence is lacking for such a division, and a late writer could not have been so accurate about first century conditions. F. C. Baur of the University of Tübingen, Germany, was the leader of that school of thought. According to the hypothesis, Petrine Christianity was legalistic, Pauline Christianity antilegalistic.

[3]Also favoring an early date of writing is the lack of allusions to the persecution under Nero in the 60s, the martyrdom of James the Lord's brother in the 60s, and the destruction of Jerusalem in A.D. 70. The undeveloped theology and the controversy over the status of Gentile Christians possibly point in the same direction, but may instead reflect Luke's accuracy in describing the primitive Church, without implications for the date of writing.

Read Acts 1. "The former treatise" (1:1) is the gospel of Luke. Theophilus may have borne the financial responsibility for the publication of Luke's two works. The purpose of the gospel of Luke was to relate the life of Jesus with emphasis on historical certainty. The main purpose of Acts is to trace the triumphant progress of the Gospel from Jerusalem, where it began, to Rome, the capital city of the empire. Acts is therefore a selective, rather than comprehensive, history of the early Church. For example, Luke does not write about the spread of Christianity to Egypt or to the East. But we do read recurring statements which summarize the success of the Gospel wherever Christians proclaimed it: "the word of God kept on spreading, and the number of the disciples continued to increase greatly . . ." (Acts 6:7; see also 9:31; 12:24; 16:5; 19:20; 28:30, 31). Behind this success was the activity of the Holy Spirit, to whom Luke repeatedly gives credit. The overall purpose of Luke-Acts, then, is the presentation of the beginnings of Christianity in Jesus' life and the extension of Christianity in early Church history so as to convince readers by the irresistible advance of the Gospel that God through His Spirit really is working in human history for the redemption of all men.

A subsidiary purpose in Acts is to show that Christianity deserves continued freedom because it is derived from Judaism, which had legal standing, and because it is not politically disloyal to Rome. Therefore Luke frequently cites favorable judgments concerning Christianity and its proponents by various kinds of local and provincial governmental officials. This apologetic was needed because Christianity started with the handicap that its founder had died as a condemned criminal under a Roman governor. And wherever Christianity spread, disturbance resulted. Already in his gospel Luke has shown that both Pilate and Herod Antipas pronounced Jesus innocent and that pressure from a mob led to a miscarriage of justice. In Acts, too, Luke shows that disturbances over Christianity arose from the violence of mobs and from false accusations, frequently by the Jews, not through any misdeeds of the Christians themselves. In this way Luke hopes to dispel prejudice against Christianity and to win sympathy from the likes of Theophilus, whose designation "most excellent" in Luke 1:3 may indicate influential political position as well as aristocratic, or at least middle class, social standing.[4]

The instruction from Jesus to wait for the coming of the Holy Spirit (1:4) referred back to His and John the Baptist's promise that He would grant the Spirit to all the disciples and referred to the fulfillment of that promise on the Day of Pentecost.

---

[4]Compare the address, "most excellent Festus," in Acts 26:25.

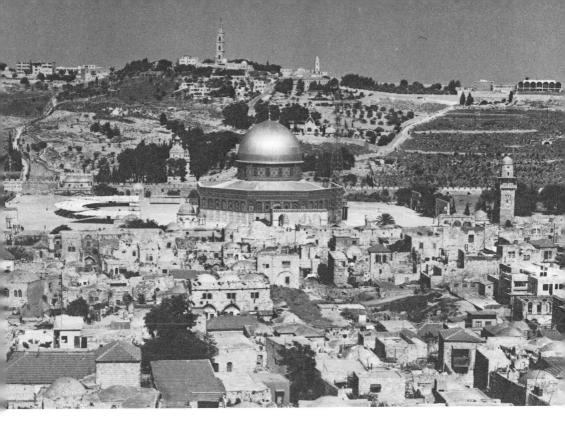

THE MOUNT OF OLIVES *in the distance as viewed across the Old City.*

There is no longer any need to wait, but only to appropriate the gift already given. The disciples wondered whether the kingdom would be restored to Israel, that is, whether the Messianic kingdom on earth with Israel in the favored position would come soon. They thought of the possibility because the Old Testament had associated the outpouring of God's Spirit with that time (Isaiah 44:3; Ezekiel 36:24-27; 39:29; Joel 2:28, 29, in their larger contexts). In effect, Jesus answered that His disciples must not waste energy wondering when those things will happen, but should evangelize the world (1:6-8).

Acts 1:8 is a key verse: "you shall receive power when the Holy Spirit has come upon you; and you shall be My witnesses both in Jerusalem, and in all Judea and Samaria, and even to the remotest part of the earth." Indeed, the verse forms a rough outline of the entire book of Acts: (1) in chapters 1-7 the Gospel goes throughout Jerusalem and Judea; (2) in chapters 8-12 to Samaria and other outlying regions; and (3) in chapters 13-28 to distant lands through Paul's missionary efforts. Just as Peter is the leading figure in evangelizing primarily the Jews in chapters 1-12, Paul is the leading figure in evangelizing primarily the Gentiles in chapters 13-28.

The Great Commission

221

In his account of the ascension (1:9-11) Luke may have intended that the two men who predicted Jesus' return be understood as angels with human appearance or perhaps as Moses and Elijah, the same individuals who had appeared with Jesus on the Mount of Transfiguration. The cloud into which Jesus ascended represents the presence of God the Father, as at Jesus' baptism, transfiguration, and Second Coming. The ascension of Jesus must have surprised the disciples, who expected an earthly Messianic kingdom almost immediately.

It is debatable whether the choice of Matthias by lot to replace Judas was wrong, as might be indicated by God's later choice of Paul. Right or wrong, the disciples thought that the number of their group, twelve, should not remain deficient, since it represented the new people of God, who were taking the place of the twelve tribes of Israel. The question also arises whether the method of choosing Matthias was wrong. The disciples intended that the use of lots should indicate the Lord's choice instead of theirs.[5]

Although the embryonic beginnings of the Church date back to the choice of The Twelve, the Pentecost after Jesus' ascension marks the birthday of the Church. The sound of wind when the Spirit came upon the disciples plays on the fact that the Greek text has only one word for "wind" and "Spirit." The tongue-shaped flames above the disciples' heads symbolized the ability to speak miraculously in unlearned foreign languages, in a reversal of the "confusion of tongues" at the Tower of Babel. The non-Palestinian pilgrims, both Jews and Gentile proselytes, amazedly recognized the languages spoken in their homelands. But the Palestinians did not understand them and so made the charge of drunken babbling. *Read Acts 2.*

The flow of argument in Peter's sermon on the Day of Pentecost is that the Jews killed Jesus, but God raised Him from the dead and exalted Him to His own right hand. The outpouring of the Spirit proves the exaltation of Jesus. The miraculous speaking in "tongues" (foreign languages) proves in turn the outpouring of the Spirit. Therefore, repent and be baptized. Although Peter quoted the prophecy of Joel as fulfilled, the fulfillment had to do only with the part about the giving of the Holy Spirit and about salvation for all who call on the name of the Lord. The celestial phenomena predicted in Joel await fulfillment at Jesus' return. The wording of 2:38 — "Repent, and let each of you be baptized in the name of Jesus Christ for the forgiveness of your sins" — sounds as though baptism is necessary for

---

[5]It is barely possible, however, that "they cast lots" should be translated, "they cast votes."

the forgiveness of sins. But since many other passages require only repentant faith in Christ, it is better to take baptism as the expected way of showing repentance and faith. The problem of unbaptized believers never arose in the New Testament.[6]

Read Acts 3:1—4:31. The Sadducees denied the doctrine of resurrection and therefore jailed the apostles for proclaiming the resurrection of Jesus as an already accomplished fact and as a guarantee of the resurrection of others.

Read Acts 4:32—5:42. To call the sharing of goods in the Jerusalem church "Christian communism" is not a happy designation. Present-day communism is atheistic and coercive. The sharing in Jerusalem stemmed from devotion to God, was purely voluntary, and was never intended to be permanent. It was only a temporary measure, which enabled the converts who had come from other countries to Jerusalem for the Festival of Pentecost to stay longer than they had provided for so that they might gain further instruction in their new-found Christian faith.

Barnabas, who sold a field and donated the entire purchase price, appears in the narrative as a foil to Ananias and Sapphira, who similarly sold a field but hypocritically pretended to donate the entire sum, while keeping part for themselves. The death of Ananias and Sapphira seems to have been harsh, at least unusual. But just as at the very beginning of Israel's history as a redeemed nation God caused the disobedient priests Nadab and Abihu to die (Leviticus 10), so also at the beginning of Church history God punished Ananias and Sapphira with death. Both times God was showing His deep concern for the pristine purity of His people. Thus, we must interpret the failure of God to continue this kind of punishment with regularity as a sign of grace, not as an indication that He condones sin in the Church.

Hellenists were Jews who had adopted Greek ways. Hebrews, or Hebraists, were Jews who had retained strictly Jewish ways of life.[7] When the Hellenistic Jewish Christians complained that their widows were being neglected in the doling out of food rations, the Hebraistic Jewish Christians graciously chose Hellenistic men, as shown by their Greek rather than Hebrew or Aramaic names, to supervise the dole. Perhaps the later

---

[6]Alternatively, we may translate "be baptized . . . *as a result of* the forgiveness of your sins." Compare Matthew 3:11; 12:41; Luke 12:32; and H. E. Dana and J. R. Mantey, *A Manual Grammar of the Greek New Testament* (New York: Macmillan, 1946), pp. 104 f.

[7]Some scholars think that the Hellenists were Gentile proselytes and God-fearers, others that the Hebrists were Samaritans. It is difficult, however, to think that many from these categories had already entered the Church.

church office of deacon ("servant, helper"), having to do with mundane matters of church life and especially the dispensing of charity, developed out of this situation. *Read Acts 6:1—8:1a.*

Stephen was not content to limit himself to the ministry of material things. The charge brought against him for his preaching implies that he had deduced the outdatedness of the Temple and its rituals from the redemptive work of Christ. Perhaps Stephen was the first Christian to arrive at this conclusion. His recorded sermon surveys the history of Israel with pointed emphasis on the fact that just as the Jews' ancestors had repeatedly rejected the messengers of God in Old Testament times, so also they had recently rejected His supreme messenger, Jesus Christ the Righteous One. The sermon also stresses the progressive nature of divine revelation — God reveals Himself in different places in a variety of ways — so that it was wrong for the Jews to regard the Temple as the be-all and end-all of true religion.

According to the account of Jesus' trial the Romans reserved the right of capital punishment. But the Roman governors spent most of their time in Caesarea on the Mediterranean seacoast. The stoning of Stephen may therefore have been an illegal action of a lynch mob, or a formal execution by the Sanhedrin overstepping its authority because of Pilate's absence. The method of stoning was first to ask the condemned for a confession in order that he might gain "a share in the world to come." He was then stripped. A witness against him pushed him face first off a ledge or platform twice the height of a man to the ground below. The victim was turned on his back. If he was not dead from the fall, a second witness dropped a stone on his chest. If death still had not occurred, others joined in dropping stones.[8] As Stephen was being stoned to death, he saw Jesus standing at the Father's right hand to greet him.

Stephen's martyrdom triggered a general persecution of Christians by unbelieving Jews. Spearheading the persecution was Saul, from Tarsus, a city in Asia Minor. His other name was Paul. Saul and Paul were *not* pre- and post-conversion names respectively. Saul is simply the Hebrew name and Paul the similar-sounding, common Roman *cognomen* (family name) simultaneously borne by the same individual.[9]

The scattering of Christians through persecution resulted in

---

[8]See the Babylonian Talmud, *Sanhedrin* 6.1-4, quoted in C. K. Barrett, *The New Testament Background,* pp. 171, 172.

[9]As a Roman citizen Paul must also have had a *praenomen* and a *nomen gentile,* but they have not survived.

widespread evangelism, such as that in Samaria by Philip, another preaching "deacon" like Stephen. *Read Acts 8:1b-40.*

The professed conversion of Simon the sorcerer was probably unreal, for he wanted to retain his lucrative influence over the people by buying with money the ability to bestow the Holy Spirit so that he in turn could demand money for doing so. Early Christian tradition traces the heretical Gnostic movement within Christendom to Simon Magus, as he was called.

The Holy Spirit did not come upon the Samaritan believers until Peter and John prayed and laid their hands upon them as a sign of solidarity between Jewish and Samaritan believers. The old antipathy was breaking down within the Christian community. The delay in the gift of the Spirit enabled the apostolic representatives of the dominant Jewish Christian group to see for themselves that God had accepted the Samaritans, as shown by their reception of the Spirit in the apostles' presence.

The story of the Ethiopian eunuch foreshadows the Gentile missions of Paul. The eunuch had been attending one of the Jewish religious festivals in Jerusalem. He was therefore at least a God-fearer, if not a full proselyte. Eunuchs lacked religious privileges in Judaism according to Deuteronomy 23:1, but the law may have been relaxed (compare Isaiah 56:3 ff.); or "eunuch" in Acts may be an official title, not a literal description. It was customary for lone travelers such as Philip to attach themselves to caravans such as the eunuch's. Reading aloud (as the eunuch was doing) was customary in ancient times even for private study.

We are brought back to Saul's persecution of "the Way" (the first name for the Christian movement because of its distinctive mode of belief and conduct) and then to Saul's conversion. *Read Acts 9:1-31.* When Jesus said to Saul, "I am Jesus, whom you are persecuting," He implied a union between Himself in heaven and His persecuted disciples on earth. The union between Christ and the believer became a vital part of Paul's theological teaching. According to 9:7 Paul's companions heard the voice of Jesus. According to a duplicate account in 22:9 they did not. But the Greek constructions in the two passages are different and may possibly mean that Paul's companions heard the sound of Jesus' voice, but did not understand the words. Alternatively, the companions of Paul heard *his* voice (9:7), but not that of Jesus (22:9).

A preaching mission in Damascus and the neighboring Arabian area (see Galatians 1:17, 18) followed Paul's conversion. Some have supposed that the stay in Arabia included a period of meditation and reception of divine revelation, but the Biblical

GATEWAY TO STRAIGHT STREET IN DAMASCUS. *While enroute here to arrest believers Paul was converted. After his conversion Paul began his preaching mission in this city.*

texts do not so indicate. Barnabas then introduced Paul to the Jerusalem church. Galatians 1:22 makes clear, however, that Paul remained unknown by face in the larger Judean area outside Jerusalem.

Paul's Background

Paul was born a Roman citizen in Tarsus in southeastern Asia Minor. See the map on page 229. How his father had obtained Roman citizenship — whether through purchase, service to the state, or some other means — we do not know. But Roman citizenship gave legal privileges and protection which served Paul well in his missionary endeavors. The father of Paul was a Pharisee (Acts 23:6)[10] who reared his son according to strict Judaism (Philippians 3:5, 6). Paul spent most of his young manhood in Jerusalem, where he studied under the famous rabbi Gamaliel (Acts 22:3). We do not know whether Paul ever saw Jesus in

---

[10]"Son of Pharisees [plural]" in Acts 23:6 implies that Paul's forebears were Pharisees even farther back than his immediate father.

person or whether he was ever married. He does not mention a wife in his epistles; but since bachelorhood was rare among Jews, we may surmise that he had been married and that his wife had died.

Read Acts 9:32—11:18. The purpose of Luke in narrating Peter's miraculous healing of Aeneas and raising of Tabitha (or Dorcas) is to show God's presence with Peter during the very period he preached to Gentiles and accepted them into the Church, actions for which narrow-minded Jewish Christians later censured him. The fact that Peter lodged with a tanner named Simon shows he had already shed some of his Judaistic scruples, for tanners were ceremonially unclean through continual contact with dead animals and were therefore to be avoided. But it took a vision to convince Peter that contact with *Gentiles* was permissible. He saw a sheet, perhaps suggested by an awning under which Peter was taking a midday nap on the rooftop. The sheet was full of ceremonially impure creatures. Then came the command of God to kill and eat, an indication that the Mosaic dietary restrictions, and indeed all other ceremonial restrictions, were now out-of-date. Finally persuaded, Peter went to preach to the Gentiles in the house of Cornelius, a Roman centurion and God-fearer.

Peter's Miracles and Vision

Peter's sermon to the household of Cornelius is C. H. Dodd's prime example of the *kerygma* (see page 73). Appropriately for the Gentile audience, the sermon sounds the new note of universality. "*Everyone* who believes in him" — the Gospel is not for Jews alone; it is for everyone! In contrast to what happened in Samaria, an apostle was already present as witness. God therefore gave His Spirit to the Gentiles immediately upon their exercise of faith, even before Peter finished preaching and before baptism or laying on of hands could be administered. In this way God dramatically demonstrated His acceptance of Gentile believers into the Church on equal terms with Jewish and Samaritan believers. Peter was later able to use God's sudden action to defend himself against parochially minded Jewish Christians in Jerusalem who criticized his going to the Gentiles. It took much longer for the Church to realize the far-reaching implications that the Mosaic law was repealed in its entirety (although many of its moral precepts were repromulgated for Christians), that the synagogues and the Temple were no longer required places for worship, and that Gentile converts did not need to be circumcised. But the incident in Cornelius' house marked a significant step in the separation of Christianity from Judaism.

Gentile Salvation in Cornelius' House

Luke now traces the spread of the Gospel as far as Antioch in Syria. He wishes to introduce Antioch as the future base for

To Antioch

227

Paul's missionary journeys, to show how Paul became associated with the church there, and to establish the link between the churches in Antioch and Jerusalem. Jerusalem was interested enough in Antioch to send Barnabas; Antioch was concerned enough to send aid to Jerusalem when famine struck. The name "Christians," first attached to believers by unbelievers in Antioch, was derisive. It also showed that the Church was gradually being recognized as something more than a Jewish sect — as a movement distinct from Judaism. By their holy and gracious living Christians eventually turned the name into a term of respect and admiration. *Read Acts 11:19—12:25.*

**Persecution by
Herod Agrippa I**

The Herod who figures in this passage is Herod Agrippa I, grandson of Herod the Great. Posing as a champion of Judaism, he martyred James the apostle and brother of John and imprisoned Peter. The first century Jewish historian Josephus confirms Luke's account of the death of Herod Agrippa from a disease which sounds like intestinal cancer.[11] The death of Herod Agrippa occurred about A.D. 44, so that the whole account represents a chronological stepping-back from the famine-relief visit (c. A.D. 46; 11:27-30).

For further discussion:

See the discussion questions and suggested collateral reading at the close of the next chapter, pages 253, 254.

---

[11]Josephus, *Antiquities* XIX. v. 1, and viii. 2.

MAP OF PAUL'S FIRST MISSIONARY JOURNEY

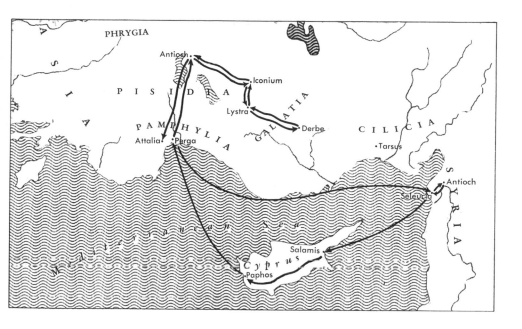

MAP OF PAUL'S SECOND MISSIONARY JOURNEY

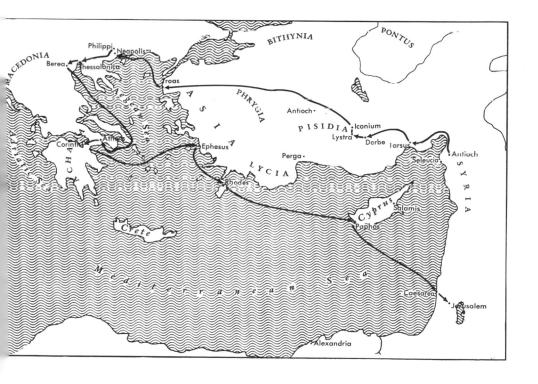

MAP OF PAUL'S THIRD MISSIONARY JOURNEY

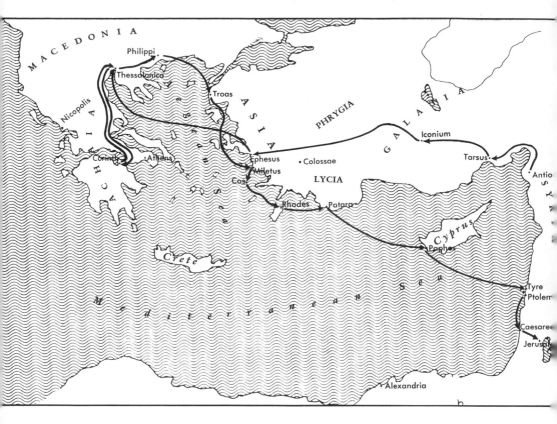

MAP OF PAUL'S JOURNEY TO ROME

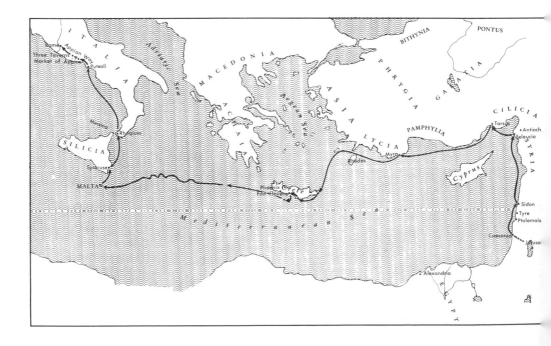

CHAPTER 13

The Acts of the Spirit of Christ Far
and Wide Through the Apostle Paul

Paul's First
Missionary
Journey

Acts 13 begins the narrative of Paul's extensive missionary endeavors. As a skillful author Luke has prepared his readers by describing the spread of the Gospel through Stephen's preaching to Hellenistic Jews in Jerusalem, the scattering of Christians through persecution with resultant expansion of the Christian witness, Philip's evangelizing Samaria and converting the Ethiopian eunuch, Saul's (Paul's) preaching in Damascus and to Hellenists in Jerusalem, Peter's going to Lydda and Joppa and to Caesarea where he converted a houseful of Gentiles, and the spread of Christianity to Antioch in Syria. Also, Luke has already presented Barnabas and Paul as partners, Barnabas having introduced Paul to the Jerusalem church and both of them having ministered in Antioch and traveled together to take famine relief from the church in Antioch to the church in Jerusalem. And finally, the contrast between the death of Herod Agrippa I, who opposed Christianity, and the successful spread of the Gospel sets the stage for Paul's wide-ranging missionary-evangelistic journeys.

Syrian Antioch

Read Acts 13, 14, following the journey on the map (page 229). Luke attributes the sending of Barnabas and Saul both to the church at Antioch and to the Holy Spirit, who inspired the church to send them. The laying on of hands was not formal ordination (Barnabas and Saul had been preaching for a long time), but an indication that the church supported their mission.

Cyprus;
Elymas and
Sergius Paulus

It was natural for Barnabas and Paul to go first to the island of Cyprus, because it was Barnabas' native land. Paul took the initiative when the Jewish magician Elymas (Bar-Jesus) tried to influence the Roman proconsul Sergius Paulus away from the Gospel (doubtless because the magician could see that his services would no longer be sought if Sergius Paulus embraced Christianity). From this point onward Luke puts the name

231

A Summary of the Main Stopping Places and Even

A.D.		
30		Jesus died and rose.
34		Paul was converted, preached in Damascus and Arabia for three years, and escaped a Jewish plot by being let down in a basket through an opening in the wall at Damascus.
		Barnabas introduced Paul to the church in Jerusalem.
		Paul returned to Tarsus.
		Barnabas brought Paul to Antioch in Syria.
47		Barnabas and Paul took famine relief to Jerusalem.

I. THE FIRST MISSIONARY JOURNEY

Antioch in Syria

Cyprus — Bar-Jesus (Elymas) was blinded and the proconsul Sergius Paulus converted.

Perga in Pamphylia — John Mark returned.

Antioch of Pisidia — Paul preached in the synagogue.

Iconium

Lystra — Paul healed a cripple; Barnabas and Paul were worshiped as Zeus and Hermes respectively; Paul was stoned.

Derbe

Lystra

Iconium

Antioch of Pisidia

Perga in Pamphylia

49   GALATIANS (under early date of South Galatian theory)   Antioch in Syria

The Jerusalem Council (Acts 15)

50-51

II. THE SECOND MISSIONARY JOURNEY

(Paul and Barnabas disagreed over whether to take John Mark; Paul took Silas.)

Antioch in Syria

Derbe

Lystra — Paul took Timothy.

Iconium

Antioch of Pisidia

} = Phrygia and South Galatia

Troas — Paul saw the man of Macedonia in a vision.

Philippi — Lydia was converted, a demon-possessed girl fortune teller delivered; Paul and Silas were jailed; a midnight earthquake occurred; the jailer was converted.

Thessalonica — a Jewish-inspired mob assaulted the house of Jason, where Paul was staying.

Beroea — The Beroeans "searched the [Old Testament] scriptures" to check Paul's message.

Athens — Paul was alone; he preached his Areopagus (Mars' Hill) sermon; Timothy and Silas rejoined Paul, but Paul sent Timothy back to Thessalonica and Silas elsewhere.

Corinth — Paul made tents with Priscilla and Aquila; Timothy and Silas rejoined Paul; Paul moved his preaching from the synagogue to the house of Titius Justus; Crispus the synagogue ruler was converted; Jesus in a vision told Paul

1 and 2 THESSALONIANS

(All dates are approximate.)

A.D.			

to stay; the Roman governor Gallio refused to condemn Paul for preaching; Paul spent one and a half years in Corinth.

Cenchreae — Paul shaved his head.

Ephesus — Priscilla and Aquila accompanied Paul this far, but stayed in Ephesus.

Caesarea

Jerusalem

Antioch in Syria

III. THE THIRD MISSIONARY JOURNEY

Antioch in Syria

Galatia and Phrygia (Derbe, Lystra, Iconium, Antioch of Pisidia)

Ephesus — disciples of John the Baptist received the Spirit; Paul preached in the school of Tyrannus; the seven sons of Sceva (unbelieving Jews) tried to use Jesus' name in exorcising demons; converts burned their books of magic; Demetrius led the silversmiths to riot in behalf of the goddess Artemis (Diana); Paul spent two years and three months in Ephesus.

1 CORINTHIANS

Macedonia (Philippi, Thessalonica, Beroea)

Greece, or Achaia (Athens and Corinth) — Jews plotted to kill Paul on a voyage to Palestine.

2 CORINTHIANS
ROMANS

Macedonia

Troas — Eutychus fell out of a window during Paul's sermon.

Miletus — Paul bade farewell to the Ephesian elders.

Tyre — Paul was warned not to go to Jerusalem.

Caesarea — Paul stayed in the house of Philip; Agabus warned Paul with a symbolic girdle about what would happen in Jerusalem.

56

Jerusalem — Paul reported to the church; involved himself in a Jewish vow to show he was not against the Mosaic law; was seized in the Temple; was rescued by Roman soldiers; spoke to the Jews from the castle stairway; spoke to the Sanhedrin; Jews plotted to ambush Paul; Claudius Lysias sent Paul to Felix in Caesarea.

Paul stood trial before Felix, Festus, and Agrippa in Caesarea, then appealed his case to Caesar.

IV. THE JOURNEY TO ROME

Caesarea

Crete — Paul's advice not to sail was rejected.

59

Storm on the Mediterranean Sea.

Malta (Melita) — shipwreck occurred; Paul shook a viper off his hand and suffered no ill effects.

PHILEMON
COLOSSIANS
EPHESIANS
PHILIPPIANS

Rome — Paul rented a house-prison; preached to Jews and Gentiles; and for two years awaited trial before Nero.

61

1 TIMOTHY
TITUS

Release from prison, further traveling.

2 TIMOTHY

Reimprisonment

64

Martyrdom

Paul before Barnabas. The lone exception occurs in a Jerusalem context at 15:12, where Luke goes back to the order "Barnabas and Paul" because in the minds of the Jerusalem Christians Barnabas was still the senior Christian and spiritual father of Paul. Luke calls Saul by the name "Paul" for the first time in 13:9. His mission to Gentiles made his Greek name more appropriate than his Semitic name.

Perga

At Perga in Pamphylia John Mark, cousin of Barnabas and helper to both Paul and Barnabas, turned back. We do not know why. Suggestions range from homesickness to fear. Whatever the reason, Paul considered it invalid, Barnabas at least excusable.

The Pauline Pattern

Paul adopted the strategy of preaching in major cities. From these centers the Gospel reverberated throughout the surrounding villages and countryside. Paul also adopted the pattern of preaching first in the Jewish synagogue (if there was one) wherever he went. He had a deep concern for his fellow Jews. As the old covenant people they had a right to hear the Gospel first. And the synagogue was the best place to find a ready-made audience, since it was a custom in the synagogues to invite qualified visitors, such as Paul, to speak. Furthermore, synagogue audiences contained large numbers of Gentile proselytes and God-fearers as well as Jews. In fact, Paul usually en-

FORUM OF THE CITY OF SALAMIS *which was an important seaport on the island of Cyprus in the days of Paul.*

PISIDIAN ANTIOCH *was supplied water through this ancient aqueduct.*

joyed his greatest success among these Gentiles, for their interest in Judaism had prepared them for his message. As a result, the unbelieving Jews regarded Paul as a poacher who seduced Gentiles from Judaism to Christianity by offering them salvation on easier terms than observance of the Mosaic law.

Paul's sermon in the synagogue at Antioch of Pisidia[1] reviewed the history of Israel to proclaim the good news that Old Testament history and prophecy had found their fulfillment in Jesus Christ. Paul also struck the note of justification by faith in Christ apart from meritorious obedience to the Mosaic law. This becomes a familiar theme in his epistles. When the Jews came to their synagogue the next Sabbath, they found crowds of Gentiles occupying the pews and eagerly awaiting another sermon from Paul. Angered, the Jews instigated persecution, and Paul and Barnabas left after ministering briefly to the Gentiles. This, too, became a pattern: preaching in the synagogue — success among the Gentile proselytes and God-fearers — Jewish hostility — withdrawal from the synagogue — further successful ministry to the Gentiles — persecution — flight.

Pisidian Antioch

---

[1]This Antioch, smaller and less important than Antioch in Syria, was near the border of Pisidia, but not quite *in* Pisidia. It nevertheless became known as Pisidian Antioch.

235

Persecution almost always came from Jewish, not Roman, sources during this early period. The Roman government still regarded Christianity as a branch of Judaism and therefore a *religio licita* (legal religion). The Roman policy was to grant freedom to all existing religions in the empire, but to ban new religions for fear of the social turmoil caused by their invasion. Only at a later date, when the Romans realized that Christianity was distinct from Judaism, did they ban Christianity as a *religio illicita*.

The people in Lystra mistook Barnabas and Paul for the Greek gods Zeus and Hermes respectively. When Paul and Barnabas refused worship, the adverse reaction of the fickle mob led to Paul's stoning and narrow escape from death. On the return trip from Derbe through Lystra, Iconium, and Antioch of Pisidia, Paul and Barnabas avoided open preaching (they had just recently been driven out of those cities) and concentrated on strengthening the believers and organizing the churches by the appointment of elders to take charge. In this way the churches were patterned after synagogues, each of which had a "Board of Elders." On the way back through Perga, Paul and Barnabas preached there, for apparently they had passed through very quickly the first time.

In their report to the home church in Syrian Antioch, Paul and Barnabas emphasized the successful evangelization of Gentiles. This sets the stage for the dispute in Acts 15 over the status of Gentile believers. Up till now Luke has shown the

THE SITE OF DERBE *today is this medium-sized habitation mound.*

unfolding divine purpose to give the Gospel to Gentiles as well as to Jews. Acts 15 shows how the problem of Gentile believers led to the separation of Christianity from Judaism as a new and separate religion against the efforts of the Judaizers. Judaizers were Jewish Christians (and their Gentile followers) who taught that Gentile believers had to be circumcised and promise to keep the Mosaic law, that is, come into the Church in the same way Gentile proselytes came into Judaism. Paul and Barnabas disagreed. The church in Antioch referred the problem to the church in Jerusalem. *Read Acts 15:1-35.*

Supported by the leaders Peter and James the half brother of Jesus, the advice of the influential mother church in Jerusalem clearly favored freedom from the Mosaic law for Gentile believers, but urged Gentiles to avoid practices which would unnecessarily offend Jews: eating meat which had been dedicated to an idol before sale; eating meat from an animal which had been strangled; eating meat that still contained the animal's blood; "fornication," or unchastity in general, but possibly here a technical term for incest (marrying relatives closer than allowed in Leviticus 18). The Jerusalem church sent back two of their own number, Judas (Barsabbas) and Silas, with Paul and Barnabas to certify to the Christians at Antioch that Paul and Barnabas were not bringing a false report in their own favor. For the crucial nature of the Judaizing controversy, see further the discussion of Galatians, pages 259 f.

The Jerusalem Council

Read Acts 15:36—18:22, following the movement on the map (page 229). Despite Paul's refusal to take John Mark again and the resultant separation of Paul from Barnabas, Mark later appears as a companion of Paul in Rome (Colossians 4:10; Philemon 24) and becomes the subject of favorable comment by Paul (2 Timothy 4:11).

Paul's Second Missionary Journey

Silas, the companion Paul did take, had come from the Jerusalem church. It was advantageous for Paul to have someone from Jerusalem who could refute the Judaizers in their claim that they resented the mother church. In the story of the imprisonment of Paul and Silas at Philippi, Silas also appears to have been a Roman citizen.

Silas

At Lystra Paul gained another companion, Timothy. In the eyes of Gentiles Timothy was a Jew because his Jewish mother had reared him in Judaism. In Jewish eyes Timothy's being the uncircumcised son of a Gentile father made him a Gentile. To regularize Timothy's status and to avoid unnecessary offense to Jews, whom he wished to evangelize, Paul had Timothy circumcised. But lest the impression be left that Paul was backing down in the Judaizing controversy, Luke emphasizes that Paul

Timothy

PHILIPPI, *a general view of the theater which dates back to the fourth century* B.C.

delivered the anti-Judaistic decision of the Jerusalem Council wherever he went.

The Man of Macedonia

Some identify the man of Macedonia in Paul's vision with Luke. But that is unlikely since Luke writes "we" in narrating the departure from Troas for Macedonia; yet the man of Macedonia calls from the other side of the Dardanelles, "Come over. . . ."

Philippi

Philippi was a city of the first of the four administrative districts of Macedonia. Antony and Octavian (later known as Augustus) settled a number of Roman army veterans in Philippi and made the city a Roman colony after their victory in 42 B.C. over Brutus and Cassius, the assassins of Julius Caesar. Octavian settled more colonists there after defeating Antony and Cleopatra at Actium (31 B.C.). The Jews in the city had only a place of prayer beside the river, apparently because their scant population did not provide the necessary ten adult men required for the establishing of a synagogue.[2]

In Philippi the charge by the masters of the fortune-telling slave girl appealed to anti-Semitic prejudice by emphasizing that Paul and Silas were Jews and falsely charged them of advo-

238   [2]Alternatively, "place of prayer" is synonymous with "synagogue."

cating practices contrary to Roman law and custom. Thus they were thrown in prison.

THE ACTS
OF THE
SPIRIT OF
CHRIST FAR
AND WIDE
THROUGH THE
APOSTLE PAUL

The Jailer

The jailer was responsible on pain of death to produce his prisoners at any time. That is the reason for his near suicide when he thought the prisoners had escaped as a result of the earthquake. The superstitious prisoners were probably awed by the strangely joyful singing of Paul and Silas in prison and by the earthquake, and so were easily persuaded by Paul and Silas not to escape. It was quite legitimate for the jailer to entertain Paul and Silas in his house, so long as he presented them when required. The baptism of the jailer's household raises the possibility of infant baptism. Against it is the argument that belief in Christ was required on the part of the household members before they were baptized.

Since a "we"-section ends after the Philippi-narrative and resumes with the return of Paul to Philippi at a later date, Luke must have stayed in Philippi, perhaps as pastor and evangelist.

The unbelieving Jews at Thessalonica were especially hostile. They not only drove Paul from their own city, but also traveled to Beroea (or Berea) to repeat their action. In Athens those who heard Paul thought that Jesus and "resurrection" were

ATHENS *with a general view of the Propylea, the entrance to the Acropolis.*

THE PARTHENON *on the Acropolis at Athens.*

two gods unfamiliar to them.[3] Paul had to present his teaching
before the Areopagus, the Athenian city council, which licensed
teachers. During that period the council met on Mars' Hill only
in cases of homicide, so that "Paul's Sermon on Mars' Hill" is
probably a misnomer. Some Athenians mocked the idea of a
resurrection of the dead. The best hope of the Greeks was immortality of the soul, and they were largely sceptical even of that.
It is questionable whether they would have wanted to believe
in resurrection of the body, for to them the body encumbered
the soul.[4] But in Biblical thought God created the body as well
as the soul. They belong together — therefore the sacredness of
the body and its coming resurrection.

Corinth;
Priscilla and
Aquila

    Corinth was a port city noted for debauchery. "To act like a
Corinthian" meant to practice immorality. "Corinthian girl" was
synonymous with "harlot." Short of funds when he arrived in
Corinth, Paul made tents with fellow Jews Priscilla and Aquila.
Since Luke does not relate their conversion, they may already

    [3]They may have confused the name Jesus with the similar-sounding Greek
word for "healing," and thus understood Paul to refer to related gods of healing
and resurrection.
    [4]See J. B. Skemp, *The Greeks and the Gospel* (London: Carey Kingsgate,
1964), pp. 78-89, for a well-balanced discussion of Greek concepts.

240

have been Christians. Around A.D. 49 or 50 the emperor Claudius had expelled them and the other Jews from Rome because of rioting in the Jewish colony over a "Chrestus," probably intra-Jewish strife over Christian preaching of "Christus" (Latin for Christ, but misspelled "Chrestus").[5]

In Corinth the decision of Gallio to allow Christian evangelism was important. Adverse decisions by civic magistrates had force only in the cities where they were made. But an adverse decision by a provincial governor, such as Gallio, would have banned the Christian witness throughout a whole province and, worse yet, established a precedent to be followed by other provincial governors throughout the empire. The Jews

THE ACTS
OF THE
SPIRIT OF
CHRIST FAR
AND WIDE
THROUGH THE
APOSTLE PAUL

Gallio

THE TEMPLE OF APOLLO *at Corinth, of the Doric order of architecture, was constructed about the mid-fifth century* B.C.

tried to persuade Gallio that Christianity was contrary to Judaism, and thus a new and therefore illegal religion. Gallio, however, dismissed the case as an intra-Jewish dispute. As the Jews

[5]Suetonius, *Claudius* xxv. 4, quoted in C. K. Barrett, *The New Testament Background,* pp. 14, 15. Suetonius seemed to think that Chrestus himself instigated the rioting. But writing seventy years after the event, he probably mistook preaching *about* Christ for preaching (or rabble-rousing) *by* Christ. Chrestus (Latin) or Chrēstos (Greek) was a very common name for slaves, meaning "useful," so that it is easy to account for the misspelling of Christus.

left the tribunal, the crowd of Gentile bystanders took advantage of Gallio's snub to the Jews by beating up the synagogue ruler Sosthenes in an anti-Semitic demonstration.[6] Gallio turned a blind eye. According to a Latin inscription found at Delphi in Greece, Gallio's proconsulship extended from about A.D. 51 to 53. Paul shaved his head in Cenchreae (or Cenchrea) just before his return trip to signify the end of a Nazirite vow he apparently had imposed on himself in Corinth. See Numbers 6: 1-21.

Paul's Third Missionary Journey

Read Acts 18:23–19:41, following the movements on the map (page 230). Paul's third missionary tour began again from Antioch in Syria. As on the second journey, Paul first of all revisited Galatia and Phrygia, regions where Derbe, Lystra, Iconium, and Pisidian Antioch were located.

Apollos

To prepare readers for Paul's ministry in Ephesus, Luke inserts a paragraph about the preaching of Apollos at Ephesus (18:24-28). This eloquent Alexandrian Jew preached about Jesus, but knew only the baptism of John the Baptist, the baptism of repentance. In other words, Apollos did not baptize his converts in the name of Jesus. After Priscilla and Aquila informed Apollos concerning Christian doctrine and practice, he went to Achaia (Greece).

Ephesus

Paul finally fulfilled his longtime desire to evangelize the important city of Ephesus. There he found some disciples who, like Apollos, knew only the baptism of John. Probably they were converts of Apollos. Nor did these disciples know that God had been giving the Holy Spirit to all believers since the Day of Pentecost. Having explained the Gospel more fully, Paul rebaptized these disciples. God in turn bestowed the Holy Spirit on them with the evidence of speaking in tongues. It is notable that the four occasions in Acts when the Holy Spirit was bestowed in spectacular manner had to do with the entrance of different groups into the Church: the original Jewish believers (chapter 2), the Samaritans (chapter 8), the Gentiles (chapter 10), the half taught disciples in Ephesus (chapter 19). God indicated His approval of each group by special manifestation of His Spirit.

According to an early tradition Paul used the school of Tyrannus from 11:00 A.M. till 4:00 P.M. Paul may have spent his mornings making tents, his afternoons teaching people interested enough in the Gospel to forego their midday siestas.

The Jewish exorcist Sceva was "high priest" (19:14) only by his own claim. Jews were highly regarded as exorcists because it

---

[6]Others think that the Jews beat up their own leader for lack of forcefulness in charging Paul. This seems doubtful.

ARCADIAN WAY *of Ephesus led from the city to the harbor. The street was lined with columns, shops, and public buildings.*

was thought that they alone could correctly pronounce the potent name Yahweh, and success in casting out demons supposedly depended largely on the correct pronunciation of the proper formulae. Sceva's seven sons, apprentices in the exorcising trade, tried to use the name "Jesus," but found the results somewhat disconcerting, for true Christian exorcism did not depend on recitation of magical names. When the converts in Ephesus burned their books of magic, they divulged the secret formulae. Such formulae then became useless to the pagans, who believed that secrecy was also necessary to the effectiveness of magical incantations.[7]

In the account of Demetrius and the silversmiths, Artemis was a local fertility goddess who had become identified with the Greek goddess Artemis (Roman name: Diana). Her image in the Ephesian temple was apparently a meteorite which the Ephesians thought resembled a many-breasted female. The temple itself, one of the seven wonders of the ancient world, had a floor area of almost 10,000 square feet. When the rioting mob filled the amphitheater, which accommodated about 25,000

Riot

[7]Compare the Paris Magical Papyrus, quoted in C. K. Barrett, *The New Testament Background*, pp. 31-35.

people, the non-Christian Jews feared they would suffer by association with the Christians because the Jews also preached against idolatry. They therefore put up a man named Alexander to tell the mob that the Jews had nothing to do with the Christians. But Alexander's voice was no match for the uproarious crowd. Only when the city clerk calmed them and warned that civil disturbance might lead to loss of civic liberties did the assembly disperse.

To Jerusalem

Read Acts 20:1—21:16 in conjunction with the map (page 230). After two years and three months in Ephesus, Paul traveled to Macedonia and Achaia, taking up an offering for the church in Jerusalem as he went. He intended to go to Rome after delivering the offering to Jerusalem. He went to Rome, but under circumstances different from those he had envisioned; for he went in chains as a prisoner. Meanwhile, he apparently planned to take a Jewish pilgrim ship from Greece to Palestine for the upcoming Passover festival. The Jews, however, plotted to do away with him during the voyage. Changing plans, he went back through Macedonia. On his way down the west coast of Asia Minor he bade farewell to the Ephesian elders, who met him at Miletus. As his journey toward Jerusalem progressed, repeated warnings came that he would be arrested and persecuted there. It is debatable whether the warnings were divinely intended to keep him from going to Jerusalem, whether he was wrong in insisting on the trip, and whether his participation in Jewish sacrifices after he arrived in Jerusalem was consistent with his theology.

ROMAN THEATER AT EPHESUS *where the riot recorded in Acts 20 occurred. Built in the first century* A.D., *the theater seated 25,000 people.*

THE ACTS
OF THE
SPIRIT OF
CHRIST FAR
AND WIDE
APOSTLE PAUL
THROUGH THE

SECTION OF THE INSCRIP-
TION *from Herod's temple
forbidding Gentiles to enter the inner court of the
temple.*

According to rumor Paul not only taught *Gentile* Christians that they were not obligated to keep the Old Testament law, but also encouraged *Jewish* believers not to circumcise their sons or keep the law. At the time Paul arrived in Jerusalem, four Jewish Christians had contracted ceremonial defilement during the period of a temporary Nazirite vow and were undergoing a seven day period of purification (Numbers 6:9-11). According to the Mosaic law these men were required to shave their heads on the seventh day and bring offerings on the eighth day before they could resume their Nazirite vow. Since the week of purification was soon to be completed, the elders of the Jerusalem church suggested that Paul join these men in the purificatory rites and pay the expenses of their offerings to demonstrate that he was not against the Mosaic law as such. Paul agreed.

Certain Jews from Asia Minor, however, had previously seen that with Paul in Jerusalem was a Gentile companion named Trophimus, an Ephesian. They mistakenly assumed that Paul had brought his Gentile companion into the Temple courts where only Jews were allowed. Gentiles were forbidden to enter the inner courts on pain of death, even for Roman citizens. The outcry of the Jews caused a riot, from which the soldiers of the Roman tribune Claudius Lysias rescued Paul. The fortress

Paul's Arrest in Jerusalem

245

of Antonia, into which Paul was taken, lay northwest of the Temple precincts. Roman soldiers garrisoned the citadel, and a double flight of stairs connected it with the outer court of the Temple. *Read Acts 21:17–23:35.*

Three years before this incident an Egyptian Jew appeared in Jerusalem claiming to be a prophet. He led a large group to the Mount of Olives and told them to wait until the walls of Jerusalem fell at his command. Then they would march into the city and overthrow the Roman garrison. The governor Felix sent troops, killed several of the Jews, and imprisoned others. However, the Egyptian Jew escaped. At first Claudius Lysias thought Paul might be that same imposter, on whom the Jews were now trying to take revenge for having duped them.

In his defense before the Jewish mob, Paul stressed what a good Jew he was and what a devout Jew Ananias, the Christian who had helped him in Damascus, was. He also emphasized the miraculous vision of Christ he had received on the road to Damascus. The Jews listened until Paul said that God had told him to preach to the Gentiles. Unable to tolerate pro-Gentilism, the Jews cried out for Paul's blood just as they had demanded the death of Jesus.

To Caesarea

To determine the reason for the riot, Claudius Lysias brought Paul before the Sanhedrin; but the session ended in confusion. When Paul's young nephew heard of a plot to ambush and kill Paul as he was being taken from place to place within the city, he informed Claudius Lysias. The tribune immediately sent Paul to Caesarea under cover of night with a large contingent of soldiers for protection. According to his letter to Governor Felix at Caesarea, Claudius Lysias had rescued Paul when he discovered that Paul was a Roman citizen. Actually, he had not discovered Paul's Roman citizenship until Paul was about to be scourged[8] for the purpose of extracting information from him, an illegal procedure against an uncondemned Roman citizen.

Roman Citizenship

The conversation between Paul and Claudius Lysias (22:27-29) reveals that Paul was a freeborn Roman citizen and that Claudius Lysias had purchased his own citizenship "for a large sum," which may have been a bribe. Paul's citizenship by birth was superior in status. The names of citizens were registered in Rome and in the place of residence. The citizens themselves possessed wax, wooden, or metal certificates with the names of witnesses. Execution was the penalty for false claim to citizenship. If a citizen was not carrying his certificate or if his certificate was suspected of forgery, the authorities might ask

---

[8]To be scourged was to be beaten with a *flagellum* (Latin), which consisted of leather thongs attached to a wooden handle and weighted with sharp bits of bone and metal. Frequently men died from the ordeal.

THIS ROMAN-BUILT AQUEDUCT *near Caesarea brought water into the city from the north.*

him to produce his witnesses. Perhaps that is one reason Paul, who traveled widely, did not frequently appeal to his Roman citizenship.[9]

A man named Tertullus acted as prosecutor for the Jews in pressing charges against Paul in Caesarea. His flattery of the governor Felix and promise of brevity were traditional ways to begin speeches. The charge against Paul was that he had disturbed the peace. Disturbing the peace was an elastically defined crime which tyrannical emperors used as a weapon of political terrorism. Almost anything could be put into this category. In his answer, Paul stated that he had nowhere agitated the people. In fact, he came to Jerusalem not in a spirit of contention, but with an offering to aid Jews who resided in Jerusalem. He especially noted the fact that the Jews from Asia Minor who provoked the riot and originally accused him had not appeared in court against him.

Then Paul argued that Christianity was not antagonistic to Judaism, but a fulfillment of Judaism. Before the Sanhedrin in Jerusalem the only "crime" with which he could be charged was his declaration of belief in the resurrection. Even the Pharisaical faction of the Sanhedrin supported Paul's position, although they of course did not believe in the resurrection *of Jesus* as did Paul. Throughout his apologies in the last part of Acts, Paul emphasizes the resurrection as a crucial point in Christian belief and as common ground between Christianity and orthodox Juda-

Before Felix

[9]See further H. J. Cadbury, *The Book of Acts in History* (New York: Harper, 1955), pp. 67 ff.; A. N. Sherwin-White, *Roman Society and Roman Law in the New Testament* (Oxford: Clarendon, 1963), pp. 144-171.

247

ism (although the Sadducees denied the doctrine). See 24:15; 26:8, 22, 23. Putting off an immediate decision concerning Paul, Felix kept him in custody but heard him again in private audience with Drusilla. *Read Acts 24.*

Before Felix and Drusilla

Drusilla was a girl bride not yet twenty years old. As a small child she had been betrothed to a crown prince in Asia Minor; but the marriage did not take place because the prince refused to embrace Judaism. Later, Drusilla married the king of a petty state in Syria. When she was sixteen, however, Felix, with the help of a magician from Cyprus, lured her from her husband to become his third wife. Very understandably, then, when Paul reasoned with Felix and Drusilla about righteousness, self-control, and the future judgment, Felix, who had expected an abstract discussion of Christianity, thought the sermon uncomfortably pointed and personal. He dismissed Paul from their presence, but still kept him in custody, hoping that Paul would offer him a bribe to be freed. But hope for a bribe from Paul was not the only factor which prevented Felix from releasing the apostle, although he was convinced of Paul's innocence. His offending the Jews on a number of previous occasions and a change of administration in the central government at Rome had made the political position of Felix as governor rather precarious. He dared not offend the Jews again by releasing Paul.

Before Festus

A man named Festus succeeded Felix in the governorship. As his first act he went to Jerusalem to make acquaintance with the leading Jews, the members of the Sanhedrin. The Sanhedrin immediately renewed charges against Paul before the new governor and asked Festus to bring Paul to Jerusalem for trial. Perhaps they planned to assassinate Paul en route as they had plotted before. Since Festus did not intend to stay very long in Jerusalem, he told the Jews to send a delegation of accusers to Caesarea. But Festus did not care whether the trial took place in Caesarea or in Jerusalem, and he wanted to establish amicable relations with the Jews. Upon his return to Caesarea, therefore, he suggested to Paul that the trial be held in Jerusalem.

But Paul may have feared assassination en route. Or perhaps he realized that the Sanhedrin might convince Festus, a novice in Jewish affairs, that they should have jurisdiction over Paul. They could support their claim by arguing that Paul was supposed to have committed sacrilege against the Temple, the kind of crime over which the Romans frequently gave jurisdiction to the Jews. Paul could easily guess the verdict should Festus turn him over to the Sanhedrin for trial. Whatever his reasoning, Paul exercised his right as a Roman citizen in appealing to Caesar in Rome, the highest court. *Read Acts 25, 26.*

THE ACTS
OF THE
SPIRIT OF
CHRIST FAR
AND WIDE
THROUGH THE
APOSTLE PAUL

Herod Agrippa II was a great-grandson of Herod the Great, a brother of Drusilla (the wife of the ex-governor Felix), and the king of a small area near Lebanon. His younger sister Bernice was living with him at Caesarea Philippi during this time. While Agrippa was paying Festus an official visit of welcome to his new governorship, Festus decided to take advantage of the situation by having Agrippa, an expert in Jewish affairs, hear Paul and help draw up a list of charges against him. Festus would send these along when Paul went to appear before Caesar.

To prove the reality of his transforming vision on the Damascus road, Paul stressed his part in the persecution of Christians. He also underscored the fact that he had once been a Pharisee who believed in the resurrection. Now he was preposterously being charged for believing in and preaching the fulfillment in Jesus Christ of the very doctrine he had always believed as a Pharisee. And of all people, those accusing him were the Jews, who, except for the Sadducees, likewise believed in the resurrection. Festus, the host, rudely interrupted Paul's speech with the charge that he had gone berserk through excessive study. But Paul appealed to Agrippa, the guest, by noting that the things about Jesus were matters of public knowledge and by asking Agrippa whether or not he believed in Messianic prophecy.

Paul's appeal embarrassed Agrippa. He could hardly say he agreed with Paul after his host Festus had just charged Paul with insanity. Neither could he say that he did not believe in the prophets without damaging his reputation for orthodoxy among the Jews. Wryly, therefore, he indicated that more persuasion than this would be required to make him a Christian. The purpose of Luke in narrating this episode is to show that the expert Jewish opinion of Agrippa agreed with the Roman opinion of Felix and Festus that Paul was not guilty of any real crime.

Read Acts 27, 28, following the journey of Paul from Caesarea to Rome on the map (page 230). The hoisting up of the boat during the storm (27:15-17) refers to the hauling aboard of a small lifeboat, which in good weather was towed behind the large ship. The sailors passed cables underneath and around the ship and tightened them to prevent the timbers from breaking apart under the leverage of the mast. The reference to lowering the gear probably means that they took down the top sails, which were used only in fair weather. But the storm sails were still set. Next the cargo was jettisoned, and finally all of the spare gear. Throughout the eleven dreary days and nights the ship was doubtless leaking badly. The only hope lay in making for shore, but the sailors did not know in what direction to steer the ship. The storm clouds had blotted out the sun and stars, and in those days they had no compasses. Despair gripped

APPIAN WAY, *south of Rome.*

those on board. Seasickness kept them from eating. But in the end God's purpose for Paul resulted in the safety of all.

In Rome

To the Jewish leaders in Rome Paul emphasized that he was there purely in self-defense. He did not intend to accuse the Jewish nation or its leaders. The Roman Jews denied knowledge of Paul and any direct knowledge of the Christian movement, although they admitted having heard negative reports of its reputation. But it seems likely that news of Paul would have reached the Jews in Rome. And they surely had come into contact with Christians in Rome, for the church there was already strongly established. It would appear that the representatives of the non-Christian Jewish community in Rome were feigning ignorance. Later, on a prearranged day, a large number of Jews heard Paul explain the Gospel. Some believed, but the majority rejected. As usual Paul then turned his attention to evangelizing Gentiles.

The delay of at least two years in Paul's trial may have been due to one or more of several factors: (1) the necessity for accusers to come from Palestine; (2) the destruction in the shipwreck of the document drawn up by Festus concerning the accusations against Paul, with the consequent need for a duplicate to be sent from Caesarea; (3) the crowded nature of Nero's court calendar.

During the period of delay Paul enjoyed considerable freedom as a prisoner. Although chained to a Roman soldier and confined to the house which he rented, he could receive visitors and any other kind of attention from his friends. The reason for this laxity was that he was a Roman citizen against whom no charge had yet been proved. Paul took advantage of his semi-freedom to preach. Luke wants his readers to note the fact that even in Rome, the capital of the empire, the Gospel was not banned as being illegal. Thus Luke has traced the triumphant march of the Gospel from Jerusalem to Rome.

A SUMMARY OUTLINE OF THE BOOK OF ACTS

Theme: the irresistible advance of the Gospel from Jerusalem to Rome

I. THE ACTS OF THE SPIRIT OF CHRIST IN AND AROUND JERUSALEM (1:1—12:25)
   A. In Jerusalem (1:1-8:3)
      1. The postresurrection ministry and ascension of Jesus (1:1-11)
      2. The replacement of Judas Iscariot with Matthias (1:12-26)
      3. The Day of Pentecost: the outpouring of the Holy Spirit, speaking in tongues, Peter's sermon, mass conversion, and Christian fellowship (2:1-47)

COLOSSEUM OF ROME *with an exterior view (above) and an interior view (below). It was completed under the rule of Titus.*

4. The healing of the lame man and Peter's sermon (3:1-26)
5. The imprisonment and release of Peter and John (4:1-31)
6. The community of goods in the Jerusalem church and the death of Ananias and Sapphira (4:32—5:11)
7. Miracles, conversions, imprisonment of the apostles, and release (5:12-42)
8. The dispute over food rations and choice of the seven "deacons" (6:1-7)
9. The sermon and martyrdom of Stephen and general persecution following (6:8—8:3)

B. Around Jerusalem (mainly) (8:4-12:25)
1. Philip's evangelization of Samaria, the Samaritan reception of the Spirit, and the story of Simon the sorcerer (8:4-25)
2. Philip's conversion of the Ethiopian eunuch (8:26-40)
3. The conversion of Saul-Paul, his preaching in and escape from Damascus, return to Jerusalem, and flight to Tarsus (9:1-31)
4. Peter's healing of Aeneas and raising of Tabitha (9:32-43)
5. The salvation of Cornelius and his Gentile household, including Peter's vision of the sheet and sermon and Gentile reception of the Spirit (10:1—11:18)
6. The spread of the Gospel to Antioch in Syria (11:19-26)
7. The bringing of famine relief from Antioch to Jerusalem by Barnabas and Saul-Paul (11:27-30)
8. Herod Agrippa I's execution of James the apostle and imprisonment of Peter, Peter's miraculous release, and Herod's death (12:1-25)

II. THE ACTS OF THE SPIRIT OF CHRIST FAR AND WIDE THROUGH THE APOSTLE PAUL (13:1—28:31)

A. The first missionary journey (13:1—14:28)
1. The sending from Antioch in Syria (13:1-3)
2. Cyprus: the blinding of Elymas and conversion of Sergius Paulus (13:4-12)
3. Perga: the departure of John Mark (13:13)
4. Antioch of Pisidia: Paul's sermon in the synagogue (13:14-52)
5. Iconium, Lystra, and Derbe: the healing of a cripple, worship of Barnabas and Paul as Zeus and Hermes, and stoning of Paul at Lystra (14:1-18)
6. The return to Antioch in Syria, with preaching in Perga (14:19-28)

B. The Judaizing controversy (15:1-35)
1. Debate in Antioch in Syria (15:1, 2)
2. The Jerusalem Council: the decision for Gentile freedom from the Mosaic law (15:3-35)

C. The second missionary journey (15:36—18:21)
1. The dispute with Barnabas over John Mark and the departure from Antioch in Syria with Silas (15:36-41)
2. The journey through South Galatia: the selection of Timothy (16:1-5)
3. Troas: the vision of the man of Macedonia (16:5-10)
4. Philippi: the conversion of Lydia, deliverance of a demon-possessed girl who told fortunes, jailing of Paul and Silas, earthquake, and conversion of the jailer and his household (16:11-40)
5. Thessalonica: a Jewish assault on the house of Jason, Paul's host (17:1-9)
6. Beroea: the checking of Paul's message by the Old Testament (17:10-15)
7. Athens: Paul's sermon before the Aeropagus [more commonly, on Mars' Hill] (17:16-34)
8. Corinth: Paul's tentmaking with Aquila and Priscilla, the favorable decision of the Roman governor Gallio, and general success (18: 1-17)

9. Return to Antioch in Syria via Cenchreae (18:18-21)

D. The third missionary journey (18:22—21:16)

1. The journey through Galatia and Phrygia (18:22, 23)

2. The preparatory ministry of Apollos in Ephesus (18:24-28)

3. Ephesus: the Christian baptism of disciples of John the Baptist, successful evangelism, and the riot led by Demetrius and the silversmiths (19:1-41)

4. The journey through Macedonia to Greece and back through Macedonia (20:1-5)

5. Troas: Eutychus' fall from a window during Paul's sermon (20:6-12)

6. The journey to Miletus, and Paul's farewell speech to the Ephesian elders (20:13-38)

7. The voyage to Caesarea, and predictions of misfortune for Paul in Jerusalem (21:1-14)

8. The journey to Jerusalem (21:14-16)

E. Events in Jerusalem (21:17—23:35)

1. Paul's involvement in a Jewish vow (21:17-26)

2. The riot in the Temple area, Paul's arrest, defense before the mob, and conversation with Claudius Lysias (21:27—22:29)

3. Paul's defense before the Sanhedrin (22:30—23:11)

4. The Jewish plot against Paul and his transfer to Caesarea (23:12-35)

F. Events in Caesarea (24:1—28:31)

1. Paul's trial before Felix (24:1-23)

2. Paul's private hearing before Felix and Drusilla (24:24-27)

3. Paul's trial before Festus and appeal to Caesar (25:1-12)

4. Paul's hearing before Festus and Herod Agrippa II (25:13—26:32)

G. Paul's stormy voyage to Rome, including shipwreck on Malta (27:1—28:16)

H. Paul's preaching to Jews and Gentiles in his Roman house-prison (28:17-31)

For further discussion:

Compare the tensions and disagreements which arose in the early Church with those in contemporary Christendom as to source, kind, and attempted solution.

Identify the similarities and differences between the structure of the early Church and that of the modern Church. What accounts for the differences?

Trace the development of the Church from a Jewish to a transethnic and international body. Are today's churches truly transethnic in character? Is today's Church truly international?

Do current methods of evangelism, missionary endeavor, and church-building follow or diverge from Pauline methods, and in what ways?

Does the activity of the present day Church lack the visible evidence of the Holy Spirit which receives repeated mention in Acts?

Would the Church in Acts be counted successful by contemporary standards?

THE ACTS OF THE SPIRIT OF CHRIST FAR AND WIDE THROUGH THE APOSTLE PAUL

For further investigation:

(Commentaries on Acts and related books)

Blaiklock, E. M. *The Acts of the Apostles.* Grand Rapids: Eerdmans, 1959.

Bruce, F. F. *Commentary on the Book of Acts. The International Commentary on the New Testament.* Grand Rapids: Eerdmans, 1954.

Ramsay, Sir William M. *St. Paul the Traveller and the Roman Citizen.* 3rd edition. Grand Rapids: Baker, 1949.

————. *The Cities of St. Paul and Their Influence on His Life and Thought.* Grand Rapids: Baker, 1949.

Van Unnik, W. C. *Tarsus or Jerusalem, the City of Paul's Youth.* Naperville, Ill.: Allenson, 1962.

(Books about Christian missionary endeavor)

Cable, M., and F. French. *Ambassadors for Christ.* Chicago: Moody, n.d.

Allen, Roland. *Missionary Methods: St. Paul's or Ours?* Grand Rapids: Eerdmans, 1962.

————. *The Spontaneous Expansion of the Church.* Grand Rapids: Eerdmans, 1962.

Lindsell, H. *Missionary Principles ana Practice.* Westood, N. J.: Revell, 1955.

Cook, H. R. *Strategy of Missions.* Chicago: Moody, 1963.

Fife, E. S., and A. F. Glasser. *Missions in Crisis.* Chicago: Inter-Varsity, 1962.

The Church's Worldwide Mission. Edited by H. Lindsell. Waco, Texas: Word Books, 1966.

Mason, David. *Reaching the Silent Billion.* Grand Rapids: Zondervan, 1967.

McGavran, D. *Church Growth and Christian Mission.* New York: Harper & Row, 1965.

Elliott, E. *Through Gates of Splendor.* New York: Harper & Row, 1957.

Hitt, R. T. *Jungle Pilot: The Life and Witness of Nate Saint.* New York: Harper & Row, 1959.

Pollock, J. C. *Hudson Taylor and Maria.* New York: McGraw-Hill, 1962.

The Journal of John Wesley. For comparison with Luke's description of Paul's missionary journeys.

PART IV

The Explanation and Implications:

Epistles and Apocalypse

ARCH OF TITUS *in Rome.*

CHAPTER 14

The Early Epistles of Paul

Leading questions:

What were the style, contents, and techniques used in the writing of letters in ancient times? How do Paul's letters compare?

Why is Galatians crucial in the history of Christianity?

Who are the addressees, and what are the dates, occasions, purposes, and contents of Paul's earlier epistles?

PAUL'S EPISTLES AND LETTER WRITING IN THE GRAECO-ROMAN WORLD

In the Graeco-Roman world private letters averaged close to ninety words in length. Literary letters, such as those by the Roman orator and statesman Cicero and by Seneca the philosopher, averaged around two hundred words. Since the usual papyrus sheet measured about 9½" x 11" (approximately the size of our ordinary notebook paper) and could accommodate 150-250 words, depending on the size of writing, most ancient letters occupied no more than one papyrus page. But the average length of Paul's epistles runs to about 1,300 words, ranging from 335 words in Philemon to 7,101 words in Romans. As can be seen, Paul's epistles are several times longer than the average letter of ancient times, so that in a sense Paul invented a new literary form, the epistle — new in its prolongation as a letter, in the theological nature of its contents, and (usually) in the communal nature of its address. From another standpoint, however, Paul's epistles are true letters in that they have genuine and specific addressees, unlike the ancient *literary* epistles, which were written for general publication, in spite of their artificial addressees.

For long documents like Paul's epistles, single papyrus sheets were joined edge to edge and rolled to form a scroll. Since the coarse grain of papyrus made writing tedious, it was usual to

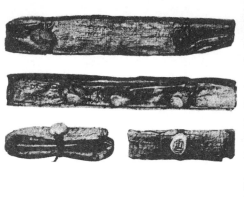

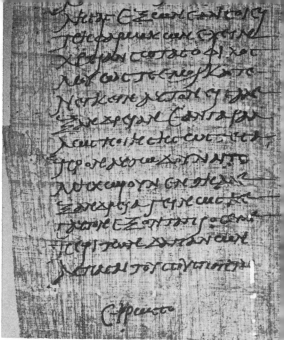

LETTERS OF PAPYRUS SHEETS *rolled, tied, and sealed (top).* A TYPICAL LETTER *of the first century* A.D. *written in a large semi-cursive hand (right).*

dictate letters to a professional scribe, called an *amanuensis,* who used shorthand during rapid dictation. The ruggedness of Pauline literary style — seen, for example, in numerous incomplete sentences — suggests that at times Paul dictated too rapidly for close attention to careful sentence structure and that his amanuensis found it difficult to keep up. Sudden breaks in thought similarly suggest temporary suspension of dictation, perhaps overnight, or for shorter or longer periods. Sometimes an author simply left oral instructions, a rough draft, or notes for his amanuensis to follow. Under such circumstances the amanuensis himself molded the exact phrasing, a factor which may account for some of the stylistic differences among epistles by the same author. The author finally edited the letter. We know for certain that Paul used amanuenses from the fact that his amanuensis once identifies himself by name (Tertius — Romans 16:22). Also, Paul's frequent statements that he is writing the final greeting with his own hand imply that the major portions of the epistles were written through an amanuensis (1 Corinthians 16:21; Galatians 6:11; Colossians 4:18; 2 Thessalonians 3:17; compare Philemon 19).

Ancient letters opened with a greeting, which included the name of the sender and that of the recipient and usually wishes for good health and success and the assurance of the sender's prayers. The main body of the letter followed, and finally the farewell and sometimes a signature. Many times the farewell included greetings from others with the author and further good wishes. Through fear that documents were being or might be

forged in his name, Paul adopted the practice of writing the farewell lines as well as a signature with his own hand to guarantee authenticity. Usually letters carried no date. The lack of public postal service made it necessary to send letters with travelers.

Paul closes several of his epistles with a section containing ethical instructions. Such instructions appear scattered throughout his other epistles and epistles by other New Testament writers. Scholars have noted striking similarities to Jewish and Stoic ethical codes of the same historical period. However, the New Testament writers rooted Christian conduct in the dynamics of Christian faith rather than throwing out a lofty but lifeless set of precepts without power to effect their own fulfillment. The fact that the exhortations in the epistles are often very similar suggests that the authors drew from a common stock of parenetic (hortatory, instructional) tradition in the Church, originally designed for catechizing newly converted candidates for baptism. On the other hand, Paul may simply have developed his own set of ethical instructions for converts and influenced later writers, such as Peter, who read at least some of his epistles (2 Peter 3:15, 16). One thing is certain. The epistolary authors drew heavily from Jesus' ethical teaching, which was preserved in oral and written tradition and frequently reflected in the phraseology and concepts of the epistles.

The order of the Pauline epistles in our present New Testament depends on length, beginning with the longest (Romans) and ending with the shortest (Philemon) — except for the Pastoral Epistles (1 and 2 Timothy and Titus), which interrupt the arrangement just before Philemon. We shall consider the epistles of Paul in the chronological order of their writing so far as it can be determined with reasonable certainty.

GALATIANS: AGAINST THE JUDAIZERS

Paul's epistle to the Galatians has to do with the Judaizing controversy about which the Jerusalem Council met (Acts 15).[1] As with that council, so also with Galatians it is almost impossible to overestimate the historical cruciality of the theological issues involved. Many of the first Christians, being Jewish, in large measure continued their Jewish mode of life, including attendance at the synagogue and Temple, offering of sacrifices, observance of Mosaic rituals and dietary taboos, and social aloofness from Gentiles. Conversion of Gentiles forced the Church to face several important questions. Should Gentile Christians be required to submit to circumcision and practice the Jewish way of life, as was required of Gentile proselytes into Judaism? For

The Crucial Issues and Theme

---

[1]Some scholars think that Paul's opponents in Galatia were semi-pagan (-gnostic), semi-Jewish syncretists.

those Gentile Christians who were unwilling to become totally Jewish, should there be a second class citizenship in the Church, as for Gentile "God-fearers" within Judaism? And most important, what makes a person Christian — faith in Christ solely, or faith in Christ plus adherence to the principles and practices of Judaism?

The answers of the Judaizers (including Jews and Gentiles who had become Jewish) insisted on the Judaistic model for Christianity. Had their view prevailed, not only would the Gospel of salvation as a free gift from God have been subverted, but also the Christian movement may well have split into a Jewish church — small, struggling, and eventually fading away — and a Gentile church, theologically rootless and tending toward pagan syncretism. Or more probably, the Gentile mission would have almost entirely ceased and Christianity would have died the death of many a Jewish sect; for most Gentiles maintained an unwillingness to live as Jews, and they regarded circumcision as an abhorrent mutilation of the human body, the beauty of which the Greeks had taught them to appreciate. But God was not to allow His purpose to be thwarted by sectarianism. And Galatians is the great charter of Christian liberty from all oppressive theologies of salvation by human effort and the great affirmation of the unity (not uniformity) and equality of all believers within the Church of Jesus Christ.

Paul wrote his epistle to the Galatians to people residing in the region known as Galatia. However, Paul's use of the term Galatia has caused debate which affects the dating of the letter. The term may refer, according to its original meaning, exclusively to the territory *north* of the cities of Pisidian Antioch, Iconium, Lystra, and Derbe; or it may also include those cities, for the Romans had added *southern* districts when they made (north) Galatia a province.

According to the North Galatian theory, Paul addressed the letter to Christians in North Galatia, which he did not visit until his second journey on his way from Pisidian Antioch to Troas. Under this view the letter could not have been written until some time after the beginning stage of the second journey and therefore after the Jerusalem Council of Acts 15, which preceded the second journey. Then the visit to Jerusalem which Paul describes in Galatians 2 probably refers to the very recent Jerusalem Council. Perhaps the strongest arguments for the North Galatian theory, with its late dating, are the original restriction of the term Galatia to the northern territory and the similarity of the statements by Paul concerning justification by faith to what he says in Romans, which he certainly wrote at a later date (see page 291).

Against the North Galatian theory is the fact that Luke no-

THRESHING FLOOR NEAR KONYA, *modern Iconium, a harvest scene typical of the Lycaonian plain. The city of Konya has a continuing history from the days of Paul and is still a prominent trading center.*

North Galatian Theory	South Galatian Theory
Paul's first missionary journey	Paul's first missionary journey
Jerusalem Council	Writing of Galatians
Paul's second missionary journey	Jerusalem Council
Writing of Galatians	Paul's second missionary journey

where suggests that Paul evangelized North Galatia. It is doubtful that Paul visited that territory on his second journey, for "the region of Phrygia and Galatia" in Acts 16:6 most naturally refers to the southern territory — a traversing of North Galatia would have required a prohibitively wide detour to the northeast. And elsewhere in his epistles Paul consistently uses geographical terms in an imperial sense, which would allow South Galatia in his epistle to the Galatians.

According to the South Galatian theory, Paul addressed his first epistle to the churches of South Galatia just after the first missionary journey, but before the Jerusalem Council. Then the visit to Jerusalem described in Galatians 2 cannot refer to the Jerusalem Council, which had not yet taken place, but refers to the famine relief visit mentioned in Acts 11:27-30. The strongest argument in favor of the South Galatian view, with its earlier dating, is that if Paul had written the letter after the Jerusalem Council, he surely would have capitalized on that council's decree in favor of Gentile Christian freedom from the Mosaic law, the main topic under discussion in Galatians. But he makes no mention at all of any such decree. The unlikely omission implies that the letter must have been written before the council had met and therefore at a time when Paul had as yet visited only South Galatia. It is also doubtful that Peter would have vacillated, as he did according to Galatians 2:11 ff., after the Jerusalem Council, where he strongly supported the position of freedom from the Mosaic law. Furthermore, Paul mentions Barnabas three times in Galatians 2, as though Barnabas were well-known to the readers. But Barnabas traveled with Paul only in South Galatia. By the time Paul went through North Galatia on his second journey, the two leaders had separated because of their disagreement over John Mark.

Introduction

The epistle opens with a greeting in which Paul stresses his apostleship, for he wishes to establish his authority against the Judaizers. In place of the usual thanksgiving for his readers, Paul immediately and violently introduces the reason for his writing. He is shocked that the Galatian Christians are deserting to another gospel, which really is not gospel ("good news") at all.

262 *Read Galatians 1:1-10.*

Paul now puts forward an autobiographical argument for the Gospel of God's grace over against the Judaizing message, which required adherence to the Mosaic law for salvation. He states that the Gospel of free grace came to him by direct revelation from Jesus Christ. It certainly could not have come from his background, he argues, for he had been a zealous Jew before his conversion. Nor did he learn it from the apostles in Jerusalem, for he did not even meet them until three years after his conversion. And when he did visit Jerusalem, he saw only Peter and James (Jesus' half brother), stayed only fifteen days, and did not become acquainted with the Judean Christians generally. Since the Gospel of grace could not have come from his background or from his contacts in Jerusalem, it must have come from God. When he again visited Jerusalem after fourteen years (either from his conversion or from his first visit to Jerusalem), the leaders there — James, Peter, and John — formally acknowledged the correctness of the Gospel of grace he preached to the Gentiles by giving him the right hand of fellowship. Furthermore, they did not require Titus, his Gentile companion, to be circumcised.

Upon coming to Antioch in Syria, Peter at first ate with Gentile Christians, but then yielded under pressure from the Judaizers. Paul publicly rebuked him. The implication is that Peter yielded to the rebuke. If not, Paul would hardly have brought up the incident as an argument in his favor. The fact that even Peter stood rebuked by Paul demonstrated the authority of Paul's Gospel of grace. *Read Galatians 1:1   2:21.*

Paul's summary of his reprimand to Peter contains the germ of his theological argument to follow. The term "justify," which appears repeatedly, means "to *regard* as righteous," only seldom "to *make* righteous."[2] In Classical Greek it meant "to deal with someone according to justice," almost the opposite from Pauline usage, which goes back to the Old Testament (especially Isaiah), where God graciously intervenes to set things right between Himself and men. God's gracious action nevertheless remains just; for Christ suffered the penalty for our sin, necessitated by divine holiness, and the imputation of divine righteousness to the believer now makes it unjust for God to condemn the believer.

Verses 17-21 in chapter two may be paraphrased as follows: "If we have to forsake the law in order to be justified by faith in Christ, does Christ encourage sin? No. Rather, if I go back to the law, I imply that I was sinning in abandoning it. But I

---

[2]To be sure, justification leads into sanctification, a change in moral behavior, so that the line of demarcation between legal standing and actual conduct is not always clearcut — but the distinction must be maintained.

did *not* sin in so doing, for Christ died under the judgment of the law against sin. As a believer, I died with Christ. That is God's viewpoint concerning me. The law has no authority over a dead man, especially one who has died under its penalty, so that I am no longer under obligation to keep the law. But Christ rose and lives within me, so that although I died in Christ when He died and thus became free from the law, yet I rose to a new life of righteousness in Christ. Therefore, if men could become righteous through keeping the law, Christ did not need to die."

Paul now develops his theological argument. If one is *converted* by faith, why not *continue* by faith rather than by the law? Abraham was justified before the law was given, so that even in the Old Testament righteousness came by faith, not by the law. The law can only curse or condemn because no one obeys it entirely. Christ died to deliver us from the law with its inevitable curse. The fact that God made His covenant with Abraham before He gave the law through Moses suggests that the Abrahamic covenant is more basic than the law. The law, then, did not annul it. The nature of the Abrahamic covenant was — on God's side — promise to bless Abraham's seed, and — on man's side — acceptance of God's promise by faith. Abraham's seed is Christ plus all those incorporated into Him by following Abraham's example of faith.

The law did have a purpose, but only a temporary one. It was to lead us to Christ as an ancient slave-tutor leading a child to school. The law accomplished this by making us keenly aware of human inability to become righteous. Being under the law, therefore, was like being minors or slaves. But in Christ we are free adults, adopted into the family of God as sons and heirs with grown-up privileges and responsibilities. Why revert to an inferior status?

Paul then recalls how the Galatians accepted his message at their conversion and pleads with them to accept his present message as they did his first. He further supports his argument in rabbinic style by an allegory on an Old Testament story. Hagar the slave woman stands for Mount Sinai, that is, the Mosaic law with its headquarters in Jerusalem, Palestine. Ishmael her slave born son stands for those who are enslaved to the law. Sarah stands for Christianity with its capital the heavenly Jerusalem. Isaac her promised and freeborn son stands for all the spiritual children of Abraham, that is, those who follow Abraham's example of faith and are therefore freed from the law in Christ. *Read Galatians 3:1—5:12.*

Responsibility
in Freedom

264

The last major section of the epistle warns against libertinism, or antinomianism (literally, "against-law-ism"), the careless attitude that freedom from the law affords license for wickedness. Liberty from the law does not mean liberty to sin. The Christian must not conduct himself according to the flesh (the sinful urge), but according to the Holy Spirit. Moreover, he must lovingly help others, especially his fellow Christians, and give liberally to those who minister the Gospel. *Read Galatians 5:13—6:10.*

The contradiction between 6:2, "Bear one another's burdens," and 6:5, "For each man will have to bear his own load," is only apparent. In the first instance Paul means that Christians should help one another in their present difficulties, and in the second instance that at the future judgment each one will answer to God for his own conduct alone.

Paul's appending numerous precepts governing Christian conduct to his prolonged attack on the legalism of the Judaizers shows that legalism does not consist in rules as such. The books of the New Testament contain many rules of behavior. Legalism is rather the imposition of wrong rules, and particularly more rules than a situation warrants, so that in a maze of minutiae people lose their ability to distinguish the more important from the less important, the principle from its application. Legalism is also the feeling of merit over one's own obedience (over against the recognition that obedience is nothing more than duty) with consequent loss of the personal dimension of fellowship with God on the basis of His grace alone.

Paul writes the conclusion in his own handwriting. The "large letters" he uses may be for emphasis, although some think that poor eyesight necessitated them. He charges that the Judaizers are motivated by desire to avoid persecution from unbelieving Jews and by ambition to boast that they are able to steal converts from Paul. By way of contrast, Paul calls attention to the sufferings he has gladly endured for his message and appeals to the Galatians that they themselves judge who has the purer motives, he or the Judaizers. *Read Galatians 6:11-18.*

Conclusion

A SUMMARY OUTLINE OF GALATIANS

Theme: justification of sinners who believe in Jesus Christ by divine grace totally apart from obedience to the law

INTRODUCTION: Greeting to the Galatians and anathema upon the Judaizing perverters of the true Gospel (1:1-10)

I. AN AUTOBIOGRAPHICAL ARGUMENT FOR THE GOSPEL OF GOD'S FREE GRACE (1:11—2:21)
   A. The direct revelation of that Gospel by Jesus to Paul (1:11, 12)
   B. The impossibility of its originating from Paul's own extremely Judaistic background (1:13)
   C. The impossibility of Paul's learning it from merely human sources, the apostles, whom Paul met not until three years after his conversion and then only for a brief time (1:14-24)

D. The later acknowledgement of Paul's Gospel by the ecclesiastical leaders in Jerusalem (2:1-10)

E. Paul's (successful) rebuke of Peter for his yielding to Judaizing pressure in Syrian Antioch (2:11-21)

II. A THEOLOGICAL ARGUMENT FOR THE GOSPEL OF GOD'S FREE GRACE (3:1—5:12)

A. The sufficiency of faith (3:1-5)

B. The example of Abraham (3:6-9)

C. The curse of the law (3:10-14)

D. The divine covenant of promise to Abraham and his offspring, or seed (Christ and those united to Him by faith), prior to the law of works (3:15-18)

E. The purpose of the law, not to provide a way of salvation through human merit, but to demonstrate the necessity of divine grace through faith in Christ (3:19—4:7)

F. A plea to retain trust in God's grace alone, with an allegory on Christian freedom based on Abraham and his two sons, slaveborn Ishmael and freeborn Isaac (4:8—5:12)

III. A WARNING AGAINST ANTINOMIANISM (5:13—6:10)

A. Christian liberty, living by the Spirit rather than according to the flesh (5:16-24)

B. Christian love (5:25—6:5)

C. Christian liberality (6:6-10)

CONCLUSION: a contrast between the Judaizers' fear of persecution and boastful pride and Paul's humiliating persecutions — and a benediction (6:11-18)

For further discussion:

What manifestations of legalism exist within contemporary Christendom?

What modern forms does antinomianism take?

Compare the Pauline concept of Christian freedom with current situational ethics, and the Christian ethic of love with the secular ethic of love.

How does Paul's emphasis on love tally with his anathema on the Judaizers?

How can Christian parents avoid both legalism and overpermissiveness in rearing their children? How can Christian educational institutions, churches, and missionary agencies avoid both legalism and libertinism?

Compare Paul's account of his visit to Jerusalem (Galatians 2:1-10) with Luke's account of the Jerusalem Council (Acts 15:1-29). How are they similar? How do they differ? Are they readily harmonized?

For further investigation:

Cole, A. *Commentary on the Epistle of Paul to the Galatians.* Grand Rapids: Eerdmans, 1965.

Neil, W. *The Letter of Paul to the Galatians.* Cambridge University Press, 1967.

Ridderbos, H. N. *The Epistle of Paul to the Churches of Galatia.* Grand Rapids: Eerdmans, 1953.

Luther, M. "The Argument of St. Paul's Epistle to the Galatians." *Luther's Works.* Vol. 26. *Lectures on Galatians 1535 Chapters 1-4.* Edited and

translated by J. Pelikan. Associate editor, W. A. Hansen. St. Louis:
Concordia, 1963. Pp. 4-12.
------------. "The Freedom of a Christian." *Luther's Works*. Vol. 31. *Career
of the Reformer*: I. Translated by W. A. Lambert. Edited and revised
by H. J. Grimm. General editor, H. T. Lehmann. Philadelphia: Muh-
lenberg, 1957. Pp. 328-377.
Bunyan, J. *Grace Abounding to the Chief of Sinners.*
Chafer, L. S. *Grace.* Grand Rapids: Zondervan, 1922.
Genesis 15-17, 21:1-21. For Old Testament passages referred to by Paul.
Danby, H. *The Mishnah.* Oxford University Press, 1933. Almost any
part of this translation of the Mishnah will give the flavor of rabbinical legalism.

FIRST THESSALONIANS: CONGRATULATIONS AND COMFORT

Paul's epistles to the church in Thessalonica are best known Theme
for their teaching about the Second Coming of Jesus Christ and
associated events. These two epistles, the Olivet Discourse of
Jesus, and the Apocalypse of John form the three major prophetic portions of the New Testament. In 1 Thessalonians
the eschatological note ties in with the second of the two overall themes, (1) congratulations to the Thessalonian believers
upon their conversion and progress in the Christian faith and
(2) exhortations toward further progress, with particular emphasis on comfort from and expectancy toward the Parousia.

Thessalonica, the capital city of Macedonia, lay on the Via Background
Egnatia, the main highway connecting Rome with the East. The
city had its own government led by politarchs, and a Jewish
settlement. Paul had evangelized the city on his second missionary journey. Some Jews and many Greeks and prominent
ladies had embraced the Christian faith. Paul's statement, "You
turned to God from idols" (1 Thessalonians 1:9), implies that
the majority of Christians there had been Gentiles before their
conversion, for Jews of that era were not idolators. (The Assyro-
Babylonian exile had cured them of idolatry.) The unbelieving
Jews in Thessalonica violently opposed the Gospel by assaulting
the house of Jason, where Paul was staying, and later traveled
to Beroea to drive Paul also out of that city.

According to Acts 17:2 Paul spent three Sabbaths preaching in
the synagogue at Thessalonica. Luke's narrative seems to imply
that the riot which forced Paul to leave occurred immediately
following his ministry in the synagogue, and Acts 17:10 indicates that the Christians sent Paul away right after the
riot. Some scholars have nevertheless put a gap between the
ministry in the synagogue and the riot because Paul mentions
having worked for his own living in Thessalonica (1 Thessalonians 2:7-11) and having received one or two gifts from
Philippi during his stay in Thessalonica (Philippians 4:16). But
Paul may have begun working immediately upon arrival in

Thessalonica and continued for three or four weeks. Likewise, two offerings could have arrived from Philippi within one month.

Another argument for a longer stay in Thessalonica is that 1 and 2 Thessalonians presuppose more doctrinal teaching than Paul could have given in a month or so. But Paul probably taught his converts intensively outside the synagogue during weekdays. And Timothy, who stayed longer in Thessalonica and after leaving returned again, taught them yet more. We therefore should probably limit Paul's ministry in Thessalonica to about a month.

Occasion

Timothy had rejoined Paul in Athens, been sent back to Thessalonica, and now rejoined Paul in Corinth. His report provided the occasion for Paul's writing 1 Thessalonians (compare 1 Thessalonians 3:1, 2 with Acts 18:5). This implies that Paul wrote 1 Thessalonians from Corinth during his second journey, not very many weeks after he had evangelized the addressees of the epistle.

ARCH OF GALERIUS, *located on the Egnatian Way in the heart of Salonika (modern Thessalonica).*

The first major section of 1 Thessalonians consists of congratulations to the Thessalonian believers upon their conversion and progress in the Christian life (chapters 1-3). Their fidelity even in the midst of persecution was proving to be an example to other Christians in Macedonia and Greece (Achaia). Timothy's report about them had indeed been good (2:17—3:9). *Read 1 Thessalonians 1-3.*

As usual, Paul combines the typical Greek greeting in a transmuted Christian form ("grace") with the typical Semitic greeting ("peace") (1:1). The form of the word "grace" which non-Christian Greeks used simply meant "Hello," but Paul changes the term to carry overtones of divine favor bestowed on ill-deserving sinners through Jesus Christ. "Peace" means more than the absence of warfare; it also carries the positive connotation of prosperity and blessing. A well-known triad of Christian virtues appears in 1:3: faith, love, and hope. Faith produces good works. Love results in labor, that is, deeds of kindness and mercy. And hope, an eschatological term referring to confident expectation of Jesus' return, generates steadfastness under trial and persecution. In the middle of the congratulatory section Paul reminds his readers in detail of his loving, self-sacrificial ministry among them. Some have thought that Paul here defends himself against slander intended to destroy his influence over the converts. More probably, Paul simply stresses how gratifying it is to him that the Thessalonians have responded well to the Gospel since he labored so fervently among them.

The second major section of 1 Thessalonians (chapters 4 and 5) consists of exhortations
    against immoral conduct (4:1-8),
    to increased mutual love (4:9, 10),
    to comfort and watchfulness in view of Jesus' return (4:11—5:11), and
    to a variety of practical matters in Christian conduct (5:12-28).

Read 1 Thessalonians 4, 5. In 4:1 Paul expertly passes from congratulation to exhortation by telling the Christians to continue progressing. The commands in 4:11, 12 to live quietly and to keep working apparently rebuke those who believed so strongly in the immediacy of Jesus' return that they were leaving their jobs. Paul's unblushing advocacy of manual labor contrasts with the view typical of the Greeks, who held that sort of work in contempt.

Rapture is the term commonly used to designate the catching up of Christians at the Second Coming, as described by Paul in 4:16, 17. *Translation* designates the immortalizing and glorifying of the bodies of Christians alive on earth when Jesus returns.

The fact that their bodies will not be resurrected from the dead will necessitate such a change in their still living, but mortal, bodies. The Thessalonian Christians were sorrowing over deceased fellow Christians, apparently because they did not realize that their deceased fellow Christians would share in the joy of Jesus' return. Perhaps they thought that death before the Parousia[3] was chastisement for sin, or even an indication of loss of salvation. Paul reassures his readers by explaining that deceased Christians will be resurrected just before the rapture so that they may be taken up along with Christians who are still alive on earth.

In chapter five Paul shifts from comfort to warning. Christians must watch for the day of the Lord (the Second Coming and following events) so that they may not be taken by surprise. Failure to watch is to put oneself in the category of the wicked, who will be caught unexpectedly. On the other hand, preparedness for the day of the Lord is more than mental awareness. It is also a mode of conduct characterized by obedience to commands such as those with which the epistle closes.

A SUMMARY OUTLINE OF FIRST THESSALONIANS

Themes: congratulations to the Thessalonian believers upon their conversion and progress in the Christian faith, and exhortations toward further progress, with particular emphasis on comfort from and expectancy toward the Parousia

INTRODUCTION: Greeting (1:1)
  I. CONGRATULATIONS (1:2—3:13)
      A. Thanksgiving for the exemplary conversion of the Thessalonian believers (1:2-10)
      B. Reminiscences by Paul over his ministry in Thessalonica (2:1-16)
      C. Timothy's glowing report about the progress of the Thessalonian Christians (2:17—3:10)
      D. A prayer for the Thessalonian believers (3:11-13)
  II. EXHORTATIONS (4:1—5:22)
      A. Morality (4:1-8)
      B. Mutual love (4:9-12)
      C. Consolation over deceased fellow Christians in view of their participation in the Parousia (4:13-18)
      D. Expectant readiness for the day of the Lord (5:1-11)
      E. Miscellaneous exhortations (5:12-22)
CONCLUSION: benediction and final instructions (5:23-28)

SECOND THESSALONIANS: CORRECTION ON THE SECOND COMING

Occasion
and Theme

Paul wrote 2 Thessalonians from Corinth on his second missionary trip, shortly after he had written 1 Thessalonians.[4] Dur-

---

[3]See the footnote on page 187.

[4]Some scholars reverse the order of 1 and 2 Thessalonians, but that view lacks manuscript evidence and (among other considerations) 2 Thessalonians 2:15 ("you were taught by us . . . by letter") seems to presuppose 1 Thessalonians.

ing the interval between the two epistles, fanaticism had increased in the church at Thessalonica. The fanaticism resulted from belief in the immediacy of the Lord's return. That belief, in turn, apparently resulted from a desire for deliverance from persecution. Paul therefore wrote this second epistle to the Thessalonians to quiet the fanaticism by correcting their eschatology.

After the initial greeting (1:1, 2), Paul again thanks God for the spiritual progress of the Thessalonian believers and for their patient endurance of persecution; but the commendation is much shorter than in 1 Thessalonians. Passing quickly to the subject of eschatology, Paul vividly describes the Second Coming when persecutors will be judged and the persecuted relieved of their sufferings. His purpose is to encourage the Thessalonians to continued endurance by pointing forward to the turning of the tables when Christ comes back. In 2:1 ff. Paul begins to deal with their misunderstandings about the Parousia by saying that it is not immediate. Therefore, they should return to their jobs and businesses. Looking for the return of Christ does not mean cessation of normal living. He *may* not return for some length of time. *Read 2 Thessalonians 1-3.*

Encouragement

Paul's warning not to be deceived by a false prophecy or by an oral or written report forged in his name (2:1, 2) suggests that the leaders of the fanaticism in Thessalonica claimed Paul's support. The phrase "man of lawlessness" (2:3) refers to the Antichrist, a world leader of wickedness and persecution in the last days. This evil figure will demand worship of himself in the Temple of God. That is, he will try to force the Jewish people to worship his image, which he will place in the (rebuilt) Temple in Jerusalem (2:4, 5; compare Mark 13:14; Matthew 24:15; Revelation 13). The suggestion that the concept of the Antichrist came from the Nero-*redivivus* myth that Nero would return from the dead stumbles against the pre-Neronian date of the concept of the Antichrist in other literature and would require us to reject without sufficient reason the authenticity of 2 Thessalonians by dating the epistle after Paul's martyrdom and Nero's death. It is also suggested that Paul had in mind the unfulfilled order of Emperor Caligula in A.D. 40 that a statue of himself be erected in the Jerusalem Temple for worship. Perhaps so, but Daniel's prophecy concerning the abomination of desolation (9:27; 11:31; 12:11), the desecration of the Temple by Antiochus Epiphanes in 168 B.C., and Jesus' allusion to a still future abomination of desolation (see the references above) provide the primary sources of Paul's statements.

Correction

What or who restrains the Antichrist from appearing until the proper time Paul felt it unnecessary to identify, for the

Thessalonians already knew the identity from Paul's oral teaching (2:5-8). The two most probable suggestions are (1) that the restraint is the institution of human government — personified in rulers, such as the Roman emperor and others — ordained by God for the protection of law and order (the Antichrist will be "lawless"), and (2) that the restraint is the activity of the Holy Spirit on earth at the present time in keeping back the Antichrist either directly or through the medium of the Church. Others think that Paul refers to missionary preaching as the restraint and to himself, the leading missionary, as the restrainer; but it is difficult to think that Paul anticipated his own special removal as a condition for the Antichrist's appearance, for elsewhere he looks for the Parousia just as other Christians do. Finally, the emphasis in 3:17 on Paul's own handwriting as an indication of the genuineness of the epistle possibly implies that an epistle had been forged in Paul's name to support the fanaticism.

A SUMMARY OUTLINE OF SECOND THESSALONIANS

Theme: the quieting of a fanatical belief, engendered apparently by persecution, that the Parousia was going to take place immediately

INTRODUCTION: Greeting (1:1, 2)

I. PERSECUTION (1:3-12)
  A. Thanksgiving for the progress of the Thessalonian believers in the midst of persecution (1:3, 4)
  B. Assurance of deliverance from persecution and of divine judgment on persecutors at the Parousia (1:5-10)
  C. Prayer for the Thessalonian believers (1:11, 12)

II. THE PAROUSIA/RAPTURE/DAY OF THE LORD (2:1-15)
  A. Denial that the Day of the Lord has arrived (2:1, 2)
  B. Affirmation of necessary precedents (2:3-15)
    1. The rebellion (2:3a)
    2. The man of lawlessness (2:3b-15)
      a. His divine claim (2:3b-5)
      b. The present restraint of his appearance (2:6, 7)
      c. His doom (2:8)
      d. His deceitfulness (2:9-12)
      e. The exemption of the Thessalonian Christians from his deceitfulness and doom (2:13-15)
  C. Benediction (2:16, 17)

III. EXHORTATIONS (3:1-15)
  A. Prayer, love, and stability (3:1-5)
  B. Industrious labor (3:6-13)
  C. Disciplinary ostracism of disobedient church members (3:14, 15)

CONCLUSION: further benediction and final greeting with emphasis on Paul's own handwriting in the last few lines as a guarantee of authenticity (3:16-18)

For further discussion:

What doctrines (and in how much depth) do the Thessalonian epistles presuppose from Paul's previous oral ministry? Compare these doctrines with the level of evangelistic preaching today.

Construct an outline of future eschatological events from the Thessalonian epistles. Why is it sketchy? Attempt to fit it with Jesus' Olivet Discourse (Mark 13; Matthew 24, 25; Luke 21) and Revelation.

Infer the Thessalonians' reaction to 1 Thessalonians from what Paul wrote in 2 Thessalonians. Then imagine what the response to 2 Thessalonians might have been.

For further investigation:

Morris, L. *The Epistles of Paul to the Thessalonians.* London: Tyndale, 1956.
_____. *The First and Second Epistles to the Thessalonians.* Grand Rapids: Eerdmans, 1959.
Walvoord, J. F. *The Thessalonian Epistles.* Grand Rapids: Zondervan [Dunham], 1958.
_____. *The Rapture Question.* Grand Rapids: Zondervan [Dunham], 1957. For the view that the rapture of the Church will occur before the tribulation.
Ladd, G. E. *The Blessed Hope.* Grand Rapids: Eerdmans, 1956. For the view that the rapture of the Church will occur not until after the tribulation.

273

CHAPTER 15

The Major Epistles of Paul

FIRST CORINTHIANS: CHURCH PROBLEMS

Leading questions:

What had been Paul's connections and communications with the Corinthian church prior to 1 Corinthians?

How did the church in Corinth sink into the deplorable condition which Paul tries to correct in 1 Corinthians?

What were the specific problems in the church at Corinth and Paul's remedies for them?

Theme
The First Epistle of Paul to the Corinthians demonstrates that lamentable conditions in the Church do not characterize the postapostolic Church alone. Aberrant beliefs and practices of astonishing variety and vulgarism flourished in the Corinthian church. It was to counter those problems that Paul wrote this epistle.

Previous Ministry in Corinth
Short of money upon his first arrival in Corinth, Paul had made tents with Priscilla and Aquila. On Sabbath days he preached in the synagogue. After Silas and Timothy rejoined him, he wrote 1 and 2 Thessalonians, moved his preaching activity next door to the house of Titus Justus, converted Crispus, chief ruler of the synagogue, received from the Roman governor Gallio a fortunate dismissal of Jewish accusations against him, and ministered altogether one and a half years in the city.

A Lost Previous Epistle
The statement in 1 Corinthians 5:9, "I wrote to you in my letter not to associate with immoral people," implies that Paul had written to the church in Corinth a previous epistle, which has since been lost. The Corinthians had misunderstood Paul to mean that they were to dissociate themselves from *all* immoral people. Paul here explains that he had in mind dissociation only from *professing Christians* who live in open and flagrant sin.

274

THE MAJOR
EPISTLES
OF PAUL

Time and
Place of
Writing

First Corinthians, then, is really the second epistle Paul wrote to the church in Corinth. He wrote it from the city of Ephesus during his third missionary journey. It was near the end of his stay there, for he was already planning to leave (16:5-8). Some have thought from 16:10, "when Timothy comes" (RSV), that Timothy carried the epistle to Corinth. However, Acts 19:22[1] suggests that Timothy was in Macedonia by this time. The New American Standard Bible gives the proper translation of 1 Corinthians 16:10: "*if* Timothy comes" [from Macedonia]. Paul would hardly have written "if" had Timothy been the carrier of the epistle. Paul had tried to induce Apollos, a very important figure, to visit Corinth, probably intending to send 1 Corinthians with him. But Apollos refused (16:12). As a result, we do not know who carried the epistle to Corinth.

The occasion for writing 1 Corinthians was twofold: (1) oral reports from the household of Chloe regarding contentions in the church (1:11); (2) the coming of a delegation from the Corinthian church — Stephanas, Fortunatus, and Achaicus — both with an offering (16:17) and with a letter asking the judgment of Paul on various problems which he takes up successively with the introductory phrase, "Now concerning . . . ," or simply, "Now . . ." (7:1, 25; 8:1; 11:2; 12:1; 15:1; 16:1). At least this is a probable inference from 16:7 ("they have supplied what was lacking on your part") and 7:1 ("now concerning the things about which you wrote"); otherwise, these men merely assuaged Paul's desire to see all the Corinthian Christians in person, and the letter from Corinth arrived through other hands. Chloe is a feminine name. The members of her household were probably slaves. Whether they had visited Paul in Ephesus, having come from Corinth, or had visited Corinth from Ephesus and reported back to Paul is uncertain.

The city of Corinth was located on a narrow isthmus between the Aegean Sea and the Adriatic Sea. The voyage around the southern tip of Greece was dangerous. Many ships were therefore carried or dragged on rollers across the isthmus and put to sea again. Several canal-digging projects were abandoned for various reasons. Being a port city, Corinth was very cosmopolitan. The athletic games at Corinth were second only to the Olympics. The outdoor theater accommodated twenty thousand people, the roofed theater three thousand. Temples, shrines, and altars dotted the city. A thousand sacred prostitutes made themselves available at the Temple of the Greek goddess Aphrodite. The south side of the marketplace was lined

---

[1] Acts 19:22: "And having sent into Macedonia . . . Timothy . . . he himself [Paul] stayed in Asia [the province in which Ephesus was located] for a while."

with taverns equipped with underground cisterns for cooling the drinks. Archaeologists have discovered many drinking vessels in these liquor lockers; some bear inscriptions such as "Health," "Security," "Love," and names of gods.

It was natural for a church in the extremely pagan society of Corinth to bristle with difficulties. Consequently, 1 Corinthians deals almost entirely with problems which plagued the church there. After the initial greeting in 1:1-9, where Paul gives thanks for the Christian faith of his readers and especially for their spiritual gifts, he launches into

1) Reproofs in response to the reports by the slaves of Chloe concerning

Divisions — the church must unite herself through humility in the light of the cross (1-4),

A specific case of immorality — the church must discipline the offender (5)

Lawsuits between Christians — the church must settle such litigations outside the secular courts (6:1-8), and

Immorality in general — Christians must live virtuously (6:9-20), and

THE CORINTHIAN CANAL *separating the Peloponnesian peninsula from the mainland of Greece was completed in 1893. In ancient times attempts to cut a ship canal across the isthmus were not successful.*

2) Replies to questions raised in the letter from the Corinthians concerning

Marriage — marriage is good, but not always the best (7),

Food, particularly meat dedicated to idols — Christians may eat, but should refrain in the presence of those in whose minds the meat is religiously contaminated (8:1—11:1),

Order of public worship, specifically,

> Veiling of women in church services — women must show submission by wearing a veil (11:2-16),
>
> Celebration of the Lord's Supper — all must participate together in a spirit of reverence and self-examination (11:17-34), and
>
> Spiritual gifts, particularly speaking in tongues — the church should de-emphasize speaking in tongues and rather emphasize prophecy and, even more, the virtue of love (12-14),

The resurrection — belief in the past resurrection of Christ and the future resurrection of believers is crucial to the Christian faith (15), and

The collection — the church should immediately start gathering the collection for the Christians in Jerusalem, so that it will be ready when Paul arrives (16:1-9).

The concluding remarks consist of miscellaneous exhortations, greetings, and news about Paul's circumstances and plans and those of Timothy and Apollos (16:10-24).

Read 1 Corinthians 1-4. The factionalism in the Corinthian **Disunity** church derived from hero worship (1:12). The admirers of Paul were loyal to him as the original founder of the church, but Paul did not side even with his own followers (see especially 1:13). The followers of Apollos apparently were spellbound by his eloquence. The followers of Cephas (Peter) may have been the Jewish segment of the church or traditionalists who rested on the authority of the first leader of the apostolic band. The so-called followers of Christ may have been those who wanted to avoid dirtying their hands in the squabbles and therefore adopted an attitude of withdrawal and superior spirituality. Alternatively, "I (am) of Christ" is Paul's own position in condemnation of those who followed merely human leaders. The details are not clear, but the factionalism appears to have arisen out of personality cults rather than from doctrinal differences. At least all factions were still meeting together, for Paul could still address a single letter to them.

In 1:14-17 Paul writes that he is glad he had not baptized very many of the Corinthians. He did not want people to be proud that they had been baptized *by him*. Paul is not denying the validity of baptism — he admits having baptized some — but is strongly denying that he or any other Christian evangelist should baptize converts to gain a personal following. On the contrary, the proper task of Christian evangelists is hardly popular, for the preaching of a Savior who died as a criminal offends human pride and worldly wisdom. Consequently, the majority of believers come from the lower strata of society. But what most of them lack by way of background and attainment Christ makes up: He is their wisdom, righteousness, sanctification, and redemption (1:18-31).

In chapter two Paul recalls that when he came to Corinth from Athens, where the worldly-wise philosophers had rejected him, he preached the cross of Christ in weakness and trembling, not with the artificial rhetorical methods of the sophistic philosophers. Such methods, designed to impress audiences with the learning and ability of the speaker, destroy the effectiveness of preaching the Gospel. Nevertheless, Paul claims to teach genuine wisdom. That wisdom comes from the Holy Spirit, who alone knows the mind of God.

Because of the factionalism in Corinth, Paul charges the Christians there with carnality, or fleshliness in the sense of sinfulness. Boasting in human leaders is wrong, he says, because they are only men. Furthermore, they are fellow-workers, not rivals (chapters 3, 4). The section closes with an admonition to unity. The implication is that Christians can achieve unity if they want it and work for it.

Immorality

Read 1 Corinthians 5-7. Paul brings up the case of a man who was living with his father's wife. Presumably she was his stepmother, since Paul does not identify her as the man's own mother. And apparently she was a non-Christian, since Paul does not prescribe punishment for her. Paul rebukes the Corinthians for their arrogant pride in condoning such flagrant sin within their number and commands discipline in the form of dismissal from the fellowship of the church, that is, social ostracism and exclusion from the Lord's Supper. Chapter six includes a section against Christians going to court against one another. Possibly that situation had some connection with the case of incest, for the discussion occurs in the middle of Paul's reproof regarding immorality. Paul cautions that ceremonial freedom does not imply moral freedom and stresses that the body is sacred as a temple of the Holy Spirit.

Marriage
and Divorce

According to chapter seven, voluntary celibacy is good; but because of the sexual impulse God has provided marriage for the avoidance of illicit relationships, so that within marriage there should be a complete giving of oneself to one's partner. Paul wishes that all might be free from marital responsibilities, as he is, not because asceticism is spiritually superior, but because the single person can devote full energy to preaching the Gospel. He realizes, however, that in this respect God's will varies for different Christians. On the question of divorce, Paul is not quite so flexible. Divorce had reached epidemic proportions in some classes of society in the Roman Empire. Paul repeats Jesus' teaching against divorce so far as Christian couples are concerned. But Jesus' words do not cover the problem of husbands or wives who have been converted after marriage and whose mates have not joined them in Christian profession. Paul therefore advises that the Christian husband or wife continue with the non-Christian mate if at all possible, at least partially because the unsaved mate and any children in the family are in a sense consecrated by the close range of the Gospel witness in the home. If the non-Christian insists on breaking up the marriage, however, the Christian is "not under bondage" (verse 15). Whether the phrase means that the Christian is not obligated to seek reconciliation or that the Christian is free to remarry within the Christian fellowship (compare the phraseology of verse 39) is debatable. Paul's indication that these instructions are his own rather than the Lord's (verses 10, 12) does not imply that they lack authority, but merely that Jesus said nothing on these points and therefore Paul must give his own teaching as one who is "trustworthy" and possessive of the Spirit (verses 25, 40).

The last part of chapter seven, especially verses 36 ff., poses difficult problems of interpretation. Is Paul referring to spiritual marriages, never physically consummated? To engaged couples? To unengaged sweethearts? Or to a Christian father, his daughter, and her suitor? The main lessons, however, are clear. On the one hand, marriage is not to be condemned on the basis of asceticism. On the other hand, marriage is not to be contracted through social pressure. Single people can often lead fuller, richer, and more productive lives than married people. In all of this Paul stresses the critical nature of the period in which Christians are living. Perhaps he had in mind the possibility of the Lord's return, a possibility which should give a sense of urgency to every generation of Christians.

It is important to understand the background of Paul's discussion concerning food associated with the worship of idols. In the ancient world pagan shrines were the main suppliers of meat for human consumption. Thus most of the meat in butcher shops had been dedicated to idols. The gods received a token portion, burned on the altar — and not usually a "choice cut" at that! After a sacramental meal with the worshiper, the priests

Food Dedicated to Idols

offered the excess meat for sale to the public. Jews, however, usually purchased meat in Jewish shops where they could be sure it had not been dedicated to a pagan god. Should Christians be as scrupulous as the Jews? *Read 1 Corinthians 8:1—11: 1.*

Paul advocates freedom to eat, but cautions his readers lest the exercise of that freedom inflict spiritual damage upon people with uninformed consciences. That is, a Christian who realizes that idols have no real divine existence may eat meat dedicated to idols without damage to his conscience. But if people who think that idols do have real divine existence happen to be observing, the better informed Christian should then refrain from eating such meat lest he damage the Christian life of the uninformed Christians and lest he mar his witness to non-Christians.

It is to be noted that the balance between freedom and the "law of love" covers only ceremonial and other questions which are neutral from the standpoint of morality. Paul warns that although he allows judicious eating of meat dedicated to idols, he by no means allows participation in idolatrous feasts in connection with heathen worship. (Pagan temples frequently had auxiliary dining rooms for social and cultic meals.) It would be blatant inconsistency for a Christian to partake both of the Lord's Supper and of suppers associated with the demonically inspired worship of false gods. Paul notes that when in Old Testament times Israel joined in heathen feasts, they also fell into forms of heathen worship which led to immoralities.

Veiling

Paul's instructions concerning the veiling of women also demand knowledge of prevailing ancient customs. It was proper in the Roman Empire for a respectable woman to veil herself in public. Tarsus, the home city of Paul, was noted for its strict adherence to this rule of propriety.[2] The veil covered the head from view, but not the face. It was at once a symbol of subordination to the male and of the respect which a woman deserves. The Christian women at Corinth, however, were quite naturally following the custom of Greek women, who left their heads uncovered when they worshiped.[3] Paul therefore states that it is disgraceful for Christian women to pray or to prophesy in church services unveiled. On the other hand, Paul goes against the practice of Jewish and Roman men, who prayed with heads covered, by commanding Christian men to pray and prophesy bareheaded as a sign of their authority. *Read 1 Corinthians 11:2-34.*

---

[2]Dio of Prusa, *Tarsica prior* §48.
[3]See *Views of the Biblical World* (Jerusalem: International, 1961), vol. 5, p. 228.

In the latter half of chapter eleven Paul states that the factionalism in the Corinthian church made mockery of their communion services, which were to be times of Christian fellowship. The Corinthians celebrated the Lord's Supper in conjunction with a love feast, a kind of church potluck supper corresponding to the Passover meal during which Jesus instituted the Lord's Supper. Some of them were coming early to the place of meeting, eating their meal, and taking their communion before the arrival of others who had longer working hours. Some were even becoming drunk. Paul, therefore, commands discontinuance of the love feasts, delay till the arrival of late-comers, introspection, and reverence. His rehearsal of the Last Supper comes from the presynoptic tradition, which originated in the action of the Lord Jesus Himself. "I received . . ." (11:23) is technical for the reception of tradition which has been handed down.

Charismata (gifts) and *glossolalia* (speaking in tongues) compose the subject matter of chapters 12-14. Many hold that the glossolalia here discussed by Paul was ecstatic speaking, not modeled after bona fide human languages. Paul does indeed state that apart from the gift of interpretation not even the speaker in tongues knows what he is saying. However, "interpretation" usually means *translation*. It would seem, therefore, that speaking in tongues was a miraculous speaking in an unlearned foreign language. The tongues were sometimes unintelligible, not because they were ecstatic non-languages, but because on some occasions neither the speaker nor anyone else present in the audience happened to possess the equally miraculous gift of translation.[4]

Through valuing glossolalia too highly the Corinthians overused the gift. Paul devalues it and insists that its use be orderly and limited. At the expense of glossolalia he magnifies superior gifts, especially prophecy, which was direct revelation from God, needed in the early Church in lieu of the New Testament Scriptures. Above all, Paul celebrates the Christian ethic of love in the prose poem of the famous thirteenth chapter. *Read 1 Corinthians 12-14.*

Paul's concept of the Church as the body of Christ stands out prominently in chapter twelve. In 14:34, 35 the prohibition against women speaking in church can hardly be absolute, for Paul has just given instructions in chapter eleven for the veiling of women so that they may pray and prophesy in public worship. "If they desire to learn anything, let them ask their own husbands at home" (14:35) suggests that Paul is prohibiting the interruption of church services by women with outspoken ques-

---

[4]See further R. H. Gundry, " 'Ecstatic Utterance' (N.E.B.)?" *Journal of Theological Studies*, N.S., 17 (1966), pp. 229-307.

tions and perhaps also by disruptive conversation among women, if they sat separately from men as in the synagogues.

Paul now takes up the topic of the resurrection of the body,
a concept foreign to Greek thought. Some of the Athenians,
entirely sceptical or hoping at best for immortality of the soul,
had mocked Paul when he spoke of bodily resurrection. If they
thought that the body encumbered the soul, they would not have
wanted to believe in resurrection.[5] This predisposition against
the doctrine of bodily resurrection was causing some Corinthians
to doubt and deny the future resurrection. They were not
yet denying the resurrection of Christ, but Paul could see that
this would be the logical outcome of their thinking. He therefore
argues from the past resurrection of Christ as an established fact
to the future resurrection of men. In particular, he has Christians in mind.

The great resurrection chapter opens with a famous summary
of the Gospel and a list of the resurrection appearances of Christ,
which Paul would not have dared to include with such reckless
confidence unless the witnesses were in fact available. By writing
"I received" concerning this material, Paul indicates that he is
quoting a confessional statement from Christian tradition even
more ancient than the date of 1 Corinthians. He continues with
a description of the resurrection body and an analogy between
death in Adam and life in Christ. Some rabbis taught that the
resurrection body will be exactly the same as the present body.
Paul says, No, the resurrection body will have continuity with
the present body, but be suited to the spiritual conditions of
eternal and heavenly existence. The chapter reaches a climax
in a burst of triumphant praise. *Read 1 Corinthians 15.*

Various explanations have been devised for the reference in
verse twenty-nine to baptism for the dead. Perhaps it refers
merely to those who were converted and baptized out of a desire to be reunited with their Christian loved ones and friends at
the resurrection. Or maybe Paul really does refer to vicarious
baptism in the full sense, but uses it as a point of argument without meaning to support the practice ("What will *they* do . . .?"
and "Why are *they* baptized for the dead?" as opposed to "we"
in the next verse). In other words, Paul was pointing out the inconsistency of those who underwent baptism for the very dead
people whose future resurrection they denied. The fighting "with
wild beasts" in verse thirty-two is probably metaphorical.[6]

The concluding chapter contains various exhortations, such
as that to lay aside money for the offering which Paul will

---

[5]See Acts 17:32 and page 240.
[6]Compare the letter of Ignatius to Rome, v. 1.

collect upon his arrival and take to Jerusalem with accredited companions. Verse twenty-two contains an important Aramaic phrase, "Maranatha," which means "O [our] Lord, come!" (compare Revelation 22:20). It shows that the designation of Jesus as Lord dates from early times in Aramaic-speaking circles and is therefore not to be attributed to later, Greek-speaking Christianity — against the claim of some modern scholars that the view of Jesus as a divine figure was a rather tardy development, not original to Jesus Himself or to the earliest Church. *Read 1 Corinthians 16.*

A SUMMARY OUTLINE OF FIRST CORINTHIANS

Theme: the problems in the church at Corinth and their solutions

INTRODUCTION: Greeting to and thanksgiving for the Corinthian church (1:1-9)

I. REPROOFS IN RESPONSE TO THE REPORTS BY THE SLAVES OF CHLOE (1:10—6:20)
   A. Divisions and the necessity of their healing by recognition of the weak humanity of Christian leaders and their followers over against the power of God in the Gospel (1:10—4:21)
   B. The case of a man cohabiting with his stepmother and the necessity of disciplining the offender by ostracism from Christian fellowship (5:1-13)
   C. Lawsuits between Christians and the necessity of their settlement by the church outside secular courts (6:1-8)
   D. Immorality in general and the necessity that Christians live virtuously by the indwelling Holy Spirit (6:9-20)

II. REPLIES TO QUESTIONS RAISED IN A LETTER FROM THE CORINTHIANS (7:1—16:9)
   A. Marriage, its essential goodness but the advantage to some of an unmarried state, restriction of divorce, and exhortation to reconciliation (7:1-40)
   B. Food, especially meat, offered to idols, its allowance for Christians provided they neither abuse their freedom by injuring the consciences of the religiously uneducated nor join in idolatrous banquets (8:1-11:1)
   C. Order of public worship (11:2—14:40)
      1. The veiling of women who participate in church services, its requirement as a sign of subordination to men (11:2-16)
      2. The Lord's Supper, its desecration in the Corinthian church by disunity and revelry and the requirements of reverence and discontinuance of the love feast (11:17-34)
      3. Spiritual gifts (12:1—14:40)
         a. The diversity of function within the unity of the Church as the body of Christ (12:1-31)
         b. The supremacy of love (13:1-13)
         c. The superiority of prophesying and inferiority of speaking in tongues, with rules for orderliness including the prohibition of interruption of church services by women (14:1-40)
   D. The resurrection, both Christ's in the past and believers' in the future, its cruciality to the Christian faith (15:1-58)
   E. The collection for the church in Jerusalem, its manner of gathering and delivery (16:1-9)

CONCLUSION: Timothy's coming visit to Corinth, Apollos' failure to visit, miscellaneous exhortations, final greetings and benediction (16:10-24)

For further discussion:

How is it possible to strike the proper balance between the unity and the purity of the Church without making the one cancel the other?

How are we to evaluate the modern ecumenical movement toward Church unity?

How do Paul's strictures against immorality and emphasis on love compare with the "new morality"?

How is Church discipline of erring members possible when today a Christian excluded from one church can gain admittance to another? How "serious" a sin requires discipline?

What current questions of Christian conduct validly fall within the area of private freedom and public responsibility?

Why do not most churches still require women participating in public services to wear veils?

Does the Holy Spirit still grant the gifts of prophecy and glossolalia, and if so, do their recipients currently exercise them in the manner prescribed by Paul?

From the standpoint of modern science, how can there be a continuity between the mortal body and the resurrection body?

For further investigation:

(Commentaries on 1 Corinthians)

Morris, L. *The First Epistle of Paul to the Corinthians.* Grand Rapids: Eerdmans, 1958.

Grosheide, F. W. *Commentary on the First Epistle to the Corinthians.* Grand Rapids: Eerdmans, 1953.

Thrall, M. E. *The First and Second Letters of Paul to the Corinthians.* Cambridge University Press, 1965.

(Books on topics appearing in 1 Corinthians)

Bromiley, G. W. *The Unity and Disunity of the Church.* Grand Rapids: Eerdmans, 1958.

Bainton, R. H. *What Christianity Says About Sex, Love and Marriage.* New York: Association, 1957. For a historical survey.

Lewis, C. S. *The Four Loves.* New York: Harcourt, Brace, 1960. For comparison with 1 Corinthians 13.

Martin, R. P. *Worship in the Early Church.* Westwood, N.J.: Revell, 1964.

Hoekema, A. A. *What About Tongue-Speaking?* Grand Rapids: Eerdmans, 1966.

Dahl, M. E. *The Resurrection of the Body.* London: SCM, 1962. For an interpretation of 1 Corinthians 15 that raises some provocative questions.

SECOND CORINTHIANS: THE CONCEPT OF PAUL CONCERNING HIS OWN MINISTRY

Leading questions:

After the writing of 1 Corinthians, what dealings between

Paul and the church in Corinth led to the writing of 2
Corinthians?

What was the mood of the Corinthian church and that of
Paul at the time he wrote 2 Corinthians?

What was Paul's apostolic self-image, as shown by his apologia in 2 Corinthians?

More than any other epistle of Paul, 2 Corinthians allows us **Theme**
a glimpse into his inner feelings about himself, his apostolic
ministry, and his relationship to the churches he had founded
and nurtured. In some respects, then, this epistle is autobiographical in tone although not in framework or total content.

After writing 1 Corinthians from Ephesus, Paul had found it **The Painful**
necessary to make a "painful visit" to Corinth and back — painful **Visit**
because of the strained relationship between Paul and the
Corinthians at the time. Luke does not record this visit in Acts.
It is to be inferred, however, from 2 Corinthians 12:14; 13:1, 2,
where Paul refers to his coming visit as the "third." Without
the inferred painful visit Paul had visited Corinth only *once*
before. The statement in 2 Corinthians 2:1, "For I made up my
mind not to make you *another* painful visit" (RSV), implies a
past painful visit which can hardly be identified with his first
coming to them with the joyful tidings of salvation through Jesus
Christ.

For whatever reason Paul made the short, painful visit, he **The Lost**
was apparently unsuccessful in bringing the church into line. **Sorrowful**
Upon returning to Ephesus, therefore, he wrote a now lost **Letter**
"sorrowful letter" to Corinth, which at first he regretted having
sent (2 Corinthians 2:4; 7:8 — the descriptions hardly fit 1 Corinthians). This is the second lost letter to Corinth. The sorrowful
letter commanded church discipline against an obstreperous individual who was leading the opposition against Paul in the
Corinthian church (2 Corinthians 2:5-10). Titus carried the
letter to Corinth. Meanwhile, knowing that Titus would return
via Macedonia and Troas and anxious to hear from Titus the
reaction of the Corinthians, Paul left Ephesus and waited in
Troas. When Titus failed to arrive quickly, Paul went on to
Macedonia, where Titus finally met him and reported the good
news that the church as a whole had repented from their re-
belliousness against Paul and had disciplined the leader of the
opposition (2 Corinthians 2:12, 13; 7:4-16).

Paul wrote 2 Corinthians from Macedonia on his third journey, **The Occasion**
then, (1) to express relief and joy at the favorable response of **for**
the majority in the Corinthian church, and in so doing describes **2 Corinthians**
his ministry in vividly personal terms (chapters 1-7); (2) to **285**

stress the collection he wants to gather from them for the Christians in Jerusalem (chapters 8, 9); and (3) to defend his apostolic authority to the still recalcitrant minority (chapters 10-13).

A SUMMARY OF PAUL'S RELATIONSHIPS WITH THE CORINTHIAN CHURCH

Paul evangelized Corinth during his second journey.

Paul wrote a lost letter to Corinth, in which he commanded dissociation from professing Christians who live immorally.

Paul wrote 1 Corinthians from Ephesus during his third journey to deal with a variety of problems in the church.

Paul made a quick, "painful" visit from Ephesus to Corinth and back to straighten out the problems at Corinth, but failed to accomplish his purpose.

Paul sent another lost letter, called the "sorrowful letter," in which he commanded the Corinthians to discipline his leading opponent in the church.

Paul left Ephesus and anxiously waited for Titus first at Troas and then in Macedonia.

Titus finally arrived with the good news that the church had disciplined Paul's opponent and that most of the Corinthians had submitted to Paul's authority.

Paul wrote 2 Corinthians from Macedonia (still on the third journey) in response to Titus' favorable report.

The Integrity of 2 Corinthians

It has been argued that 2 Corinthians 10-13 is at least part of the "lost" sorrowful letter, because Paul changes from a tone of happiness in chapters 1-9 to self-defense in chapters 10-13. But the distinction does not entirely hold true, for there is self-defense also in chapters 1-9 (see 1:17 ff.; 2:6, 17; 4:2-5; 5:12, 13). The difference in emphasis is due to Paul's addressing primarily the repentant majority in chapters 1-9, primarily the still recalcitrant minority in chapters 10-13. (Others suggest that fresh news of revived opposition forced Paul to change his tone from the tenth chapter onward.) A number of considerations militate against dividing 2 Corinthians into two originally separate epistles: (1) we would have expected chapters 10-13 to have preceded chapters 1-9 if they had been written before as the sorrowful letter; (2) although firm in tone, chapters 10-13 are hardly sorrowful; (3) chapters 10-13 contain nothing about the insulting behavior of the leader of Paul's opposition, yet that was the subject matter of the sorrowful letter according to 2:1 ff.; (4) 12:18 mentions a *previous* visit of Titus, which must have been for delivering the sorrowful letter, but according to the partition theory 12:18 is itself part of the sorrowful letter!

A Review of Past and Present Relationships

Paul opens the epistle with a greeting and thanksgiving for comfort from God in persecutions and hardships. He then begins to describe his ministry as sincere and holy. He defends himself against the charge of vacillation — failure to carry out a

286

threatened further visit — by claiming that his words are just as affirmative as the promises of God in Christ and by explaining that he has delayed his visit to give them time for repentance, so that he may arrive under happier circumstances than otherwise. Pleased that the Corinthian church has disciplined his leading opponent, Paul advises restoration of the man into the fellowship of the church. This would be shown especially by allowance to participate again in the Lord's Supper. The section closes with a metaphor of Christ as a victorious general entering Rome in triumphal procession, and another metaphor in which the Corinthian Christians, as Paul's converts, are a letter of recommendation for Paul written by Christ Himself. *Read 2 Corinthians 1:1—3:3.*

The Ministry of the Gospel

Paul now describes the superiority of the Gospel over the Mosaic law. The fading of God's glory from the face of Moses when he descended from Mount Sinai represents the temporary nature of the Mosaic covenant. We are now free from the law and its condemnation. But just as Moses reflected the fading glory of the old covenant, we should reflect the permanent, greater, and increasing glory of the new covenant. How amazing that God should entrust the preaching of this glorious Gospel of the new covenant to poor, weak human beings! But although we feel our inadequacy, writes Paul, we do not despair. The hope of resurrection makes us overlook our present physical dangers in preaching the Gospel. With feelings of tremendous privilege and responsibility as a minister of the new covenant, Paul claims conscientiousness and integrity no matter how adverse or favorable the conditions of his ministry. *Read 2 Corinthians 3:4—7:16.*

Separation

In the digression of 6:11—7:1 Paul portrays the life of separation from sin as an enlarging rather than confining experience. Some have thought that this digression is part of Paul's first lost letter to Corinth, referred to in 1 Corinthians 5:9: "I wrote to you in my letter not to associate with immoral people." But why an excerpt from that letter should have been inserted here is difficult to say; and manuscript evidence is lacking to indicate that 6:11—7:1 did not originally belong to 2 Corinthians.

The Offering

Pleading for a generous offering for the church in Jerusalem, Paul presents the liberality of the Macedonian Christians as worthy of imitation, and even more so is the self-sacrifice of Christ. Sometime *you* may need help, Paul argues. Furthermore, you eagerly seized on the idea of such an offering when I first mentioned it some time ago. Do not prove that my bragging to the Macedonians about your zeal was unfounded. *Read 2 Corinthians 8, 9.*

The opponents of Paul had accused him of boldness when absent, cowardice when present. He therefore reminds his readers that meekness is a virtue of Christ; but like Christ he can be bold in their presence if he wants, and *will* be if necessary, though in the Lord, not in himself. *Read 2 Corinthians 10-13.* In these chapters Paul presents the credentials of his apostolic ministry: his sincerity as a preacher (he did not even accept wages from the Corinthians), his extensive sufferings, special revelations from God, and miracle-working powers. But Paul carefully guards against boastful pride by repeatedly insisting that the recalcitrants are forcing him to write in this vein and also by mentioning his weakness, particularly his "thorn in the flesh" (12:7-10). Among the proposed identifications of Paul's thorn in the flesh are epilepsy, eye disease, malaria, leprosy, migraine headaches, depression, stammering, and false teachers. The epistle closes with an appeal that his next visit may not have to be an occasion for rebuking the Corinthians again.[7]

A SUMMARY OUTLINE OF SECOND CORINTHIANS

Theme: the concept of Paul concerning his own ministry as reflected in his relationships to the church at Corinth

INTRODUCTION: Greeting (1:1, 2)

I. THE RELATIONSHIP BETWEEN PAUL AND THE CORINTHIAN CHURCH WITH SPECIAL REFERENCE TO THE NOW AGREEABLE MAJORITY (1:3—7:16)
   A. Thanksgiving for divine comfort and protection (1:3-11)
   B. Explanation of Paul's failure to visit Corinth again, not fearful vacillation but desire to avoid another painful visit (1:12—2:4)
   C. Instruction to restore the disciplined, penitent leading opponent of Paul, with a statement of forgiveness by Paul (2:5-11)
   D. Inner description of Paul's ministry (2:12—6:10)
      1. Anxiety over Titus' failure to come to Troas (2:12, 13)
      2. Thanksgiving for triumphant confidence in Christ (2:14-17)
      3. The living recommendation of Paul's ministry in the Corinthian converts themselves (3:1-3)
      4. The superiority of the new covenant over the old (3:4-18)
      5. The determination of Paul to carry out his ministry (4:1—6:10)
   E. Plea for mutual affection and separation from unbelievers (6:11—7:4)
   F. Joy over Titus' report in Macedonia that the majority in the Corinthian church had repented of their opposition to Paul (7:5-16)

II. EXHORTATION TO CONTRIBUTE TO THE COLLECTION FOR THE CHURCH IN JERUSALEM (8:1—9:15)
   A. The example of the Macedonian Christians (8:1-7)
   B. The example of Jesus (8:8, 9)
   C. The ideal of equality (8:10-15)
   D. The coming of Titus and others to receive the collection (8:16—9:5)
   E. The divine reward for liberality (9:6-15)

---

[7]Some scholars identify the Corinthian opponents of Paul at least partially with Gnostics because of his counteremphasis on true spiritual knowledge; but the appeal of Paul to his Jewishness (11:21, 22) seems to be aimed at Judaizers, who also would have claimed to possess the truth.

III. THE RELATIONSHIP BETWEEN PAUL AND THE CORINTHIAN CHURCH
WITH SPECIAL REFERENCE TO THE STILL RECALCITRANT MINORITY
(10:1—13:10)
   A. The defense of Paul against charges of weakness and cowardice
      (10:1-11)
   B. The rightful claim of Paul over the Corinthians as his converts
      (10:12-18)
   C. Paul's concern over the danger of false teachers at Corinth (11:1-6)
   D. Paul's refusal to take financial support from the Corinthians (11:7-15)
   E. Paul's pedigrees of Jewish ancestry and Christian service, including the
      suffering of persecution (11:16-33)
   F. Paul's visions and thorn in the flesh (12:1-10)
   G. The apostolic miracles of Paul (12:11-13)
   H. The coming visit of Paul to Corinth, with a threat of harshness and an
      appeal for repentance (12:14—13:10)
CONCLUSION: farewell exhortations and greeting, and a benediction (13:
11-14)

For further discussion:

For what historical and theological reasons might two of
Paul's letters to the Corinthian church have been lost? Is it
likely that had they been preserved, the Church would
have accepted them into the canon? How should they now
be received if somehow discovered?

How do Paul's remarks about Christian stewardship of
money (2 Corinthians 8, 9) compare with the Old Testament law of the tithe?

Why did not Paul "turn the other cheek" instead of defending himself from personal attack?

Construct a personality profile of Paul from this most self-
revealing of his epistles.

For further investigation:

Tasker, R. V. G. *The Second Epistle of Paul to the Corinthians.* London:
Tyndale, 1958.
Hughes, P. E. *Paul's Second Epistle to the Corinthians.* Grand Rapids:
Eerdmans, 1962.
Thrall, M. E. *The First and Second Letters of Paul to the Corinthians.*
Cambridge University Press, 1965.

ROMANS: THE GIFT OF GOD'S RIGHTEOUSNESS
THROUGH FAITH IN CHRIST

Leading questions:

What was the origin and composition of the church in
Rome?

What led Paul to write to the church in Rome although he
had never visited there?

What is the step by step progression in this most systematic
of Paul's explanations of the Gospel?

Theme

The great theme of Romans is justification by divine grace through faith in Jesus Christ. Jesus implied this doctrine in the parables of the prodigal son, the Pharisee and the publican, the laborers in the vineyard who received equal wages, and the great supper. The same implication lies behind His statement, "I came not to call the righteous, but sinners to repentance" (Mark 2:17), and behind His dealings with Zacchaeus (Luke 19:1-10). Thus, Paul did not innovate the doctrine of free forgiveness, but developed its statement in his own distinctive style. The doctrine receives its most systematic treatment by Paul in his epistle to the church in Rome.

The Founding
of the Church
in Rome

The early Church father Clement of Rome suggested that Paul and Peter were martyred in Rome. By the time of Tertullian (early third century) the Church had generally accepted this tradition. However, the local church in Rome was probably not founded by an apostle, certainly not by Paul and almost

SYNAGOGUE RUINS *believed to date back to the first century* A.D. *were uncovered at Ostia, an old Roman port city southwest of Rome.*

certainly not by Peter. As previously noted, the Roman historian Suetonius wrote that the emperor Claudius banished the Jews from Rome in A.D. 49 or 50 because of rioting at the instigation of one called "Chrestus," probably a misspelling of "Christus" (Latin for Christ).[8] If so, Christianity had already gone to Rome. But Peter was still in Jerusalem at the Jerusalem Council in about A.D. 49. Furthermore, Paul makes no reference and sends no greeting to the Apostle Peter in writing Romans. Perhaps some of the Jews and proselytes from Rome who were in Jerusalem on the Day of Pentecost became Christians and carried the Gospel back to Rome at the very dawn of Church history (Acts 2:10).

Some scholars maintain that the Roman church consisted mainly of Jewish Christians. They argue that the emphasis on the Jewish nation in chapters 9-11, the appeal to the example of Abraham, the quotations of the Old Testament, and the passages in which Paul appears to be arguing against Jewish objections (2:17—3:8; 3:21-31; 6:1—7:6; 14:1—15:3) imply a Jewish congregation. But according to chapters 9-11 God has temporarily *set aside* the Jewish nation *for the sake of the Gentiles,* so that these chapters may rather indicate that the original readers of the epistle were mainly Gentiles. Paul's appeals to Abraham and to the Old Testament may reflect his own Jewish background, not the background of his readers. And his answering typical Jewish objections may stem from his frequent debates with unbelieving Jews and with Judaizers rather than from Jewish addressees.

A number of passages demonstrate the predominantly Gentile composition of the Roman church. Paul writes in 15:5, 6, "among all the Gentiles . . . including yourselves." In 1:13 he writes, "You as well as . . . the *rest of* the Gentiles." "I am speaking to you Gentiles" (11:13) characterizes the Roman church in general, not a minority within the church; for in 11:28-31 the readers are said to have obtained mercy because of Jewish unbelief. In 15:15, 16 Paul speaks of his writing to them in conjunction with his ministry "to the Gentiles."

Paul had just completed gathering the collection for Jerusalem during his third missionary journey (15:25, 26). He wrote from Corinth, for Gaius the Corinthian was his host at the time (16: 23; 1 Corinthians 1:14). The mention of Erastus, the city treasurer (16:23), confirms that Corinth was the place of writing. An inscription discovered in Corinth and dating from the first century reads, "Erastus, the commissioner of public works, laid this pavement at his own expense." Strictly, "commissioner of

---

[8]See page 241.

public works" is not the same as "city treasurer," but it is natural to think either that Erastus advanced from commissioner to treasurer or that he was demoted from treasurer to commissioner because of his Christian profession. It also remains possible that the two titles are roughly synonymous. Further confirmation that Paul wrote Romans from Corinth comes from the commendation of Phoebe, who belonged to the church at Cenchrea near Corinth. This commendation probably indicates that Phoebe carried the letter from Corinth to Rome (16:1, 2).

Purpose

Paul wrote Romans as a preparation for his first visit to that city and to the Christian community there. For a long time he had been intending to visit Rome, but had been prevented (1:13; 15:22-24a). The purpose of his coming was to strengthen the Roman Christians in the faith (1:11, 15) and to win their financial support for his projected mission to Spain after visiting Rome (15:24, 28). Romans, then, is a treatise on the Gospel designed to prepare the readers for Paul's coming oral ministry among them.

The Personal Greetings

Because Paul knew only certain of the Christians in Rome — those who had moved there since he had become acquainted with them — Romans is more formal than any of Paul's other epistles. In chapter sixteen the personal greetings which Paul nevertheless sends to individuals although he has never visited Rome have caused some scholars to think that the sixteenth chapter is an epistle or part of an epistle originally sent to Ephesus. But the chapter is hardly a whole epistle (it consists almost entirely of greetings), and there is no manuscript evidence that it ever circulated independently either as a whole epistle or as part of one. The only other long series of greetings in Paul's epistles occurs in Colossians, sent to another city Paul had never visited. Probably Paul emphasized his previous acquaintance elsewhere with Christians who had moved to churches he had never visited to establish friendly relationships with those churches, and omitted individual greetings in epistles to churches he had visited to avoid favoritism. There is insufficient reason, then, to think that chapter sixteen originally belonged to another epistle.

Textual Confusion

Ancient manuscripts vary widely, however, on the position of the doxology in 16:25-27 (in our English Bibles) and on the position of the benediction in 16:20. The confusion may be due to the heretic Marcion, who possibly omitted chapters fifteen and sixteen because of Old Testament and Jewish references disagreeable to his anti-Jewish way of thinking. The confusion may be compounded by a truncated form of the epistle lacking chapter sixteen, for which there is ancient textual evidence. Probably some editions omitted that chapter with its

personal greetings to make the epistle adaptable for general circulation throughout the Church.

THE LOGICAL DEVELOPMENT OF THOUGHT IN ROMANS

In the opening part of the epistle Paul greets his readers and
mentions his hope of visiting them so that he may preach the
Gospel in Rome as elsewhere (1:1-15). Paul then states his
theme in 1:16, 17: the good news of deliverance from sin by the
giving of God's righteousness to everyone who believes in Jesus
Christ.

The first major section delineates the need for justification because of human sinfulness (1:18—3:20). The latter half of
chapter one describes the wickedness of the Gentile world,
chapter two the sinful self-righteousness of the Jewish world,
and the first half of chapter three summarizes the guilt of humanity in general. It should be noted that for Paul sins (plural)
are only symptomatic of the real problem, which is sin (singular)
as a dominating principle in human experience.

Justification is God's remedy according to the second major
section (3:21—5:21). The latter half of chapter three presents
the sacrificial death of Christ as the basis of our justification and
faith as the means of appropriating the benefits of His death.
Chapter four portrays Abraham as the great example of faith,
against the rabbinical doctrine of Abraham's store of merit so
excessive that Jews could draw upon it. Chapter five lists the
manifold blessings of justification — peace, joy, hope, the gift of
the Holy Spirit, and others — and contrasts the unbeliever's position in Adam, where there is sin and death, and the believer's
position in Christ, where there is righteousness and life eternal.

In the third major section the discussion progresses to the
topic of sanctification, or holy Christian living (chapters 6-8).
Should we sin so that God may exercise His grace all the more
and thus gain more praise for Himself? No! Baptism illustrates
our death to sin and our coming alive to righteousness (chapter
6). But sanctification has nothing to do with keeping the Old
Testament law, which could only give a sense of defeat with
no ability to overcome the demonic control of sin over our conduct (chapter 7). Rather, the Spirit of Christ gives the power to
overcome, so that chapter eight climaxes with a burst of praise:
"Who shall separate us from the love of Christ?" Paul lists the
possibilities and denies them all.

The discussion turns to the problem of Israel in the fourth major section of Romans (chapters 9-11). Because of his own Jewish background Paul was keenly concerned about the unbelief
of the majority of his fellow Jews. In this, Paul faced a logical

problem. He had been affirming that the Gospel was no innovation, but derived from the Old Testament and constituted the fulfillment of all that Abraham, David, and the prophets stood for. But if this was so, why did the Jews by and large not recognize the truth of the claim? Did the general rejection of the Gospel by Jews imply a flaw in Paul's argument? In answer, chapter nine stresses the doctrine of election, the right of God to choose whomever He wishes. It is perfectly legitimate, argues Paul, for the sovereign God to do with Israel and the Gentiles what He wants to do. And it is God's prerogative to choose the Gentiles now as it was for Him to choose the Jews previously. But God's current rejection of Israel is not capricious, for Israel deserves it because of her self-righteousness and refusal to believe what she has both heard and understood in the Gospel (chapter 10). Furthermore, Israel's setting aside is only temporary and partial. A Jew may gain salvation as easily as a Gentile by believing in Christ, and God will restore the whole nation to His favor in the future. Meanwhile, the Gentiles enjoy equality with them (chapter 11).

The Obligation: Christian Precepts

The fifth major section contains practical exhortations for Christian living, including commands to obey civil authorities and to allow freedom on ceremonial issues (chapters 12-14).

Conclusion

Paul concludes the letter by stating his plans and sending greetings (chapters 15, 16).

THE MAIN DOCTRINES IN ROMANS

Human Guilt

Read Romans 1:1—3:20. Paul carefully notes by his quotation of Habakkuk 2:4 that the Old Testament supports the fundamental truth that righteousness comes through faith (1:17). He also states that nature itself reveals the power and deity of God, so that the heathen have no excuse (1:19, 20). The rest of chapter one describes the retrograde nature of sin. The statement, "God gave them up," tolls like a death knell three times throughout the passage (verses 24, 26, 28).

In chapter two Paul describes the self-righteous Jew, who delighted in pointing out the sins of the pagan world. The Jews are just as guilty in their own proud way, argues Paul. Furthermore, genuine Jewishness does not consist in physical ancestry or in the rite of circumcision, but in a proper spiritual relationship to God. In fact, Gentiles who follow the law of God written in their consciences demonstrate a right relationship with God that many Jews lack. The word "Jew" means "Praise." The true Jew, therefore, is the man whose life is praiseworthy by divine criteria (2:17).

In 3:1 Paul anticipates a Jewish objection: If Jews are no better than Gentiles, why did God choose the Jewish nation? Does

not the whole Old Testament imply that God has specially favored the Jews? Yet you, Paul, are saying that God treats
Jews and Gentiles in the same way! Paul freely admits that Jews
do have the advantage of standing closest to divine revelation
in the Scriptures. But higher privilege does not imply less sinfulness. With a string of Old Testament quotations Paul concludes the section by charging the entire human race with guilt
before God.

The next paragraph is the core of the book. "The law and Propitiation
the prophets" refers to the Old Testament. Paul emphasizes that
although righteousness comes through faith in Jesus Christ rather
than through keeping the law, yet the law and the rest of the
Old Testament do attest the righteousness by faith. "The glory
of God," which mankind lacks (3:23), is the splendor of God's
character. The term "propitiation" (3:25) refers to the sacrificial
death of Jesus as that which appeased the holy anger of God
against human wickedness. "Expiation" is a synonymous term
which fails, however, to emphasize the element of God's righteous indignation. Whether translated "propitiation" or "expiation," the term may also refer to the mercy seat, the golden lid
over the ark of the covenant, on which the Jewish high priest
sprinkled sacrificial blood once a year to atone for the sins of
Israel. Paul indicates that God forgave sins during the Old Testament period only in anticipation of Christ's death. When he
states that God is both "just and the justifier of the one who
has faith in Jesus," he means that God's holiness has been satisfied because Jesus paid the penalty for human guilt and that
God's love has likewise been satisfied because the death of Jesus
provides a way by which the sinner may be forgiven. Divine
justice is rigid enough to demand the infliction of penalty for
the upholding of justice, elastic enough to allow the righteous
to act in behalf of the unrighteous for the exercise of mercy.
Read Romans 3:21-31.

Again Paul anticipates a Jewish objection: if one gains right- *Faith*
eousness merely by faith in Christ, there is no advantage in being a Jew or in keeping the law as a Jew. Paul essentially agrees
with that conclusion, but argues that the Old Testament itself indicates that righteousness comes by faith, as in the examples of
Abraham and David. *Read Romans 4, 5.*

In the first verses of chapter five Paul lists the blessings *Blessings*
which accompany justification: peace with God through Jesus
Christ; introduction into the sphere of God's grace; joy in the
hope of the glory of God ("hope" means confident expectation
that Jesus will return, and "the glory of God" here means the
divine splendor Christians will enter at the Second Coming);
joy in present persecution; perseverance; proven character;

hope (repeated); and the love of God in our hearts through the gift of the Holy Spirit. The terms "reconcile" and "reconciliation" in verses 10 and 11 refer to the turning of the sinner from hatred against God to love for God.

**Original
Sin**

In verses 12-14 Paul argues that the reign of death before God gave the law through Moses proves the whole human race was implicated in Adam's original sin; for before the time of Moses there was no written law to break. A contrast between "the one" and "the many" follows: one man (Adam) sinned in Eden — the many (a Semitic expression for "all") sinned and died in Adam; one man (Jesus Christ) performed an act of righteousness on the cross — the many (all who believe in Him) are regarded as righteous and live eternally.

**Adam vs.
Christ**

**Union with
Christ**

The primary objection to this easy way of salvation, justification by faith alone, is that it logically implies a patently false line of reasoning with a ridiculous conclusion: the more we sin, the more God exercises His grace and gains greater glory for so doing — therefore we should sin as much as possible for the glory of God! Paul's horrified repudiation of such reasoning stems from the doctrine of the believer's union with Christ as dramatized through Christian baptism. In baptism the believer confesses his death to sin through identification with Christ in His death and also confesses his coming alive to righteousness through identification with Christ in His resurrection. So far as God is concerned, then, the Christian died when Christ died; he rose when Christ rose. That fact places the Christian under obligation to live as a person who is dead to sin and alive to righteousness. He must therefore form his self-image according to God's viewpoint. *Read Romans 6-8.*

**Christian
Liberty**

In the last part of chapter six Paul writes that freedom from the law does not imply freedom to sin, because freedom and slavery are relative terms. A non-Christian is free from the restrictions of living as a Christian, but is a slave to the control of sin. On the other hand, a Christian is free from the control of sin, but a slave to the restrictions of holy living. In reality, captivity to holiness is the truest kind of freedom, freedom not to sin, freedom to live righteously.

In chapter seven Paul illustrates his argument from marriage law. A mate is free to marry another person when the other mate has died, because death cancels the marriage relationship. Similarly, the death of Christ cancels the believer's relationship to the Mosaic law, freeing him to belong to Christ and bear fruit for God. Why then was the law given? It was given to prompt dependence on Christ for righteousness by increasing awareness of sin and moral incapability. Paul does not deny that God intended the Mosaic law to be a way of life for Old Testament believers. But so far as forgiveness of sins is concerned, the law was never supposed to be a system of human merit, but a means of inducing men to cast themselves on divine grace.

The last part of chapter seven classically describes the frustration of a person who wants to do good, but cannot, because of the demonic power of sin aggravated by the law. Frustration changes to triumph for believers, however, because they have the Spirit of Christ (chapter 8). As in Galatians, Paul contrasts the flesh and the Spirit. The Spirit of Christ empowers believers to conquer the sinful urge, assures them of salvation, will someday glorify them, and helps them to pray. Chapter eight climaxes with a burst of praise and confidence. The only One who has a right to accuse us — because He is holy — is the very One who justifies us. God would not be righteous if He *did* condemn us now that we are in Christ!

Frustration to Triumph

Read Romans 9-11. In discussing the problem of Israel, Paul maintains that God has a right to choose and to reject as He wants. Sinners have no claim on God. But God does not exercise His prerogative arbitrarily. He has rejected Israel because they sought self-righteousness rather than the righteousness of God. The invitation to salvation is thus open to all, Jews and Gentiles alike. But divine rejection of Israel at the present time is not as bad as it might seem. There are several mitigating factors: (1) a remnant of Jews do believe; (2) rejection of Israel as a nation provides Gentiles with better opportunity than they had before; (3) Jewish jealousy over the widespread salvation of Gentiles will compel the Jews to repent; and (4) the nation of Israel will yet be saved at the return of Christ, that is, those who are alive at His return will accept His messiahship and thereby receive salvation.

The Election and Rejection of Israel

Practical exhortations occupy the next major section of the epistle. For Paul theology always affects life, and to maintain a high level of Christian conduct in the churches he never leaves his readers to guess the practical import of his doctrinal teaching. After an appeal for Christians to offer themselves as "living [as opposed to slain] sacrifices" to God, Paul exhorts his readers not to imitate the outward conduct of non-Christians, but to live pleasingly before God as the result of a renewal of mental attitudes (12:1, 2).

Christian Commitment

Individual consecration leads to the various ministries of preaching, teaching, serving, giving, and leading — all according to the particular abilities God has given to individual Christians and all to be performed modestly and harmoniously (12:3-8). Harmony within a church depends, however, on mutual Christian love, which includes sincerity, hatred of evil, retention of right standards (goodness), affection, respect, industriousness, devotion to God, joy in hope, patience, prayer, generosity, and hospitality (12:9-13).

Similarly, Christians must maintain good relationships with non-Christians through prayer for their welfare, empathy with their joys, sympathy with their sorrows, and respectful and forgiving attitudes toward them. If the non-Christians still persecute, God Himself will judge them and vindicate His people (12: 14-21). Paul also commands submission to the state by obedience and payment of taxes; but his words must not be taken as blind support of totalitarianism. The stated presupposition is that the governing authorities are carrying out justice by punishing wrongdoers and praising rightdoers. Thus, resistance for purely political or selfish reasons deserves censure, but not resistance for moral-religious reasons (13:1-7). God requires love not only for one's fellow Christians, but also for one's fellow men in general. This includes payment of debts[9] and avoidance of adultery, murder, theft, and covetousness (13:8-10). The prospect of Jesus' return sharpens all of these ethical commands (13:11-14). Finally, as in 1 Corinthians Paul indicates that Christians must allow one another freedom to differ on ceremonial questions so long as damage is not done to weaker, uninformed people (14:1—15:3). *Read Romans 12:1—15:13.*

Concluding Remarks

Stating his plans with more detail than in chapter one, Paul now relates his hopes to deliver an offering to the church in Jerusalem and to evangelize Spain after visiting Rome. The commendation of Phoebe in 16:1, 2 reflects the Christian practice in which a home church recommends one of its members to a church in the locality to which that member is moving or paying a visit. The greeting to Prisca (a shortened form of Priscilla) and Aquila in 16:3 implies that they had returned to Rome. We know from secular sources, also, that Claudius' edict expelling the Jews from Rome was not permanently effective. Greetings, warning against false teachers, a benediction, further greetings, and a doxology complete the epistle. *Read Romans 15:14—16: 27.*

A SUMMARY OUTLINE OF ROMANS

Theme: the Gospel of justification by faith, or the gift of God's righteousness to sinners who believe in Jesus Christ

INTRODUCTION (1:1-17)
  A. Greeting (1:1-7)
  B. Paul's plan to visit Rome (1:8-15)

---

[9]Paul does not prohibit incurring of debts, but commands that debts incurred must not be left unpaid.

C. Statement of theme (1:16, 17)

I. THE SINFULNESS OF ALL MEN (1:18—3:20)
   A. The sinfulness of Gentiles (1:18-32)
   B. The sinfulness of Jews (2:1—3:8)
   C. The sinfulness of Jews and Gentiles together (3:9-20)

II. THE JUSTIFICATION OF SINNERS WHO BELIEVE IN JESUS CHRIST (3:21—5:21)
   A. The basis of justification in the propitiatory death of Jesus (3:21-26)
   B. Faith as the means of obtaining justification (3:27—4:25)
      1. Its exclusion of boasting in one's works (3:27-31)
      2. Its Old Testament examples in Abraham (especially) and David (4:1-25)
   C. The many blessings of justification (5:1-11)
   D. A contrast between Adam, in whom there is sin and death, and Christ, in whom there is righteousness and life (5:12-21)

III. THE SANCTIFICATION OF SINNERS JUSTIFIED BY FAITH IN JESUS (6:1—8:39)
   A. Baptism as a representation of the believer's union with Christ in His death with reference to sin and coming alive with reference to righteousness (6:1-14)
   B. Slavery to sin and freedom from righteousness versus slavery to righteousness and freedom from sin (6:15-23)
   C. Death to the law through union with Christ in His death as illustrated by the cancellation of marriage through the death of one's spouse (7:1-6)
   D. The failure of the law to produce righteousness because of the inability of human beings to overcome their own sinful bent (7:7-25)
   E. Righteous living through the Spirit by those who are justified by faith in Jesus Christ, with a description of life in the Spirit (8:1-27)
   F. A statement of confidence and triumph (8:28-39)

IV. THE UNBELIEF OF ISRAEL (9:1—11:36)
   A. The concern of Paul for Israel (9:1-5)
   B. The unbelief of Israel as a matter of God's predetermined plan (9:6-33)
   C. The unbelief of Israel as a matter of her own self-righteousness (10:1-21)
   D. The present remnant of believers in Israel (11:1-10)
   E. The future restoration and salvation of Israel (11:11-32)
   F. A doxology to God for His ways of wisdom (11:33-36)

V. PRACTICAL EXHORTATIONS (12:1—15:13)
   A. Consecration to God (12:1, 2)
   B. Ministries in the church (12:3-8)
   C. Love within the Christian community, with attendant virtues (12:9-13)
   D. Relationships with non-Christians (12:14-21)
   E. Obedience to the state (13:1-7)
   F. Love (13:8-10)
   G. Eschatological watchfulness (13:11-14)
   H. Freedom and avoidance of offence on ceremonial questions, such as the eating of certain food and the observance of sacred days (14:1—15:13)

CONCLUSION (15:14—16:27)
   A. Paul's plan to visit Rome after taking a gift of money to the Christians in Jerusalem (15:14-33)
   B. Commendation of Phoebe (16:1, 2)
   C. Greetings (16:3-16)
   D. Warning against false teachers (16:17-20a)
   E. Benediction (16:20b)
   F. Further greetings (16:21-23)
   G. Doxology (16:25-27)

For further discussion:

Does Paul's doctrine of human sinfulness degrade the dignity and nobility of man?

Does Paul contradict himself in appealing to the Gentile's good works performed out of conscience (2:12-16), and contending for total depravity of Jews and Gentiles alike (3:9-20)?

Is the transference of a penalty from a guilty to an innocent party legally defensible?

How can God rightly blame the whole human race for the original sin of Adam?

How can God rightly attribute the righteousness of Christ to all believers?

Is justification possible without sanctification?

Does the inner struggle between right and wrong depicted in Romans 7:7-25 characterize Christians or non-Christians? Compare Romans 8.

How can God maintain His sovereignty and yet allow man enough freedom of action to be held responsible?

Are men saved because they decide to believe in Christ or because God decides to make them believe? Is there another alternative?

Relate Pauline statements about the future of Israel (Romans 11) to recent Middle Eastern events.

What should be the attitude of the Christian toward his government in the face of current social problems and international politics?

For further investigation:

(Commentaries on Romans)

Bruce, F. F. *The Epistle of Paul to the Romans.* London: Tyndale, 1963.

Murray, J. *The Epistle to the Romans.* 2 volumes. Grand Rapids: Eerdmans, 1959-65.

(Books on topics appearing in Romans)

St. Augustine. *Confessions.* Especially the first several "books" for the problem of guilt.

Lewis, C. S. *The Case for Christianity.* Part I. New York: Macmillan, 1950. Or *Mere Christianity.* Book I. London: G. Bles, 1952. On human moral consciousness.

Luther, M. *Commentary* [or *Lectures*] *on Romans.* On 3:21-31.

Calvin, J., and J. Sadoleto. *Reformation Debate: Sadoleto's Letter to the Genevans and Calvin's Reply.* Edited by J. C. Olin. New York: Harper & Row, 1966. For justification by faith as a disputed point during the Reformation.

Calvin, J. *Institutes of the Christian Religion,* Book I, chapter 15; Book

II, chapters 1-5; Book III, chapters 21-24. For the Calvinistic view of divine sovereignty and human free will.

Arminius, J. *Declaration of Sentiments,* I-IV, and *Apology Against Thirty-One Defamatory Articles,* Articles I, IV-VIII, XIII-XVII. For the Arminian view of divine sovereignty and human free will.

Chafer, L. S. *He That Is Spiritual.* Grand Rapids: Zondervan [Dunham], 1918. On sanctification.

Walvoord, J. F. *Israel in Prophecy.* Grand Rapids: Zondervan, 1962. For comparison with Paul's discussion of Israel in Romans 9-11.

CHAPTER 16

The Prison Epistles of Paul

Leading questions:

From which of his various imprisonments did Paul probably write his Prison Epistles?

What are the interrelationships of the Prison Epistles?

What circumstances led Paul to plead with Philemon on behalf of a runaway slave?

Why did Paul write to the church in Colossae although he was unacquainted with them? What was the nature of the "Colossian heresy" as inferred from Pauline correctives?

What was the destination of the probably misnamed "Ephesians"? How do its structure and distinctive theological emphasis compare with that of Colossians?

What prompted the writing of Philippians? What were the attitudes and prospects of Paul at the time — and his concerns for the church in Philippi?

Paul's Imprisonments

Ephesians, Philippians, Colossians, and Philemon comprise the Prison (or Captivity) Epistles, so called because Paul was in prison when he wrote them. There are two known imprisonments of Paul, one in Caesarea under the governorships of Felix and Festus (Acts 23-26) and another in Rome while Paul awaited trial before Caesar (Acts 28). Supported by a small amount of early Church tradition, some scholars have conjectured another imprisonment in Ephesus during Paul's extended ministry there. Paul does mention "frequent" imprisonments in 2 Corinthians 11:23, but these probably refer to overnight stays in jail, as at Philippi (Acts 16:19-40). The traditional view assigns all of the Prison Epistles to the Roman imprisonment, but the Ephesian and Caesarean possibilities must at least be kept in mind for each of the Prison Epistles.

PHILEMON: PLEA FOR A RUNAWAY SLAVE

In the Epistle to Philemon, Paul asks a Christian slavemaster to receive kindly, perhaps even to release, a recently converted runaway slave now returning. There is hardly a more striking example of the salutary sociological effects of the Gospel in the entire New Testament.

Philemon, a resident of Colossae, had become a Christian through Paul ("you owe me even your own self," verse 19). This probably happened in nearby Ephesus during Paul's ministry there. A church met in the house of Philemon (verse 2). The early Christians had no church buildings and therefore met in homes. (If the number of believers was too large for one home to accommodate them, they used several.)

THE GATE OF ST. PAUL *at Rome stands in the southern part of the city.*

A slave of Philemon named Onesimus had absconded with some of his master's money and fled to Rome, where somehow he came into contact with Paul.[1] The apostle converted Onesimus and convinced him that as a Christian he should return to his master to live up to the meaning of his name, for "Onesimus"

---

[1]See the discussions on page 305 about the place of origin for Ephesians and Colossians, written at the same time as Philemon.

means "useful" (verses 10-12). With great tact and Christian courtesy, therefore, Paul writes to persuade Philemon not only to take back Onesimus without punishing him or putting him to death (the usual treatment of runaway slaves), but also to welcome Onesimus "as a beloved brother . . . in the Lord" (verse 16). Paul wants to retain Onesimus as a helper (verse 13). It has been suggested that the confident "you will do even more than what I say" (verse 21) broadly hints that Philemon should liberate Onesimus; but perhaps Paul is suggesting only that Philemon loan Onesimus for missionary work. Paul promises to pay Philemon the financial loss caused by Onesimus' theft; however, the immediate mention of Philemon's greater spiritual debt to Paul invites Philemon to cancel the financial debt which Paul has just assumed (verses 18-20). *Read Philemon.*

Archippus

Professors John Knox and E. J. Goodspeed have suggested that Philemon was overseer of the churches in the Lycus Valley, where Colossae, Laodicea, and Hierapolis were located; that he lived probably in Laodicea rather than in Colossae; that Archippus, not Philemon, was the owner of Onesimus and therefore the primary recipient of the letter; but that Paul sent Onesimus back with the letter *via Philemon* so that this influential churchman might exert pressure on Archippus, a stranger to Paul, to release Onesimus for missionary service with Paul. The epistle "to Philemon" then becomes the letter "from Laodicea" mentioned in Colossians 4:16, for it had first gone to Philemon in Laodicea and was then forwarded to Archippus and the church in his house. The "ministry" Archippus is commanded to fulfill in Colossians 4:17 is nothing else than the granting of Paul's request that Onesimus be released to become Paul's helper.[2] Against the theory, however, Archippus' "ministry," which he has "received in the Lord" and is to "fulfill," sounds more active and official than the release of a slave. Furthermore, the mention of Philemon first, rather than Archippus, appears to make Philemon the primary recipient of the letter (verses 1, 2: Philemon, Apphia his wife, Archippus the leader of the church and possibly Philemon's son, and the church which met in Philemon's house). Paul addresses the others, including the church, to exert public pressure on Philemon.

A SUMMARY OUTLINE OF PHILEMON

Theme: mercy for a runaway slave who had become a Christian

INTRODUCTION: greeting (1-3)

---

[2]Goodspeed, *New Solutions of New Testament Problems* (University of Chicago, 1927); Knox, *Philemon among the Letters of Paul,* 2nd edition (Nashville: Abingdon, 1959).

I. THANKSGIVING FOR PHILEMON (4-7)

THE PRISON

II. PLEA FOR ONESIMUS (8-22)

EPISTLES

CONCLUSION: greetings and benediction (23-25)

OF PAUL

For further investigation:

Blaiklock, E. M. *From Prison in Rome.* Grand Rapids: Zondervan, 1964.
Carson, H. M. *The Epistles of Paul to the Colossians and Philemon.* Grand Rapids: Eerdmans, 1960.
Moule, C. F. D. *The Epistles of Paul the Apostle to the Colossians and to Philemon.* Cambridge University Press, 1958.

COLOSSIANS: CHRIST THE HEAD OF THE CHURCH

In his Epistle to the Colossians Paul highlights the divine person and creative and redemptive work of Christ against devaluation of Christ by a particular brand of heresy which threatened the church in Colossae. Then Paul draws out the practical implications of this high Christology for everyday life and conduct.

Theme

The ancient Marcionite prologue[3] to Colossians says that Paul wrote the epistle from Ephesus. This tradition is doubtful, however, because it also says that Paul wrote Philemon from Rome. Yet Colossians and Philemon are inseparably linked, for both letters mention Timothy, Aristarchus, Mark, Epaphras, Luke, Demas, Archippus, and Onesimus (Colossians 1:1 and Philemon 1; Colossians 4:10-14 and Philemon 23, 24; Colossians 4:17 and Philemon 2; Colossians 4:9 and Philemon 10 ff.). The duplication of so many names must indicate that Paul wrote and sent both letters at the same time and from the same place.

Ephesian Origin

Furthermore, if Paul wrote Colossians and Philemon from an Ephesian imprisonment, the slave Onesimus had absconded with his master's money only one hundred miles distance to Ephesus; yet that is improbable, for Onesimus would have known he might easily be captured so close to home. It is far more likely that Onesimus fled far away to the larger city of Rome to hide himself in the crowds. Moreover, Luke was with Paul when Paul wrote Colossians (Colossians 4:14); but the description of Paul's Ephesian ministry is not one of Luke's "we"-sections in Acts. We should therefore reject an Ephesian imprisonment as the place of origin for Colossians, despite partial support from the Marcionite tradition.

It is even more improbable that Colossians came from the Caesarean imprisonment. Caesarea was also a smaller and less likely city than Rome as a place to which a runaway slave might flee to escape detection. Onesimus would scarcely have

Caesarean Origin

---

[3] An introduction to the epistle written from the standpoint of Marcionism, a brand of Gnosticism.

SITE OF ANCIENT COLOSSAE *with a view of the city mound and the Taurus Mountains in the background.*

come into contact with Paul in Caesarea, for only Paul's friends could see him there (Acts 24:23). Also, the expectation of Paul that he would soon be released (he asks Philemon to prepare lodging for him! — Philemon 22) does not tally with the Caesarean imprisonment, where Paul came to realize that his only hope lay in appealing to Caesar.

Roman Origin

Several considerations favor the Roman imprisonment: (1) it is most likely that to hide his identity Onesimus fled to Rome, the most populous city in the empire; (2) Luke's presence with Paul at the writing of Colossians agrees with Luke's accompanying Paul to Rome in Acts; (3) the difference in doctrinal emphases between Colossians, where Paul is not preoccupied with the Judaizing controversy, and the Epistles to the Galatians, Romans, and Corinthians, where he strongly emphasizes freedom from the Mosaic law, suggests that Paul wrote Colossians during the later period of the Roman imprisonment, when the Judaizing controversy no longer dominated his thinking.

Founding of the Church in Colossae

The city of Colossae lay in the valley of the Lycus River in a mountainous district about one hundred miles east of Ephesus. See the map on page 230. The neighboring cities of Laodicea and Hierapolis overshadowed Colossae in importance. The distant way in which Paul writes that he has "heard" of his readers' Christian faith (1:4) and his inclusion of the readers among those who have never seen him face to face (2:1) imply that Paul had neither founded the church in Colossae nor visited it. Since the Colossians had learned the grace of God from Epaphras (1:6, 7), he must have been the founder of the church. Yet Epaphras was with Paul at the time of writing

306

(4:12, 13). We may surmise that Epaphras became a Christian through Paul's Ephesian ministry, evangelized the neighboring region of Colossae, Laodicea, and Hierapolis, and visited Paul in prison to solicit his advice concerning a dangerous heresy threatening the Colossian church (see below). Apparently Archippus had been left in charge of the church (4:17). Under this hypothesis we can understand why Paul assumed authority over the Colossian church even though he had never been there; he was "grandfather" of the church through his convert Epaphras, and as such his judgment had been sought.

The Christians in Colossae were predominantly Gentile. Paul classes them among the uncircumcised (2:13). In 1:27 the phrases "among the Gentiles" and "in you" seem to be synonymous. And the description of the Colossians as once "estranged and hostile in mind" (1:21) recalls similar phraseology in Ephesians 2:11 ff., where Paul indubitably refers to Gentiles.

A Gentile Church

The Epistle to the Colossians centers around the so-called "Colossian heresy." We can infer certain features of the false teaching from the counter-emphases of Paul. In fact, Paul probably borrows words and phrases used by the false teachers, such as "knowledge" and "fulness," and turns them against the heresy by filling them with orthodox content. The heresy

The Colossian Heresy

> detracted from the person of Christ, so that Paul stresses the preeminence of Christ (1:15-19);
>
> emphasized human philosophy, that is, empty speculations apart from divine revelation (2:8);
>
> contained elements of Judaism, such as circumcision (2:11; 3:11), rabbinical tradition (2:8), dietary regulations and Sabbath and festival observances (2:16);
>
> included worship of angels as intermediaries to keep the highest God (pure Spirit) unsullied by contact with the physical universe (2:18) — a pagan feature, since although orthodox Jews had developed a hierarchy of angels, they did not worship them nor did they regard the physical nature of the universe as evil; and
>
> flaunted an exclusivistic air of secrecy and superiority, against which Paul stresses the all-inclusiveness and public nature of the Gospel (1:20, 23, 28; 3:11).

The Colossian heresy, then, blended Jewish legalism, Greek philosophic speculation, and Oriental mysticism. Perhaps the location of Colossae on an important trade route linking East and West contributed to the mixed character of the false teaching. Most of the features appear fullblown in later Gnosticism and in the Greek and Oriental mystery religions. However, the presence of Judaistic features prevents simple equation of the Colossian heresy with that which later came to be known as Gnosticism and with the mystery religions, both of which were either un- or anti-Judaistic. The heresy at Colossae rather represented an attempted invasion of Christianity by a syncretistic gnostic Judaism which lacked the redeemer motif of later, anti-Judaistic Gnosticism.

Doctrine, Especially Christology

Colossians has two sections: doctrine (chapters 1, 2) and exhortation (chapters 3, 4). Paul puts the doctrinal accent on Christology. The epistle opens with a greeting, thanksgiving, and prayer. Then begins the great Christological discussion. *Read Colossians 1, 2.*

Paul's laudatory statements about Christ mention
His kingdom (1:13),

His redemptive work (1:14),

His being the outward representation ("image") of God in human form (1:15),

His supremacy over creation as its Master and Heir (since first-born sons received twice as much inheritance as other sons, "first-born" came to denote priority and supremacy, so that "first-born of all creation" [1:15] need not imply that Jesus was the first to be created),

His creatorship (1:16),

His preexistence and cohesion of the universe (1:17),

His headship over the new creation, the Church, and

His primacy in rising from the dead never to die again (1:18).

Some scholars take verses 15-20 as a quotation from an early hymn of praise to Christ. The "fulness of God" dwelling in Christ is the totality of divine nature. When Paul writes that his own sufferings complete "what is lacking in Christ's afflictions" (1:24), he does not imply that Christ failed to accomplish redemption fully. He means that sufferings endured in spreading the Gospel are also necessary if men are to be saved and that Christ continues to suffer with His persecuted witnesses because of their union, or solidarity, with Him. The term "mystery" ("this mystery, . . . Christ in you," 1:27) refers to spiritual truth hidden from unbelievers, but revealed to believers.

In his polemic against the Colossian heresy (2:8-23) Paul charges that the false teaching obscures the preeminence of Christ, that its ritual observances, taken from Judaism, only foreshadow the spiritual realities in Christ, and that its asceticism and angel-worship foster human pride and detract from the glory of Christ.

The union of the believer with Christ in His death, resurrection, and ascension forms the basis for practical exhortations. Christians are to adopt God's viewpoint by regarding themselves as dead to sin in Christ and alive in Him to righteousness. *Read Colossians 3, 4.* "Scythians" (3:11) were regarded as particularly uncouth barbarians. Since salt retards corruption, speech "seasoned with salt" (4:6) probably means speech which is not corrupt or obscene.

A SUMMARY OUTLINE OF COLOSSIANS

Theme: the preeminence of Christ

INTRODUCTION: (1:1-12)
- A. Greeting (1:1, 2)
- B. Thanksgiving (1:3-8)
- C. Prayer (1:9-12)

I. THE PREEMINENCE OF CHRIST IN CHRISTIAN DOCTRINE (1:13—2:23)
- A. His creative and redemptive work (1:13-23)
- B. His proclamation by Paul (1:24—2:6)
- C. His sufficiency over against the Colossian heresy (2:8-23)

II. THE PREEMINENCE OF CHRIST IN CHRISTIAN CONDUCT (3:1—4:6)
- A. Union with Christ in His death, resurrection, and exaltation (3:1-4)
- B. Application of death with Christ to sinful actions (3:5-11)
- C. Application of resurrection with Christ to righteous actions (3:12—4:6)

CONCLUSION (4:7-18)
- A. The coming of Tychicus and Onesimus (4:7-9)
- B. Greetings and final instructions (4.10-17)
- C. Farewell and benediction (4:18)

For further investigation:

Simpson, E. K., and F. F. Bruce. *Commentary on the Epistles to the Ephesians and the Colossians.* Grand Rapids: Eerdmans, 1957.
Carson, H. M. *The Epistles of Paul to the Colossians and Philemon.* Grand Rapids: Eerdmans, 1960.
Moule, C. F. D. *The Epistles of Paul the Apostle to the Colossians and to Philemon.* Cambridge University Press, 1958.

EPHESIANS: THE CHURCH — THE BODY OF CHRIST

Ephesians was not written in response to a specific circumstance or controversy as were most of Paul's epistles. It has almost a meditative quality. In the theme shared with Colossians — Christ the head of the Church His body — Ephesians emphasizes the Church as Christ's body, whereas Colossians emphasizes the headship of Christ. Colossians warns against false doctrine which diminishes Christ, while Ephesians expresses praise for the unity and blessings shared by all believers in Christ.

The indication that Tychicus will add further details about Paul's circumstances by word of mouth implies that Tychicus carried the epistle known as "Ephesians" to its destination (Ephesians 6:21, 22). Paul's self-identification as "a prisoner of the Lord" demonstrates both his being in prison at the time of writing and his awareness of the Lord's purpose in his imprisonment.

Relation to Colossians

Paul must have written Ephesians and Colossians at approximately the same time because the subject matter in the two epistles is quite similar (Christ the head of the Church His body) and because the verses about Tychicus recur in almost identical form in Colossians 4:7, 8. Tychicus must therefore have carried both letters at once. (Colossae was about one hundred miles east of Ephesus.)

Ephesian, Caesarean, or Roman Origin

Although Ephesians may have been directed to the region around Ephesus rather than to Ephesus itself (see below), it is hardly possible that Paul wrote from an Ephesian imprisonment. So far as the Caesarean imprisonment is concerned, Paul's reference to preaching boldly as "an ambassador in chains" implies that he was still proclaiming the Gospel in spite of his being a prisoner (Ephesians 6:20); yet in Caesarea only his friends could visit him (Acts 24:22, 23). In Rome, however, Paul preached to a steady stream of visitors who came to his house-prison (Acts 28:30, 31). Ephesians therefore was written during the Roman imprisonment, just as the closely related Colossians and Philemon.

Goodspeed's Theory

The American scholar E. J. Goodspeed has theorized that an admirer of Paul wrote Ephesians toward the end of the first century A.D. Goodspeed goes so far as to suggest that the admirer was Onesimus, the converted slave about whom Paul wrote to Philemon.[4] According to this theory, the writer designed Ephesians to summarize Pauline theology as an introduction to a collection of Paul's genuine epistles. The collection of the Pauline corpus was prompted by the prominence of Paul in the recently written book of Acts. However, manuscript evidence is lacking that Ephesians ever stood first in the collection of Pauline epistles, as we would expect if Goodspeed's hypothesis were true. Moreover, very early Church tradition assigns Ephesians to Paul himself.

Destination not Ephesus

The phrase "in Ephesus," which refers to the locale of the readers (1:1), is missing in the most ancient manuscripts. Thus Paul omits the geographical location of the addressees altogether.

---

[4]*The Key to Ephesians* (University of Chicago Press, 1956) and other works by Goodspeed and by those following his lead.

Furthermore, the distant way in which Paul speaks of his having "heard" about the readers' faith (1:15) and their having "heard" of his ministry (3:2) and the lack of his usual terms of endearment rule out Ephesus as the destination; for Paul had labored there for over two years and knew the Ephesian Christians intimately, as they also knew him.

Some early tradition identifies the church in Laodicea as the recipient of the epistle. The German scholar Harnack suggested that early copyists suppressed the name Laodicea because of the condemnation of the Laodicean church in Revelation 3:14-22 and that later copyists substituted the name Ephesus because of Paul's close association with the church in that city. Paul does mention a letter to Laodicea in Colossians 4:16. But since no manuscript mentions Laodicea in Ephesians 1:1, the making of "Ephesians" into "Laodiceans" in early tradition was probably an attempt to identify the letter to Laodicea mentioned in Colossians.

More likely, "Ephesians" was a circular epistle addressed to various churches in Asia Minor in the general vicinity of Ephesus. Under this view Paul's mention of the epistle to Laodicea in Colossians 4:16 possibly refers to our "Ephesians," but would not imply that the epistle was addressed only to Laodicea. Rather, in its circulation to the churches throughout the area the epistle had reached Laodicea and was to go next to Colossae. The circular nature of the epistle, then, explains the omission of a city name in the address (1:1). If a single copy of the letter circulated from Ephesus and came back to Ephesus, the name of that city could have easily become linked to the epistle.

Like Colossians, Ephesians falls into two parts. Ephesians 1-3 is doctrinal: the spiritual privileges of the Church. Ephesians 4-6 is hortatory: the spiritual responsibilities of Christians.

After the greeting (1:1, 2) Paul launches into a doxology of praise to God for spiritual blessings in Christ "in the heavenly places" (1:3-14). In other words, the believer's union with Christ involves a share in His exaltation as well as in His death, burial, and resurrection. The doxology delineates the parts played by all three members of the Trinity in salvation: the Father chose believers (the doctrine of election, verse 4); the Son redeemed them (verse 7); the Holy Spirit "sealed" them, that is, the gift of the Spirit is God's downpayment, or guarantee, that He will complete their salvation at the return of Christ (verses 13, 14). A thanksgiving and prayer that Christians may comprehend and appreciate the immensity of God's grace and wisdom follow the doxology (1:15-23). *Read Ephesians 1.*

Divine
Grace

To help his readers appreciate the magnitude of divine grace, Paul contrasts their domination by sin before conversion and their freedom from that tyranny after conversion. He also emphasizes that salvation is wholly unearned; it comes by divine grace, through faith, and apart from meritorious good works. God's action does produce good works, but they are a consequence rather than a means of salvation. Divine grace reveals itself especially in the redemption of Gentiles from paganism and in their equality with Jews in the Church. The dividing wall of hostility between the two groups, symbolized by the wall in the Temple courtyards beyond which Gentiles were not allowed, does not exist in the Church.[5] But however grand the plan of salvation, Paul and his readers faced the unpleasant reality of present persecution. Nevertheless, he writes that his awareness of God's grace and of his privilege in spreading the good news prevents discouragement. Similar awareness on the part of his readers will likewise prevent their discouragement. The section therefore closes with another doxology and prayer that the readers may be stabilized by increased spiritual knowledge. *Read Ephesians 2, 3.*

Unity and
Diversity

The practical exhortations begin with a plea for outward unity growing out of the already existing spiritual unity of the Church. Yet this unity includes a diversity of function for the growth of the body, or Church. Each Christian has a ministerial function, for which leaders of the Church are to equip him. *Read Ephesians 4:1-16.*

Holy
Conduct

Miscellaneous instructions on holiness follow: Tell the truth. Be righteously indignant when necessary, but do not sin by failing to control anger. Do not steal. Avoid obscene speech and risqué humor. The section closes with a metrical triplet which may have come from an early baptismal hymn, sung at the moment of rising from the waters:

> "Awake, sleeper,
> And arise from the dead,
> And Christ will shine on you."

Read Ephesians 4:17—5:14.

The Filling
With the
Spirit

Paul's exhortation to be filled with the Holy Spirit indicates that this will show itself in the avoidance of drunkenness (unlike the orgiastic enthusiasm of Hellenistic cults) and in joyful singing, witnessing, and submission to one another. Mutual submission includes the social obligations of wifely subordination to the husband modeled after the Church's subordination to Christ

---

[5]Alternatively, the dividing wall represents the old barrier between God and man, now broken down by Christ.

the head, husbandly love toward the wife modeled after Christ's love for the Church His body, obedience to parents by children, fatherly patience with children, obedience of slaves to masters, and kindness of masters toward slaves.

Paul then unites the metaphors of head and body with a picture of the Church as the bride and wife of Christ, who is the groom and husband. Just as husband and wife become "one flesh" (or body) in the marital relationship, Christ and the Church are spiritually one. Scholars have suggested various sources for the Pauline metaphor of the Church as Christ's body: the Stoic notion that the universe is a body with many different parts, the rabbinical idea that men are the members of Adam's body in a very literalistic sense, the symbolic or sacramental union of the believer with Christ's body when he eats the bread in the Lord's Supper. Whatever the source(s) — if any be needed for a man of Paul's originality — it is certain that the Hebrew concept of corporate personality underlies the metaphor, and indeed the whole Pauline doctrine of the union between the believer and Christ.

Before the farewell, Paul urges his readers to don the spiritual armor provided by God and to fight the satanic powers which dominate the world. Perhaps the sight of the soldier to whom Paul was handcuffed while dictating Ephesians in his house-prison suggested "the full armor of God." The word for "shield" denotes the large kind which covered the whole body, not the small circular shield of the Greeks. "Flaming missiles" refers to darts and arrows dipped in pitch or some other combustible material, set aflame, and hurled or shot toward the enemy. *Read Ephesians 5:15—6:24.*

A SUMMARY OUTLINE OF EPHESIANS

Theme: the spiritual privileges and responsibilities of the Church

INTRODUCTION: greeting (1:1, 2)
  I. THE SPIRITUAL PRIVILEGES OF THE CHURCH (1:3—3:21)
    A. Praise for spiritual blessings originating in the Father's plan, the Son's accomplishment, and the Spirit's application (1:3-14)
    B. Thanksgiving and prayer for increased comprehension of divine grace (1:15-23)
    C. The regeneration of sinners by divine grace alone (2:1-10)
    D. The reconciliation of Gentiles with God and with Jews in the Church (2:11-22)
    E. Paul's sense of privilege in proclaiming the Gospel (3:1-13)
    F. Prayer for stability through increased comprehension (3:14-19)
    G. Doxology (3:20, 21)
  II. THE SPIRITUAL RESPONSIBILITIES OF THE CHURCH (4:1—6:20)
    A. Maintenance of unity through diversity of edificatory ministry (4:1-16)
    B. Moral conduct (4:17—5:14)
    C. The filling with the Spirit (5:15-20)
    D. Submission to one another (5:21—6:9)

1. Submission of wives to husbands, as the Church's to Christ (5:22-24)
2. Love of husbands to wives, as Christ's to the Church (5:25-33)
3. Obedience of children to parents (6:1-3)
4. Parental authority with patience (6:4)
5. Obedience of slaves to masters (6:5-8)
6. Fairness of masters to slaves (6:9)

E. Spiritual warfare utilizing the whole armor of God against satanic forces (6:10-20)

CONCLUSION: the coming of Tychicus, a final greeting, and benediction (6:21-24)

For further investigation:

Foulkes, F. *The Epistle of Paul to the Ephesians.* Grand Rapids: Eerdmans, 1963.

Bruce, F. F. *The Epistle to the Ephesians.* London: Pickering and Inglis, 1961.

Simpson, E. K., and F. F. Bruce. *Commentary on the Epistles to the Ephesians and the Colossians.* Grand Rapids: Eerdmans, 1957.

PHILIPPIANS: A FRIENDLY THANK YOU NOTE

Theme and Occasion

The church at Philippi appears to have been Paul's favorite. He received regular assistance from it (Philippians 4:15 ff.; 2 Corinthians 11:8 ff.). The Epistle to the Philippians is thus the most personal of any which Paul wrote to a church. It is, in

STREAM NEAR PHILIPPI *at or near the traditional place where Paul met Lydia and the other women in a prayer meeting.*

fact, a thank you note for their most recent financial gift (4: 10, 14), which they had sent through Epaphroditus (2:25). During his trip or after his arrival with the offering, Epaphroditus had fallen almost fatally ill (2:27). The Philippians heard of his illness, and word came back to Epaphroditus that they were concerned about him. Paul sensed that Epaphroditus wanted to return to Philippi and therefore sent him with the epistle (2:25-30).

Subsidiary Purposes

The return of Epaphroditus not only enabled Paul to write his gratitude for their financial assistance, but also gave him opportunity to counteract a tendency toward divisiveness in the Philippian church (2:2; 4:2), to warn against Judaizers (chapter 3), and to prepare the Philippians for approaching visits by Timothy and, hopefully, by Paul himself (2:19-24).[6]

Caesarean Origin

Paul was in prison at the time of writing ("my imprisonment," 1:7, 13). But to which of his imprisonments does Paul refer? Probably not to the Caesarean, because there Paul would not have been able to preach so freely as implied in 1:12, 13 (compare Acts 24:23). Also, Paul would have known that release in Caesarea would mean almost instant lynching by the Jews in the area, so that his only prospect of safety lay in appealing to Caesar and thus going to Rome under guard. Yet in Philippians 1:25; 2:24 (and Philemon 22) Paul hopes for quick release.

Ephesian Origin

Ephesus presents a better possibility, for several reasons. Paul writes that he hopes to send Timothy to Philippi (2:19, 23); and Luke writes that Paul sent Timothy and Erastus to Philippi *from Ephesus* (Acts 19:22). (But if the two passages are really parallel, why does Paul omit mentioning Erastus in Philippians 2:19 ff.?) A further argument for an Ephesian imprisonment is that the polemic against the Judaizers in chapter three is similar to Paul's earlier pattern of thought. (It remains possible, however, that a later Judaizing threat revived Paul's earlier polemics against the Judaizers.)

Inscriptions testify that a detachment of the Praetorian Guard once was stationed in Ephesus, and Paul mentions the Praetorian Guard in 1:13. Similarly, "Caesar's household" (4:22) might refer to imperial civil servants in Ephesus.

According to Acts, Luke accompanied Paul to Rome, but was not with him in Ephesus. That Paul does not mention Luke in Philippians as he does in Colossians 4:14 and Philemon 24 therefore suggests that he wrote Philippians from an Ephesian im-

---

[6]"Epaphroditus" is the full form of the name "Epaphras," which appears in Colossians. But we do not have sufficient evidence to identify Epaphras, founder of the church in Colossae, with Epaphroditus, messenger of the church in Philippi.

prisonment. (But if Philippians was written toward the end of the Roman imprisonment [see below], Luke might have left Paul by then, so that this argument from silence is not decisive.)

It is also argued for an Ephesian imprisonment that if Paul had written Philippians later, from Rome, he could hardly have said that his readers had for some time "lacked opportunity" to support him financially (4:10). So much time had elapsed by the time of the Roman imprisonment that they would have had prolonged opportunity; but an earlier Ephesian imprisonment allows for such a statement. However, we do not know all the financial circumstances of Paul and the Philippians. To avoid the charge of embezzlement, Paul may have refused personal gifts during the period he was collecting money for the church in Jerusalem. That may be the reason why the Philippians "lacked opportunity."

Generally considered as the strongest argument in favor of an Ephesian imprisonment over against the Roman is that Philippians presupposes too many journeys between Rome and Philippi (about a month's journey apart), whereas the short distance between Ephesus and Philippi makes the numerous journeys within a short period of time more conceivable. The journeys presupposed in Philippians are

1) the message carried from Rome to Philippi that Paul had been imprisoned there;
2) the bringing of the gift by Epaphroditus;
3) the delivery back to Philippi of the report that Epaphroditus had fallen ill; and
4) the return of the word that the Philippians were concerned about Epaphroditus.

In reality, however, this argument for Ephesus against Rome is not substantial. Time for the journeys between Rome and Philippi would require only four to six months *in toto*. Allowances for intervals between the journeys still keep the total amount of time required well within the minimal two years (or longer) which we know Paul spent in Rome (Acts 28:30). And Paul wrote Philippians toward the end of his imprisonment, for he expected to be released soon (1:19-26) and to visit Philippi (2:23, 24). His transfer from his own rented house (Acts 28:16, 23, 30) to the barracks of the Praetorian Guard on the Palatine (Philippians 1:13) indicates that his trial was finally in progress and near conclusion.

Furthermore, the Philippians may have known that Paul was going as a prisoner to Rome before he arrived there, so that Epaphroditus could already have started toward Rome. Or, since the shipwreck delayed Paul at Malta, Epaphroditus may have arrived in Rome before Paul. The Christians in Rome knew beforehand of Paul's coming, for they met Paul outside the city and escorted him the rest of the way (Acts 28:15, 16). Had Epaphroditus informed them? Only journeys 2-4 are necessarily presupposed, and the temporal factor does not at all hinder the view that Paul wrote to the Philippians from Rome.

Against the Ephesian imprisonment, Paul fails to mention the collection for Jerusalem (which was very much on his mind throughout his third missionary tour, during which he ministered in Ephesus) and his writing about money matters in Philippians would have made reference to the collection almost certain had he been writing during that period from Ephesus. Also, we must bear in mind that an Ephesian imprisonment of Paul is entirely conjectural and is not mentioned in Acts although Luke goes into great detail about Paul's ministry in Ephesus (Acts 19).

In favor of Rome, "Praetorian Guard" (1:13) and "Caesar's **Roman** household" (4:22) most likely point to Rome.[7] According to **Origin** 1:19 ff., Paul's life was at stake in the trial. The trial must therefore have been before Caesar in Rome, for in any other place Paul could always exercise his right of appeal to Caesar. The early tradition of the Marcionite prologue likewise assigns the epistle to Rome. For all these reasons and because of the weakness of arguments to the contrary, the traditional view that Paul wrote Philippians from Rome remains the best.

The informality of this thank you note makes it difficult **Joy in** to outline. Throughout, the dominant emotional note is one of **Hardship** joy. In the first chapter, after the customary greeting, thanksgiving, and prayer, Paul describes the ministry he is carrying on in spite of his imprisonment, even because of it. The palace guard and Roman officialdom in general are hearing the Gospel. Moreover, the boldness of Paul's witness inspires other Christians, even those who do not like Paul. The latter are not false teachers, however, for Paul calls them "brethren" (1: 14, 15). *Read Philippians 1.*

Read Philippians 2. This chapter is famous for the passage on **The Kenosis** Jesus' self-emptying, or humiliation, and exaltation (2:6-11). **Hymn** Many scholars think Paul is quoting an early Christian hymn. The passage is incidental, however, to an exhortation to ecclesiastical unity through humility, for which Jesus is the great example. The ancient world despised humility; Christian teach-

---

[7]Since the Praetorian Guard in Rome numbered about nine thousand, but in Ephesus far fewer, the fact that the "whole" Praetorian Guard had heard of Paul's imprisonment for Christ (1:13) has been thought to favor Ephesus over Rome. But the success of Paul's witness elsewhere suggests that the whole guard in Rome may have heard, especially if Paul succeeded in converting some of them. Or, "praetorium" may refer to the emperor's palace rather than to the large group of soldiers who comprised the guard.

ing made it a virtue. The passage clearly implies the preexistence of Christ before His incarnation. But of what did He empty Himself? According to the *kenosis*[8] theory He emptied Himself of divine metaphysical (but not moral) attributes such as omnipotence, omniscience, and omnipresence. However, since Jesus frequently displayed these attributes according to the gospel accounts of His earthly ministry, a better answer to the question is that Jesus emptied Himself solely of the independent exercise of those attributes (compare John 5:19) or simply of the outward glory of His deity. Or perhaps the self-emptying in verse seven does not refer to the incarnation at all, but to Jesus' expiring on the cross, in synonymous parallelism with the reference to Jesus' death in the following verse. Under the last interpretation, Paul is allusively quoting Isaiah 53:12: "he poured out [emptied!] his soul [frequently equivalent to the reflexive pronoun 'himself'] to death."

**Against
Judaizers**

The "Finally, my brethren" in 3:1 sounds so much like the closing part of an epistle — yet two more chapters follow — and Paul changes tone so suddenly that some scholars posit a long interpolation, beginning in 3:2, from another epistle. But the theory lacks manuscript evidence. It is better to suppose a break in dictation, perhaps with fresh news from Philippi about a threat of false teachers there. Paul had intended to close, but then thought it necessary to prolong the epistle with warning against the Judaizers.

Chapter three contains another famous passage. It is Paul's autobiographical review of his Jewish background and the revolution in his scale of values when Christ became the goal of his life (3:3-14). Again, however, the passage is incidental — this time to a warning against the Judaizers, who practice, according to Paul's sarcastic term, "mutilation" instead of circumcision (3:2). Paul also calls them "dogs," regarded then as despicable creatures, the very term by which Jews regularly referred to Gentiles. Still another designation is "evil-workers," an ironic counterthrust at their belief in salvation by good works. True circumcision, however, consists of inward faith in Christ Jesus without self-merit.

Paul's Jewish background had been impeccable: (1) circumcision on the eighth day exactly as prescribed by the Mosaic law (Leviticus 12:3); (2) Israelite ancestry; (3) tribal origin in Benjamin, from which came the first king of Israel, Saul (also a name of Paul); (4) Hebraistic rather than Hellenistic practice and heritage;[9] (5) Phariseeism; (6) zealousness to the point of persecuting the Church; (7) blamelessness in formal observance

---

[8]*Kenosis* is the Greek word for *emptying.*

[9]Compare page 52.

of the law. The entrance of Christ into his life caused Paul not merely to dismiss, but to renounce as liabilities all his former assets as a Jew. And he continued to do so, growing to regard them as "refuse" (3:8), that he might experience increasing union with Christ in His sufferings, death, and resurrection.

Realizing that his readers might misunderstand him to claim perfection, Paul disclaims it and expresses the ardor with which, forgetting the past, he is pursuing the heavenly goal (3:12-16). "Forgetting" does not mean banishing from memory (if that were possible), but disregarding as having any present potency.

The discussion again comes around to the Judaizers, who opposed the cross of Christ by requiring works of the law, who worshiped their belly by insisting on adherence to the dietary restrictions of the law, who gloried in their shame by exposing nakedness for the rite of circumcision, and who set their minds on earthly things by occupying themselves with forms and ceremonies (3:17-19).[10] Chapter three closes with a reference to the Christian "commonwealth" or "citizenship" in heaven, a particularly meaningful figure of speech to the Philippians, whose own city was a colony populated largely with Roman citizens living away from their true home in Italy. *Read Philippians* 3, 4.

Exhortations

The various exhortations in chapter four include a plea for unity between two women of the church, Euodia and Syntyche, former helpers of Paul. The man who is to aid their reconciliation is a "true yokefellow," unknown by name unless that *is* his name with a play on its meaning: "*Syzygos* [Greek for *yokefellow, comrade*], truly so called." At any rate, Paul asks him to live up to his name or description by promoting the reconciliation. Exhortations to joy, patience, trust, prayer, thanksgiving, and nobility of thought follow — with promises of divine presence and peace and the return of Jesus.

Then Paul expresses thanks for the recent gift to him from the Philippian church, as well as for previous contributions. Throughout this section Paul maintains disinterestedness in money for its own sake or for his selfish benefit, but indicates a concern for and confidence in the reward of the Philippians for having given so generously. Finally, greetings and a benediction conclude the epistle.

A SUMMARY OUTLINE OF PHILIPPIANS

Theme: thanks for financial assistance with personal news and exhortations

INTRODUCTION: greeting (1:1, 2)

I. PERSONAL MATTERS (1:3-26)

---

[10]Some scholars see antinomian and/or perfectionist gnostics as the target of these remarks; but Paul's appeal to his own Judaistic, indeed Pharisaical, background favors identification with the Judaizers throughout the chapter.

A. Paul's thanksgiving, prayer, and affection for the Christians in Philippi (1:3-11)
B. Paul's prison-preaching, prospect of release, and readiness to die (1:12-26)

II. EXHORTATIONS (1:27—2:30)
    A. Worthy conduct (1:27-30)
    B. Unity by humility, with the example of Christ's self-emptying (2:1-18)

III. THE SENDING OF TIMOTHY AND EPAPHRODITUS TO PHILIPPI (2:19-30)

IV. WARNING AGAINST THE JUDAIZERS, WITH A FAMOUS AUTOBIOGRAPHICAL PASSAGE (3:1-21)

V. EXHORTATIONS (4:1-9)
    A. Unity between Euodia and Syntyche (4:1-3)
    B. Joy and trust (4:4-7)
    C. Nobility of thought (4:8,9)

VI. THANKS FOR FINANCIAL ASSISTANCE (4:10-20)

CONCLUSION: greetings and benediction (4:21-23)

For further discussion:

Should Paul and the early Christians have crusaded against slavery? Why did they not? What should be the involvement or noninvolvement of the Church in the curing of social ills — within the Church, outside the Church, officially, individually?

Compare current neomysticism and intellectualism with the Colossian heresy.

Why do people tend to react against the Ephesian emphasis on salvation through the sheer grace of God by constructing their own systems of salvation by meritorious works?

What was the key to Paul's joy in hardship, as expressed in Philippians?

For further investigation:

Blaiklock, E. M. *From Prison in Rome.* Grand Rapids: Zondervan, 1964.
Martin, R. P. *The Epistle of Paul to the Philippians.* Grand Rapids: Eerdmans, 1959.

CHAPTER 17

The Pastoral Epistles of Paul

Leading questions:

What are the pros and cons of Pauline authorship of the Pastorals?

Where do the Pastorals fit into the chronology of Paul's life?

What instructions does Paul give for the ongoing life of the Church and the maintenance of Christian belief?

FIRST AND SECOND TIMOTHY AND TITUS: ADVICE TO YOUNG PREACHERS

Theme — 1 and 2 Timothy and Titus comprise the Pastoral Epistles, so called because Paul wrote them to young pastors. They contain instructions concerning the administrative responsibilities of Timothy and Titus in the churches.

Authenticity — Modern higher critical scholarship casts more doubt on the authenticity of these epistles than upon any of the others claiming authorship by Paul. According to the view which denies Pauline authorship of the Pastorals, the pseudonymous writer used the authority of Paul's name to combat rising Gnosticism in the second century. It is said either that the Pastorals are wholly pseudonymous (but why then the presence of very personal items about Paul which have the ring of authenticity?) or, more often, that an admirer of Paul incorporated authentic Pauline notes in writing the epistles after Paul's lifetime.

The Theory of Pauline Fragments — Disagreement exists concerning what sections of the Pastorals contain the supposed scraps of material really written by Paul.[1] Moreover, it is unlikely that mere fragments of genuine Pauline epistles would be preserved, especially since most of them are of a personal nature and lack theological appeal. It is still more

---

[1]The fragments commonly claimed are 2 Timothy 1:16-18; 3:10, 11; 4:1, 2a, 5b-22; Titus 3:12-15.

unlikely that they would later be incorporated into longer pseudepigraphal epistles in a haphazard way. And why did the supposed forger concentrate almost all of the fragments in 2 Timothy instead of distributing them evenly throughout the three Pastorals? For that matter, why did he write *three* Pastorals? Their contents do not differ sufficiently to indicate why he should have written three epistles in Paul's name instead of just one.

Pseudonymity

In favor of authorship by Paul is the claim in the first verse of each Pastoral Epistle that Paul is writing. Against the claim, it is argued that pseudonymous writing was an accepted literary practice ("pious forgery") in ancient times and in the early Church. But the facts are that pseudonymous writing was only an occasional practice and that it was not acceptable in the early Church. Paul warns against forgeries in his name (2 Thessalonians 2:2; 3:17). The early Church expelled an elder from ecclesiastical office for writing pseudonymously[2] and was very concerned with questions of authorship, as shown, for example, by the debate over the authorship of Hebrews and by hesitancy in adopting a book of unknown authorship into the New Testament canon.

Furthermore, it is highly improbable that a late admirer of Paul would have called him "the foremost of sinners" (1 Timothy 1:15). The Pastorals are much closer in style and content to Paul's other epistles than are the noncanonical and indubitably pseudonymous books to the authentic writings of those in whose name they were forged. Added to the claim of the Pastorals themselves that they were written by Paul and the concern of the early Church with questions of authorship is the very strong and early tradition that Paul himself wrote the Pastorals. Only Romans and 1 Corinthians have any stronger attestation.

Vocabulary and Style

Doubt about Pauline authorship stems primarily from differences in vocabulary and grammatical style which appear when the Pastorals are compared with other Pauline epistles. Comparisons consist of statistical tables, sometimes drawn up with the aid of computers. However, this "scientific" objection to Pauline authorship does not take into account differences in vocabulary and style caused by differences in subject matter and addressees and changes in a person's writing style because of environment, age, experience, and the sheer passage of time. Perhaps even more significant is the possibility that stylistic differences stem from different *amanuenses* and from Paul's giving greater freedom to his amanuenses in the exact wording of his

---

[2]See Tertullian, *On Baptism* XVII. For a full discussion of pseudonymity, see D. Guthrie, *New Testament Introduction: Pauline Epistles* (Chicago: Inter-Varsity, 1961), Appendix C, "Epistolary Pseudepigraphy," pp. 282-294.

thoughts at some times than at other times. The explanation by means of amanuenses is sometimes scorned as being too easy. But it is realistic, for we know positively that Paul did dictate his epistles.

Furthermore, the generally accepted Pauline epistles or extended passages within them exhibit the same kinds of stylistic differences which assertedly disprove Pauline authorship of the Pastorals. And most of the words occurring only in the Pastorals among Paul's epistles also occur in the Septuagint and in extra-Biblical Greek literature of the first century, so that the words must have been part of the vocabulary of Paul and his amanuenses.

Doubters of Pauline authorship also contend that the Gnostic heretic Marcion omitted them from his New Testament canon because they were non-Pauline. But Marcion had a propensity for rejecting parts of the New Testament accepted by orthodox Christians. He rejected Matthew, Mark, and John, for example, and excised portions of Luke. The statement that "the law is good" (1 Timothy 1:8) must have offended Marcion's radical rejection of the Old Testament, and the disparaging reference to "what is falsely called 'knowledge [Greek: *gnōsis*]'" (1 Timothy 6:20) must have antagonized Marcion, who called his own system of doctrine *gnosis* — ample reasons for Marcion's omission of the Pastorals from his canon without the implication that they were pseudonymous.

Marcion's Omission

Also, some assert that the Pastorals attack a type of Gnosticism which arose only after Paul's lifetime. To be sure, the asceticism criticized in 1 Timothy 4:3 ("who forbid marriage and advocate abstaining from foods") sounds somewhat like later Gnosticism. Nevertheless, the prominent Jewish element in the false teaching — "those of the circumcision," "Jewish myths," "disputes about the law" (Titus 1:10, 14; 3:9, respectively) — disproves that the Pastorals necessarily attack later Gnosticism; for Judaistic features, though spilling over into the second century, were more characteristic of the earlier phase of the movement. The Pastorals rather strike at the mixed kind of heresy rebutted earlier in Colossians and now known to have originated in syncretistic Judaism of a pre-Christian gnostic variety. Thus, an early date for the Pastorals is preferable; and an early date favors authorship by Paul since a pious forger would not have dared use the apostle's name so close to Paul's lifetime.

Gnosticism

It is claimed that the Pastorals reflect a more highly organized ecclesiastical structure than had developed during the lifetime of Paul. But the Pastorals mention only elders (or bishops), deacons, and widows, all of whom figure earlier in the New Testament period as distinct classes within the Church. See, for

Ecclesiastical Structure

example, Acts 6:1; 9:39, 41; 1 Corinthians 7:8; Philippians 1:1. Moreover, the pre-Christian Dead Sea Scrolls describe an officer in the Qumran community who bears remarkable similarity to the bishops who appear in the Pastorals. Instructions for the appointment of elders by Timothy and Titus (1 Timothy 5:22; Titus 1:5) are due not to advanced hierarchical Church government, but to the starting of new churches under missionary conditions, just as Paul and Barnabas at a very early date appointed elders for the new churches in South Galatia (Acts 14:23).

Orthodoxy

In the same way, it is argued that the Pastorals' emphasis on orthodoxy of doctrine implies a post-Pauline stage of theological development when Christian doctrine was considered complete and therefore to be defended from corruption rather than widened in scope. However, the defense of traditional Christian orthodoxy characterized Paul's epistles from the very earliest. Galatians as a whole and the fifteenth chapter of 1 Corinthians are examples.

Conflicting
Data

Finally, some maintain that the Pastorals give historical and geographical data which do not harmonize with Paul's career as recorded in Acts and the other epistles. These are supposed to be the telltale mistakes of a pious forger. The conflicting data are that Paul had left Timothy in Ephesus when he traveled on to Macedonia (1 Timothy 1:3 — contrast Acts 20:4-6), that Demas had deserted Paul (2 Timothy 4:10 — Demas is still with Paul in Philemon 24), and that Paul had left Titus in Crete (Titus 1:5) and gone to Nicopolis (Titus 3:12) while Titus had proceeded to Dalmatia (2 Timothy 4:10 — whereas in Acts Paul visited neither Crete nor Nicopolis).

Two Roman
Imprisonments

The answer to this argument is the hypothesis that Paul was acquitted and released from his first Roman imprisonment, that he enjoyed a period of freedom, into which the travel data of the Pastorals fit, and that he was reimprisoned and condemned to die as a martyr for the Christian faith, which in the meantime had been outlawed. *Thus, the historical and geographical data in the Pastorals do not conflict with Acts, but refer to events which took place after the close of Acts.* The Pastorals themselves constitute evidence in favor of the hypothesis of two separate Roman imprisonments. So also does Paul's expectation of being released in Philippians 1:19, 25; 2:24, written during the first Roman imprisonment, in contrast with Paul's failure to entertain any possibility of release in 2 Timothy 4:6-8, written during the hypothesized second imprisonment.

Order of
Writing

We conclude that Paul wrote 1 Timothy and Titus between the imprisonments and 2 Timothy during his second imprisonment, just before his martyrdom. Whether or not he ever reached

Spain, as planned in Romans 15:24, 28, remains unknown. The early Church father Clement of Rome wrote that Paul "reached the limits of the West" (1 Clement 5:7), a statement which may be interpreted as a reference either to Rome or to Spain at the far western end of the Mediterranean Basin.

In addition to the instructions concerning the administrative responsibilities of Timothy and Titus in the churches, Paul summons Titus to come to him in Nicopolis on the west coast of Greece. See the map on page 230. And in 2 Timothy, Paul, reminiscing over his past career and expecting his execution soon, asks Timothy to come to him in Rome before winter (4:6-9, 21; 1:17). Paul feared that otherwise he might never see Timothy again, since navigation ceased during the winter and the execution might occur in the meantime.

FIRST TIMOTHY

1 Timothy, after the greeting, opens with a warning against false teachers who mishandle the law. Paul then recalls his own experience of conversion and commission to apostleship and charges Timothy to cling tenaciously to the orthodox Christian faith. Timothy must take warning from two false teachers whom Paul had ejected from the Church into the world, which is Satan's territory ("whom I have delivered to Satan that they may learn not to blaspheme," 1:20). *Read 1 Timothy 1.* The clause, "It is a trustworthy statement," leading into the declaration, "Christ Jesus came into the world to save sinners" (verse 15), is a formula which introduces early Christian confessions, slogans, and hymns (also in 1 Timothy 3:1; 4:9, 10; 2 Timothy 2:11-13; and Titus 3:5-8a).

Chapter two begins with an exhortation to public prayer for all men, especially for governmental authorities. There follow instructions that Christian women dress modestly, rather than extravagantly, and that in the church they not occupy authoritative teaching positions over men. The statement "woman will be saved through bearing children" (2:15) probably means that in spite of the pain suffered in childbearing, a lingering result of the original curse on human sin (Genesis 3:16), the Christian woman is still saved from the eternal judgment of God against sin. That is, the continued painfulness of giving birth to children does not contradict the salvation of Christian mothers. Under this view "through" means "through the midst of" rather than "by means of (bearing children)."[3]

---

[3]Other interpretations are (1) that believing women are saved through the supreme childbirth, that of Christ; (2) that Christian women work out their salvation by bearing and rearing children in a godly manner; and (3) that Paul does not promise spiritual salvation, but deliverance from the physical dangers of child-bearing (so apparently the New American Standard Bible).

Paul then lists the qualifications for bishops and deacons. "Bishop (*episcopos*)" means "overseer, superintendent," and refers to the office filled by men called "elders (*presbyters*)." Thus, although "bishop" and "elder" go back to different Greek words, they are synonymous. "Deacon" means "servant, helper" and refers to the bishops' assistants, who took care of the mundane matters of church life, particularly the distribution of charity. The listing of qualifications for "women" in 3:11 may imply a feminine order of deaconesses, or may refer to deacons' wives, who were expected to help in the charitable work of their husbands. The section closes with the quotation of an early Christian hymn or creed, which traces the career of Christ from incarnation to ascension ("He was revealed in the flesh . . . taken up in glory," 3:16). *Read 1 Timothy 2, 3.*

A further warning against false doctrine (chapter 4) is followed in chapter five by discussions of Timothy's proper relationship to different age-groups in the church, the status of widows, and the treatment of elders. As a young man, Timothy is to treat other young men as brothers, older men as fathers, older women as mothers, and young ladies as sisters.

Widows should be supported by their families. But godly widows sixty or more years old and without family support should receive economic assistance from the church. Younger widows should marry, lest they fall into the temptation of resorting to an immoral life as a means of support.

Faithful elders, especially those who preach and teach, merit financial support. Elders are not to be impeached except on the testimony of two or three witnesses, but those who are duly convicted must be rebuked publicly. Timothy is not to ordain ("lay hands on") a man to eldership hastily without first proving the man's character over a period of time (unless the reference is to restoration of disciplined members of the church). The epistle closes in chapter six with miscellaneous instructions about Christian slaves, false teachers, wealthy Christians, and Timothy's own spiritual responsibilities. *Read 1 Timothy 4-6.*

A SUMMARY OUTLINE OF FIRST TIMOTHY

Theme: the organization and administration of churches by Timothy

INTRODUCTION: greeting (1:1, 2)
I. WARNING AGAINST HERESY, WITH PERSONAL REMINISCENCES (1:3-20)
II. THE ORGANIZATION OF THE CHURCH BY TIMOTHY (2:1—3:13)
    A. Public prayer (2:1-8)
    B. Modesty and subordination of women (2:9-15)
    C. Qualifications for bishops (3:1-7)
    D. Qualifications for deacons (3:8-13)
III. THE ADMINISTRATION OF THE CHURCH BY TIMOTHY (3:14—6:19)

A. Preserving the Church as the bastion of orthodoxy against heterodoxy (3:14—4:16)
B. Pastoring the members of the church (5:1—6:26)
1. Men and women, young and old (5:1, 2)
2. Widows (5:3-16)
3. Elders, with an aside regarding Timothy (5:17-25)
4. Slaves (6:1-2b)
C. Teaching and urging of Christian duties (6:2c-10)
D. Leading by example (6:11-16)
E. Warning the wealthy (6:17-19)
CONCLUSION: final charge to Timothy and benediction (6:20, 21)

TITUS

Paul wrote this epistle from Nicopolis, on the west coast of Greece, to Titus, whom he had left on the Island of Crete to organize the church there. As in 1 Timothy, he warns against false teachers and issues instructions to various classes of Christians on proper conduct. The doctrinal basis for these instructions is the grace of God, which brings salvation, leads to godly living, and offers the "blessed hope" of Jesus' return (2:11 14). The experiential basis for the instructions is regeneration by the Holy Spirit (3:3-7). *Read Titus 1-3.*

A SUMMARY OUTLINE OF TITUS

Theme: the organization and administration of the churches in Crete by Titus

INTRODUCTION: greeting (1:1-4)
I. THE APPOINTMENT AND QUALIFICATIONS OF BISHOPS (1:5-9)
II. THE SUPPRESSION OF FALSE TEACHERS (1:10-16)
III. THE TEACHING OF GOOD CONDUCT (2:1—3.8a)
CONCLUSION (3:8b-15)
A. Summary (3:8b-11)
B. Request for Titus to come to Nicopolis and other instructions (3:12-14)
C. Greetings and benediction (3:15)

SECOND TIMOTHY

The last epistle of Paul opens with reminiscences of God's call to Timothy and to Paul interspersed with exhortations and a sidelight on some who had forsaken Paul in prison and others who had stood by him. The further directions to Timothy draw comparisons with the hard work and self-discipline required of soldiers, athletes, and farmers. Against heretical teaching, Paul stresses that "all scripture is inspired by God and profitable" (3:16). A final charge to preach the word of God, a statement of readiness to die, and personal news and requests conclude Paul's farewell epistle. *Read 2 Timothy 1-4.*

Jannes and Jambres (3:8) were two of Pharaoh's magicians

---

[4]Just as orthodoxy means "right belief," orthopraxis means "right doing or conduct."

who opposed Moses, according to Targum Jonathan on Exodus 7:11 and early Christian literature outside the New Testament. The parchments Paul asks Timothy to bring (4:13) must have had important contents, for parchment was expensive. Perhaps they were Paul's legal papers, such as his certificate of Roman citizenship, or copies of the Old Testament Scriptures, or records of Jesus' life and teachings.

We are probably to understand the deliverance of Paul "out of the lion's mouth" figuratively rather than literally, for the lion was a common metaphor for extreme danger (4:17; compare Psalm 22:21). More specifically, the lion has been taken as a symbol for the devil, as in 1 Peter 5:8, or the emperor Nero.

A SUMMARY OUTLINE OF SECOND TIMOTHY

Theme: the commission of Timothy to carry on the work of Paul

INTRODUCTION: greeting (1:1, 2)
   I. EXHORTATION TO STRENGTH OF MINISTRY, AGAINST TIMOTHY'S TENDENCY TO TIMIDITY (1:3—2:7)
   II. EXHORTATION TO ORTHODOXY, AGAINST FALSE TEACHING AND PRACTICE (2:8—4:8)

CONCLUSION (4:9-22)
   A. A request for Timothy to come soon (4:9-13)
   B. News about Paul's trial (4:14-18)
   C. Greetings, with a further plea for Timothy to come and a benediction (4:19-22)

For further discussion:

What differences are noticeable between the structure of modern churches and the early Church as reflected in the Pastorals? How do we account for these differences?

How binding are the ecclesiastical structure and functional style of the ancient Church upon the modern? Conversely, do changing circumstances and different cultures allow the Church freedom of operation and innovation — and if so, within what limits, provided there are limits?

Evaluate the charge that Paul's concern for orthodoxy in the Pastorals sounds negative and overly defensive.

For further investigation:

Guthrie, D. *The Pastoral Epistles and the Mind of Paul.* London: Tyndale, 1956.
————. *The Pastoral Epistles.* Grand Rapids: Eerdmans, 1957.
Kelly, J. N. D. *A Commentary on the Pastoral Epistles.* New York: Harper & Row, 1963.
For a summary chart of the Pauline epistles, see "A Chart of the Books in the New Testament," page 384.

EXCURSUS: A RESUME OF PAULINE THEOLOGY

Since Paul's theology is distributed throughout a number of epistles written under missionary circumstances, it remains for us to summarize his thought. Some scholars earlier believed that Paul borrowed extensively from Greek concepts and from the mystery religions for the content and form of his theology. There is general agreement now, however, that his debt to the Old Testament and rabbinical Judaism far exceeds his debt to Greek and mystical sources. These same scholars also believed that Paul was the great innovator, who transformed Jesus from what He actually had been, a prophetic rabbi and martyr, into a cosmic Savior with divine attributes. But closer study of the Pauline literature has shown that Paul drew on earlier Christian tradition — hymns, creeds, baptismal confessions, catechetical instructions concerning Christian conduct, and the oral and written traditions about Jesus' life and teaching before the writing of the gospels. A study of the gospels, Acts, and the non-Pauline epistles leads to the same conclusion: Paul developed an already existing Christian theology which originated with Jesus and which grew out of the Scriptures of the Old Testament, regarded as fully authoritative.

From Judaism and the Old Testament came Paul's concept of one true God who is omnipotent, holy, and gracious. This God is a person. Those who know Him through Christ may address Him affectionately as Father ("Abba"). But there is multiplicity within the personality of the one God; so Paul writes in the trinitarian terms of Father, Son, and Holy Spirit. God the Father created the universe and all beings in it through and for His Son. The material universe is therefore inherently good; sin is an intruder. All men sinned in Adam, and sin has such a firm grip on men that the good law of God provokes transgression rather than obedience. The result is death, both physical and spiritual. As part of the material creation, the human body is inherently good; but because sin works itself out through the body, Paul calls the sinful urge "the flesh."[5]

Jesus, the eternally preexistent Son of God, came from heaven to rescue men from slavery to sin and its consequences. To do so, He became a human being and died to satisfy both the divine anger against sin and the divine love for sinners. God raised Him from the dead and exalted Him as LORD (from "Yahweh" or "Jehovah") in heaven to demonstrate His satisfaction. Now the "call" of God comes to those people whom He

---

[5]"The flesh" does not always refer to the propensity to sin. Other meanings include bodily flesh, mankind, natural human descent or relationship, and human nature as such (whether weak and sinful or not).

has chosen beforehand. Yet the divine election of some men does not contradict the open invitation to all men for salvation. Men accept this invitation by sincere sorrow for sin (repentance) and faith in Jesus Christ, which involves mental assent to what Christianity says about His identity, exclusive trust in His death and resurrection for the remission (removal) of sins, and moral commitment to the kind of life He demands. The repentant believer immediately comes to be "in Christ," so that his sin is transferred to Christ and the righteousness of Christ is transferred to him. Solidarity with Christ replaces solidarity with Adam. In this way God can lovingly treat the believer as righteous (justification), while still upholding His own righteous standard of justice. Jesus as LORD "redeems" believers, that is, He sets them free from the slavery of sin by the payment of a price, just as Yahweh redeemed Israel from bondage in Egypt at the Exodus. God and the believer are reconciled; their broken fellowship is restored. All of this happens by divine grace, the favor of God toward ill-deserving men, without meritorious good works on their part.

The Spirit, Christians and the Church

To the believer God gives His Spirit as a guarantee of future and eternal glory and as an aid to individual and corporate Christian living. The Spirit enables believers to conquer the sinful urge ("the flesh"), to live virtuously, to pray, and to minister to others. The body, once dominated by the flesh, becomes the sacred temple of the divine Spirit, destined for the resurrection to life eternal. But just as the body of the individual Christian is the temple of the Holy Spirit, so also is the Church as a whole. Indeed, the body with its various parts is Paul's great metaphor for the Church in her organic unity, diversity of function, and subordination to Christ the head. And churches (from the Greek word *ecclesia*) are not buildings, but local assemblies of those whose higher citizenship belongs to the kingdom of God. These are the holy ones ("saints"), the "brethren," into whose hearts have shone the open secrets ("mysteries") of the Gospel. They confess their union with Christ in His death, burial, and resurrection by baptism, and the continuance of that union by the Lord's Supper, which also looks forward to the Messianic banquet at the Parousia.

Eschatology

The forces of evil — Satan, demonic spirits, and men dominated by them — control this present age. But it will not be so forever; the day of the Lord is coming. Then *He* will take control. When the man of sin (Antichrist) leads a great rebellion against God, Christ the Lord will return to judge the wicked, vindicate the godly, and restore the nation of Israel. For this event Christians must watch. It is their confident "hope," and a possibility for each generation. After the day of the Lord, the

age to come begins, a never-ending succession of ages called
eternity, in which God will enjoy His people and they Him —
forever.[6]

For further discussion:

Why did not Paul and other early Christian authors write
theological books in systematic form rather than occasional
letters and tracts?

What particular aspects of his theology kept Paul from becoming an armchair theologian, and compelled him to
travel far and wide at great personal cost for the sake of
evangelism?

For further investigation:

Machen, J. G. *The Origin of Paul's Religion.* Grand Rapids: Eerdmans,
1925.
Bouttier, M. *Christianity according to Paul.* Translated by F. Clarke. London:
SCM, 1966.
Scott, C. A. A. *Christianity according to St. Paul.* Cambridge University
Press, 1961.
Barclay, W. *The Mind of St. Paul.* New York: Harper & Row, 1958.
Hunter, A. M. *Paul and His Predecessors.* Philadelphia: Westminster, 1961.
——————. *The Gospel According to St. Paul.* Philadelphia: Westminster, 1967.
Whiteley, D. E. H. *The Theology of St. Paul.* Philadelphia: Fortress, 1964.
Stewart, J. S. *A Man in Christ.* New York: Harper & Row, n.d.
Longenecker, R. N. *Paul, Apostle of Liberty.* New York: Harper & Row,
1964.
Davies, W. D. *Paul and Rabbinic Judaism.* London: S.P.C.K., 1962. For
more advanced study.

---

[6]Paul drew the three terms, "this (present) age," "the day of the Lord,"
and "that (or, the coming) age," from rabbinic parlance and filled them with
Christian concepts.

CHAPTER 18

Hebrews: Jesus Our Great High Priest

Leading questions:

Who are the leading candidates for the authorship of Hebrews?

To whom was Hebrews written, where did they live, and what was their spiritual state?

What is the distinctive Christological emphasis in Hebrews, and how does it relate to the dissuasion of the readers from apostasy?

Theme

The author of Hebrews distinctively portrays Jesus Christ as the great high priest who, having offered none other than Himself as the completely sufficient sacrifice for sins, ministers in the heavenly sanctuary. The purpose of this portrait, which presents the superiority of Christ over every aspect and hero of Old Testament religion, was to prevent the first readers of the epistle from reverting to Judaism.

Authorship

Early Church tradition is uncertain about the authorship of the anonymous book of Hebrews. Nevertheless, at a very early date (c. A.D. 95) Hebrews was known and used in 1 Clement.

Paul

In the eastern part of the Roman Empire, Paul was usually regarded as the author. The theology of Hebrews does resemble that of Paul when we compare the preexistence and creatorship of Christ in Hebrews 1:1-4 and Colossians 1:15-17, the humiliation of Christ in Hebrews 2:14-17 and Philippians 2:5-8, the new covenant in Hebrews 8:6 and 2 Corinthians 3:4-11, and the distribution of gifts by the Holy Spirit in Hebrews 2:4 and 1 Corinthians 12:11. However, the western segment of the Church doubted Pauline authorship and even excluded Hebrews from the canon at first because of the uncertain authorship. This fact shows that the early Church did not gullibly accept books into the canon without first examining their credentials as to authorship, trustworthiness, and doctrinal purity.

The western Church had good reasons to doubt authorship by Paul. None of the acknowledged epistles of Paul are anonymous like Hebrews. The polished Greek style of Hebrews differs radically from Paul's rugged style, much more than can be explained by a difference in amanuenses. And Paul constantly appeals to his own apostolic authority, but the writer of Hebrews appeals to the authority of those who were eye-witnesses to Jesus' ministry (Hebrews 2:3). HEBREWS: JESUS OUR GREAT HIGH PRIEST

Others have suggested Barnabas, whose Levitical background (Acts 4:36) fits the interest in priestly functions exhibited throughout Hebrews and whose association with Paul would explain the similarities to Pauline theology. But as a resident of Jerusalem (Acts 4:36, 37), Barnabas probably heard and saw Jesus, whereas the author of Hebrews includes himself among those who had to depend on others for eyewitness testimony (Hebrews 2:3). Barnabas

Luke, another companion of Paul, is also a candidate for the authorship of Hebrews because of similarities in the polished Greek style of Hebrews and that of Luke-Acts. But Luke-Acts is Gentile in outlook, Hebrews highly Jewish. Luke

Martin Luther suggested Apollos, whose acquaintance with Paul (1 Corinthians 16:12) and tutoring by Priscilla and Aquila (Acts 18:26) would account for the likenesses to Pauline theology in Hebrews. Apollos' eloquence (Acts 18:24, 27, 28) could have produced the high literary style of Hebrews. Also, his Alexandrian background fits Hebrews' exclusive use of the Septuagint in Old Testament quotations, for the Septuagint was produced in Alexandria, Egypt.[1] But the lack of early tradition favoring Apollos leaves us in doubt. Apollos

To suppose that Paul's companion Silvanus (Silas) was the author again would explain the similarities to Pauline theology. Not much more can be said for or against authorship by Silvanus. Silvanus

The same is true of the suggestion that Philip wrote Hebrews. Philip

Harnack suggested Priscilla because of her close association with Paul and ingeniously argued that she left the book anonymous because female authorship was unacceptable to the public. Priscilla

The likenesses between Hebrews and 1 Clement make Clem- Clement

---

[1]Some scholars draw a parallel between the allegorical interpretation of the Old Testament by the Jewish philosopher Philo, a contemporary of Apollos and fellow native of Alexandria, and the treatment of the Old Testament in Hebrews. However, Hebrews treats the Old Testament as typological history rather than allegory.

ent of Rome a possibility. But there are many differences in outlook, and Clement probably borrowed from Hebrews. With the early Church father Origen, we conclude that only God now knows who wrote Hebrews.

Addressees

In spite of the traditional appendant heading "To the Hebrews," some have thought Hebrews was originally addressed to Gentile Christians. For support, an appeal is made to the polished Greek style and the extensive use of the Septuagint with only an occasional departure from that Greek translation of the Old Testament. But these phenomena imply nothing about the original addressees. They indicate only the background of the author. The frequent appeal to the Old Testament, the presupposed knowledge of Jewish ritual, the warning not to relapse into Judaism, and the early traditional title all point to Jewish Christians as the original recipients.

Destination

Prima facie it might seem most likely that these Jewish Christians lived in Palestine. But according to 2:3 they had neither seen nor heard Jesus for themselves during His earthly ministry, as many Palestinian Christians had doubtless done; and according to 6:10 they had materially assisted other Christians, whereas Palestinian Christians were poor and had to receive aid (Acts 11:27-30; Romans 15:26; 2 Corinthians 8, 9). Furthermore, the readers' knowledge of Jewish ritual appears to have come from the Old Testament in its Septuagintal version rather than from attendance at the Temple services in Jerusalem. And the statement "Those from Italy greet you" (13:24) sounds as though Italians away from Italy are sending greetings back home. In that case, Rome is the probable destination. Substantiating this conclusion is the fact that evidence for the knowledge of Hebrews first appears in Rome (1 Clement).[2]

Recently, H. Montefiore has proposed that Apollos wrote Hebrews in A.D. 52-54 from Ephesus to the church in Corinth, especially to its Jewish Christian members.[3] He draws numerous parallels between Hebrews and Paul's Corinthian correspondence. In his view "those from Italy" (13:24) are Priscilla and Aquila, who had originally moved to Corinth from Rome, but had subsequently accompanied Paul from Corinth to Ephesus. One wonders, however, why the author of Hebrews did not mention Priscilla and Aquila by name rather than by a generalizing phrase, especially since he had just mentioned Timothy by name. Nevertheless, Montefiore's arguments deserve serious consideration.

---

[2]See further W. Manson, *The Epistle to the Hebrews* (London: Hodder & Stoughton, 1951).

[3]*A Commentary on the Epistle to the Hebrews* (London: Black, 1964).

Wherever the addressees lived, they were well-known to the author. He writes about their generosity (6:10), their persecution (10:32-34; 12:4), their immaturity (5:11—6:12), and his hope of revisiting them soon (13:19, 23). Two additional details may be significant: (1) the readers are exhorted to greet not only the leaders and fellow Christians in their own assembly, but "*all* the saints" (13:24); (2) they are rebuked for not meeting together often enough (10:25). Possibly, then, they were a Jewish Christian group or house-church who had broken away from the main body of Christians in their locality and who stood in danger of lapsing into Judaism to avoid persecution.[4] The main purpose of the epistle is to prevent such apostasy and to bring them back into the mainstream of Christian fellowship.

The use of Hebrews in 1 Clement requires a date of writing before c. A.D. 95, the date of 1 Clement. It is sometimes further argued that the present tenses of verbs in Hebrews describing sacrificial rituals implies a date before A.D. 70, when Titus destroyed the Temple and sacrifices ceased to be offered. But other writings that must certainly date from after A.D. 70 continue to use the present tense about Mosaic rituals (1 Clement, Josephus, Justin Martyr, the Talmud). Furthermore, Hebrews does not describe the ritual of the Temple, but the ritual of the pre-Solomonic "Tabernacle," so that the present tense is merely vivid literary style and cannot very well imply anything about the date of Hebrews. What *does* strongly favor a date of writing before A.D. 70, however, is the lack of any reference in Hebrews to the destruction of the Temple as a divine indication that the Old Testament sacrificial system had been outmoded. Surely the author would have used such a historical argument had he written after that event.

Date

As other epistles, Hebrews concludes with personal allusions; but unlike other epistles, it has no introductory greeting. The oratorical style and remarks such as "time would fail me to tell" (11:32) might seem to indicate a sermon. But the statement, "I have written to you briefly" (13:22), requires us to think that Hebrews is an epistle after all, written in sermonic style.

Literary Form

To keep his readers from lapsing back into Judaism, the writer of Hebrews emphasizes the superiority of Christ over all else, especially over the various features of Judaism arising out of the Old Testament. The phrase "better than" epito-

Christ's Superiority

---

[4]The immediate fading of a sure tradition of authorship may be due to the separatism of the original addressees. Other identifications of the addressees are that they were a group of converted Jewish priests (Acts 6:7) or a group of converts from the Qumran sect, which produced the Dead Sea Scrolls.

mizes the dominant theme of Christ's superiority, a theme punctuated throughout the book by exhortations not to apostatize.

Over the Prophets

Christ is better than the Old Testament prophets because He is the Son of God, the heir of the universe, the creator, the exact representation of divine nature, the sustainer of the world, the purifier from sins, the exalted One — and therefore God's last and best word to man (1:1-3a).

Over Angels

Christ is also better than the angels, whom contemporary Jews regarded as the mediators of the Mosaic law on Mount Sinai (Acts 7:53; Galatians 3:19); for Christ is the divine Son and eternal creator, but angels are servants and created beings (1:3b—2:18). Even His becoming lower than the angels through incarnation and death was only temporary. He had to become a human being to qualify as the one who by His death could lift fallen man to the dignity in which God originally created man. For that sacrificial act, Christ has received great honor. In the middle of this section occurs an exhortation not to drift away from Christian profession (2:1-4). *Read Hebrews 1, 2.*

Over Moses

As the divine *Son over* God's household, Christ is better than Moses, a *servant in* God's household (3:1-6). The exhortation, therefore, is to avoid incurring God's judgment as a result of unbelief. The Israelite generation who came out of Egypt under Moses but died in the wilderness because of God's anger against their rebellion provides a warning example (3:7-19).

Over Joshua

Christ is better than Joshua; for although Joshua brought Israel into Canaan, Christ will bring believers into the eternal resting place of heaven, where God rests from His work of creation (4:1-10). It is obvious that Joshua did not bring Israel into this heavenly rest; for long after Joshua lived and died, David spoke of Israel's resting place as yet to be entered (Psalm 95:7, 8).[5] The comparison between Jesus and Joshua is all the more pointed in the Greek New Testament in that the Hebrew name "Joshua" has "Jesus" as its Greek form. In other words, the Greek text knows no distinction between the names of the Old Testament Joshua and the New Testament Jesus.

---

[5]Another interpretation is that the "rest" into which Jesus leads Christians is not the future heavenly rest from the good works of Christian living, but the *present* spiritual rest, or cessation from self-righteous works of the law, because of the redemption already accomplished through Christ. However, the closely connected warning against apostasy, with its dire consequences, and the parallel between God's resting from His (good) work of creation and our resting from work both favor the interpretation given above. Yet another view is that the Christian's rest is not salvation itself (whether present or future), but successful Christian living as typified by the conquest of Canaan under Joshua. But again, the interpretation tends to cut the connection of the passage with the warnings not to apostatize.

The author then exhorts his readers to enter the heavenly rest by fidelity to their Christian profession (4:11-16). Later emphasis on the all-sufficiency of Jesus' sacrifice eliminates any implication that the continuance of good works in the Christian life merits salvation. However, good works and the avoidance of apostasy are necessary to demonstrate the genuineness of Christian profession. Verse twelve contains the famous comparison of God's word with a double edged sword that pierces into and lays bare man's innermost being. Christians must therefore prove that their outward profession springs from inward reality. *Read Hebrews 3, 4.*

Christ is better than Aaron and his successors in the priesthood (5:1—12:29). The author of Hebrews first indicates two points of similarity between the Aaronic priests and Christ: (1) like Aaron, Christ was divinely appointed to priesthood, and (2) by sharing our human experiences, Christ has a sympathy for us at least equal to that of Aaron (5:1-10). The outstanding example of Jesus' human feelings is His instinctive shrinking from death while praying in Gethsemane (but not blameworthy terror of death, and obviously not refusal to accept the cross).

Next comes a lengthy exhortation (5:11—6:20) to progress from spiritual infancy to maturity by advancing beyond elementary doctrines of the Jewish faith which form the foundation for Christian belief and gain new significance in their Christian context. Failure to grow increases the danger of apostasy. And if a Christian renounces Christ in a public, willful, and final way, all possibility of salvation forever ceases to exist. The author describes his readers as Christians from the standpoint of their present profession (not knowing their hearts, how else could he describe them?), but goes on to point out that apostasy would both demonstrate the unreality of that profession and incur an irrevocable judgment for false profession. It should be noted that apostasy carries a much stronger meaning than temporary disobedience. *Read Hebrews 5, 6.*

Points of Christ's superiority over Aaron are that (1) Christ became priest with a divine oath, but not the Aaronites (Aaron and his priestly descendants); (2) Christ is eternal, whereas the Aaronites died and had to be succeeded; (3) Christ is sinless, but the Aaronites were not; (4) the priestly functions of Christ deal with heavenly realities, those of the Aaronites only with earthly symbols; (5) Christ offered Himself voluntarily as a sacrifice which will never need to be repeated, whereas the repetitiousness of animal offerings exposes their ineffectiveness as inferior creatures to take away sins; and (6) the Old Testament itself, written during the period of the Aaronic priesthood, predicted a new covenant which would make obsolete the old covenant under which the Aaronites functioned (Jeremiah 31: 31-34).

Interpretive dispute has raged about the warning in 6:1-12:

(1) Those who believe that the passage teaches the terrifying possibility of a true Christian's reverting to a lost condition struggle against the stated impossibility of restoration (6:4), against those New Testament passages which assure believers, the elect, of eternal security (John 6:39, 40; 10:27-29; Romans 11:29; Philippians 1:6; 1 Peter 1:5; 1 John 2:1), and against the entire doctrine of regeneration.

(2) Those who feel that the author of Hebrews poses a hypothetical rather than a realistic possibility find the repetition of this urgent warning here and elsewhere in Hebrews (especially 10:26-31) embarrassing.

(3) Those who tone down the severity of the threatened judgment from loss of salvation to loss of reward (with bare retention of salvation — compare 1 Corinthians 3:12-15) run against the implication of 6:9 that the threatened judgment is the opposite of salvation: "Though we speak thus, yet in your case, beloved, we feel sure of better things that belong to salvation," (compare 10:27: "a fearful prospect of judgment, and a fury of fire which will consume the adversaries").

(4) Those who view the warning as addressed to near Christians rather than to full Christians must minimize the force of the phrases "those who have once been enlightened [compare 10:32; 2 Corinthians 4:4, 6; 1 Peter 2:9; *et passim*], who have tasted the heavenly gift [compare Christ's 'tasting' death for every man (2:9), certainly a full experience], and have become partakers of the Holy Spirit [compare Christ's partaking of human nature (2:14), surely not a partial incarnation], and have tasted the goodness of the word of God and the powers of the age to come [compare 1 Peter 2:3]." They also find difficult the appeal for maturity instead of conversion, the warning against "apostasy" (6:6) instead of failure to confess Christ initially, and the address to the readers by the distinctively Christian term "beloved" (6:9; compare 10:30: "The Lord will judge *his people*").

(5) The most promising interpretation views the warning as directed to professing Christians with the implication that they must show the genuineness of their profession by withstanding pressure to apostatize. Whereas assurances of eternal security reflect a divine perspective (God, who knows the hearts of men perfectly, will forever keep His own), this warning and others like it reflect a human perspective (Christians, who know their own hearts imperfectly, must outwardly demonstrate to themselves and others that their profession is real, not by sin-

less perfection but by perseverance against opposition and temptation). Thus the author of Hebrews addresses his readers as Christians, as he must since at the time of writing they all profess to be Christians. Yet, unlike God, he cannot know their inward spiritual state. He must warn against the danger of false profession, ultimate apostasy by willful and final denial of previously professed Christian faith, and the resultant irrevocable judgment. It is not *really* possible to be saved and lost, but it is *apparently* possible — and the "apparently" must be treated with all gravity because human beings move largely on the level of appearances.

For the distinction between divine and human perspectives, we may consult 1 Samuel 16:7b ("man looks on the outward appearance, but the Lord looks on the heart") and compare Paul's doctrine of justification by faith (in the sight of God) and James' doctrine of justification by works (in the sight of men). It is important to recognize the validity and seriousness of *both* perspectives. Finally, the purpose of warnings like this is not to upset conscientious Christians, but to caution careless Christians lest they turn out not to be Christians at all.

Taking his cue from the statement in Psalm 110:4 that the Messianic king will be a priest after the pattern of Melchizedek, the author of Hebrews draws several parallels between Christ and that shadowy Old Testament figure, to whom Abraham gave a tenth of the spoils of battle after rescuing Lot (Genesis 14). Melchizedek was a priest of God; so also is Christ. The name "Melchizedek" means "King of Righteousness" (more literally, "my king is righteous"); the man by that name was king of "Salem" (probably a short form of "Jerusalem"), which means "peace" (in the sense of full divine blessing); and righteousness and peace are characteristics and results of Christ's priestly ministry. The absence in the Old Testament of a *recorded* genealogy for Melchizedek and of accounts of his birth and death (of course he had parents and ancestors, was born, and died) typifies the *real* eternality of Christ as the Son of God, in contrast to the dying of all Aaronic priests. The superiority of Christ over Aaron is further symbolized by the giving of a tenth of the battle spoils to Melchizedek by Abraham, from whom Aaron later descended. Solidarity with one's ancestors is here presupposed. The same superiority appears again in Melchizedek's blessing Abraham, rather than vice versa, for the greater man blesses the lesser. *Read Hebrews 7:1—10:18.*

Melchizedek

Hebrews closes with a long hortatory section and final greetings (10:19—13:25). The author urges his readers to use the superior method of approaching God through Christ rather than the outdated Old Testament method, especially in collective

Exhortation

worship, which they were neglecting (10:19-22). He warns them again, as in chapter six, of the terrifying judgment which comes on those who openly and finally repudiate their Christian profession, but states his confidence, based on previous endurance of persecution by his readers, that they will not fall into apostasy (10:23-31).

He then encourages them to continued steadfastness by citing as examples the Old Testament heroes of faith,[6] by linking his readers to them, and finally by citing Jesus as the most outstanding example of patient endurance of suffering and ultimate reception of reward (10:32—12:3). Suffering is good discipline and a sign of sonship (12:4-13). Esau becomes a warning example of the faithless apostate (12:14-17).

In conclusion, the writer again stresses the superiority of the new covenant, rooted in the blood of Christ (12:18-29), and exhorts his readers to mutual love, hospitality (especially needed in those days by itinerant preachers), sympathy, the healthy and moral use of sex within marriage, avoidance of avarice, imitation of godly church leaders, avoidance of false teaching, acceptance of persecution, thanksgiving, generosity, obedience to ecclesiastical leaders, and prayer. *Read Hebrews 10:19—13:25.*

A SUMMARY OUTLINE OF HEBREWS

Theme: the superiority of Christ as a deterrent against apostasy from Christianity back to Judaism

I. THE SUPERIORITY OF CHRIST OVER THE OLD TESTAMENT PROPHETS (1:1-3a)

II. THE SUPERIORITY OF CHRIST OVER ANGELS (1:3b—2:18), AND A WARNING AGAINST APOSTASY (2:1-4)

III. THE SUPERIORITY OF CHRIST OVER MOSES (3:1-6), AND A WARNING AGAINST APOSTASY (3:7-19)

IV. THE SUPERIORITY OF CHRIST OVER JOSHUA (4:1-10), AND A WARNING AGAINST APOSTASY (4:11-16)

V. THE SUPERIORITY OF CHRIST OVER THE AARONITES AND WARNINGS AGAINST APOSTASY (5:1—12:29)
   A. Christ's human sympathy and divine appointment to priesthood (5:1-10)
   B. Warning against apostasy with exhortation to maturation (5:11—6:20)
   C. The Melchizedek pattern of Christ's priesthood (7:1-10)
   D. The transitoriness of the Aaronic priesthood (7:11-28)
   E. The heavenly realties of Christ's priesthood (8:1—10:18)
   F. Warning against apostasy (10:19-39)
   G. Encouragement from Old Testament heroes of faith (11:1-40)
   H. Encouragement from the example of Christ (12:1-11)

---

[6]Chapter eleven is sometimes considered to be the great faith chapter of the New Testament, just as 1 Corinthians 13 is the love chapter and 1 Corinthians 15 the resurrection chapter.

1. Warning against apostasy with the example of Esau (12:12-29)

VI. PRACTICAL EXHORTATIONS (13:1-19)

CONCLUSION: greetings, news of Timothy's release, and benedictions (13:20-25)

For further discussion:

How important is it to determine the authorship of Hebrews, and the date, geographical destination, and original reading audience of the epistle?

What would be the likely apologia by the author of Hebrews to the modern charge that salvation by sacrificial blood is a primitive religious concept?

If God accurately sees the inward spiritual state of a professing Christian but other people judge with only relative certainty by outward appearances, in what ways does the Christian know his own spiritual state, and with what degree of sureness?

For further investigation:

Bruce, F. F. *The Epistle to the Hebrews.* Grand Rapids: Eerdmans, 1964.

Hewitt, T. *The Epistle to the Hebrews.* Grand Rapids: Eerdmans, 1960.

Manson, W. *The Epistle to the Hebrews.* London: Hodder & Stoughton, 1951.

Filson, F. V. *'Yesterday': A study of Hebrews in the Light of Chapter 13.* London: SCM, 1967.

CHAPTER 19

The Catholic or General Epistles

Leading questions:

Why are the Catholic, or General, Epistles so called?

Which James wrote the epistle bearing that name? Whom did he address? What is the practical value of his epistle? How does his doctrine of works compare with the Pauline view of faith?

What was the nature of the persecution being suffered by the first readers of 1 Peter? How does Peter encourage them? Where was the "Babylon" from which he wrote?

How are we to evaluate modern doubts over Petrine authorship and the canonicity of 2 Peter? What common theme and relation does the epistle have with Jude?

Who was Jude? Why did he change his mind regarding the contents of his epistle? How are we to understand his quotation from pseudepigraphal sources?

To whom and against whom did John address his first epistle?

What are the Johannine criteria of genuine Christianity?

Who are "the elect lady and her children" whom John warns in his second epistle not to entertain false teachers?

What roles did Gaius, Diotrephes, and Demetrius play in the ecclesiastical dispute around which 3 John centers?

The term "Catholic," meaning "general, universal," came to be applied by the early Church to James, 1 and 2 Peter, 1-3 John, and Jude, because these epistles (with the exceptions of 2 and 3 John) lack indications of limited address to a single locality. It should be noted that they are titled according to their traditional authors, like the gospels, but unlike the Pauline epistles and Hebrews, which take their titles after the traditional addressees.

342

The Epistle of James is the least doctrinal and most practical book in the New Testament. (That fact should lead us neither to underrate nor to overrate the value of the book, for doctrine and practice are equally important.) We are dealing, then, with a manual of Christian conduct which assumes a foundation of faith on the part of the readers.

This epistle bears the name of its author James (Greek for the Hebrew name "Jacob"), a leader in the early Jerusalem church (Acts 15:12 ff.; 21:18; Galatians 2:9, 12) and usually considered to be the half brother of Jesus.[1] It is possible however, that James was an older stepbrother of Jesus by a (conjectural) marriage of Joseph previous to his marriage to Mary. The latter view, which excludes any blood relationship to Jesus, might better explain the failure of Jesus' brothers to believe in Him during His lifetime (Mark 3:21; John 7:2-8); and their lack of concern for Mary because she was only their stepmother, might also better explain why Jesus, from the cross, committed His mother to the Apostle John (John 19:25-27). However, the reason may have been that Mary's discipleship alienated her from her other children, who still did not believe in Jesus.

To maintain the doctrine of the perpetual virginity of Mary, the traditional Roman Catholic view is that "brother" means "cousin." But the associations between Jesus and His brothers in Matthew 13:55; Mark 6:3; and John 2:12; 7:2-10 imply a closer relationship than that of cousins, and probably also closer than that of stepbrothers. The view that the James who wrote this epistle was Jesus' half brother therefore remains the most probable.

Although not a believer in Jesus during His public ministry, James witnessed the risen Christ (1 Corinthians 15:7) and was among those who were awaiting the Holy Spirit on the day of Pentecost (Acts 1:14). This implies that James and the other brothers of Jesus became believers some time during the very last stage of Jesus' earthly career. Although James himself carefully practiced the Mosaic law (Galatians 2:12; Acts 21:17-26), at the Jerusalem Council he supported Paul's position that Gentile converts should not have to keep the law (Acts 15:12-21).

The subject matter of James and its Jewish tone, especially the stress on the law, harmonize with what we know of James

---

[1] James the son of Zebedee and one of the Twelve Disciples suffered martyrdom in A.D. 44 (Acts 12:2), probably too early for us to think that he wrote the epistle. The tone of authority in the Epistle of James fairly well rules out the lesser known Jameses in the New Testament, the son of Alphaeus, the younger and son of Mary (not the mother of Jesus), and the father of Judas (not Iscariot). See a concordance for references.

the Lord's brother from Acts, Galatians, and other sources. Also, there are some significant verbal parallels between the Epistle of James and the words of James in Acts 15, such as the term "greeting" (Greek: *chairein*, used in the New Testament only in James 1:1 and Acts 15:23, the decree drafted under James' leadership), the term "visit," or "concerned himself about" (James 1:27 and Acts 15:14, the speech of James before the Jerusalem Council), and others (compare James 2:5, 7 with Acts 15:13, 17). Those who regard the epistle as a late first or early second century pseudepigraphal work maintain that a simple Galilean, such as James, could not have written the well-styled Greek of the epistle. However, the objection overestimates the literary quality of the Greek style and, more importantly, fails to take account of the fact that Palestinian Jews, especially Galileans, who lived in a predominantly Gentile region, knew and used Greek along with Aramaic and Hebrew.[2]

Canonicity

The Epistle of James encountered some difficulty in gaining canonical status. Several factors help to explain the hesitancy of the early Church: (1) the brevity of the epistle, its dominantly practical rather than doctrinal nature, and the limitation of its address to Jewish Christians — all of which doubtless retarded wide circulation; (2) the fact that James was not one of the twelve apostles; and (3) uncertainty about the identity of James in 1:1, for several men by that name appear in the New Testament. The mistaken impression (voiced by Martin Luther) that the doctrine of works in James contradicts Paul's doctrine of faith did not seriously disturb the early Church so far as we can tell. When it came to be realized that the author almost surely was James the Lord's brother, the final verdict was favorable toward the canonicity of the Epistle of James.

Jewish Christian Address

James writes "to the twelve tribes who are dispersed abroad" (1:1). This designation may be taken metaphorically, as in 1 Peter,[3] for the predominantly Gentile Church scattered throughout the Roman Empire. In James, however, the reference is more probably to Jewish Christians living outside Palestine, as favored by a number of items in the epistle: the specific reference to "the twelve tribes"; the use in 2:2 of the Greek word for synagogue, translated in its untechnical sense of "assembly"; the five quotations of and numerous allusions to the Old Testament; Jewish idioms, such as "Lord of Sabaoth [hosts]" (5:4); stress on several permanent principles of the Jewish law (2:8-13; 4:11, 12) and monotheism (2:19); and the omission of any

---

[2]See the article cited on page 21, and J. N. Sevenster, *Do You Know Greek?* (Leiden: Brill, 1968).

[3]See pages 350 f.

allusion to slavery and of any polemic against idolatry, neither of which was characteristic of first century Jews, but both of which Gentiles commonly practiced.

Josephus places the martyrdom of James at A.D. 62,[4] so that the epistle must be dated earlier. Some scholars advance arguments for a date so early (A.D. 45-50) that the Epistle of James could be considered the first book of the New Testament to be written. For example, the lack of any reference to the Judaizing controversy is said to imply a date before the controversy arose just prior to the Jerusalem Council of about A.D. 49; and the Jewish tone of the epistle is said to imply a date before Christianity had expanded outside of Palestine. But the limitation of the address to Jewish Christians and the strongly Jewish outlook of James himself can account for both phenomena, so that we must content ourselves with an indeterminate date before James' martyrdom.

Notably, James contains numerous allusions to sayings of Jesus recorded in the gospels, especially material associated with the Sermon on the Mount. For example, the contrast in 1:22 between hearers and doers of the word recalls the parable of the wise man, who builds on a solid foundation by hearing and doing the words of Jesus, and the foolish man, who builds on the sand by hearing and failing to do His words (Matthew 7:24-27; Luke 6:47-49)..

It is difficult to outline James. This epistle shares the rambling and moralistic style of Proverbs and other wisdom literature; but the precepts are delivered in the fashion of a fiery prophetic sermon. After the initial greeting (1:1) one can only list the series of practical exhortations on various topics:

Rejoice in trials (1:2-4).

Believingly ask God for wisdom (1:5-8).

Do not desire wealth (1:9-11).

Distinguish between trials, which come from God, and temptations, which come from human lusts, for God gives only good gifts (1:12-18).

Be doers of the word in speech and action, not mere hearers (1:19-27).

Do not show partiality toward the rich, but love all equally and as yourselves (2:1-13). As in the Old Testament, the emphasis in "the rich" lies more on their wicked persecution of the righteous than on their wealth, just as "poor" frequently means "pious and persecuted" more than "poverty-stricken."

---

[4]*Antiquities* XX. ix. 1. Less likely is the date A.D. 68 given by Hegesippus, as recorded in Eusebius, *Ecclesiastical History* II. xxiii. 18.

**Works and
Faith**

Demonstrate the genuineness of your faith by good works (2:14-26). James writes of justification by works as the outward evidence *before men* of inward faith. He is not contradicting Paul, who writes of justification by faith *before God*. Knowing the hearts of all men, God does not need to see the outward evidence of works. Some of the scholars who think that James wrote the epistle late in his lifetime argue that he was correcting antinomian perversion of Paul's teaching about justification by faith. Others, failing to see that James and Paul complement each other (Paul, too, emphasizes good works as a consequence of true faith!), hold that James or a later forger is attacking not merely a distortion of the Pauline doctrine, but Paul's own formulation. *Read James 1, 2.*

**Controlling
the Tongue**

Produce the qualities of genuine wisdom required of Christian teachers: control of the tongue, that is, its speech; meekness, which avoids quarrelsomeness; and purity, which avoids worldliness (3:1—4:10).

Do not slander one another (4:11, 12).

Do not plan overconfidently by not taking into account the will of God and the possibility of death (4:13-17).

Be patient until Jesus returns, for then God will punish the rich and powerful persecutors (5:1-11).

Earn a reputation for honesty, so that you will not have to reinforce your speech with oaths (5:12).

**Anointing
the Sick**

Share your concerns and joys with one another (5:13-18). In particular, let the elders of the church believingly pray for the healing of the sick as they anoint the sick with oil in the name of the Lord. If the sick person has sinned and confesses, healing will demonstrate that God has forgiven. (The reverse — that sickness is always a direct chastisement for sin and that failure to recover implies God has not forgiven — does not logically follow.) Since olive oil was a common household remedy, James may have had its medicinal properties in mind, as if to say, "Treat with medicine and pray for recovery." The command to anoint with oil forms the basis for the Roman Catholic sacrament of extreme unction, in which the priest anoints the eyes, ears, nostrils, hands, and feet of a person about to die as a medium of forgiveness if the person cannot consciously confess his sins to receive priestly absolution. But James speaks of "elders," not priests. Nor does he speak of people already in the throes of death. Similarly, the command, "Confess your sins to one another" (5:16), is a Roman Catholic prooftext for auricular confession. But James writes "to one another" (a strange name for a priest, according to Martin Luther) and probably refers to resolving differences among Christians rather than to exposing one's private sins either to a priest or to the whole church.

**Confessing
Sins**

Prevent fellow-professing Christians from apostatizing and incurring eternal judgment (5:19, 20).[5] *Read James 3-5.* The one
"who turns a sinner from the error of his way" will save from
death not his own soul, but that of the straying Christian (by
profession), and "will cover a multitude" not of his own sins,
but those of the person who is tending toward apostasy.

A SUMMARY OUTLINE OF JAMES[6]

Theme: Christian conduct in everyday life

INTRODUCTION: greeting to Jewish Christians of the Dispersion (1:1)
  I. JOY IN TRIAL (1:2-4)
  II. PRAYER FOR WISDOM (1:5-8)
  III. DISINTERESTEDNESS IN WEALTH (1:9-11)
  IV. DIFFERENTIATION OF TRIALS AND TEMPTATIONS (1:12-18)
  V. OBEDIENCE TO THE WORD (1:19-27)
  VI. LOVE WITHOUT PARTIALITY TO THE RICH (2:1-13)
  VII. WORKS AS A DEMONSTRATION OF FAITH (2:14-26)
  VIII. WISDOM (3:1—4:10)
      A. Wisdom in the control of the tongue (3:1-12)
      B. The wisdom of meekness and unworldliness (3:13—4:10)
  IX. AVOIDANCE OF SLANDER (4:11, 12)
  X. OVERCONFIDENCE (4:13-17)
  XI. PATIENCE (5:1-11)
  XII. HONESTY (5:12)
  XIII. COMMUNALITY, INCLUDING PRAYER FOR THE SICK AND MUTUAL CON-
      FESSION OF SINS (5:13-18)
  XIV. RECLAMATION OF ERRING FELLOW CHRISTIANS (5:19, 20)

For further investigation:

Tasker, R. V. G. *A Commentary on the General Epistle of James.* Grand
  Rapids: Eerdmans, 1957.
Robertson, A. T. *Studies in the Epistle of James.* New York: Doran, 1915.
Ross, A. *The Epistles of James and John.* Grand Rapids: Eerdmans, 1954.
Mitton, C. L. *The Epistle of James.* Grand Rapids: Eerdmans, 1966.
Romans 4, for comparison with James 2:14-26 on faith and works.

FIRST PETER: SALVATION AND SUFFERING

The readers to whom this epistle was first directed were suffering persecution. The emphases therefore fall on proper Christian conduct in the face of anti-Christian hostility and on the
compensatory gift of salvation which will reach completion in
the future.

The author of the epistle identifies himself as Peter (1:1).
This identification remarkably agrees with two phenomena:
(1) a number of phrases in 1 Peter recall the phraseology of

---

[5]See the remarks on apostasy in connection with Hebrews, pages 338 f.
[6]Because of the style of James it is doubtful whether the usual outline of only
a few major points can be imposed without violating the nature of the book.

Peter's sermons recorded in Acts[7] and (2) allusions to Jesus' sayings and deeds as recorded in the gospels come from the situations in which Peter played a special part or would have a special interest.[8] Therefore, although some modern scholars have theorized that 1 Peter originally was a baptismal sermon or liturgy (1:3—4:11) transformed into an epistle by the addition of 1:1, 2 and 4:12—5:14, and hence probably non-Petrine, it is better to accept the epistle's own claim to have been written by the Apostle Peter, a claim supported by early Church tradition.

Date

The theme of persecution which runs throughout the epistle suggests that Peter wrote it around A.D. 63, shortly before his martyrdom in Rome under Nero in A.D. 64.

Persecution

The persecution presupposed in 1 Peter seems not to have originated from an imperial ban on Christianity, for Peter still speaks of the government as a protector (3:13; 2:13-17). The empire-wide ban came later. The persecution rather took the forms of slanderous accusations, social ostracism, mob riots, and local police action. Scholars who deny Petrine authorship usually date the epistle during the persecutions under Domitian (A.D. 81-96) or Trajan (A.D. 98-117). However, during these later periods the dominant issue was the refusal of Christians to sacrifice to the emperor. Since this topic does not appear in 1 Peter, the early date, with Petrine authorship, is preferable.

Silvanus the Amanuensis

Silvanus acted as Peter's amanuensis for this epistle ("I have written . . . through Silvanus," 5:12) and may have been responsible for the fair style of Greek, although we must not think that Palestinian Jews, such as Peter, were incapable of handling that language well.[9] "Silvanus" probably is another (perhaps Latin) form of the name "Silas" and refers to the Silas who accompanied Paul on his second missionary journey; for Paul mentions a "Silvanus" as his companion during the second journey (1 Thessalonians 1:1; 2 Thessalonians 1:1; 2 Co-

---

[7]Compare, for example, Acts 2:23 and 1 Peter 1:20 on the foreordination of Christ's death; Acts 10:42 and 1 Peter 4:5 on the judgment of "the living and the dead"; and the distinctive use of the Greek word *xylon* (literally, "wood") for the cross in Acts 5:30; 10:39 and 1 Peter 2:24.

[8]For example, the exhortation in 2:13-17 to live as freemen, but at the same time to live in subjection to civil authority in order to avoid giving offence, goes back to the incident recorded in Matthew 17:24-27, where Jesus said that he and his disciples were really free from human authority; but to avoid giving offence he paid the Temple tax with "Peter's Penny," found by Peter in the mouth of a fish. For further examples, see R. H. Gundry, " 'Verba Christi' in I Peter: Their Implications Concerning the Authorship of I Peter and the Authenticity of the Gospel Tradition," *New Testament Studies,* 13 (1967), pp. 336-350.

[9]See the article cited on page 21.

rinthians 1:19), and in Luke's narrative of the second journey the name is "Silas" (nine times in Acts 15:40—18:5). The similarity of Peter's ethical exhortations to those in the Pauline literature suggests that Peter was influenced by Paul's writings, perhaps known to him through Silvanus, or that both apostles drew from a common stock of more or less stereotyped catechetical instruction — oral or written, prebaptismal or postbaptismal.

Peter writes from "Babylon" (5:13), probably not the city by that name in Mesopotamia, but Rome. (Mesopotamian Babylon was almost devoid of inhabitants by the beginning of the Christian era.) "Babylon" occurs as a symbolic name for Rome in Revelation 17:4-6, 9, 18, obviously, as Rome was the *ruling* city in the New Testament period (verse 18), the city of seven hills (verse 9 — Babylon in Mesopotamia was situated on a plain, its ruins still visible today), and the persecutor of the Church (verse 6). Rome was called "Babylon" because it was the world capital of idolatry, a position once held by the Mesopotamian city.[10] Extrabiblical references to Rome as "Babylon" also suggest that Peter uses a well-known designation of the imperial

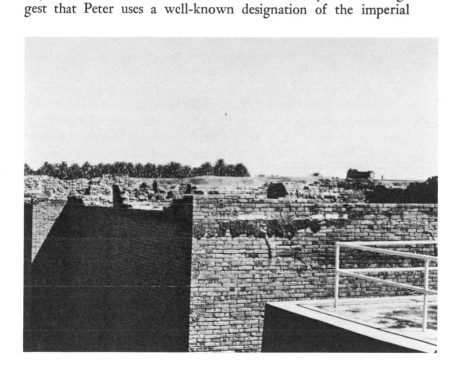

ANCIENT BABYLON, *the glorious Chaldean capital of Old Testament times, was in ruins and almost uninhabited in the days of Peter and Paul.*

---

[10]Compare the calling of Jerusalem "Sodom and Gomorrah" because of Jerusalem's wickedness (Revelation 11:8).

city. Furthermore, the early Church fathers understood "Babylon" as a reference to Rome.

Tradition knows of no church in Mesopotamian Babylon or of Peter's ever going there, but tradition does indicate that Peter died in Rome. When the fact that John Mark was in Rome during Paul's imprisonment there (Colossians 4:10) is connected with his presence with Peter at the writing of 1 Peter (1 Peter 5:13), another formidable argument for the Roman origin of the epistle appears. Finally, the order of provinces in the address (1:1) suggests that the bearer of the epistle came from Rome in the West, made a circuit of certain provinces in Asia Minor with the epistle, and returned westward to Rome. This can be seen by tracing Pontus, Galatia, Cappadocia, Asia, and Bithynia on the map. See page 230.

Addressees

The phrases "exiles of the Dispersion" (1:1), "among the Gentiles" (2:12), and "the Gentiles" (as a third party, 4:3) at first glance seem to imply that the original addressees were *Jewish* Christians. But the references to their preconversion sin of idolatry (4:3 — the Jews in New Testament times did not practice idolatry) and "passions of your former ignorance" and "futile way of life" (1:14, 18; compare Ephesians 4:17, where similar phraseology applies to Gentiles) clearly indicate the predominantly Gentile background of the intended readers. This conclusion is confirmed by 2:10: "once you were not a people [this could hardly be said of the Jews, God's covenant nation], but now you are the people of God." Just as Peter uses the term "Babylon" figuratively for Rome, he also uses the term "Gentiles" figuratively for non-Christians and the phrase "exiles of the Dispersion" for Christians scattered throughout the world. Because the Church has displaced Israel (for the present), Jewish designations can be applied to the predominantly Gentile church.

After the greeting, Peter praises God for the prospect of a glorious heavenly inheritance which makes present persecution bearable. Christ also had to suffer before glorification, something the Old Testament prophets did not understand because they did not discern the distinction between Jesus' first Advent, for death, and His Second Advent, for dominion. *Read 1 Peter 1:1-12.*

In view of future glory, it is imperative for Christians to be holy in conduct. They have been liberated ("redeemed") from the slavery of sin by Jesus' blood, which is the evidence of His life sacrificed for sinners. It is also imperative for Christians to love one another on the basis of the fact that they have all been born into the family of God through His word, to grow like newborn infants, and to be built up like a temple with Christ as the corner- or capstone. Furthermore, Christians are to make a favorable impression on the unbelieving world by good behaviour. This involves exemplary citizenship, obedience of slaves to masters without back talk, self-adornment of Christian wives with obedience to their husbands rather than with gaudy fashions, the honoring of wives by husbands, and, once again, mutual love within the Christian fellowship. *Read 1 Peter 1:13—3:22.*

The preaching of Christ to the spirits in prison (3:18 ff.) most probably means that during the time between His death and resurrection Christ descended in spirit form into hell[11] to proclaim His triumph over the demonic spirits whom God had imprisoned there because of their corruptive influence among men in the time of Noah immediately prior to the Deluge. The preaching need not refer to an offer of salvation. When unqualified, the term "spirits" in the Bible refers to supernatural beings, not to departed human spirits. The point of the passage is that just as God vindicated Christ before the very spirits who had tried to thwart the divine purpose in history, so also God will someday vindicate Christians before their persecutors.

An alternate interpretation is that the preincarnate Christ offered salvation through Noah's preaching to the antediluvian generation, who are now confined to hell because they rejected the message. In this interpretation the point of the passage lies

---

[11]A slight variation is that the prison is not hell, but the atmosphere of the earth, to which demonic spirits are now confined. Compare Ephesians 2:2; 6:12; but for the above view, see 2 Peter 2:4; Jude 6.

in the parallel between God's vindication of Noah (rather than Christ) and His vindication of Christians. But the succession of mainly verbal phrases about Christ — "put to death," "made alive in the spirit," "went," "preached," "the resurrection of Jesus Christ," "has gone into heaven," "is at the right hand of God" — makes a backward reference to an activity of Christ millennia before His incarnation exceedingly awkward.

Baptism

In comparing baptism to the Flood, Peter carefully indicates that the contact with water does not remove sin ("not the removal of dirt from the flesh"); rather, the inward attitude of repentance and faith, which shows itself by submission to the baptismal rite ("an appeal to God for a good conscience," 3:21), leads to remission.

Exhortations

The next section begins with a summary exhortation not to sin, but to love one another. The statement that "he who has suffered [= died[12]] in the flesh has ceased from sin" (4:1) plays on the double meaning of the term "flesh": (1) the body and (2) the sinful urge. When Jesus died *bodily*, the *sinful nature* of believers also died so far as God is concerned. Every believer, then, has already died to sin by union with Christ in His death. But it remains to translate the divine viewpoint into the actuality of day-to-day conduct. Compare Romans 6:1-14. "The dead" to whom the Gospel was preached (4:6) are not "the spirits in prison" of 3:18 ff. They are Christians who have been martyred ("judged in the flesh [by their persecutors]") and, as a result, now enjoy the life of heaven ("live in the spirit"). The final exhortations are to rejoice in suffering for Christ, to make sure that suffering is incurred by Christian testimony rather than by bad conduct, to show humility, and to resist with courage Satanically inspired persecution. *Read 1 Peter 4:1—5:14.*

A SUMMARY OUTLINE OF FIRST PETER

Theme: the salvation and conduct of suffering Christians

INTRODUCTION: greeting (1:1, 2)

I. PRAISE FOR THE HEAVENLY INHERITANCE OF PERSECUTED CHRISTIANS (1:3-12)
II. EXHORTATION TO PERSONAL HOLINESS (1:13-21)
III. EXHORTATION TO MUTUAL LOVE (1:22-25)
IV. EXHORTATION TO ADVANCEMENT WITHIN SALVATION (2:1-10)
V. EXHORTATION TO CHRISTIAN CONDUCT IN NON-CHRISTIAN SOCIETY (2:11—4:19)
   A. Good deeds (2:11, 12)
   B. Good citizenship (2:13-17)

---

[12]See 2:21 and, according to many ancient manuscripts, 3:18, where suffering and death are equivalent.

C. Submission of slaves, with the example of Christ (2:18-25)
D. Submission of wives (3:1-6)
E. Considerateness of husbands (3:7)
F. Sympathetic and loving unity (3:8-12)
G. Innocent suffering, with the example of Christ and His vindication in hell (3:13—4:6)
H. Joyful suffering (4:12-19)

VI. EXHORTATION TO HUMILITY WITHIN THE CHURCH AND RESISTANCE TO PERSECUTION (5:1-11)

CONCLUSION: Silvanus' function as amanuensis, greetings, and benediction (5:12-14)

For further investigation:

Stibbs, A. M., and A. F. Walls. *The First Epistle General of Peter.* Grand Rapids: Eerdmans, 1959.
Thomas à Kempis. *The Imitation of Christ.* For comparison with the same theme in 1 Peter.
Foxe, John. *Book of Martyrs.*
Lewis, C. S. *The Problem of Pain.* New York: Macmillan, 1962.
1 Enoch 6-21, 67-69; Jubilees 10, in R. H. Charles' edition of *The Apocrypha and Pseudepigrapha of the Old Testament.* For comparison with Christ's preaching to the spirits in prison according to 1 Peter 3:19.

SECOND PETER: IN DEFENSE OF ORTHODOXY

Heretical teachers who peddled false doctrine and practiced easy morality were beginning to make serious inroads into the Church. 2 Peter is a polemic against them, and particularly against their denial of the return of Jesus. Peter affirms the true knowledge of Christian belief to counter heretical teachings.

Theme

Widespread doubt exists among modern scholars that the Apostle Peter wrote this epistle. The early Church exhibited some hesitancy in accepting it into the canon. However, this may be explained by the comparative brevity of the epistle, which perhaps limited widespread distribution of and acquaintance with it. We must not forget that the early Church *did* finally accept it as a genuine and canonical writing from the pen of Peter. It is worth noting, moreover, that two books of the New Testament apocrypha, the Gospel of Truth and the Apocryphon of John, contain probable quotations from or allusions to 2 Peter and thus show an early acceptance of 2 Peter as an authoritative book already in the second century.[13] Similarly, the very early (third century) Bodmer papyrus designated P[72] shows acceptance of 2 Peter as canonical; for in that manuscript 2 Peter shares with 1 Peter and Jude a blessing on the readers of these sacred books and receives even more elaborate support than the other two epistles. The style of 2 Peter

Authenticity and Canonicity

---

[13]See A. Helmbold, *The Nag Hammadi Gnostic Texts and the Bible* (Grand Rapids: Baker, 1967), pp. 90, 91.

is different from that of 1 Peter; but a difference in amanuenses may account for that. Remarkable similarities of phraseology between 2 Peter and 1 Peter and the Petrine speeches in Acts point to a common source, the Apostle Peter.[14]

**Relation
to Jude**

It is also argued that 2 Peter borrows from Jude, especially in the description of false teachers, and that a man of Peter's apostolic stature would not have borrowed from a comparatively insignificant writer, such as Jude. But one may question the last part of the argument. Literary history is full of examples of prominent writers who borrowed from obscure sources (Shakespeare is one who did). Furthermore, a number of scholars have argued very cogently that Jude wrote his epistle later and borrowed from 2 Peter. For example, the fact that 2 Peter speaks of the coming of the false teachers predominantly in the future tense and Jude in the past tense seems to indicate that 2 Peter was written *before* widespread heresy, Jude *afterwards*. It is also possible that their similar phraseology comes from a common source unknown to us.

**The Allusion
to Paul's
Letters**

A further objection to Petrine authorship is that the reference to Paul's epistles in 2 Peter 3:15, 16 implies that all of them had been written, collected, and published together; and that could have happened only after the martyrdom of Peter and Paul, for Paul was writing up to the very end of his life. But the reference to Paul's epistles need imply the existence of only those epistles he had written up to the time Peter wrote his second epistle. Peter's knowledge of them probably came from his travels, from the circulation of Pauline epistles, and from Silvanus (or Silas), who was both Paul's missionary companion and Peter's amanuensis (1 Peter 5:12). The description of Paul as "our beloved brother" (2 Peter 3:15) is what an apostolic contemporary and equal would write and not what a later pseudonymous author would write about an ecclesiastical hero of a preceding generation. Despite modern doubt, then, we may accept the final verdict of the early Church that shortly after the Apostle Peter wrote his first epistle and shortly before his martyrdom in A.D. 64, he wrote this second epistle which bears his name.

**The Reliability
of Orthodoxy**

2 Peter asserts the true knowledge of Christian belief in opposition to false teaching. After the salutation, Peter glories in

---

[14]See E. M. B. Green, *2 Peter Reconsidered* (London: Tyndale, 1961), pp. 12-14, and the entire monograph for a full discussion of all aspects of the problem. See also D. Guthrie, *New Testament Introduction: Hebrews to Revelation* (Chicago: Inter-Varsity, 1962), pp. 137-185; and for conceptual similarities with the pre-Christian Dead Sea Scrolls, W. F. Albright, *From the Stone Age to Christianity,* 2nd edition (Garden City, New York: Doubleday, 1957), pp. 22, 23.

the magnitude of God's promises to believers, by which they come to share the divine nature, and points out the resultant necessity of developing Christian virtues. Correct conduct must undergird correct belief. He reminds his readers of the reliability of the Christian faith, as supported by eyewitness testimony to the events of Jesus' life (Peter singles out his own observation of the transfiguration, 1:16-18) and as proved by the fulfillment of divinely inspired prophecy. *Read 2 Peter 1.* "No prophecy of scripture is a matter of one's own interpretation" (1:20) probably means that the Old Testament predictions of Messianic events did not arise out of the prophets' own interpretation of the future, but from the influence of the Holy Spirit. Compare 1:21: "for no prophecy was ever made by an act of human will, but men moved by the Holy Spirit spoke from God."[15]

The mention of true prophecy at the end of chapter one leads to a condemnation of false prophecy. Current and future false teachers stand in the tradition of the Old Testament false prophets and will incur the same divine judgment on themselves. Their licentious living demonstrates their depravity and slavery to lust, even though they promise freedom. True Christians, however, should recall the predictions of judgment at the Second Coming after the pattern of the Flood, but with fire instead of water. The delay in Jesus' return should not be misinterpreted as cancellation. It is rather due to God's patience in giving each generation more time for repentance. After all, what is a thousand years to the eternal God? Since the present scheme of things will be destroyed, Christians should live uprightly by eternal values in anticipation of Jesus' return. The classification of Paul's epistles among "the other scriptures" (3: 15, 16) shows that they were already regarded as inspired. *Read 2 Peter 2, 3.*

A SUMMARY OUTLINE OF SECOND PETER

Theme: the true knowledge of Christian belief versus false teachers and their denial of the Parousia

INTRODUCTION: greeting (1:1,2)
  I. THE TRUE KNOWLEDGE OF CHRISTIAN BELIEF (1:3-21)
     A. The moral undergirding of Christian belief with correct conduct (1:3-11)
     B. The historical reliability of Christian belief, supported by eyewitness

---

[15]Other interpretations are that (1) prophetic predictions should not be interpreted in isolation from other Scriptures; (2) prophetic predictions were not addressed exclusively to the generation contemporary with their issuance; (3) the Holy Spirit interprets prophecy, as well as inspires it; (4) the Christian as a private individual does not have the ability or right to interpret Scripture, but needs ecclesiastical direction.

testimony (particularly of the transfiguration) and fulfilled prophecy
(1:12-21)

II. FALSE TEACHERS (2:1-22)
   A. Their coming appearance in the Church (2:1-3)
   B. Their future judgment (2:4-10a)
   C. Their immoral ways (2:10b-22)
III. THE PAROUSIA AND FINAL DISSOLUTION (3:1-18a)
   A. Its certainty in spite of delay and denials by false teachers (3:1-10)
   B. Its call to godliness (3:11-18a)
CONCLUSION: doxology (3:18b)

For further investigation:

McNab, A. "II Peter," in *The New Bible Commentary.* Edited by F. Davidson, A. M. Stibbs, and E. F. Kevan. 2nd edition. Grand Rapids: Eerdmans, 1963. Pp. 1143-1150.
Paine, S. W. "The Second Epistle of Peter," in *The Wycliffe Bible Commentary.* Edited by C. F. Pfeiffer and E. F. Harrison. Chicago: Moody, 1963. Pp. 1453-1462.

JUDE: DANGER! FALSE TEACHERS!

Theme

Like 2 Peter, the Epistle of Jude polemicizes against false teachers who had penetrated the Church — in greater numbers, it would appear, than at the time 2 Peter was written.[16] The particular heresies receive no detailed description or rebuttal, but the heretics themselves draw vehement castigation.

The Author

The author of the epistle identifies himself as Jude, "the brother of James" (verse 1). He is probably not referring to the Apostle James of the well-known trio, Peter, James, and John. Herod Agrippa I had martyred the Apostle James at an early date (Acts 12:1, 2). The writer refers rather to James the leader of the Jerusalem church (Acts 15; Galations 1, 2) and half brother of Jesus. Thus, Jude was also a half brother of Jesus, but with modesty he describes himself as "a servant of Jesus Christ" (1:1). The date of the epistle is uncertain, but it is late enough for heretics to have made serious inroads into the Church.

**False
Teachers**

Jude had intended to write a doctrinal treatise, but the infiltration of false teachers into the Church compelled him to change his epistle into an exhortation to fight vigorously for the truth of the Gospel. In vivid terms he describes both the wickedness of the false teachers and their doom by citing past examples of divine judgment: the generation of Israel who perished in the wilderness for their faithless ways, the fallen angels (probably the demonic spirits who corrupted the human race just before the Flood [Genesis 6:1 ff.; 1 Peter 3:18 ff.]), and Sodom and Gomorrah. The false teachers' lack of reverence for spiritual things and for superhuman beings stands in contrast to the care with which the archangel Michael disputed with Satan over

[16]The point is disputed; see page 354.

Moses' corpse. The letter closes with a stirring doxology. *Read Jude.*

In verses 14 and 15 Jude quotes the pseudepigraphal apocalypse of 1 Enoch ("Enoch . . . prophesied, saying, 'Behold the Lord came with many thousands of His holy ones, etc.,' " from 1 Enoch 1:9). In the allusion to the dispute between Michael and Satan (verse 9) he seems to refer to another pseudepigraphal book, the Assumption of Moses. Although the full text of the Assumption of Moses has not survived and the extant fragments do not contain this story, it seems likely that Jude's reference is from that source. We should not be surprised that a canonical writer quotes noncanonical writings. Paul refers to a rabbinical midrash (exposition) on the water-giving rock that "followed" Israel in the wilderness (1 Corinthians 10:4), quotes heathen poets in his sermon at Athens (Acts 17:28), and apparently borrows the names of Pharaoh's magicians who opposed Moses (Jannes and Jambres, 2 Timothy 3:8) from some noncanonical source. Quotations from such material does not imply belief in its divine inspiration. It does not necessarily have to imply historicity of the material; for the New Testament writers may simply be illustrating a point, just as John Milton (to take one of many possible examples) utilized Greek myths without implying belief in them as literal history.

A SUMMARY OUTLINE OF JUDE

Theme: warning against false teachers in the Church

INTRODUCTION: greeting (1, 2)

I. THE ENTRANCE OF FALSE TEACHERS INTO THE CHURCH (3, 4)
II. THE UNGODLY CHARACTER AND COMING JUDGMENT OF THE FALSE TEACHERS (5-16)
III. RESISTANCE AGAINST THE FALSE TEACHERS (17-23)

CONCLUSION: benediction (24, 25)

For further investigation:

Robertson, R. "The General Epistle of Jude," in *The New Bible Commentary.* Edited by F. Davidson, A. M. Stibbs, and E. F. Kevan. 2nd edition. Grand Rapids: Eerdmans, 1963. Pp. 1161-1167.

Wallace, D. H. "Jude," in *The Wycliffe Bible Commentary.* Edited by C. F. Pfeiffer and E. F. Harrison. Chicago: Moody, 1963. Pp. 1487-1490.

Henry, C. F. H. *Frontiers in Modern Theology.* Chicago: Moody, 1966. For current theologies which might fall under the strictures of 2 Peter and Jude.

FIRST JOHN: FATHERLY INSTRUCTION TO "LITTLE CHILDREN"

For the early Christian, heresy in the Church posed the problem of distinguishing orthodoxy from heterodoxy, faithful ministers of the word from false teachers. The Epistle of 1 John formulates several primary criteria — righteousness, love, and correct Christology — for testing the Christian profession of teachers and of oneself.

Literary Form and Address

Written probably toward the end of the first century A.D. by the Apostle John, 1 John has no introduction, author's greetings, or concluding salutations. Yet the statements "I am writing" (2:1) and "These things I have written to you" (2:26) show that originally 1 John was not an oral sermon, but a written composition. It might have been a general tract for the whole Church. However, the affectionate "my little children," by which the writer repeatedly addresses his readers, implies a limited circle of Christians with whom the writer was closely acquainted. According to early Church tradition John lived in Ephesus during his old age. Therefore, 1 John was probably a general letter written in sermonic style to Christians he had come to know in Asia Minor in the area surrounding Ephesus (compare with Paul's circular letter to the "Ephesians" and the sermonic style of Hebrews).[17] John clearly states that his purpose in writing is to strengthen his readers' knowledge, joy, and assurance in the Christian faith (1:3, 4; 5:13) over against false teaching (2:1 ff.; 4:1 ff.).

Purpose

Antignostic Polemic

The heresy of Gnosticism was probably developing within Christendom by the time John wrote. Indeed, according to early tradition John hurriedly left a public bath in Ephesus upon hearing that the Gnostic leader Cerinthus had entered.[18] Building on the notion that matter is inherently evil, Cerinthus distinguished between an immaterial divine Christ-spirit and a human Jesus with a physical body, and said that the Christ-spirit came upon the human Jesus right after His baptism and left just before the crucifixion.

Against this Cerinthian doctrine John stresses that it was the one person "Jesus Christ" who began His public manifestation by being baptized and finished it by being crucified: "This is the one who came by water and blood, Jesus Christ; not with the water only, but with the water and with the blood" (5:6). That is, Jesus Christ really died as well as entered His ministry by the water of baptism. The water also refers to the water

---

[17]It is also possible that 1 John represents a Western Asiatic letter-form which lacked opening address and closing greeting.

[18]Irenaeus, *Against Heresies* III. iii. 4: "There are also those who heard from him [Polycarp] that John, the disciple of the Lord, going to bathe at Ephesus, and perceiving Cerinthus within, rushed out of the bath-house without bathing, exclaiming, 'Let us fly, lest even the bath-house fall down, because Cerinthus, the enemy of the truth is within'" (translation from the edition of Roberts and Donaldson).

which with the blood flowed from Jesus' pierced side in proof of the reality of His death.

Working on the same presupposition that anything material and physical must necessarily be evil, other Gnostics also tried to avoid the incarnation and bodily death of Jesus Christ by saying that He only *seemed* to be human (so-called doceticism, from the Greek word *dokeō, to seem*). John therefore emphasizes the reality of the incarnation: "what we have heard, what we have seen with our eyes, what we beheld and our hands handled, . . . and we have seen" (1:1, 2). Ironically, the first major Christian heresy attacked the humanity rather than the deity of Jesus.

To accomplish his purpose of strengthening the readers by combating heresy with truth, John discusses three criteria for determining genuine Christian profession: (1) righteous living; (2) love for other believers; (3) belief in Jesus as the incarnate Christ. Just as the criterion of belief in Jesus as the incarnate Christ is directed against Gnosticism, so also is the criterion of righteous conduct directed against the moral laxity of Gnostics and the criterion of love toward fellow Christians directed against the haughty exclusivism of Gnostics.

Criteria of Christian Experience

After claiming firsthand knowledge of Jesus' life (1:1-4), John insists that true Christians, although not sinless, live righteously (1:5—2:6), love one another instead of the world (2:7-17), and believe the truth concerning Christ. Thus they reject false teachers, called "antichrists" because they are precursors of *the* Antichrist (2:18-28), who will appear during the tribulation just before the end of this age. Then John discusses the criteria again: righteousness (2:29—3:10a); love (3:10b-24a); truth (3:24b—4:6); love (4:7—5:3); righteousness (5:4-21). *Read 1 John 1-5.*

In chapter three the strong language about Christians' not sinning cannot denote flawlessness in the light of 1:8: "If we say we have no sin, we deceive ourselves, and the truth is not in us" (compare 1:10; 2:1). The Greek present tenses in the third chapter may indicate that the conduct of true Christians is not *predominantly* sinful. Perhaps John also means that a Christian cannot sin *as a Christian*. When he does sin, he temporarily denies his new nature. This is not to say that he ceases to be a Christian, but that he ceases to act like the Christian he is. The Gnostics prided themselves on their "Christian freedom" to do anything they pleased, including freedom to sin.

Sinlessness?

The enigmatic mention of a sin leading to death, a sin undeserving of intercessory prayer (5:16, 17), probably refers to the final apostasy, warned against in Hebrews and exhibited by

The Sin Unto Death

the Gnostic teachers, that results in irrevocable condemnation. Alternatively, John refers to physical (not eternal) death as a chastisement for disobedient Christians (compare 1 Corinthians 5:5; 11:27-34).

A SUMMARY OUTLINE OF FIRST JOHN

Theme: the criteria of true Christian belief and practice over against Gnosticism

PROLOGUE: the eyewitnessed incarnation of Christ, the word of life, as the basis for Christian fellowship (1:1-4)

    I. THE CRITERION OF RIGHTEOUS CONDUCT (1:5—2:6)
   II. THE CRITERION OF MUTUAL CHRISTIAN LOVE (2:7-17)
  III. THE CRITERION OF INCARNATIONAL CHRISTOLOGY (2:18-28)
  IV. THE CRITERION OF RIGHTEOUS CONDUCT (2:29—3:10a)
   V. THE CRITERION OF MUTUAL CHRISTIAN LOVE (3:10b-24a)
 VI. THE CRITERION OF INCARNATIONAL CHRISTOLOGY (3:24b—4:6)
VII. THE CRITERION OF MUTUAL CHRISTIAN LOVE (4:7—5:3)
VIII. THE CRITERION OF RIGHTEOUS CONDUCT (5:4-21)

SECOND AND THIRD JOHN: FATHERLY INSTRUCTION TO CHRISTIAN PEOPLE

Canonicity and Authorship of 2 and 3 John

The attestation of 2 and 3 John in patristic writings is somewhat weak, doubtless because of the brevity of these letters. The earliest Church fathers exhibited no doubt that the Apostle John wrote them. In both letters John identifies himself as "the elder," not in the sense of an officer in a local church, but in the sense of an elder statesman of the church, that is, an apostle (compare 1 Peter 5:1). The term stands in contrast to John's favorite designation of his readers, "my little children."

Themes, Purpose, and Address of 2 John

The themes of Christian love and truth dominate 2 John. The purpose is to warn against showing hospitality to any false teacher ("do not receive him into the house or give him any greeting," verse 10). The addressees are "the elect [or chosen] lady and her children" (verse 1). Some interpreters consider them to be personal acquaintances of the apostle. It is far more likely that "the elect lady" is a personification of a local church and "her children" the individual members of that church; for the lady and her children are beloved by "all who know the truth" (verse 1). It is improbable that one family enjoyed such a wide reputation in Christendom, but quite conceivable that a prominent church did. Furthermore, neither the lady's children nor her nephews (verse 13) are mentioned by personal names,[19] and the pronoun "you" in verses 8, 10, and 12 is plural. All this

---

[19]Some have treated the words "elect" and "lady" as proper names of a woman, giving "Electa" or "Kyria" or both. But "elect" can hardly be a proper name, for the lady's sister is also "elect" (verse 13). Two sisters would not have the same name "Electa"! Also, the considerations in the text above militate against taking "lady" either as the name or as a description of an individual Christian woman.

data plus the warning against false teachers and the command to love one another are more appropriate to a church than to a family (compare 1 John). Where the church was located we do not know. *Read 2 John.*

A SUMMARY OUTLINE OF SECOND JOHN

Themes: Christian love and Christian truth

INTRODUCTION: greeting (1-3)

I. EXHORTATION TO CHRISTIAN LOVE (4-6)

II. WARNING AGAINST FALSE DOCTRINE AND ENTERTAINMENT OF FALSE TEACHERS (7-11)

CONCLUSION: the hope for a coming visit and another greeting (12, 13)

Third John focuses on an ecclesiastical dispute. The place where the recipient lived is unknown, but it was most likely in the region around Ephesus. John sends the letter to Gaius (1) to commend Gaius' hospitality to "the brethren" (probably itinerant teachers sent by John); (2) to rebuke Diotrephes, a self-assertive leader in the church, for his lack of hospitality toward "the brethren," for his dictatorial ways, and for his opposition to the apostolic authority of John; and (3) to praise Demetrius, who probably carried the letter. Demetrius may have needed a recommendation because he was moving from the Ephesian church, with which John was associated, to the church where Gaius was (compare the commendation of Phoebe in Romans 16:1, 2) or because he was one of the itinerant teachers of the kind to whom Diotrephes had refused hospitality. Indeed, Diotrephes had expelled from the church those who dared to give them food and lodging. John indicates that he has written another letter to the whole church to which Gaius belongs (verse 9). This other letter may be 2 John, the circular 1 John, or an epistle which has since been lost. Verse ten contains the threat of a personal visit by John for a direct confrontation with Diotrephes. *Read 3 John.*

Theme, Address, and Purposes of 3 John

A SUMMARY OUTLINE OF THIRD JOHN

Theme: an ecclesiastical dispute

INTRODUCTION: greeting (1)

I. COMMENDATION OF GAIUS' HOSPITALITY TO TRAVELING CHRISTIAN WORKERS (2-8)

II. CONDEMNATION OF THE REBELLION OF DIOTREPHES AGAINST JOHANNINE APOSTOLIC AUTHORITY AND HIS REFUSAL OF HOSPITALITY TO TRAVELING CHRISTIAN WORKERS (9-11)

III. COMMENDATION OF DEMETRIUS, PROBABLE CARRIER OF THE LETTER AND ENVOY OF JOHN (12)

CONCLUSION: the prospect of a coming visit and final greetings (13-15)

For further discussion:

Is there anything specifically Christian (rather than merely Jewish) about the Epistle of James? If any, why so little?

What relevance can an epistle that arose out of persecution, such as 1 Peter, have for the Church in a free society?

How should false teachers in the Church be treated? And how serious a deviation is required to merit the opprobrious epithet "false teacher" or "heretic"?

What are the logical connections between righteousness, love, and orthodoxy in 1 John?

For further investigation:

Ross, A. *The Epistles of James and John.* Grand Rapids: Eerdmans, 1954.
Law, R. *The Tests of Life.* Edinburgh: T. & T. Clark, 1909.

CHAPTER 20

Revelation: He Is Coming!

Leading questions:

Why does the style of Revelation differ from that of the Gospel and Epistles of John if John was the author of all?

What historical circumstance evoked the writing of Revelation?

What are the major interpretive approaches to Revelation, and their strengths and weaknesses?

What local background enlivens our understanding of the seven messages to churches in Asia?

What meanings do the apocalyptic symbols in Revelation bear?

What are the sources of the plagues described in Revelation?

Who are the 144,000, the two witnesses, the woman, the child, the beast, and the false prophet?

With what events will present history finally conclude and the eternal state begin?

The Apocalypse (Greek for "unveiling"), or Book of Revelation, contains more extended prophecies about the future than any other part of the New Testament. These prophecies focus on the eschatological triumph of Christ over the antichristian forces of the world — beginning with the tribulation, climaxing with the Parousia, and reaching completion with the full realization of God's kingdom — all to the great encouragement of Christians who face the antagonism of an unbelieving society. Theme

Revelation is strongly attested as canonical and apostolic in the earliest post-New Testament period of Church history, from Hermas in the early second century through Origen in the first half of the third century. Doubts arose later, largely because of Canonicity and Authorship

363

ISLAND OF PATMOS *with a view to the open sea from the monastery.*

Dionysius' argument that differences between Revelation and the Gospel and Epistles of John exclude common authorship: the Apostle John cannot therefore have written Revelation. It is true that from a grammatical and literary standpoint the Greek style of Revelation is inferior to that of the Johannine gospel and epistles. But R. H. Charles, perhaps the greatest expert on apocalyptic literature, regarded the "bad grammar" as deliberate, for purposes of emphasis and allusion to Old Testament passages in Hebraic style, rather than due to ignorance or blundering.[1] Others have thought that the "bad grammar" resulted from an ecstatic emotional state of John when he received his prophecies in the form of visions. The simplest solution is to say that as a prisoner on the Island of Patmos in the Aegean Sea, John did not have the advantage of an amanuensis to smooth out his rough style, as he apparently had for his gospel and epistles. It is not impossible that all three above factors contributed to the different style in Revelation.

Date   Concerning the date of writing, one view maintains that Nero's

---

[1]R. H. Charles, *A Critical and Exegetical Commentary on the Revelation of St. John;* The International Critical Commentary (Edinburgh: T. & T. Clark, 1920), vol. I, pp. cxvii-clix.

persecution of Christians after the burning of Rome in A.D. 64 evoked Revelation as an encouragement to persecuted Christians. In support of this view is the observation that the numerical value of the Hebrew letters spelling Nero Caesar totals 666, the very number which appears in Revelation 13:18 as symbolic of "the Beast." However, technical problems cast doubt on the numerical value of Nero's title.

It is also argued in favor of an early (Neronian) date that the smoother literary style of the Gospel and Epistles of John exhibit an improvement in his command of the Greek language and thus imply that Revelation dates from an earlier period when John was still struggling with Greek as a language less familiar to him. But there are other explanations for the rough style in Revelation (see the preceding section); and archaeological discoveries and literary studies have recently demonstrated that along with Aramaic and Hebrew, Greek was commonly spoken among first century Palestinians. Thus John must have known and used Greek since his youth.[2]

The traditional and probable date of Revelation is the reign of Domitian (A.D. 81-96). Although Domitian did not persecute Christians on a wide scale, his attempt to enforce emperor worship presaged the violent persecutions to come. Revelation was designed, then, to prepare Christians for resistance. The early Church father Irenaeus explicitly dated the writing of Revelation during Domitian's emperorship.[3] The testimony of Irenaeus is very impressive, because he was a protégé of Polycarp (A.D. 60-155), the bishop of Smyrna who had sat under the tutelage of John.

Apocalyptic Style

In style typical of apocalyptic literature, Revelation displays highly symbolic language in the description of visions. The visions portray the end of history when evil will have reached its limit, and God will intervene to commence His kingdom, judge the wicked, and reward the righteous. All this is presented not to satisfy idle curiosity about the future, but to encourage the people of God to endure in a world dominated by wickedness. Very frequently John utilizes phraseology from the Old Testament, especially from Daniel, Ezekiel, and Isaiah.

The extravagant figures of speech used throughout the Apocalypse may sound strange to modern ears, but they convey the cosmic proportions of the described events far more effectively than prosaic language could ever do. Interestingly, the strange figures are comparable in style to creations of our contemporary cartoonists, which we readily accept and understand.

---

[2]See the article cited on page 21.
[3]Irenaeus, *Against Heresies* V. xxx. 3.

Interpreters usually follow one of four main approaches to Revelation:

The idealist view strips the symbolic language of any value in the prediction of future events and reduces the prophecy to a symbolic picture of the continuous struggle between good and evil, the Church and paganism, and of the eventual triumph of Christianity. This interpretation contains a kernel of truth, but it arises mainly from the presupposition that genuine predictive prophecy is impossible and from embarrassment over the extravagance of apocalyptic language.

The preterist view, sharing the same presupposition with the idealist, limits Revelation to a description of the persecution of Christianity by ancient Rome and to what was expected to happen by way of the destruction of the Roman Empire and the vindication of Christians at the supposedly near return of Christ. Of course, under this view Revelation turned out to be mistaken — Jesus did not return quickly although the Roman Empire did fall and Christianity continued. Consequently preterists attempt to salvage the significance of the book for modern times by resorting also to the idealist view. Preterists are prone to infer a utilization of pagan mythology throughout Revelation.

The historicist view interprets Revelation as a symbolic pre-narration of Church history from apostolic times till the return of Christ and the final judgment. Thus, the breaking of the seals represents the fall of the Roman Empire, the locusts from the bottomless pit stand for the Mohammedan invasions, the beast represents the papacy (according to the Reformers), and so on. But the explanations of the individual symbols vary so widely among interpreters of this school that doubt is cast on the interpretive method itself. For although prophetic language is somewhat opaque before the predicted events come to pass, the fulfilling events should clarify the language sufficiently to prevent the breadth of interpretive variations which exists among historicists.[4] Generally, historicists hold to postmillennialism, the utopian idea that Christ will return *after* a lengthy golden age (the millennium) resulting from conversion of the world to Christianity — a view popular in the nineteenth century; or they hold to amillennialism (the more usual view today), which denies a literal thousand years' reign of Christ over a restored Israel and the Gentile nations, and transmutes the thousand years' reign of Christ into His present spiritual rulership while seated at the right hand of God the Father.

---

[4]For example, historicists have variously identified the locusts from the abyss in 9:1 ff. with the Vandals, Goths, Persians, Mohammedans, heretics, and others.

The futurist view recognizes that Revelation arose out of pressure on the Church from Rome during the first century and that the book spoke to that situation; but it holds that the bulk of Revelation describes a future distressing and chaotic time called "the tribulation" immediately followed by the return of Christ, the coming of God's kingdom, the final judgment, and the eternal state. Futurists usually calculate the tribulation, or Daniel's seventieth week (Daniel 9:24-27), as seven years in length, with perhaps only the latter three and one half years intensely distressing. Also, they usually hold to the premillennial view that upon His return Christ will reestablish the Davidic kingdom of Israel and rule the world for one thousand paradisiacal years (the millennium), crush a Satanically inspired rebellion at the close of the millennium, and preside at the final judgment before the eternal state begins.

Disagreement exists among futurists (or premillennialists) over whether the Church will continue on earth throughout the tribulation (posttribulationism), will be evacuated from the earth by a preliminary coming of Christ before the tribulation (pretribulationism), or at its halfway mark (midtribulationism), or whether only the godly part of the Church will be evacuated beforehand (partial rapturism).[5] Pretribulationism and posttribulationism are the most widely held views among futurists. Broadly speaking, the more strictly an interpreter separates God's dealings with the Church from His dealings with Israel, the more inclined he is to see the Church removed from the tribulation, during which Israel figures prominently. Posttribulationists view the tribulation as a time when God concurrently finishes His earthly dealings with the Church and begins to deal with Israel again in preparation for the millennial kingdom. Entire loss (or nearly so) of distinction between the Church and Israel usually results in historicism, the denial that there will be a future period of seven years' tribulation, so that it becomes meaningless to ask whether the rapture occurs before, during, or after the tribulation. Some historicists, however, believe in a literal millennium after Jesus' return.

The view here adopted is primarily futurist with a reminder that John was writing not only for the end of the age, but also for the Christians of his own time and indeed for Christians of every generation. In particular, the struggle between Christianity and the Caesars corresponds to the struggle between God's people in the tribulation (whether the Church or others) and the Antichrist, who will rule the revived Roman Empire.

REVELATION:
HE IS COMING!

4) Futurist

The Rapture
Question

Perspective

---

[5]On the term *rapture*, see page 269.

A SURVEY
OF THE
NEW TESTAMENT

Origin,
Address, and
Contents

Revelation retains its relevance because of the possibility for each successive generation to see the fulfillment of the book.

After the address, the first chapter contains an account of John's vision of Christ on a certain Sunday ("Lord's day," 1:10) during his exile on Patmos because of his Christian witness. Early Church tradition seems to imply that John was later released from Patmos and spent his last years in Ephesus. Chapters 2 and 3 contain seven messages dictated to John by Christ for seven churches in Asia in and around Ephesus.[6] "Asia" refers to the Roman province by that name in Asia Minor. Then follows a vision of God, His heavenly court, and the appearance of Christ as a lamb still bearing the scars of sacrificial death (chapters 4, 5). Chapters 6-19 describe mainly the plagues of the tribulation and the subsequent return of Christ. Finally, John tells about the reign of Christ and the saints for a thousand years, the last judgment, and the New Jerusalem (chapters 20-22).

Read Revelation 1-3. The seven spirits of God mentioned in the introductory remarks (1:4; cf. 4:5) are probably not seven different spirits, but the one Holy Spirit according to His sevenfold relationship to the seven churches addressed or according to Isaiah's sevenfold characterization of Him as the Spirit (1) of the Lord, (2) of wisdom, (3) of understanding, (4) of counsel, (5) of might, (6) of knowledge, and (7) of the fear of the Lord (Isaiah 11:2). John did not intend his description of Christ to be taken with a strict literalness, which here would be grotesque. The figures of speech are rather to be translated into the various characteristics and functions of Christ. His clothing represents royal priesthood, His white hair eternal age, His flaming eyes the piercing gaze of omniscience, His bronze-like feet the stamping down of judgmental activity, His thunderous voice divine authority, the two-edged sword His word, and His shining face the glory of His deity.

The seven golden lampstands symbolize the seven addressed churches, for whom Christ cares. The seven stars in His hand represent the "angels" of the seven churches, either guardian angels for each local assembly, or human "messengers" (another possible translation) sent from the churches to visit John on Patmos. The translation "messengers" gains favor from their being addressed and exhorted throughout chapters two and three — how could John write to and exhort angels?

---

[6]These messages are somewhat incorrectly called "letters," since that would imply separate communications to each church, whereas John is to write and send the entire contents of Revelation with the seven messages embedded within it (1:11).

The command given John to "write the things which you have seen, and the things which are, and the things which shall take place after these things" (1:19) is sometimes taken as a built-in, threefold outline of the book: (1) the past things, or John's vision of Christ (chapter 1); (2) the present things, or the messages to the seven churches representing the entire age of the Church (chapters 2, 3); and (3) the future things, or the return of Christ with preceding and following connected events (chapters 4-22). But at the time Jesus spoke the words recorded in 1:19, "the things which are" still had to do with the vision of Christ, for the dictation of the messages had not yet started. Chapters 1-3 describe a single vision. The statement in 1:19 should not, then, be taken as a formal outline of the book, but as a simple statement that John was to write the things he had just seen, was seeing, and was about to see.

Each of the seven messages contains an address, self-designation, analysis (with commendation and/or rebuke), exhortation, and promise. Christ carefully chooses His self-designating titles to suit the situation in each of the churches. For example, to the suffering church at Smyrna He is the one "who died and came to life" (2:8).

The Seven Messages

The Nicolaitans, opposed by the Ephesian church, reputedly were heretical followers of Nicolaus of Antioch (an assumption based perhaps on the similarity of the names), one of the seven men chosen to wait on tables in the early Jerusalem church (Acts 6:5). If so, he had turned apostate. We gather from scattered statements in Revelation 2 and 3 that the Nicolaitans participated in pagan worship and immorality. Perhaps the commendable opposition to them by the Ephesian church led to divisiveness, which made the orthodox Christians lose their former love ("first love") toward one another.

Ephesus

The "ten days" of persecution for the church in Smyrna (2:10) refers to a short period of persecution or to ten waves of persecution.

Smyrna

"Satan's throne" in Pergamum (2:13) alludes to the facts that that city was the center of the emperor cult in the province of Asia and that a huge altar to Zeus on the hill nearby dominated the city. The "manna" which is promised to overcomers symbolizes eternal life (2:17). Compare Jesus' self-designation as the "bread of life" in typological fulfillment of the Old Testament manna (John 6). The symbolism of the "white stone" inscribed with a new name and given to overcomers (also 2:17) signifies their right to enter eternal life, but the specific background is difficult to ascertain (see the commentaries).

Pergamum

The numerous trade guilds in the industrial city of Thyatira caused many Christians who were members of the guilds to

Thyatira

369

REMAINS OF THE ALTAR TO ZEUS *in a commanding position above the city of Pergamum. The altar was described as "Satan's Seat" by early Christians.*

PERGAMUM'S ALTAR TO ZEUS *as reconstructed is displayed in a museum in East Berlin.*

IN SARDIS, *an Ionic capital from a column of the Temple of Artemis.
This section is approximately six feet high.*

participate in the heathen festivities that formed part of the
guilds' activities. It appears that a false prophetess, sarcastically
called "Jezebel" after King Ahab's wicked Tyrian wife, encouraged this licentious type of "freedom" (2:20).

Sardis was noted for its immorality; the effect on the church
was that only ". . . a few people in Sardis . . . have not soiled
their garments" (3:4). The city was noted also for its dyeing of
woolen garments; Christ therefore promises that overcomers will
walk with Him, contrastingly, "in *white* garments" (3:4, 5). **Sardis**

The population of Philadelphia was small because of frequent
earthquakes. The church there was correspondingly small ("you
have a little power," 3:8). As the One who has authority to
admit or deny entrance into the Messianic kingdom ("he . . .
who has the key of David," 3:7), the Lord promises admittance
to the Philadelphian Christians, whom He does not criticize at
all. Pretribulationists take the promise to the church at Philadelphia, "I also will keep you from the hour of testing" (3:10),
as an indication that true Christians will be removed from the
world before the tribulation. Posttribulationists, comparing the
phraseology of John 17:15 ("I do not pray that thou shouldst take
them out of the world, but that thou shouldst keep them from
the evil one"), regard it as a promise of protection on earth
from divine wrath. **Philadelphia**

Laodicea was a prosperous center of banking, a place of manu-
facture of clothing from the raven-black wool of sheep raised in
the area, and a center for medical studies. In particular, a
famous Phrygian powder used to cure eye diseases came from **Laodicea**

the region. So self-sufficient was Laodicea that after a destructive earthquake in A.D. 60, the city did not need the financial aid given by Rome to neighboring cities for reconstruction. In clear allusion to these facts Christ castigates the Laodicean Christians for their spiritual poverty and nakedness in the midst of affluence and advises them to acquire spiritual wealth, to clothe themselves with *white* clothing (righteousness), and to treat their defective spiritual eyesight, or distorted sense of values, with spiritual medicine (3:18). Cold water is refreshing; hot water is useful. But the Laodiceans were like the water from nearby hot springs, which in flowing through the aqueduct became tepid — and nauseating.

The Seven
Churches and
Church
History

The churches addressed in the seven messages existed as local assemblies in Asia during the first century. They also represent types of churches which have existed throughout Church history. It has been suggested even further — although not all agree — that the dominant characteristics of the seven churches in the order of their mention represent the distinctive characteristics and developments within Christendom during successive eras of Church history:

AT HIERAPOLIS *these formations are produced by lime from mineral hot springs. The spring water has been celebrated from ancient times as a cure for eye trouble. The hot springs also provided lukewarm drinking water for the nearby Laodiceans.*

372

Ephesus, the hardworking apostolic church;

Smyrna, the heavily persecuted postapostolic church;

Pergamum, the increasingly worldly church after Emperor Constantine made Christianity virtually the Roman state religion;

Thyatira, the corrupt church of the Middle Ages;

Sardis, the Reformation church with a reputation for orthodoxy, but a lack of spiritual vitality;

Philadelphia, the church of modern revivals and global missionary enterprise; and

Laodicea, the contemporary church made lukewarm by apostasy and affluence.

However, this interpretation suffers from the criticisms that Thyatira receives some higher marks than are usually given to the Middle Ages, that the Reformation church hardly merits the message of almost total rebuke directed to Sardis, that the open door mentioned in the letter to Philadelphia probably refers to entrance into the Messianic kingdom rather than to missionary enterprise, and that the lengthening of Church history requires repeated adjustments of the interpretation. Nevertheless some of the similarities remain tantalizing.

A difference of opinion exists concerning John's being caught up to heaven in 4:1. Posttribulationists treat it as a purely personal experience for the reception of further visions; many pretribulationists as a symbol of the rapture of the entire Church before the tribulation. Moreover, pretribulationists usually regard the twenty-four "elders" in the heavenly throne room as representative of the just-raptured Church. To posttribulationists they are no more than human or angelic leaders in the heavenly worship of God and Christ. *Read Revelation 4, 5.* **John's Rapture**

The book, or scroll, with seven seals contains the prophecies which follow in Revelation, prophecies which only the action of Christ can bring to pass. Christ's taking the scroll, breaking its seals, and unrolling it therefore represent His beginning to wrest control of the world from the Satanic forces of persecution and wickedness by accomplishing the prophecies. This activity climaxes at the Parousia and establishment of God's kingdom on earth. **The Scroll**

The next chapters (6-16) contain three series of seven plagues each: seals, trumpets, and bowls. Some interpreters think that their fulfillment will be consecutive. The plagues under the trumpets will come to pass after those under the seals, and the plagues in the bowls after those of the trumpets. The Second Coming and Battle of Armageddon form the climax. In this scheme the trumpets constitute the seventh seal, the bowls con- **Seals, Trumpets, and Bowls** stitute the seventh trumpet, and the Parousia (coming of Christ) and Armageddon constitute the seventh bowl:

Seals 1 2 3 4 5 6 7
           Trumpets 1 2 3 4 5 6 7
                      Bowls 1 2 3 4 5 6 7
                                 Parousia

But the fact that the contents of the seventh in each series are practically identical and seem to indicate finality — thunder, lightning, an earthquake, and various indications that the end has come — suggests that the seals, trumpets, and bowls are at least partially concurrent in their fulfillment. The plagues of the seals will be spread out over the whole tribulation period, those of the trumpets over the last part, and those of the bowls concentrated at the end, so that the seventh in each series is identical and leads right up to the Parousia:

                                              Parousia
Seals   1   2   3   4   5   6   7
               Trumpets 1 2 3 4 5 6 7
                    Bowls 1 2 3 4 5 6 7

Seals

For the most part, the contents of the seals appear to stem from human depravity:

Seal 1: militarism, perhaps on the part of the wicked Antichrist, who dominates the tribulation period;

Seal 2: warfare, resulting from militarism;

Seal 3: famine, resulting from warfare;

Seal 4: death, resulting from famine and other ravages of war (the first four seals portray the famous "Four Horsemen of the Apocalypse");

Seal 5: persecution and martyrdom of the saints (the last generation of the Church according to posttribulationism; others who have turned to God after the rapture of the Church according to pretribulationism);

Seal 6: the celestial phenomena which Jesus said would immediately precede His return (Mark 13:24-26; Matthew 24:29, 30; Luke 21:25-27);

Seal 7: silence in heaven, thunder, lightning, and an earthquake.

Read Revelation 6:1—8:5.

144,000

Some interpreters regard the 144,000 Israelites who are marked for protection during the tribulation as symbolic of the Church. Against that view, however, is the explicit enumeration of the twelve tribes in contrast to the stated international character of the multitude of saints who come victoriously out of the tribulation in the very next vision. Pretribulationists usually cast the 144,000 in the role of Israelite evangelists who spread the Gospel throughout the world in the absence of the Church, with the result that a vast multitude of Gentiles believe and are saved. Others regard the 144,000 as orthodox Jews whom God will protect during the tribulation, especially when they are being persecuted for refusal to worship the image of the Antichrist which will be placed in the rebuilt Temple. As a result of divine protection, this Jewish remnant will survive to become the nucleus of the reestablished Davidic kingdom during the millennium.

The trumpets appear to stem primarily from Satanic and demonic activity:

Trumpet 1: hail, fire (or lightning), and blood, resulting in the burning of one third of the earth;

Trumpet 2: the throwing of an erupting volcano ("burning mountain") into the sea, resulting in the turning into blood of one third of the sea and in death and destruction to one third of life and ships at sea;

Trumpet 3: the falling of a meteorite, described as a blazing star named "Wormwood," on one third of the water supply on land (rivers and springs), turning them bitter and poisonous with widespread loss of life;

Trumpet 4: the darkening of the sun, moon, and stars by one third;

Trumpet 5: the opening of the bottomless pit by a star (probably Satan) which has fallen from heaven to earth, resulting in demonic torment of human beings, the demons being likened to locusts with the stinging tails of scorpions;

Trumpet 6: a further plague, in which demonic horsemen slaughter one third of mankind;

Trumpet 7: the turning of the kingdoms of the world into the kingdom of Christ, lightning, thunder, an earthquake, and the time of judgment and reward.

It is obvious that much of the language in these descriptions is meant to be taken symbolically. Nonetheless symbolic language conveys literal truth, so that the interpreter must avoid overspiritualization. The burning mountain, or volcano, and the blazing star, or meteorite, probably refer to fallen angels, perhaps to Satan himself, as does the star which falls from heaven to earth under the sixth trumpet. Satan and his demonic hosts vent their wrath upon the earth in ways which are impossible for us to anticipate with certainty. *Read Revelation 8:6—11:19.*

The two witnesses in the first part of chapter eleven probably minister during the latter three and one half years (1,260 days, or forty-two months) of the tribulation because during the time of their preaching the Gentiles "will tread under foot the holy city" (11:2). This must refer to the persecution of the Jewish nation in the second half of the tribulation after the Antichrist has broken his covenant with Israel (Daniel 9:27).

The two witnesses are usually identified by futurists as Moses and Elijah, who will reappear and represent the law and the prophets. Elijah's return for ministry to Israel was predicted by Malachi (4:5) and confirmed by Jesus (Matthew 17:11; Mark 9:12a). Moses and Elijah appeared together on the Mount of Transfiguration during Jesus' first advent; and the miracles of the two witnesses in Revelation 11:6 correspond to the Old Testament miracles of Moses (turning water to blood and smiting the earth with plagues — compare Exodus 7-12) and Elijah (striking their enemies with lightning, or "fire" — compare 2 Kings 1:9-12 — and producing drought — compare 1 Kings 17:1). Sometimes the two witnesses are identified as Enoch and Elijah, the only Biblical characters to avoid physical death (by translation to heaven) and therefore sent back during the tribulation to preach until martyred. However, the last generation of the Church will not experience physical death, so that we need not suppose both Enoch and Elijah having to die to maintain the general rule of physical death as part of the curse on sin. Interpreted still differently and perhaps too symbolically, the two witnesses stand for the collective testimony of God's people on earth during the tribulation.

Woman and Child

In chapter twelve the woman represents Israel (alternatively, the Church), the twelve stars of her crown the twelve tribes of Israel (alternatively, the twelve apostles of the Church), and the birth of her child the birth of the Messiah Jesus, who came from the nation of Israel. The dragon represents Satan. The one third of the stars represent fallen angels, who by following Satan become demonic beings. The catching up of the child to heaven represents the ascension of Jesus at the close of His earthly career. And the protection of the woman from the dragon for 1,260 days in the wilderness represents the protection of the Jewish remnant (the 144,000?) from Satanically instigated persecution at the hands of the Antichrist during the latter half of the tribulation. *Read Revelation 12.*

Beast and False Prophet

In chapter thirteen the beast and the false prophet have been interpreted to represent the revived Roman Empire and the Antichrist respectively. More probably, the beast represents the revived Roman Empire personified in its ruler the Antichrist, and the false prophet is the Jewish high priest of the Antichrist cult, who will place an image of the Antichrist (an "image" of the revived Roman Empire is hardly conceivable) in the rebuilt Jerusalem Temple and will try to force the worship of it upon the Israelites (compare 2 Thessalonians 2:3, 4, 9; Mark 13:14;

Matthew 24:15; Daniel 9:27). In 19:20 both the beast and the
false prophet appear to be individuals, since both are thrown
into the lake of fire: "and the beast was seized, and with him
the false prophet who performed the signs in his presence, by
which he deceived . . . those who worshiped his image; these
two were thrown alive into the lake of fire." *Read Revelation
13, 14.*

The 144,000 appear again in chapter fourteen, this time on
Mount Zion with Christ the Lamb, celebrating their triumphant
passage through the tribulation. This implies a point of time at
the close of the tribulation, after Christ's descent, and con-
stitutes an indication (among others) that John's visions dart
back and forth chronologically.

The two harvests reaped in 14:14 ff. may both symbolize
judgment at the Second Coming. Or, according to posttribulationists, the first harvest, reaped by "one like a son of man"
sitting on a white cloud, represents the rapture of the Church
at the coming of Christ after the tribulation; and because of the
phrase mentioning "the wrath of God," the second reaping
represents the immediately following outburst of judgment at
Armageddon.

John explicitly states that the bowls represent plagues which
originate in the wrath of God, probably concentrated at the end
of the tribulation ("seven plagues, which are the last," 15:1):

Bowl 1: malignant sores;

Bowl 2: the turning of the sea to blood, resulting in death
to all life at sea and in it (an intensification of the second
trumpet);

Bowl 3: the turning of all rivers and springs to blood
(an intensification of the third trumpet);

Bowl 4: scorching heat;

Bowl 5: darkness and pain;

Bowl 6: the gathering of hordes from the East for the
Battle of Armageddon, a converging of Gentile nations to
Palestine either to fight unitedly against Israel or to fight
against one another for Palestine as a prize — but Christ
returns to rescue Israel in the nick of time;

Bowl 7: "It is done," an earthquake, thunder, lightning,
and the downfall of heathen powers.

Read Revelation 15, 16.

The collapse of the revived Roman Empire is now celebrated.
"Babylon" is symbolic for Rome since Rome had taken the
place of that Mesopotamian city as the world's center for idol-

atry, immorality, and persecution of God's people.[7] Chapter seventeen places the emphasis on the *false religion* of pagan Rome; chapter eighteen on the *commercialism and materialism* of Rome. Much of the phraseology in these chapters comes from the prophecies against Babylon in Isaiah 13, 14, 46-48 and (especially) Jeremiah 50, 51 and the prophecy against Tyre in Ezekiel 26-28. *Read Revelation 17, 18.*

Marriage Supper

The marriage supper of the Lamb represents the uniting of the saints with their Savior at the long-awaited Messianic banquet. Pretribulationists see the event as having taken place in heaven during the tribulation since all the Church will have been taken to heaven by that time. Posttribulationists see it as on the verge of taking place at the return of Christ following the tribulation, because the last generation of the Church will still be on earth.

Parousia

At His coming, Christ destroys the gathered armies of the wicked nations. The beast and the false prophet are thrown into the lake of fire. Satan is confined for one thousand years.

Millennium

The righteous dead rise and share in Christ's millennial rule

THE PLAIN OF ESDRAELON *viewed from the hills of Nazareth. An historic commercial crossroad and the site of important battles in Israel's history, this plain is designated to be the scene of the vast conflict pictured in Revelation 16.*

---

[7]See the discussion on pages 349 f. concerning the application of "Babylon" to Rome in 1 Peter.

over the earth. John singles out the martyrs for special mention in order to encourage the willingness of God's people to undergo martyrdom, if necessary, in maintaining fidelity to Christ. Satan, loosed after the thousand years, instigates a revolt against the rule of Christ among the many who have been forced to submit to his political dominion, but have not submitted to his spiritual lordship. The revolt is crushed, and the last judgment takes place. *Read Revelation 19, 20.*[8]

The new Jerusalem, the spotless bride and wife of the Lamb, contrasts sharply with the harlot Babylon (Rome) of the preceding chapters. That "the kings of the earth shall bring their glory into it" (21:24) may indicate that the new Jerusalem descends to earth at the beginning of the millennial kingdom. But the abolishing of death, grief, crying, pain, and all "the first things" associated with the world in which evil resides (21:4) points to the eternal state after the millennium and the final elimination of sin with all its results.

And so the New Testament ends with the beatific vision ("they shall see His face," 22:4), an invitation to eternal life (22:17), a curse on anyone who adds or subtracts from the prophecies of Revelation (22:18, 19), a promise of and prayer for Jesus' return (22:20), and a benediction (22:21). *Read Revelation 21, 22.*

A SUMMARY OUTLINE OF REVELATION

Theme: visions of the eschatological triumph of Christ over the antichristian forces of the world.

INTRODUCTION (1:1-8)

    A. Title and means of revelation (1:1, 2)
    B. A blessing on the public reader and audience (1:3)
    C. Greeting (1:4, 5a)
    D. Doxology (1:5b, 6)
    E. Statement of theme (1:7, 8)

  I. CHRIST THE ROYAL PRIEST TENDING THE SEVEN LAMPSTANDS (CHURCHES) AND HOLDING THE SEVEN STARS (ANGELS OR MESSENGERS OF THE CHURCHES) (1:9-20)

 II. THE SEVEN MESSAGES TO CHURCHES IN ASIA (2:1—3:22)

    A. The message to the church in Ephesus (2:1-7)
    B. The message to the church in Smyrna (2:8-11)
    C. The message to the church in Pergamum (2:12-17)
    D. The message to the church in Thyatira (2:18-29)
    E. The message to the church in Sardis (3:1-6)
    F. The message to the church in Philadelphia (3:7-13)

---

[8]Amillenialists refer the binding of Satan to the work of Christ during His *first* advent, the first resurrection to the *spiritual* coming alive of those who believe in Christ, the thousand years' reign with Christ to the *present spiritual* kingship of Christ and the saints (one thousand being a round number for a long period of time), the crushing of the revolt to the Second Coming, and the second resurrection to the *physical,* general resurrection of both the righteous and the wicked at the Second Coming.

G. The message to the church in Laodicea (3:14-22)

III. THE HEAVENLY COURT (4:1—5:14)

    A. The worship of God by the four living creatures and the twenty-four elders (4:1-11)

    B. The appearance of Christ the Lamb to take the scroll with seven seals, and further praise (5:1-14)

IV. THE PLAGUES OF THE TRIBULATION (6:1—16:21)

    A. The first six seals, stemming from human depravity (6:1-17)

        1. The first seal: militarism (6:1, 2)

        2. The second seal: warfare (6:3, 4)

        3. The third seal: famine (6:5, 6)

        4. The fourth seal: death (6:7, 8)

               The Four Horsemen of the Apocalpyse

        5. The fifth seal: persecution and martyrdom (6:9-11)

        6. The sixth seal: celestial phenomena (6:12-17)

    B. The sealing of the 144,000 for protection (7:1-8)

    C. The white-robed multitude of saints who came out of the tribulation (7:9-17)

    D. The seventh seal: silence in heaven, thunder, lightning, and an earthquake (8:1-5)

    E. The first six trumpets, stemming from Satanic and demonic activity (8:6—9:21)

        1. The first trumpet: hail, fire (or lightning), blood, and burning of one third of the earth (8:7)

        2. The second trumpet: the throwing of an erupting volcano into the sea, the turning into blood of one third of the sea, and destruction of one third of life and ships at sea (8:8, 9)

        3. The third trumpet: the falling of a meteorite on one third of the water supply on land, turning them poisonous and causing widespread loss of life (8:10, 11)

        4. The fourth trumpet: the darkening of the sun, moon, and stars by one third (8:12)

        5. Announcement that the last three trumpets constitute the three woes (8:13)

        6. The fifth trumpet: the locusts from the bottomless pit (9:1-12)

        7. The sixth trumpet: the slaughter of one third of mankind by demonic horsemen (9:13-21)

    F. The cancelling of the seven thunders to avoid further delay (10:1-7)

    G. John's eating a scroll of prophecies about the nations (10:8-11)

    H. The two witnesses (11:1-13)

    I. The seventh trumpet: the transfer of the world to Christ's rule, lightning, thunder, an earthquake, judgment, and reward (11:14-19)

    J. The protection of the woman (Israel) who bore the male child (Christ) from the dragon (Satan) (12:1-17)

    K. The two beasts (13:1-18)

        1. The beast out of the sea with seven heads and ten diadems (the revived Roman Empire and its leader the Antichrist) (13:1-10)

        2. The beast out of the earth, or land (of Palestine), with two horns (a Jewish high priestly collaborator with the Antichrist) (13:11-18)

    L. The 144,000 with Christ the Lamb on Mount Zion, singing (14:1-5)

    M. Three angelic messages (14:6-12)

        1. The eternal Gospel (14:6, 7)

        2. The fall of Babylon (Rome) (14:8)

        3. Warning against worship of the beast (14:9-12)

    N. Two harvests (14:14-20)

        1. By "one like a son of man" (14:14-16)

        2. By an angel, with much bloodshed (14:17-20)

    O. The seven bowls, stemming from divine wrath (15:1—16:21)

        1. Preparation (15:1—16:1)

2. The first bowl: malignant sores (16:2)
3. The second bowl: the turning of the sea into blood and death to all life at sea and in it (16:3)
4. The third bowl: the turning of all rivers and springs into blood (16:4-7)
5. The fourth bowl: scorching heat (16:8,9)
6. The fifth bowl: darkness and pain (16:10,11)
7. The sixth bowl: the gathering of eastern hordes for the Battle of Armageddon (16:12-16)
8. The seventh bowl: "It is done," an earthquake, thunder, lightning, and the downfall of heathen powers (16:17-21)

V. THE FALL OF BABYLON (ROME) AND THE RETURN OF CHRIST (17:1-19:21)
   A. A description of the harlot Babylon, with emphasis on her paganism and a prediction of her downfall (17:1-18)
   B. The destruction of Babylon, with emphasis on her commercialism (18:1—19:5)
   C. The marriage supper of the Lamb (19:6-10)
   D. The descent of Christ (19:11-16)
   E. The defeat of the wicked hordes and the casting of the beast and the false prophet into the lake of fire (19:17-21)

VI. THE KINGDOM OF CHRIST AND GOD (20:1—22:5)
   A. The binding of Satan for one thousand years (20:1-3)
   B. The millennial reign of Christ and the saints (20:4-6)
   C. The loosing of Satan, a rebellion, and its defeat (20:7-10)
   D. The judgment at the great white throne (20:11-15)
   E. The new Jerusalem, new heaven, and new earth (21:1—22:5)

CONCLUSION (22:6-21)
   A. The trustworthiness of Revelation, with warnings and invitation (22:6-20)
   B. Benediction (22:21)

For further discussion:

How are we to understand "what must soon take place" and "the time is near" (1:1, 3) in view of almost two thousand years of Church history?

Why is predictive prophecy at least partially opaque in meaning until after its fulfillment?

Assign the various branches of Christendom, including denominations, to the categories represented by the seven churches in Asia.

What guidelines might help to settle the question of literal versus figurative interpretation of the Apocalypse?

What developments in recent and current history may be a stage-setting for events predicted in Revelation — or should we even attempt to engage in such speculation?

Why are so few clearly understandable details about heaven and hell given to us? Is the assumption of the question false?

For further investigation:

Tenney, M. C. *Interpreting Revelation.* Grand Rapids: Eerdmans, 1957.

Beasley-Murray, G. R. "The Revelation," in the *New Bible Commentary.* Edited by F. Davidson, A. M. Stibbs, and E. F. Kevan. 2nd edition. Grand Rapids: Eerdmans, 1963. Pp. 1168-1199.

Walvoord, John F. *The Revelation of Jesus Christ.* Chicago: Moody,· 1966.

Pentecost, J. D. *Things to Come.* Grand Rapids: Zondervan, 1958. For an extensive survey of Biblical eschatology from a premillennial, dispensational standpoint.

Allis, O. T. *Prophecy and the Church.* Philadelphia: Presbyterian and Reformed, 1945. For an amillennial, antidispensational viewpoint.

Ludwigson, R. *Bible Prophecy Notes.* 3rd edition. Grand Rapids: Zondervan, 1951. For the pros and cons of various schemes of prophetic interpretation.

Morris, Leon. *The Biblical Doctrine of Judgment.* Grand Rapids: Eerdmans, 1960.

Smith, Wilbur M. *The Biblical Doctrine of Heaven.* Chicago: Moody, 1968.

Lewis, C. S. *The Great Divorce, A Dream.* London: Bles, 1945. For a modern allegory on heaven and hell.

CHAPTER 21

In Retrospect

Jesus Christ came into the world at a time of religious and philosophical malaise. His own people the Jews, under the heel of Roman domination, were looking for a political Messiah. When Jesus largely avoided the politically loaded term "Messiah" and presented Himself as a spiritual Redeemer (the Son of Man who must suffer and die as the Servant of the Lord before exaltation to dominion), not even His own disciples understood Him. The Jews in general and the Sanhedrin in particular rejected Him for Barabbas, who *was* a political revolutionary. Thus Jesus died by Roman crucifixion.

But the resurrection vindicated Jesus before His disciples. After His ascension and the outpouring of the Holy Spirit on the Day of Pentecost, they began to proclaim Him as Lord and Savior. They apparently expected Him to return within a short time, however, and in a continued (but understandable) spirit of Jewish nationalism set about evangelizing their own nation in preparation for a soon-to-be-established kingdom in which Israel would dominate the Gentiles. The Parousia was delayed and converted Hellenistic Jews (especially in Syrian Antioch), with less anti-Gentile bias than most Palestinian Jewish Christians, sent out Barnabas and Paul for the first concerted effort to win Gentiles. Success inspired further missions, and the gospel eventually spread over the entire Roman Empire.

Evangelistic success necessitated organization of local groups of converts for instruction and worship. The structure of the institutional church began to take shape. Doctrinal and ethical instruction was amplified by those elements in the Old Testament not outmoded through New Testament fulfillment, and by the recall, application, and extension of Jesus' teaching and example. This led, under the guidance of the Holy Spirit, to deeper reflection on the nature of the person and work of Christ, the significance of the Church, and the eschatological future.

Except for some scattered and now lost writings, the early communication of Christian doctrine and ethics was oral. The

A CHART OF THE BOOKS IN THE NEW TESTAMENT

Book	Author	Time of Writing (A.D.)[1]	Place of Writing	Addressees	Themes and Distinctive Emphases
Galatians	Paul	49, just after Paul's 1st missionary journey	Antioch in Syria (?)	Christians in Pisidian Antioch, Iconium, Lystra, and Derbe, South Galatia	Justification by divine grace through faith in Jesus Christ — against the Judaizing doctrine of meritorious works of the law
1 Thessalonians	Paul	50-51, during the 2nd missionary journey	Corinth	Christians in Thessalonica	Congratulations upon conversion and Christian growth and exhortations to further progress, with emphasis on comfort from and expectancy toward the Parousia
2 Thessalonians	Paul	50-51, during the 2nd missionary journey	Corinth	Christians in Thessalonica	Quieting of a fanatical belief (engendered by persecution) in the immediacy of the Parousia
1 Corinthians	Paul	54, during the 3rd missionary journey	Ephesus	Christians in Corinth	Problems of manners, morals, and beliefs within the church
2 Corinthians	Paul	55, during the 3rd missionary journey	Macedonia	Christians in Corinth	Paul's inner feelings about his apostolic ministry; the offering for the church in Jerusalem
Romans	Paul	55, during the 3rd missionary journey	Corinth	Christians in Rome	Justification by divine grace through faith in Jesus Christ
James	James the half brother of Jesus	40s or 50s	Jerusalem	Jewish Christians of the Dispersion	Exhortations to Christian conduct in everyday life
Mark	John Mark	late 50s or early 60s	Rome	Non-Christian Romans	The redemptive activity of Jesus
Philemon	Paul	60	Rome	Philemon, his family, and the church in his house — all in Colossae	Mercy for a runaway slave, Onesimus, who had become a Christian
Colossians	Paul	60	Rome	Christians in Colossae	The preeminence of Christ
Ephesians	Paul	60	Rome	Christians in the region around Ephesus	The spiritual privileges and responsibilities of the Church
Luke	Luke	60	Rome	Non-Christian Gentiles, especially those with some culture and interest in Christianity	The historical certainty of the Gospel
Acts	Luke	61	Rome		The irresistible advance of the Gospel from Jerusalem to Rome

Book	Author	Date	Place of writing	Destination	Purpose
Philippians	Paul	61	Rome	Christians in Philippi	Thanks for financial assistance with personal news and exhortations
1 Timothy	Paul	62	Macedonia	Timothy in Ephesus	The organization and administration of churches by Timothy
Titus	Paul	62	Nicopolis	Titus in Crete	The administration of the churches in Crete by Titus
2 Timothy	Paul	63	Rome	Timothy in Ephesus	The commission of Timothy to carry on Paul's work
1 Peter	Peter	63	Rome	Christians in Asia Minor	The salvation and conduct of suffering Christians
2 Peter	Peter	63-64	Rome	Christians in Asia Minor	The true knowledge of Christian belief versus false teachers and their denial of the Parousia
Matthew	Matthew	60s	Antioch in Syria	Jews in Syria	The Messiah and the new people of God
Hebrews	unknown (Apollos?)	60s	unknown	Jewish Christians in Rome	The superiority of Christ as a deterrent against apostasy from Christianity back to Judaism
Jude	Jude the half brother of Jesus	60s or 70s	unknown	Christians everywhere	Warning against false teachers in the Church
John	John	late 80s or early 90s	Ephesus	Christians and/or non-Christians in the region around Ephesus	Believing in Jesus as the Christ and Son of God for eternal life
1 John	John	late 80s or early 90s	Ephesus	Christians in the region around Ephesus	The criteria of true Christian belief and practice over against Gnosticism
2 John	John	late 80s or early 90s	Ephesus	A church near Ephesus	Christian love and Christian truth
3 John	John	late 80s or early 90s	Ephesus	Gaius, a Christian in the region around Ephesus	An ecclesiastical dispute, involving Gaius, Diotrephes, Demetrius, and John himself
Revelation	John	late 80s or early 90s	Ephesus	Seven churches in western Asia Minor	Visions of the eschatological triumph of Christ over the antichristian forces of the world

1Datings are approximate and often disputed. They presuppose the discussions throughout this book. Places of writing and identification of authors are also disputed.

geographical spread of the Gospel created the need to instruct from a distance. Thus the writing of the New Testament epistolary literature started. Somewhat later the writing of the gospels[1] began as a literary means of evangelizing unbelievers, confirming the faith of believers, and providing an authoritative record of Jesus' life and ministry as the number of eyewitnesses decreased through death in the passing of time. Finally, toward the close of the first century, the last surviving apostle, John, contributed the last of the New Testament writings with both literary forms of gospel and epistle, and added a book unique in form within the New Testament — the visionary, forward-looking Apocalypse. Then began the process of collection and canonization. For a final conspectus of New Testament literature, see the chart on page 384.

---

[2]The Book of Acts should really be thought of as Part Two of Luke's gospel.

General
Index

General Index

This index excludes items in the Table of Contents and the various charts.

Scripture
Index

Index to Passages
Treated in the Harmonistic
Studies of the Gospels

INDEX TO
PASSAGES
TREATED IN
THE HARMONISTIC
STUDY OF THE
GOSPELS

For passages in Acts, the epistles, and Revelation, see the Table of Contents.